Praise for *The Bishop & The Seeker*

What happens when a left-leaning, New-Age-friendly critic of Christian faith engages in dialogue with a conservative, biblical-literalist, African-American Evangelical preacher? A shouting match? Insults and damnation? No—something more powerful and hopeful: honest conversation, mutual and respectful listening, and fresh insights for both parties. If you honestly think that people don't think honestly anymore, but just react out of tired old scripts, this book will make you think again. A hopeful sign on many levels, and a beautiful, well-told, and fun story too—this book will do you good, whether you identify more with Teri or the Bishop.

Brian McLaren, author/activist, brianmclaren.net

Reads like a mystery novel. A courageous attempt to cross lines and see into depths that are rarely explored.

Laurie Bolster, PhD, Educator

A joyful and intelligent journey from cover to cover.

Susan Kendrick, President, Write to Your Market, Inc.

WOW!! This book is fantastic!!!! I couldn't put it down—and when my husband saw me reading it, he picked up the first page, sat down next to me, and the two of us sat on the couch and read till the sun set. We both enjoyed it so much! The style is vivid, the stories are compelling, and we are learning so much.

Nancy Leidy, Healthcare executive, Washington D.C.

This changes the way I think about people in other religions and makes me realize how different they think. I will be reaching out to them in a whole new way.

Pastor William D. Lottahall, Jr.,
New Birth Community Church, Manassas, VA

Whether you are on the outside look… you will be rewarded by passionately-told st…

…**nt**, Host,
The Q… …BC News

This renewed my zeal for the Lord. I loved the transparency, like I was eavesdropping on their very private thoughts. This book will touch many lives.

Caroline June, Upper Marlboro, MD

I think they're on to something here. This looks like it is going to cover all the reasons I stopped going to church and all the reasons I still love Jesus.

Sandy Capps, traditional military mom, Jacksonville, FL

Was I offended? Yes. Did I laugh? Oh yes! Especially when they took Bishop Thomas to that New Age movie. I am a dyed-in-the-wool Christian, and Bishop Thomas is my ideal pastor; I would LOVE to meet both him and Teri.

Lindsey Antle, Parker, CO

I was inspired by the grace and patience Bishop Thomas shows in trying to reach Teri. It's so amazing to learn what some people can believe. In fact, I've been sharing the chapters with my Bible studies group; we could all learn a lesson from Bishop Thomas.

Sue Bartlett, Bible studies teacher, Annapolis, MD

There were times I wanted Teri to tell the bishop to cut the crap; she was caving in to him. But I saw something deeper going on. When his words sounded preposterous to her, she drilled into his heart, and saw that it was good. Sensing his integrity gave her the space to trust and listen for what he meant in terms she could understand. There were times she even articulated it for him, helping open his eyes to his own values. She wasn't caving, she was dancing.

Laurie S. Hall, author of "An Affair of the Mind"

This is really an amazing and eye-opening work. Christians may not come away with a greater acceptance of New Age thought, but they will come away with a clearer vision of how the two belief systems both support and challenge one another. This, in itself, is a great accomplishment and has potential to help smooth some of the rough spots between the two groups.

Laurie Higgs, former Couples Ministry Director,
McLean Baptist Church

Few authors can address several different audiences at once. This book will move you to explore your beliefs in a new way—whichever "side of the fence" you are on. If you're not afraid to re-examine your basic assumptions so as to understand others better in our pluralistic culture, read this book!

Diane Eble, publishing coach and author of "Abundant Gifts," www.yourbookpublishingcoach.com

The magic of this book shows up early when Teri writes, "We were deadlocked, the energy was blocked. The question hung in the air as to why we were pursuing this difficult venture of trying to understand each other. The bishop spoke, 'Well, I'm just riding this wave to see where it goes.' It felt wrong to let facts come between us while an underlying Truth was calling."

If you "ride the wave" of this dialogue, you, too, will feel the Truth that is calling you. In some cases it may disturb you, in others exhilarate. But the promise of this journey is the clarifying of your Faith and its practice in service to a larger world.

James R. Jones, Director, Personal Awareness Institute

A testimony to the power of love to honor and bridge seemingly opposing views. This book models that through seeking to understand, we can each do our part to transform the world.

Rev. Trish Hall, Celebration Center for Spiritual Living, Falls Church, VA, www.celebrationcenter.org

Wow. Couldn't put the book down last night until I finished it. Very engrossing, very easy to read, very thoughtful—even though I disagree with almost everything you say about New Age and New Thought.

Kay Pentecost, RScP, New Thought Practitioner, Religious Science

A vivid example of how exploring what we mean by our words can reveal our common struggles and aspirations. It can show us to see the world—and each other—with more compassionate eyes.

Dr. Susanne Cook-Greuter, Co-founder, Integral Institute; author, "Transcendence and Mature Thought in Adulthood"

This book articulates deep, complex, and personal concepts in fluid prose lubricated by surprises and compelling stories. Teri's adventures with the ladies of Highview and their fundamental views are both fun and peculiar—just when I am ready to hear her mock their backward attitudes, she makes me see them in new, sympathetic ways, forcing me to examine my prejudices. I loved tracing the evolution that I witnessed in both Teri and the Bishop. It was subtle and positive and enlightening. I loved the Bishop. For me his character, his wisdom, his goodness was essential to my "fundamental" enlightenment, as a secularist. I would love to meet this man.

Zack Kincheloe, English Department Chair, Chico High, CA

In keeping with her "integral" principles, Teri's growth was not abandonment of the places she'd been, but an invitation to come along. It's as if one hand is reaching back to where she's been, and the other hand is reaching out to where she's going; and in the middle is Teri, weaving the old and the new into a seamless garment and holding the space for the people she loves.

Laurie S. Hall, author of "An Affair of the Mind"

I love this Bishop. He really knows the Bible. But why are you asking all these niggling questions? "Fear of the Lord" is just an expression. Everybody knows that. Nobody is actually afraid of him. I don't understand the purpose of this book. Could you just send me some tapes of the Bishop, please?

Elodie Ling, Anglican, retired British school teacher
living in the Bahamas

The Bishop & The Seeker

Wrestling for the Soul of the 21st Century

The Bishop & The Seeker

Published by:
Intermedia Publishing Group, Inc.
P.O. Box 2825
Peoria, Arizona 85380
www.intermediapub.com

ISBN 978-1-935529-44-6

Printed in the United States of America

Scripture sources are indicated as follows:
(ASV) American Standard Version
(CEV) Contemporary English Version
(ESV) English Standard Version
(HCSB) Holman Christian Standard Bible
(KJV) King James Version
(LAM) Holy Bible from Ancient Eastern Manuscripts by George M. Lamsa
(NASB) New American Standard Bible
(NKJV) New King James Version
(NIV) New International Version
(NWT) New World Translation

Graphic treatment by Nathan Freeman of Gustave Doré's *Jacob Wrestling the Angel*

The Bishop & The Seeker

Wrestling for the Soul of the 21st Century

Teri Murphy and Bishop Phillip O. Thomas

Introduction by Bishop Phillip O. Thomas

When the Murphys first visited my church in September of 2003, I was excited at the hint that God was addressing my prayer for a multiracial ministry in which everyone could experience the love of God and each other, regardless of race or culture. I was eager to discover what attracted them to a predominately Black congregation. Though I expected differences, little did I anticipate what was in store. I now think God was testing just how much difference I was ready to handle.

Our perspectives were so different that the day Teri told me she was leaving over how I treated a gay man, I wasn't sure at first what she was talking about. But unlike many people who come to a pastor with complaints, Teri seemed open to listen. And so I tried to share the biblical point of view in a constructive way. Her sincere commitment to truth made me want to continue taking time to minister to her. In fact, I came to enjoy our candid discussions as Teri's quick mind, irreverent humor, and willingness to confront sensitive issues squarely gave me a rare opportunity to sharpen my own thinking and expand my understanding. And I have been bountifully rewarded to see most of Teri's prejudices about Christianity fall away. She and her husband may still have a few strange ideas about God, but we are blessed to have them in our midst.

As for myself, I've learned that many people turn their back on Christianity because the Bible interpretation they are exposed to is restricting rather than liberating. I've also learned that some of the forms of alternative spirituality or ethics that they turn to can put them on a moral path very similar to that of Christianity. I believe my fellow evangelists will be more effective in bringing these good people to God's kingdom if they start by seeking this common ground.

For this book, Teri took the notes and served as editor of our dialogues, so it is her voice you will hear predominately. But we have worked closely to be sure the text accurately reflects our spirited discussions. Some dialogues have been condensed and reorganized to make for better flow. And sometimes Teri might have been a bit overzealous in whittling down some of my finer pronouncements. But we have purposely left in some discussions that were incomplete or included points one of us thought better of later. It is in the nature of a conversation like this to never reach a perfect endpoint.

I am grateful to Teri for spearheading this project and giving me an unusual venue for sharing the gospel of Jesus Christ the way he intended it to be shared.

Introduction by Teri Murphy

When my husband Andy and I first dropped in on Highview for the passionate music, I had no idea that I was embarking on an extraordinary journey that would show me how to have it all—tradition and progress, individuality and group, faith and works, union and communion with God. My searingly candid dialogues with Bishop Thomas spilled over into encounters with renowned scholars, gay followers of Jesus, an imam who champions freedom, debates in a Bahamas Internet café run by Jehovah's Witnesses, and a revelation in the "Eden" of a California walnut orchard. These adventures propelled me to reconsider every assumption of my generation and to expand my heart to embrace a much wider circle as brethren. They gave me a vision of fresh possibilities to heal religious conflict while bringing us all closer to God.

I thus hope that this book will resonate with people of varied religious and spiritual perspectives. For those of you who have felt frustrated by conservative Christians who see you as "lost" while you see them as naive or worse, you will find here ideas for getting along better with those whose religion seems to have built walls between you. You may find as I did that doors appear where before you saw only the walls.

For those of you who feel that religion threatens our freedoms, my experience with Bishop Thomas offers a fresh look at ways we might integrate faith and reason peacefully in public life. Regardless of the extent to which you may believe the Bible is based on myth, learning to speak its language can help identify common values for bridging our most problematic differences.

I also hope to reach out to those of you who, like me, have benefited from "New Age" or alternative spirituality and are now looking to expand your perspective. Bishop Thomas and I have blazed a trail that can permit you to reconsider traditional values from a new and higher perspective, a perspective that integrates postmodern consciousness with tradition. If, like me, you yearn to balance surrender and action, intuition and reason, self and group, you may find that traditionalists can offer valuable lessons. And what better way to use the inner peace and open mind we like to think we've cultivated than by reaching out to the one group from which we most often feel separate? This story shows how to make brothers and sisters of those in traditional religion.

For Christians of all stripes, I hope you will be as inspired as I was by the way Bishop Thomas breathes life and relevance into the full body of Biblical values. His approach can indeed give you a more successful way of witnessing to those of your "prodigal children" from the New Age who may be ready to hear the Christian message in a whole new way. Like you, they reject the modern claim that science holds the only truth, so they carve paths that put "Spirit" back at the center of life. Whatever errors you may think they make, along the way some of them get pretty good at developing values many Christians are still working on. If you are willing to walk with them awhile on the spiritual path, you may be surprised at how many values you have in common and at the usefulness of some of their techniques for your own faith walk.

And finally, I hope to extend a hand to those of all other faiths. As we find ourselves living, working, and playing with people whose religions can seem so "other," interfaith friendships bring richness to life and peace to communities. I believe there are things we can all learn from each other as we mature in our understanding of this magnificent and mysterious life we find ourselves in.

Author's Note: What's a Fundamentalist?

When I first met Bishop Thomas, my definition of a "fundamentalist" was anyone who believed any holy book was literally "the Word of God." That is the way you will find "fundamentalist" used throughout most of this book. By the end of this extraordinary journey, however, I came to appreciate that I was commingling a rich breadth of human attempts to know truth into just that one word. So I apologize if some uses of "fundamentalist" give offense; my understanding continues to mature.

To forestall either of us from jumping ship prematurely in our dialogues, Bishop Thomas and I negotiated a definition of "fundamentalist" and other key terms we could both support with varying mixtures of reluctance and enthusiasm. You will find these definitions in the back of the book as a "Glossary for Non-fundamentalists."

Teri Murphy

Contents

Part I

Setup

1

How a "New Ager" Landed in a Fundamentalist Church

It's what we learn after we know it all that counts.
Earl Weaver, Baltimore Orioles

Not far from my home in an upper middle class neighborhood of Arlington, Virginia, is a pocket of modest homes in a mostly Black neighborhood that was once officially segregated. In that neighborhood my husband, Andy, found a hundred-year-old church doing old-time religion complete with shouting, fainting, and jubilant, electric praise music that could be heard a block away. It was named for the neighborhood it sat in: Highview Park Christian Assembly.

We were among the last people you'd expect to be attracted to such a place. We had spent decades dabbling in every positive thinking, self-improvement, and spirituality movement of the postmodern era. The past 15 years we were active in a church of Religious Science where the theology was rational, the music was mostly soft, and the preferred form of worship was silent meditation. All paths to God were honored equally, and the congregation included those who thought of themselves as Christians, Buddhists, Hindus, Jews, and even a few neo-Pagans.

Andy was drawn to Highview at least partly because of how it recreated our experience of the great music and passionate expression of churches in the Bahamas. We had vacationed on a tiny island there shortly after we met. Harbour Island is only four blocks wide, and there isn't much to do there on Sunday. So we visited the churches to check out a *Washington Post* travel piece that reported, "When the singing gets going, the paint seems to jump off the walls." We found ourselves a seat directly under a ceiling fan with a view of a palm tree. And that was it; we were hooked—on the passion, the people, and the sense of community that's possible in such a tiny place. We started returning to the island several times a year, and I developed some web design clients there. We visited all of the island's eight churches, and settled in to a few we particularly liked—without paying much attention to their theology.

Meanwhile at home, we were feeling less comfortable with our own congregation, a metaphysical group called the Celebration Center of Religious Science in Falls Church, Virginia. Andy had discovered it for us shortly after we met, and we both fell in love with the place the day we walked in. As strong individualists, we were hooked by music that said, "It's in every one of us to be wise" and by the slogan, "Wouldn't it be wonderful if a group of people somewhere were for something and against nothing." The favored name for God was "Universal Mind" or "the Universe" for short, and they taught that our thoughts create our reality and thus we are 100% responsible for our experience of life. We joined on the spot and spent 15 years as eager participants in both the philosophy and the community with its skits, spaghetti suppers, budget committees, and hospital visits.

But now we were taking some time out from the Celebration Center, yearning for something new. The Religious Science movement was shifting—in some ways we were comfortable with and some we weren't. Andy wanted more community action. I wanted to integrate the community's "feminine" values of surrender, forgiveness, and trust of intuition, with the traditionally masculine values of action, courage, and reason.

During this time out from the Center, Andy and I both missed having a community to celebrate with on Sunday. So Andy set out to find something like we had experienced in the Bahamas. I went with him to Highview thinking we'd just visit a few times while we were figuring out what was next. But the Universe had something else in mind.

Greeted with open arms

The Highview congregation of about 100 was all Black but for an occasional visitor or spouse of a member, while Andy and I are White. And although I felt we might be intruding, they welcomed us with open arms—especially the pastor, Bishop Phillip Thomas, who seemed ready to diversify his congregation. Not only did he frequently announce how happy he was to have us visit, but he singled us out for asides when he made in-the-family Black references in his sermons. For example, "Don't you take abuse from that Nnn… *(glancing at us)* ...Black person." These caused hysterical laughter with folks hugging and high-fiving us.

When we had been attending for a couple months, one of the senior "mothers," Mother Hafta, took me aside and told me, "Teri, we don't often get people of your racial, uh, well sometimes they visit, but they don't come back, but…Well, might just as well come right out and say it: We love you just as much as if you were Black." I blinked a moment before finding the presence of mind to answer honestly. "That's about the sweetest thing anybody ever said to me."

On a similar note, the Sunday that Andy asked to join Highview, Bishop Thomas warned the congregation only half-jokingly, "Any of you got a problem with Andy joining this church, you come see me in my office."

Each of these moments typified an unspoiled genuineness that kept us coming back.

Old time preaching with a twist

The Bishop was a great speaker. His style ranged from quiet and thoughtful to high speed shouting and stomping up the aisle. He intermixed sophisticated word play, bawdy street references, and searing satire—all delivered with a smile that frequently brought down the house with laughter, "Amens!" and high-fiving to affirm, "He got me on that one."

His themes represented the flip side of everything we were used to hearing. Religious Science calls itself "a teaching church, not a preaching church." Now we were in for heavy-duty preaching with calls for faith, character, and morality. In a sermon on sexual chastity Bishop Thomas got the single women chanting, "Click click! Lock lock!" We laughed till we cried. Like many of his points, it was so preposterous as to preclude niceties of political correctness. Other themes were largely directed to concerns of the mostly blue-collar congregation, but there was plenty that was universal, and I felt harpooned myself several times. When he made fun of the "Mind-over-matter, name-it-and-claim-it, gab-it and grab-it crowd," I joined in the laughter feeling a stab of truth. And when he satirized people who were always looking for a better church, I considered hiding under my seat.

On the surface, it was raw, primitive. Yet there was the scent of something *higher,* as if a richer message was being communicated on the subspace channel. *What is going on here?* I wondered.

Excellence, accountability, and community

Andy and I were also impressed by the focus on excellence in action. In our metaphysical circles, the focus was on visioning a perfect outcome more than on acting to make it happen. But now I was back in the land of the Protestant work ethic. The Highview congregation worked to live up to its mission statement, "Providing world class ministry." Before service, white-gloved ushers practiced pirouetting clockwise, not counterclockwise, after taking each person to a seat. Ministry leaders were required to submit annual goals, and the pastor was following a long-term plan that covered everything from increasing the percentage of children in the choir to fixing cracks in the baptismal pool.

That plan also included a "Mark of Excellence" outreach ministry that provides job training, counseling, and transitional housing for those who needed a hand up before they were ready to be saved. This was extremely impressive for a small congregation, with many members working two or three jobs to make ends meet.

Also to our surprise, there was rarely a mention of prejudice or of politics—other than to encourage people to vote for "whoever best reflects your values." Once when a visiting speaker told a sly little tale about who his cat voted for, Bishop Thomas deftly followed up by saying he had spoken with several cats in the congregation and the feline vote seemed to be split. Indeed, the focus at Highview was entirely on changing one's self. Bishop Thomas declared in a booming barrage one Sunday, "It ain't about what the government did to you. It ain't about what the White man did to you. It's about what you can do for yourself with Jesus." This seemed to echo the personal accountability that had attracted Andy and me to Religious Science.

Upbeat and offbeat with fabulous music

Andy and I like things that are upbeat and offbeat, and so Highview seemed a good harbor for a while. The name, Highview, struck me as a good sign for us positive thinkers. (A year later when the church moved to the Fairfax suburbs, the name was shifted to Highview Christian Fellowship.)

And the music was fabulous. There was no palm tree out the window, but the jubilant, electric, passionate praise was like worship in the Bahamas with more consistently upbeat lyrics.

I'm trading my sorrow

I'm trading my shame

I'm trading it all for the glory of the Lord

Yes Lord,

Yes Lord,

Yes Lord,

Yes!

Taken together the package bespoke excellence in both spirit and form.

Getting comfortable with hellfire and damnation

The only problem was the theology. Andy and I are pretty good about translating old-style Christian terminology into parallels we can be comfortable with. We had joked about implanting *Star Trek*-style translators in our heads such that "Lord" becomes "Spirit"; "sin" becomes any action that does not serve the highest good of self and others; and "salvation" becomes transformation. In our richly blessed lives and in appreciation for what Andy calls "theater of the world," we had no need to translate "Our God is an awesome God" or "Make a joyful noise for his many blessings." It even began to feel natural to add "Thank you Jesus!" to most any sentence. Andy moved faster than I did in this translation process.

But when you start going to a church regularly, the specifics become more important. We passed a couple hurdles easily. There was very little talk about End Times. The Bishop rarely mentioned Satan, and the first time he did he caught himself in a way that impressed me. "When the devil leads you...or rather, I should say, when you *let* the devil lead you..." Another time he said, "It's true that if you don't follow God's Word you'll go to hell, but I'd rather focus on the positive side of things." Maybe this was a version of hellfire and damnation *lite* that we could live with for what I assumed would be a short stay.

The attention to ourselves, the cut-loose worship style, the unapologetic focus on action, and the inside peek at another culture all felt like forbidden pleasures. But I knew from the moment I walked in the door and began enjoying them that there would be a price to pay, and that I was headed inevitably to a tight spot. Weeks turned into months. Andy joined the church and started volunteer teaching GED classes through the church's Mark of Excellence outreach ministry while I tried to keep a low profile. The early warning signs that it was time to move on were pronouncements that Jesus is the *only* way, and an announcement of a new ministry to help gays turn from their sins. After about 6 months the line was crossed, bam bam, two Sundays in a row. And we were forced to choose.

Pushed over the edge

On that first troubled Sunday a visiting minister gave a blistering accounting of all the "cults" that a Christian has to beware of. She had done her homework well: she hit the religions of most of my friends and accurately summarized their beliefs. She did a good enough job on "New Age"— "They believe that God is in everything and that their thoughts can influence reality!"—that Andy and I exchanged a glance of "Sounds good to me." The speaker's tone, however, was one of anger and dire warnings.

But that sour note was only a prelude to the following Sunday. At the end of a typically long service, Bishop Thomas said he needed to say goodbye to a young man who was leaving the congregation. "He and I have had some emails," the pastor said, "and I want to take one last chance to challenge him to turn away from sin." He then launched into a mini sermon on the evils of homosexuality: "Those teenage girls kissing each other thinking it's a fad. It's not a fad, it's a sin." (He was referring to a recently televised kiss between Madonna and Britney Spears.) Then he asked the young man to come up to the front so people could pray for him. The fellow kept his head down as a dozen congregants surrounded him, hugging him, and praying aloud.

"That's it," I thought. "The party's over. I can't come back here, and I'm ashamed to be here now." I considered but rejected the possibility of walking up close enough to the young man to say, "Don't let them get to you. You're a perfect child of God just as you are."

The question facing me was *how* to leave. If I simply never came back, people would make up their own stories about why that White lady disappeared, perhaps thinking that the church was just too Black for her. The decision was further complicated by knowing that anything I did would affect Andy who had become more actively involved and was more inclined to allow the good aspects to outweigh the bad. If I spoke up, I would be outing him, too, as someone whose beliefs did not fall in line. He told me he was conflicted, and I told him I would support however he wanted to handle it. But when it became clear in a few days that his preference was long-term mulling, I asked if it would be all right if I made an appointment with Bishop Thomas, and he said it would. So I gathered my courage and set up an appointment via email.

"The battle is joined," said Andy, "and I'll support you however it turns out."

2

Confrontation

Love is work or courage directed toward the nurture of our own or another's spiritual growth.
Scott Peck, *Road Less Traveled*

Courage is nine-tenths context. What is courageous in one setting can be foolhardy in another and even cowardly in a third.
Joseph Epstein, *Women's Quarterly*

Preparing

The good news was that I was in an excellent position for my mission of speaking my truth. I had little to lose, and more important, here at last was a pure case in my long history of being a church troublemaker: I knew for certain I was right—something unacceptable had happened. Other times when I've brought an issue to the head of whatever group I was in, I felt there was a good chance that I was being pigheaded, bucking something for my own ego, or limited view. But this time I had no doubt about being *right*.

Just as liberating was the fact that this was not my community so I could "release results"; I had no responsibility to help change things. To the contrary, the church appeared to be doing a lot of good within its own community, including running a shelter, and I had respect and fondness for many of the people I had met, especially the pastor, although I had never spoken to him one-on-one.

So checking my feelings, I had no righteous anger. But I did have a lot of fear—fear that because I was an outsider, any action was inappropriate and might only cause trouble for myself and others. Under similar circumstances I had been told that my complaints reflected only my own need for control. Those instances were in an environment where everyone bent over backward to not make each other wrong. How much stronger might the reaction be here? Then of course, there was the whole cross-cultural racial thing; how dare I?

But the values I hold highest include being willing to say what's hard to say and being willing to hear what's hard to hear. And thus the choice to say something felt inescapable.

For preparation I turned to a book that I'd been meaning to read for a decade: Peter McWilliams' *Ain't Nobody's Business if You Do*. It's an argument for why no consensual act should ever be a crime in a free society. In the middle is a funny and brilliant 200-page "book report" on the Bible, arguing that it does not prohibit consensual acts such as homosexuality when the relevant verses are viewed in context. I wrote out notes of what I would say. The morning of the appointment I awoke feeling inspired by this thought, "Don't present your departure from Highview as a *fait accompli*—a done deed. Leave an opening."

I once heard that when you face a challenge, you should say to yourself, "My whole life has prepared me for this moment." That rang true in this case. Sitting on the church steps waiting for the pastor to arrive for our appointment, I said one last prayer for divine support. The slightly mocking response that popped into my head was, "You get yourself into these things. You'd better know by now how to handle them."

Lion's den

Bishop Thomas arrived late from a traffic jam, apologetic but buoyant. The moment he drove up—wearing a baseball cap and smiling and waving through the open window of his sporty jeep—I had a sharp impression that this was not the formidable figure I saw on the pulpit on Sundays. I suddenly got a cold-feet feeling that I was making some kind of mistake. This couldn't be the person who had publicly shamed that young man. *Too late. Can't turn back.*

He led me into his small office where I sat across from him at his desk. On the wall were paintings of a riverside baptism among a rural, Black congregation. Scattered on his bookcase among Bible commentaries were whimsical trinkets like Mickey Mouse ears and some colorful paper decorations from a cruise ship.

I started by passing him an envelope with my contribution to the building fund—it contained the amount he had recently asked every employed congregant to give.

"I want to start by giving you this because I have received many benefits from being here and I don't want to be eating any free fish." I was referring to a hysterically funny sermon he had given about congregants who come for the free loaves and fishes but never give anything back. He got us all chanting, "No more free fish!"

Then with my voice a half octave higher than usual I said, "And I wanted to give this to you first because there's a good chance you'll throw me out of here before we're done."

"Oh, I doubt that," he said, his voice now a half octave higher than usual as well.

I started by listing all the things I admired about the church and all the things I had gotten from his sermons. He responded to each one with the kind of distracted "uh-huh" that made me think I made a mistake in signaling that bad news lay ahead.

Outing myself as a New Ager

I launched into my prepared remarks. "You would call the church I've come from New Age, though New Thought is more accurate," I said. "We are very much positive thinkers; our slogan is "There's a power for good in the universe, and it works through my thinking." In fact, you would probably include us in the group you once referred to as 'The mind-over-matter, name-it-and-claim-it, gab-it-and-grab-it crowd.' I was able to laugh at that because I think we do sometimes fall prey to self-centeredness. In fact, part of the reason I've appreciated being here at Highview is that you provide the other side of the story on a few things I'm sorting through. You might say I'm taking a time out from my Religious Science congregation to do that."

"Uh-huh."

"So that means I see Christianity as just one of the paths to God—one our founder called 'probably the most appropriate for Western man.' And thus being here at Highview has felt like being an orphan piglet that took shelter amidst a warm litter of puppies. I figured one day the Mama dog was going to look at me and say, 'What? You ain't growed no hair yet?' She'd shake me by the neck and toss me out of that basket." (He didn't laugh at this attempt to establish a light tone, and my voice went up another half octave.)

"And then I knew the time had come to leave the basket on my own power last week when you called up that young man. I was extremely uncomfortable being in the presence of that. It doesn't accord with my reading of the Bible, and it doesn't accord with my understanding of the spirit of Jesus. I felt ashamed to be there."

"So the question now is whether you want to throw me out yourself or if I should just leave of my own power—unless I've missed something.... And I'm finished with my prepared remarks now," I said, folding up my outline and bracing myself.

An astonishing response

"Well first of all," he said, "I want you to know that I appreciate all the positive things you said. I shouldn't be beholden to what people think, but I'm human, and I do like positive feedback. But I also appreciate negative feedback. So let me ask you, with that incident last Sunday, what exactly were you uncomfortable about?"

"The fact that you shamed and outted that young man publicly."

"Oh, you mean it was clear to you that he is..."

"Gay? Well it most certainly was."

"Oh. Well then, perhaps I overstepped. I thought I was being careful about what I said. But if you as a relative newcomer picked it up, perhaps I said more than I meant to. In fact, I was a little concerned that I might have gone too far, which is why I asked him to my office to talk after service, and I think we got to a pretty good place about it."

"Well I'm glad to hear that."

"And the background is that I was just on a cruise with his family and some other congregants. He and his friends engaged in some pretty flagrant displays, potentially embarrassing his mother. I didn't say anything at the time, though I think I should have. But afterwards he came to me convicted about it."

"Convicted?" I asked.

"He knew that he had gone too far, and he felt bad about it. So he came to me to talk about it."

So "convicted" means "guilty"?

"No, no. Guilt is a feeling you hang onto after you've set things right. There's no point in that."

I was feeling the ground shift beneath me. My sense that I was 100% right began to show cracks.

Busting

"That's the way we handle things like that here—publicly. If you were from the 'hood,' you might call it 'busting' someone. But it's never supposed to be punitive. It's holding the person accountable publicly and offering support for getting back on track. It should never be done in a way that makes someone feel exposed or shamed. If I do it right, the person involved eventually comes to thank me."

I felt another shift. Fresh in my mind was a definition of fundamentalism by my favorite contemporary philosopher Ken Wilber, "...relies on shame to enforce the rules." And here was a self-described fundamentalist telling me that shame was bad.

In fact, I had witnessed some other "bustings" at Highview—one that I would read between the lines was about relapsing to drug use and another about spouse abuse. In both cases the spouses of the busted parties seemed very happy to have the support of the community in such an intervention. In a different kind of public support, I had also seen resources garnered for a new member who declared herself to be an unemployed mother of four. Bishop Thomas started calling out assignments to people: "Deacon Hafta, you'll be her care group deacon; make sure she gets whatever she needs. And Sister Basil, you're good at getting people jobs. Let's guarantee her that if she stays with us, by this time next year she'll be moving toward her dream of a better life."

"Well... It's an interesting way to do community," I said tentatively. "I've always thought we should try to work out our differences voluntarily rather than being so quick to call in outside authorities... But everybody would have to know upfront what they're getting into."

"Yes," he said. "Everybody's got to know upfront. It's a hard balance for me to strike, and sometimes I get it wrong. And I'm sorry for that."

The conversation paused until I said, "Well, uh, I wasn't prepared for you to apologize."

Homosexuality and sin

"But homosexuality is a sin," he said. "It says so in the Bible. I believe the Bible is the inerrant Word of God, and I have devoted my life to living and teaching it as it is."

His tone was not dogmatic but one of grounded conviction. He was standing in his truth, and feeling that, I was moved. And I was even more struck by the fact that he seemed eager to hear my reply.

"How do you determine what's right and wrong?" he asked me.

"First of all, I'm not convinced the Bible does condemn homosexuality as sin when the relevant passages are viewed in context," I said, hoping I wouldn't have to remember the citations I had studied the night before. "And even if the Bible does condemn it, my conscience tells me otherwise. The teachings of

Jesus are the highest ethical teachings I know. But I get divine guidance every day. And that present-day guidance tells me it's not consistent with the spirit of Jesus to call homosexuality a sin."

"What we think of as divine guidance.... I'm sorry, did I interrupt you?" he asked. "Were you finished?" I nodded, silently giving him another point for being a good listener.

"What we think of as divine guidance from conscience or intuition is just an experience," he said. "It could be coming from other sources; there are... other spirits."

He dropped his voice on "other spirits" as if he knew I wouldn't like it. I was also off balance from his reference to "just an experience"—having spent 20 years in an environment in which being conscious of our experience is a primary goal.

"There's a million beliefs out there that we can be tossed and turned by," he continued. "That's why we need one standard that stays firm. And when there's something in the Bible that I don't understand, I take it as a sign that I need to do more growth so I can live up to its standard, rather than bringing it down to mine."

His tone remained personal, genuine, present—not the least bit preachy. And I was struck by the fact that he was addressing a question I had been asking for several years. When I base decisions on my experience or my intuition, how do I distinguish that from ego needs or the subtle groupthink influences to which we humans are so very vulnerable? And when New Thought or any other transcendental movement teaches people to "follow their hearts" how do we avoid encouraging those who hear their hearts telling them to kill the infidels? Meanwhile my favorite philosopher Ken Wilber was shaking things up by critiquing over-reliance on personal experience as producing a generation of self-focused narcissists.

I didn't like the Bishop's answer, but I liked that he had zeroed in on the question.

An unexpected place to draw a line

"Okay, so what if I brought gay friends to your service?" I said.

"I would be respectful and welcome them. It's not like I'd say anything... unless my guidance for the week was to speak about that topic. But chances are they wouldn't be comfortable here knowing we believe their lifestyle is a sin."

"Well, I don't believe homosexuality is a sin, and I do believe I need to follow reason and my experience in determining that. So I guess this is your opportunity to throw me out."

"I'm not going to throw you out," he said.

"You might want to reconsider that. If I stay I'm likely to be trouble."

"Oh I doubt that."

Only slightly less controversial topics

Both of our voices had returned to their normal pitch—his returning quicker than mine—and we began to cover other topics more casually. I told him about having clients in the Bahamas who were Jehovah's Witnesses, and that they were among the most likeable, and creative people of high integrity I had ever had as friends. He started pointing to doctrinal errors of the Jehovah's Witnesses, and I told him I didn't want to get into that level of "angels on the head of a pin." I did say that I'd pay money some day to see a debate between him and my Witness friends, and he laughed at that.

We were both starting to enjoy the conversation.

"Let me ask you," he said. "How well do you know the Bible?"

"Well, growing up Catholic I learned the major themes and stories. And, uh, I studied up for this meeting last night. I feel like I know the big picture of what the Bible says, and I do live by it."

"But living by it is not enough," he said, leading us to a discussion of being saved by faith alone versus by works. I had a prepared answer for that from my McWilliams homework of the night before, but the Bishop was late for a class, so I didn't try to squeeze it in.

He said, "My challenge to you would be to study the Word of God in the Bible so you can get to know him better." This was said in a tone of, "She's put herself in the position of being my congregant, how can I best serve her?" But the prospect of Bible study had no appeal to me, especially in this congregation where all my attitudes would be alien.

What am I doing here?

Perplexed, I said, "I really don't know why I was drawn here to Highview. Maybe it has to do with assisting your homeless shelter; I could teach some basic computer classes."

"I know you were drawn here for a reason," he said, "for me as well as for you."

A bell sounded in my head. The concept of being drawn to situations that reflect our own mental state and hold lessons for us is a major theme in Religious Science.

"But it's not the contribution of your talents I'm interested in," he continued. "It's how much we can assist you in moving closer to God. I would be eager to meet like this again when we can get into more detail."

As our talk came to a close, one little sticky matter remained, and he cleaned it up diplomatically. He had put out a feeler to Andy and me about helping with the couples ministry based on our book *The Husband's Manual*. "Let's wait on the couples ministry," he said, "until you've had a chance to get to know your way around here."

"That makes sense." Pointing to the Bible on his desk I said, "I think everything Andy and I would say would be wholly consistent with that, but the terms we use would be alien."

"I believe you," he said. "I trust you and Andy. Not because of intuition, but just because of a good feeling in my heart."

He said this in all sincerity, despite the apparent blatant contradiction with everything he had just said about not trusting one's experience.

We hugged as we parted. And I could already feel the pull of ambivalent feelings. On the one hand, his offer that we follow up on some of the issues we had opened was tempting. But I didn't want to waste his time by giving him the impression that he could "save" me. As I walked down the church steps, the quirky voice in my head asked, "What have you gotten yourself into now, Kingfish?" (This was a reference dredged up by my subconscious to one of the first television shows with an all-Black cast before the days of political correctness.)

I had no idea that I was about to enter one of the juiciest adventures of my life. It would lead me to reassess every assumption of my generation, and it would lead Bishop Thomas to stretch his definition of salvation.

In the months ahead, two issues from this first conversation would resurface continually: following your heart versus following The Book, and the line between using shame for control and seeking excellence via holding people accountable. One year later, the Bishop's ability to draw that line would be put to the ultimate test in how he dealt with a member of his own family.

3

Background: No Coincidences?

Coincidence is God's way of remaining anonymous.
Albert Einstein

I arrived home dizzy with exhilaration over having created a new kind of opening and disoriented over where it might lead. I went to my email, and there I found an invitation from my other congregation, The Celebration Center, to sign up for a metaphysical Bible class. In my 15 years of being at the Celebration Center, a Bible class had never been offered.

"Law of attraction"

Now I was doubly disoriented by the coincidence. New Thought teaches there are no coincidences; everything that happens to us is a reflection of our thought. But the philosophy takes a neutral stance toward the meaning of such coincidences, seeing them as the natural result of "The Law of Attraction." A version of this "law" was popularized by the best-selling book and video *The Secret*. Our version of the law of attraction would say that I was wrestling with a challenge about looking at the Bible, and so I attracted an opportunity to do so—with there being no preference by the Universe as to whether I should take it or not.

But this coincidence did not smell "neutral." Surely taking a "Metaphysical" Bible class was not what Bishop Thomas had in mind when he recommended that I get to know the Bible. I couldn't imagine that he would consider anything in such a class to be less than heretical, and therefore, possibly worse than not looking at the Bible at all. On the other hand, if he thought my taking the class was a good idea, the "coincidence" would look to him like divine guidance and would thus be the best possible example that all of our guidance is not pre-written in a 2,000 year-old book. Surely this example would force the Bishop to admit that intuitive guidance is more than "just an experience" and is always freshly and directly available to everyone.

Neutral schmeutral. The invitation to the class was a trail marker. And I'd have to be an idiot not to see that the juicy stuff in life was down that path.

My religious background

The best way to establish the unusual perspective I would bring to such a class is to summarize my religious background. It reflects an ongoing push-pull between enjoying the benefits of orthodoxy and community and then striking out on my own when pursuit of truth seems to require it. Eventually this felt less like a zigzag pattern and more like a spiral—always looping back to core values, but at a higher level of understanding.

Growing up Catholic

As a child, I walked to Catholic mass every Sunday with my family in the picture-perfect town of Los Gatos, nestled in the foothills of Northern California. My experience at St. Mary's Catholic School was largely positive. Discipline was strict—50 to a room, we sat up straight, hands folded on our desktops, and we marched out to recess in an orderly line in our uniforms. But this discipline was never harsh, and I believe it gave me an ability to focus that has always served me well.

As to theology, answers to the great questions were learned by memorizing the catechism.

> *Who made me?*
>
> God made me.
>
> *Why did God make me?*
>
> God made me to know, love, and serve him.

We did not study the Bible directly but rather took "Bible History" lessons that recapped the major stories and themes. One year the parish sponsored a Bible sale, and everyone was encouraged to buy a leather-bound copy for the home. My parents chose one of the largest, a volume the size of two phone books with a white leather cover marbled with gold to look old. After a few weeks the novelty wore off, and we never opened it again.

Religion was never discussed at home; we simply did whatever was on the church calendar. My dad was an engineer for IBM, a quiet and competent man with a gentle sense of humor. And my mother was a schemer—buying real estate with the pennies she saved on our grocery bills. My parents spent weekends renovating whichever old house was Mom's latest project; but we never missed church.

The sacred aspect of the Catholic Church moved me: stained glass, ceremony, and incense evoked my reverence. At about age 9, I had the first of my life's two mystical experiences. I was walking alone to weekday mass, something I did only occasionally since it was not required. On that morning I was dawdling, not sure I wanted to go. A small breeze touched my back, and suddenly I had a sense of the presence of the Virgin Mary. In my mind, her blue-robed image filled the horizon; her outstretched arms encircled the town, and her hand reached all the way around to give the gentlest nudge to that spot on my back. My family was stable and loving, but this was the most safe, loved, and valued I had ever felt. I hurried to get to mass on time.

Authority vs. independence

Despite this experience—or perhaps because of it—at age 13 I stood nervously on the school steps awaiting the pastor. I had recently graduated into the public high school where a maverick history teacher was telling us about Eastern Religions. When the pastor came by that day, I told him I would not be returning for weekly religion classes because we were not allowed to discuss other religions or "social issues" there, such as abortion. Instead, friends and I had persuaded one of our parents to hold alternate discussions in their home. The pastor warned me about being exposed to false doctrines, but he was not forcefully opposed. I think he was too surprised to know what to say.

At about the same time, my Girl Scout troop broke away to operate independently. We were running a profitable pancake breakfast once a month to save money for a trip to Mexico. Girl Scout Headquarters wanted a portion of the profit that we considered unreasonable, so we decided to continue operating as an independent troop. It was years later before I would see the pattern developing: moving back and forth from community to independence.

In college, I fell away from going to church altogether, not because I rejected it, but because it had become a tight-fitting shirt that no longer seemed relevant. I was having sex with my boyfriend in the "free love" 70s and couldn't believe I would go to hell for it. Still, I remained grateful to Catholicism for both the discipline and the interest in the sacred that it had given me. When I moved to Washington, D.C. for a career in communications, I lived mostly as a secular humanist, dabbling in meditation and reading an occasional book on the interplay of psychology and spirituality. My friends were all people pretty much like me.

A mid-life transformation

Then at age 36 I took one of the major personal growth workshops that were sweeping the country in the 80s, and I had my second mystical experience, or actually a set of them, as I will relate later. The focus of the workshop was on taking 100% personal responsibility for our lives and recognizing that "the Universe" reflected our thoughts back to us in our experience. The facilitators challenged us to consider everything that took place within the workshop as a microcosm of how our lives worked.

That backdrop produced a vortex of apparent coincidences. One of the most striking occurred when the facilitator was working with one young man to point out how his thoughts had contributed to all the problems in his life. The man grew increasingly uncomfortable as he began to see how this might be so. Then the facilitator asked him a particularly pointed question about his divorce, and the man said, "I'd do anything to get out of here right now." At that moment, the hotel's fire alarm sounded, and loudspeakers asked us to evacuate the room. We filed out in a state that elsewhere might have been called, "Fear of the Lord." Possibly that alarm was only a coincidence. But from that day forward, I began to see such coincidences regularly in my life. And as I paid attention to the lessons I could impute from them, my life got immeasurably richer and more joyous.

Secular friends tell me that such apparent coincidences are only a product of the human mind's capacity to make a story out of whatever material is presented to it. And they may be right. But there was another aspect to the workshop experience that hooked me: the sense of connection with other people and with this "Universe" with which we were interacting.

There was nothing explicitly spiritual about the workshop, quite the contrary. But one of its intense interpersonal exercises had us just look at each other in silence. For many of us, this produced a profound sense of connection, both between us and to something beyond. Eventually I would realize that I had reconnected with the sense of Divine love I had glimpsed in my childhood vision. The result for me was a hugely expanded view of life and an ability to see the Divine spark in other people, especially those *not* like me.

A husband on a similar path

Two years later I used a personal ad to meet my husband, Andy Murphy. The ad said, in part, that I was looking for someone who, "lived by his word(s)," and who "laughed at himself easily, was willing to say what was hard to say, and who believed that life is what you make it." That ad netted me a husband who had been on a trajectory remarkably similar to mine: from Catholicism to humanism to a sense of the power of the mind when it becomes aware of a connection to "the Universe." Together we celebrated the sense expressed by Emerson in his famous essay *Self Reliance* that,

> We lie in the lap of immense intelligence, which makes us receivers of its truth and organs of its activity. When we discern

> justice, when we discern truth, we do nothing of ourselves, but allow a passage to its beams. If we ask whence this comes, if we seek to pry into the soul that causes, all philosophy is at fault. Its presence or its absence is all we can affirm.

Andy and I went looking for a community in which to share this radical sense of spirituality. He found the Celebration Center of Religious Science, which I described briefly earlier, via a newspaper ad.

Celebration Center of Religious Science

The Celebration Center leased a building that was designed as a bank at the edge of a strip mall. Every Sunday morning about 100 of us sat in hotel-style chairs facing the "platform" from which the minister gave "encouragements" instead of "sermons." We were mostly middle age and White, with every kind of religious background, but an odd preponderance of ex-Catholics.

The only permanent adornment in the lilac-painted room was a colorful piece of fabric art at the front. A circle surrounding a heart that burst forth glittering rays symbolized the interaction of human and divine thought taking form in the universe. After an encouragement, a reading chosen by a member, a brief silent prayer, and some upbeat music, we pushed the chairs aside to enjoy socializing and whatever refreshments anyone had brought.

The small bookstore at the entrance carried texts by our founder Ernest Holmes for those who were taking evening classes plus other self-help and spiritual titles. Completion of a four-year program of study made one eligible to be licensed as a Religious Science Practitioner. These practitioners coach people in the five-step affirmative prayer technique that is the hallmark of Religious Science, "Spiritual Mind Treatment." The day I first learned of the technique—which I will describe later— I felt a forehead-slapping surge of, "This is so obviously right, why didn't anybody ever tell me about this?" And indeed, with guidance from the practitioners, I came to rely on affirmative prayer to uplift me when I was irritated or upset about something.

Church politics was one of the main things I let myself get irritated about. It was the same as anywhere: a small number of volunteers doing most the work, a few tithers who carried the load of paying the rent, and endless committee meetings to determine things such as whether someone's workshop on psychic pets was sufficiently aligned with our belief system to be announced in the Sunday bulletin. (It wasn't.)

At its most uncomfortable, church politics was about drawing lines between the authority of the minister and that of the board. (Believe me, I could write another book on how this issue is the white hot flash point in attempts to balance community and individuality, faith and reason, surrender and taking a stand.) Two years before our story begins, the community had a nasty confrontation when the board decided not to renew the contract of a minister. My impression was that some of the unpleasantness stemmed from the fact that our reliance on "keeping the higher thought" left many of us with no response to persistent conflict but avoidance and passive aggression: standing behind trees throwing rocks packaged to look like roses. I was guilty of my share of this, and some of my friends at The Center might say that if I and a few others were better at holding the higher thought, the conflict would have resolved itself. But I also had the impression that in another time and place, our "higher consciousness" might have called some of us to burn others at the stake—which would have been done with the highest motives of "purifying consciousness." Still, I was unable to garner much support for bringing the parties together to negotiate. And this was one reason I was feeling out of step.

Andy's sense of being out of step stemmed partly from a desire for more social action; it was limited to an annual Christmas basket for a needy family and a cleanup that Andy started of the local roadway. But the Celebration Center did keep a full calendar of social activities—film nights, tubing trips down the Shenandoah River, and playful skits that I wrote and directed.

Despite our recent yearnings for something new, Andy and I loved The Center. As freelance teachers and editors, we had no regular office community, and we had no children at home. So being a part of this community and helping to keep it running at its best had been deeply satisfying.

Religious Science and New Thought

Also satisfying was being surrounded by people with whom we could explore all the questions that arise from the twin assertions of Science of Mind that

1. Everything is connected, or "God is all there is"
2. Therefore, our thoughts create our reality

Congregants encouraged each other to focus on the "higher thought"—the most positive and loving outcome for any situation. For example, a person dealing with a difficult boss might be encouraged to envision both himself and the boss as being in a satisfying and rewarding work environment. Such a focus tended to produce daily demonstrations that many "challenges" (we never said "problems") could indeed be overcome solely by changing our thinking about them. Curiously enough, this had the effect of producing a community that I believe has more "faith" than the average church in which everyone has been a member for life. This was not the faith of our fathers in various doctrines. Rather it was a stripped-down faith that there was something out there that interacts with us. We acquired this "faith" not from a book, but from personal experience in our lives that the principles worked—most of the time. In fact, we were reluctant to use the word "faith," normally preferring the phrase, "Trust the Universe."

The philosophy we were practicing, Science of Mind, was one of several in the New Thought movement that emerged after the 1850s when it began to look like man had to choose between science and God. The theory of evolution convinced many people that we didn't need God to explain how life began; the Industrial Revolution made it appear that we wouldn't need God to solve our problems once science figured everything out; and it looked like psychology could cure our neuroses without needing God to forgive our sins. In fact, it was beginning to look like God was a pre-modern superstition.

But a lot of problems turned out to be more stubborn than we expected. So along came several thinkers to reconcile science with "the ancient wisdom traditions" of philosophy and world religions. (A brief history of New Thought is in the endnotes.[1])

New Thought vs. New Age: an old "Secret"

The founder of Religious Science was one of those reconcilers. In 1936 Ernest Holmes wrote *Science of Mind*, which became the basis of the SOM philosophy and of the church of Religious Science. One summary of Religious Science is, "There is a power for good in the universe, and you can use it; it works through your thinking." This core concept is present in many of the alternative religions generally labeled today as "New Age." The difference, as my friend Ed Preston once put it, is that a "New Ager" may believe that healing happens because there is power in the crystal, herb, or Indian chant used for it. The New Thought adherent believes the power is solely in one's thought about the crystal, herb, or chant.

In Ernest Holmes's model of New Thought, as I understood it, all thought passes through a "creative medium," which can also be called the Law of God, and there it attracts everything necessary to manifest in form. Newcomers to New Thought tend to focus on using these principles to improve their finances, relationships, or health. Those were the benefits highlighted in the popular book and film, *The Secret*. But with long experience in New Thought, some people come to believe that this "law of attraction" works particularly well when one aligns one's intention with what Holmes and others identified as the evolutionary direction of the universe—to ever more diversity, consciousness, and love. These seasoned followers work to align themselves with this universal, evolutionary flow. They may even begin to call this bigger picture of what they want "seeking first the Kingdom of Heaven."

This last fact is the reason I've diverged from our story to set all this background. I came to realize that for some people, the more they advanced in New Thought, the more their conceptions of "the Universe" began to converge with traditional views of God. And this would prove to be a major factor in my interest in hard-core Christianity.

Allergic to Christianity

In addition to the fact that the New Thought model of the universe seemed more rational than traditional religion, another reason many people were drawn to it is that they felt battered by the Christianity they grew up with. Here was a philosophy that focused on my status as a "co-creator" with God rather than as "a loathsome spider dangling over the pit of hell"—a line from Jonathan Edwards' 18th century sermon that appeared in my high school rhetoric text.

I personally never felt repressed by my religious upbringing. In fact, Andy and I coordinated a "Return to our Religious Roots" activity for Christians while we were still at the Celebration Center. But it was not received warmly by those whose wounds were still unhealed. In fact, it was ironic that a group that thought of itself as "honoring all religious paths" would eagerly celebrate any religious tradition *except* a purely Christian one. Founder Ernest Holmes had stated that Christianity was "the most appropriate religion for Western man." But at Christmas and Easter, we found ways to integrate other religious symbols into the service so no first-timer could conclude we thought Christianity was *better* than other religions. (People who want New Thought from a Christian perspective usually attend Unity, a larger New Thought group that teaches affirmative prayer as an interpretation of the Gospels.)

Breaking away... again

After Andy and I spent a couple years living these ideas at the Center, some church politics caused a few of us to break away and form an independent group. We actually ran a small church for five years, renting space from Presbyterians. Then we rejoined the Center a few years later when the situation we were uncomfortable with there shifted. It was at that point I saw my personal pattern regarding community—either I was a troublemaker who insisted on having things her own way, or I was committed strongly to both principle *and* community. How was I to know which it was? Hard core New Thought said it actually *was* whatever I chose it to be.

Yearning for a different mix

After returning to Celebration Center, Andy and I enjoyed its fellowship and encouragement for several more years before we began to yearn for a different mix. Religious Science as it is currently being practiced is extraordinarily good at developing one set of virtues. We began to yearn for balance with the complementary virtues.

- Balance between the **self-esteem** that builds a strong individual and the **humility** it takes for individuals to serve each other in community
- Balance between the traditionally "**feminine**" virtues of forgiveness, non-judgment, surrender, and compassion

versus the "**masculine**" virtues of courage to make hard choices and then stretch ourselves in *taking action* to fulfill them.

- Balance between **intuition** and **reason**.

Regarding the last issue, we had been attracted to Religious Science by the premise that reason never has to be sacrificed in our concept of the Divine. But more and more, we were hearing the value of "releasing" logic in favor of Divine guidance. And some of the guidance my friends received seemed suspect. Frequently this had to do with quitting a job or starting a new venture with no preparation. An article in New Republic satirized the phenomenon I was sensing:

> *God grant me the enthusiasm to pursue the things I excel at, the humility to set aside the things I stink at, and the wisdom to know that there really is a difference.*

For example, a group of us decided Washington needed a peace institute. There was lots of excitement about gathering to envision it, but no effort was taken to research similar ideas that had already been tried. Nothing ever came of the idea while I was at the Center.*

Taken together, the imbalances I was sensing created a stew in which we were so surrendered to everything that we were rarely moved to take action to improve a situation. And when we were moved to improve a situation, we spent so much time seeking divine guidance and each other's opinions that the original *gumption* behind a movement often got lost.** In another example, I was working on a committee at the Center to raise funds for our own building. We developed what we considered a pretty ambitious plan. But one of the congregants admonished us for having too small a vision. If we trusted the Universe, he said, we would call the local headquarters of Mobil Oil and ask them to donate $10 million to us. Okay, we said, why don't you make that call and let us know what happens? "Oh no," he replied, "That's the job of the committee."

This ungrounded idealism mixed with lack of personal responsibility was the opposite of the qualities that had attracted Andy and me to New Thought. It gave me a very non-spiritual desire to throw something at someone—which seemed to be an example of when it would not be a good idea to "follow my bliss."

I was wrestling with issues like these when the Center held a dinner for a young woman who was candidating for the post of minister. Rev. Harriet Quigley has both a sharp mind and a glow about her that bespeaks close contact with the Divine—a glow that she attributes to regular meditation and the intention to "put

---

* Several years later, a bill to establish a peace institute was passed in Congress

** Like Robert Pirsig in his Zen and the Art of Motorcycle Maintenance, I prefer "gumption" to "enthusiasm" as a more sturdy term to convey the original meaning from the Greek "filled with Theos," filled with God.

God first." I overheard her saying something that struck me like a ship's foghorn to a shipwrecked sailor. "We confuse the pre-rational with the transrational," she said. I had never heard these words before, but my heart leapt at recognition of a truth. I was about to become acquainted with a body of work that gave me a roadmap through my spiritual questions and set me up for my coming adventure at Highview.

4

Rescuing Truth, Beauty, and Goodness from Postmodernists

If you think that all values and
virtues are "merely subjective,"
you should not be surprised if
your own lifeworld starts to look
hollow and empty. To complain
about this state of affairs is like
murdering your parents and then
complaining you're an orphan.
Ken Wilber, *A Brief History of Everything*

Beauty, truth, and goodness act
as compass headings
for the improvement of the
human condition.
Steve Mcintosh, *The Natural Theology of*
Beauty, Truth, and Goodness

Ken Wilber to the rescue

Rev. Harriet was quoting Ken Wilber, a controversial philosopher who seeks to re-establish the place of Truth, Beauty, and Goodness at the center of life. Like my beloved Ernest Holmes before him, Wilber is an integrator. But he has the benefit of an additional hundred years of advances in all the ways we know about ourselves. Wilber created a "map" of human development that integrates the best work in psychology, philosophy, anthropology, science, and world religions. The comprehensiveness of his resulting "Integral Theory" has caused some to call him "The Einstein of Consciousness."

A key feature of Wilber's theory is that there is a *direction* to growth—for individuals, for societies, and for history. There is a *forward* and a *back*, and thus, a good and a better, a true and a more true, a beautiful and a more beautiful.

This puts Wilber at odds with some aspects of New Age thinking and the academic, postmodern culture of political correctness and extreme moral relativism. And while criticism of these movements was already coming from social conservatives, Wilber's insights carry more weight with "my people" because they come from the *inside*. For the academics among my peers, Wilber has written dozens of books praised by top scholars. And for those in alternative spirituality who value "higher consciousness," his lifelong practice of meditation makes him a credible reporter of those states.

Wilber's work put wind back in my sails for the spiritual journey. His influence will show up throughout this book, but two ideas in particular gave me the traction I needed to push off. He gave me a map that I could use for telling which direction is *forward* and a scale for weighing the guidance I hear along the way.

Except it's not exactly true to say Wilber's work *gave* me those abilities, because I already had an internal compass that was telling me something was off track in my experience of New Thought. I can't say for sure if that compass was set by the divine, by the nuns in Los Gatos, or by some hidden neurosis of my own. I had purposefully ignored its rumblings in order to do the last decade's work in becoming less judgmental. And now, almost everything Wilber said was making my internal compass spin wildly in recognition. Wilber was going to give me permission to *go back* and reactivate my navigation tools at a new level of awareness. And the wonder of it was that those two tools, for choosing direction and for weighing guidance, would also be the two uses of the Bible that Pastor Thomas would lay out for me.

(Please note that the next several pages sketch the theory behind these two tools. If you just want to continue with the story, skip ahead to the next chapter at *Another coincidence next door*, page 34.)

Growth to goodness

As to the first of these ideas, Wilber's model of human development includes higher levels that must be *grown into*: spiritually, ethically, socially, physically, etc. Most notably, in terms of ethics, studies show that in all cultures, we grow from being concerned only with ourselves, to being concerned with our families and our tribes, to being concerned with the good of everyone. The sociologists call it moving from egocentric, to ethnocentric, to world centric. Looked at in another way, our behavior grows through stages that have been called pre-conventional, then conventional, then post-conventional. Children and tribes are *pre-conventional* before they know the rules; *conventional* when they learn and follow the rules; and *post-conventional* when they put the higher good above following a specific rule.[2]

Because every child must start at the beginning and pass through these stages, the stages point the way toward growth. But Wilber says that many New Agers and secularists have it backwards. They are under the mistaken idea that childhood is a state of spiritual wholeness that we must move *back* to. Their mistake is to confuse a child's initial fusion with union. The babe smiles glowingly, he says, not because it senses its union with the Divine, but because it hasn't yet realized there is anybody else out there separate from it. Take the child's rattle away, and you bust this illusion and get a very undivine reaction. Only after a lifetime of disciplined devotion to sensing the connectedness of life do some adults reach a state in which no stress can permanently "rattle" them. That is genuine union with something beyond our personal egos. To look *backwards* for this state is to risk becoming self-focused narcissists on a "regress express."

This mistake leads us to spend too much time healing childhood wounds and not enough time on the moment-to-moment work of "growth to goodness," Wilber further says. This rang true for me in that I had become uncomfortable with the amount of focus on recapturing childhood wholeness among some of my peers. This was valuable work, no question. But "seeking our bliss" should offer us opportunities to work through these challenges, not sidestep them. Most of us were near 50; I was itching for the next phase of going out to contribute something with whatever portion of ourselves was functional. I expressed this sense in a spoof of *Peter Pan* at The Celebration Center in which I had Tiger Lily advise Peter, "It's time to connect with your inner adult."

Pre-rational vs. transrational

The second way Wilber set me up for something new was to give me a tool for distinguishing between intuitions that are concocted by my own mind and those that come from somewhere *beyond.* In Wilber's model, as children we are pre-rational—we believe in magic because we don't know better. Then we become rational; we learn reason and can test what's behind the magic tricks. But there is a form of knowing *beyond* reason that involves direct experience of the truth—whether you call it intuition or divine revelation. Wilber calls this form of knowing "transrational." Thus, it is beyond reason rather than opposed it. It always *includes* the rational.

The trouble is that it's very difficult to distinguish the transrational from the pre-rational, he says. They both look alike from the point of view of the purely rational; they're both non-rational. This "pre-trans" confusion, as Wilber calls it, leads to two kinds of errors, both of which I was suffering from.

The first error is *elevating* the pre-rational. In New Thought we put so much emphasis on following intuition that every whim, dream, or impulse gets full attention and respect. This made for some very long committee meetings, but I didn't know how to express the discomfort I was feeling. As a fellow board member once confided to me, "Nothing is ever just plain crap."

The second half of the pre-trans confusion leads to the opposite problem: we negate genuine transrational inspirations. An example of this problem is the childhood experience of the Virgin Mary that I described earlier. Wilber would call my vision a "peek" experience (as opposed to "peak") because it offered a glimpse of a higher realm of consciousness that I interpreted based on my culture and level of development at the time. A Native American child might have "seen" a great protective hunter. An experienced meditator might have felt a sense of oneness with no imagery attached. But that doesn't mean we weren't each touching something real. Each of us could take a lifetime to fully integrate such a glimpse into a fuller view of reality.

A child having that same experience in today's rational society, however, might be told he or she was simply imagining it. Wilber says that the consequences for society have been devastating as humanity's rich inner life of values around Truth, Beauty, and Goodness collapses into what he calls the "flatland" of things we can test by our senses.

The first part of the solution is simply to be aware that *there is a distinction* between transrational gold and pre-rational gunk. Other parts of the solution are explored throughout this book.

Godless science meets the New Age

Wilber also helped me see my confusions in historical context. In college philosophy class, I never quite followed all the abstract readings. But I did come away knowing that Truth, Beauty, and Goodness were somehow the sum of all values. Now Wilber showed me an inarguable *realness* for these "big three"—and their opposites. The quest for Truth, Beauty, and Goodness can serve as a compass for the quest for God.

Historically, Wilber shows me, the Enlightenment was a fight between science and religion to define Truth, Beauty, and Goodness. Science won and began the modern era without God. It promised us that Truth, Beauty, and Goodness would flow from technology and education. But then along came postmodern critics who "trashed" the definitions of the Big Three from both science *and* religion by proving that every perception is shaped by context in the eye of the beholder. Thus, those critics said, not only does God not exist, but Truth, Beauty, and Goodness don't really exist either. Wilber says the postmodernists were right up to a point, but then he moves on to show how "the Big Three" *still do* sit at the center of life, calling us.

Throughout these battles over definitions, people who heard the call of the Big Three (Truth, Beauty, and Goodness) split in different directions. The Transcendentalists and their children in the New Age movement rejected all religious authority and took intuitive knowing as their guide. We should "follow our bliss" and listen to our hearts.

But having broken the iron grip of both dogma and reason, these movements fell prey to confusion. Where was the dividing line between the pre-rational and the transrational? How am I to know if a feeling that draws me flows from divine intuition or from my subconscious ego needs?—from God or the devil, as my new Christian friends would ask. Without some means of drawing such a line, it was a slippery slope to extreme moral relativism, political correctness run amok, and tongue rings on preteens.

No wonder I was confused.

But my new hero Ken Wilber insists there *is* truth, and it can be *measured* from the outside and *experienced* from the inside. This perspective saved my sanity later in our story when Bishop Thomas grilled me about what *standard* I use to measure value.

Seeking a new balance

Wilber's perspective also helped me to make sense of the thirst I was feeling for a new balance among competing pairs of values.

- Yes, we must reclaim our self-esteem if it is damaged, but then we must grow *forward* to take our place in community.
- Yes, avoid judging others, but then *act* on your best determination of what serves the highest good.
- And yes, we all have access to guidance from a higher realm. But when that guidance tells us to kill the neighboring villagers or bet your paycheck on a particular horse, consider whether there might be some *other standard* against which you can measure the trustworthiness of your source.

Paradox rocks

The newly hired Rev. Harriet was a drink of water to this thirst for balance. She preached that we should transcend "either-or" thinking in favor of integral, "both-and" thinking that accepts paradox. And thus we must simultaneously cultivate both sets of values in ourselves. My friend Ed Preston turned this attitude into the slogan "Paradox rocks."

Rev. Harriet's fresh approach came partly from her mentor, Rev. Michael Beckwith, who was the biggest star in Religious Science at the time. Reverend Beckwith was the nephew of a Baptist preacher, and he heads a multiracial congregation of 9,000 at his Agape International Spiritual Center in Los Angeles. I had heard him speak and been intrigued by his focus on "seeking first the kingdom," an emphasis that came with absolutely no dogma attached. (Rev. Beckwith has since left Religious Science for an independent ministry, and the organization our Center belongs to has renamed itself United Centers for Spiritual Living.)

But while our new minister's approach released the tension I felt around one set of paradoxes, she increased it around another: the tension between the glory of the individual and the glory of God. No longer were Sunday encouragements about the thrilling freedom and responsibility of co-creating our path with God, but rather they were about meditating to hear the plan God had already set for us—and for the church. And I didn't much care for the sound of that.

I had tried meditation over the years, and I gave it another try now. But it just didn't stick as my regular spiritual practice. I much preferred the written "spiritual mind treatment" prayers that were the hallmark of Religious Science. This put me at a disadvantage both in the congregation and in my studies of Ken Wilber. He and many other spiritual teachers I respect recommend meditation for growth in consciousness. Wasn't there another way?

I was casting about for a different means to integrate the mounting paradoxes. When Andy and I started attending Highview, it was like going from the ice chest to the lobster pot on each of these sets of issues. For the first 6 months, the water had felt pretty good…

5

We Have Each Other's Attention, Now What?

Each eye was placed where one
ray should fall,
that it might testify of that
particular ray.
Ralph Waldo Emerson, *Self Reliance*

Note: the first half of this chapter is all social theory. If you want to continue with the story skip to *Another coincidence next door* page 34.

Spiritual slumming

I told myself that my interest in Highview expressed a search for *balance* in the masculine/feminine value pairs discussed in the previous chapter. But some of my friends had another word in mind: *regression*. It is near-universally assumed in secular and New Thought circles that fundamentalism ranks barely higher than magic in the levels of spiritual consciousness—and some New Agers would rank it lower. A few friends thought it was just another interesting Murphy adventure that we were crossing a line that few had crossed before. But other friends, people who would have asked polite questions if we said we were dabbling in Voodoo, changed the subject abruptly when we told them we were visiting a fundamentalist church. Their shock was palpable.

Was I in fact spiritually slumming—regressing to a belief system that offered the comfort of certainty and pandered to my desire to meditate less and act more?

Transcend and include

Once again, Wilber's map provided a useful check on my internal compass. At first glance, the map showed Highview on a street going the wrong way for me. It ranks fundamentalism low: allowing the authority of a holy book to trump reason makes fundamentalism pre-rational, and believing that "only our people are chosen to be saved" makes it ethnocentric. However, a closer look at the map—and at Highview—was going to suggest that my initial reading was wrong on both counts—or at least incomplete.

For one thing, Wilber is one of the few voices in intellectual circles calling for secularists to respect the contributions of religion at *every* level. He starts with the assumption that *no perspective is 100% wrong; even lunatics get some things right*. My friend Connee Chandler passed along this image: Each of us is a lighthouse with an arc we illuminate and an area of darkness behind or beyond us. Each of us has areas of brilliance and blindness.

In Wilber's model, these varying perspectives can be ranked in terms of development. The most reliable way to do so, he says, is to note that each level of truth will "transcend and include" levels below it: each level will *transcend* the lower level's limitations but *include* its benefits.

Wilber further insists that each level of truth makes a critical contribution to the growth of both the individual and the society as a whole. To extend the lighthouse analogy, imagine an array of lighthouses in a rocky bay. A taller lighthouse might cover more ground. But when I'm negotiating a particular reef, I may be better served by the shorter lighthouse whose beam shines directly on my position.

Thus it makes no sense to disparage the contributions at any level. Just as it would make no sense to condemn crawling once one learns to walk, so it makes no sense to reject the constructive values of fundamentalism: structure, order, loyalty, and mastery of the sex and power drives that rule at the lower levels.

In fact, Wilber says, religion is the only "conveyor belt" capable of moving most of humanity up through the various levels of growth. In *Integral Spirituality: A Startling New Role for Religion in the Modern and Postmodern World*, he says that intellectuals' disdain for religion is hampering the conveyor belt's movement.[3] Among our social problems, he calls this cultural clash "the single greatest problem facing the world." Instead of dismissing religion as "merely myth," we should be seeking to grease the conveyor belt: to applaud every religion's efforts to keep people moving *up*.

Another coincidence next door

As the first night of Metaphysical Bible class at Celebration Center approached, I got a call from a woman I had seen a few times at the Center. Miriam Wilson is a delightful, retired clown who spent many years volunteering in hospitals. Her "heartsy" interest in crystals, costumes, and energy vortices contrasts with my cooler interest in ideas. She said she was considering taking the Bible class, and that people at the Center told her to talk to me about it—presumably my Highview connection made me an authority.

As we talked, I was amazed to hear her story. Miriam told me that she had always had a close relationship with Jesus, and that it had taken an abrupt turn when she had a near death experience 20 years ago. Afterwards, Jesus spoke to her directly, she said. And one of the "assignments" he gave her was to set aside her crystals and infiltrate a Bible College. She didn't use the word "infiltrate," but I got a sense of covertness from the story she told. She said she learned a lot during the five years she was there, and that she enjoyed the passionate praise and the hands-on healings she participated in. But she was never comfortable with the fear-based aspects of hellfire and damnation. In fact, she said she helped a couple of people to "get out" when they wanted to but couldn't withstand the group pressure to stay.

Bridges in the invisible

I asked Miriam why she stayed in a place where she wasn't thoroughly comfortable. She said she felt she was "building bridges in the invisible." She said that even if she never shared any of her own gentler beliefs about Jesus, that she believed her presence at the Bible College made a difference.

I was struck by the parallels between her story and mine. And I liked that she hadn't been on a mission to change anyone's mind. Building bridges in the invisible sounded like a pretty good intention for my time at Highview. I adopted it until something better came along.

Considering Miriam's story, I thought perhaps I should stay at Highview at least long enough to have a few more discussions with Bishop Thomas. But I was concerned that I would be wasting the time of this very busy man if his sole reason for meeting with me again was to convert me. On the other hand, I was intrigued by a chance to expose him to another point of view. And the only honorable way to do that would be to keep an open mind myself, even if that meant risking being seduced into his beliefs. Didn't the Buddhists counsel us to keep a "beginner's mind"? I could ask friends at Celebration Center to tie a rope around my waist.

Looking for loopholes

Shortly after my initial meeting with the Bishop, Andy and I left on one of our regular trips to the Bahamas. I took with me the Peter McWilliams book that I had studied in preparation for that first meeting, *Ain't Nobody's Business if You Do*. McWilliams, who was gay, died after being imprisoned for flouting the law against medical marijuana for his cancer pain. That made him a genuine martyr in my eyes. So his witty but respectful Bible commentary felt like a trustworthy starting point for putting my toe into the Bible. McWilliams stood in awe of the Jesus who

> ...made one of the most brilliant moves in the history of human thought. He gave a series of examples that illustrated

> a being *so* loving, *so* giving, and *so* trusting in God that it was *absolutely impossible* for a *human* being to achieve the ideal. He then *specifically prohibited* any attempts to improve others until you, yourself, were entirely loving, giving, and trusting.[4]

At one point McWilliams recounts the deathbed scene of Vaudeville's W.C. Fields—an unrepentant, hard-drinking womanizer not unlike Denny Crane in TV's *Boston Legal.* If the Bible is right about hell, Fields had cause to be nervous. Supposedly a friend came in and found Fields reading a Bible. "What are you doing?" asked the friend. "I thought you didn't believe in God."

"Looking for loopholes," Fields said.

I realized that looking for loopholes was exactly what I was doing.

Testing the waters

But still I was mired in doubt about approaching the Bishop again. Could I really be myself in any subsequent communication? Perhaps the very special opening we had created was a one-time wormhole across our universes that would close off as soon as he realized how different my universe was.

I decided to test the water by sending him an email. I said how much I appreciated the openness of our discussion, and I told him about the coincidence of the Bible class invitation from Celebration Center. And I teased a bit:

>> So doesn't that sound to you like I got direct guidance from a source other than the Bible? Huh? Gotcha, huh? <<

He replied,

>> Bless you, Teri. The pleasure was all mine. Let's do it again sometime. God really does speak to us. And the more we listen, the more he speaks.

Love ya,

Bishop T. <<

Emboldened by this response, I ramped it up a bit, sending another email with a couple of provocative statements about my beliefs, for example,

>> Religious Science, that's my cult. We believe that all thoughts are prayers and all prayers are answered… <<

The response I got back couldn't have been better:

>> Well now Teri, I am sitting here reading your email and grinning from ear to ear and asking myself, What am I going to do with you? <<

I had poked the bear expecting to flush out rigid defensiveness or judgment, and instead I got willingness to "play." If we could both maintain this level of openness in future communications, interesting things just might happen.

Dueling fundamentalists

Another overlay of irony to this situation was the fact that my best client in the Bahamas was a family of Jehovah's Witnesses who owned a bakery. I created and managed a website for them that made their key lime tarts a first stop for many tourists arriving at the island. In exchange, Andy and I stayed in their apartment over the bakery and ate all the baked goods we wanted. (Have I mentioned that we seem to lead a charmed life?)

Initially I had all the common preconceptions about Witnesses: that they are rigid, narrow minded, and pushy. But this family's qualities are as far from that stereotype as possible. Robert Arthur and his wife Anna gave up careers in television production to come here. Starting with nothing, they opened a bakery from which they also now run a real estate business.

Robert has suggested to Andy the possibility that they co-write a sitcom based on life in the bakery. And so, on a typical morning, I sit in the bakery with my laptop and my banana pancakes watching what Andy and I call "The Robert Show." One of the bakers didn't show up, so Robert has been up since dawn rolling out jalapeno cheese bread, setting some aside for the poor family next door. Now he is helping school children buy donuts while appeasing a tense New York tourist whose latte came with whole milk instead of skim. He's also swapping hilarious stories with some wealthy captain of industry who owns a house here and wants advice on fixing his water pump. Then a local guy who started drinking too early comes in to panhandle, and Robert deftly escorts him outside and points him to someone who is hiring day laborers. The phone rings and Robert cradles the receiver to counsel a pregnant teen while serving another order and motioning some homeowners to start without him a meeting to form a fire protection committee. (When a bad hurricane hit several years ago, the bakery served as relief headquarters, distributing supplies contributed by Witnesses overseas.) Robert moves deftly between the bakery and his house next door tending to his chronically ill wife who nevertheless dresses fashionably each day and helps out as much as she can. After the bakery closes, I overhear another phone conversation in which Robert negotiates with someone who is trying to cheat him out of a real estate commission. Robert is firm, calm, persistent. Even when he hangs up, the only tension he releases is to say, "*Some* people."

"Robert, don't you ever get upset about anything?" I ask.

"What's there to get upset about?" is his reply.

This was a life balanced between action and surrender.

Even my impression of the family's proselytizing shifted when I realized that they regularly worked a full day and then spent several hours studying their Bible via scholarly cross-references to the many other translations. Then they went out sharing what they learned with the elderly, the sick, drunks on the corner, and anyone who wouldn't turn them away at the door. These people were experts in the Bible, and they had more energy to live their beliefs than I had ever had.

So on a theory somewhat akin to, "It takes a thief to catch a thief," I asked them to comment on some of Bishop Thomas's Bible interpretations. I got an earful—some of it surprising, like the fact that Witnesses don't find justification in the Bible for hell as everlasting conscious punishment. Clearly the world of fundamentalism was more complex than I realized.

It seemed ironic that Bishop Thomas had indeed motivated me to look into the Bible, although probably not via the kind of resources he had in mind. My team now included a Jehovah's Witness, a gay drug user, a "metaphysical" Bible class, and a bald, meditating, postmodern philosopher. I thought they had pointed me toward a few loopholes, and I was eager to request a second appointment with the Bishop when I returned home.

A bad start: busted and going to hell

Upon my return from the Bahamas, I went to Sunday service at Highview eager to try on my new status of being open about my beliefs—and to set up a second meeting with the Bishop. But to my horror near the end of service, he went on a tear about how "Some people think they can believe in any version of God they want, but they're going to hell. Being a good person has nothing to do with it. You can be a Boy Scout or a sweet little old lady on her cane and still go to hell."

With dismay I assumed this was directed at me, and that my communication with Pastor Thomas had actually made the situation worse by causing him to focus on hell, which he normally didn't do. I lost my nerve about asking for a second meeting.

That would have been the end of this story but for some advice I got from my dear friend Ed Preston. Ed is a retired army colonel, a Practitioner at the Celebration Center, and an interfaith hospital chaplain. Thus he often walks the interfaith tightrope and was intrigued by my intention to build bridges. He helped me to realize that if I wanted to dance with someone who believed in the devil, I had to be able to withstand the heat. He suggested that my best response to being told publicly I was going to hell was to say, "Well, now Pastor, I'm sitting here grinning from ear to ear and asking myself, what am I going to do with you?"

I laughed and requested a second appointment.

And then I prepared by writing a spiritual mind treatment, modified slightly to pass muster as a Christian prayer.

Purpose: To engage in dialogue with Bishop Thomas that serves the highest good of myself and others.

Dear Spirit, Universe, Higher Power, One Mind, Lord Jesus,

There is only one God, one Power, one Life animating and illuminating all things.

I stand in that Power, that Life, receiving passage of its beams.

I know that nothing can threaten my connection with this Source. And so I enter eagerly into exchange with Bishop Thomas, knowing that each of us has eyes placed to receive one beam of truth. I help him to see through my eyes, and he helps me to see through his. My lips speak clearly the truth as I know it. My ears are open to hear truth in a new way. And my heart is open to give and receive love with Bishop Thomas and with all my new brothers and sisters at Highview. Our exchange uplifts us both and flows outward to uplift all those whose lives we touch.

I am so grateful for this opportunity to expand the light.

I release this intention, knowing it is already done. And I await its outcome with joyful expectation.

And so it is.

In Jesus' name.

Amen.

I was ready for my second meeting with the Bishop.

Part II

God

6

How Could You Love a God Like That?

The Law is not thrust upon man. It rests deep within him, to waken when the call comes.
Martin Buber

I arrived for our appointment intending to go as far as I could to honor Bishop's understanding of God without betraying my own. I also planned to move slowly in revealing my non-traditional beliefs, waiting until we established common ground. We settled in to his small office on a Thursday night prior to a ministerial class he was scheduled to teach an hour later.

Teri: I should tell you right off that I believe there is a great deal of wisdom in the Bible, and that the ethical teachings of Jesus are one of the best guides for living on the planet. But I understand most of the Bible as metaphors, not the literal truth.

Bishop: Well some portions of the Bible are metaphorical, but it's important to know which ones.

Teri: That's where reason helps me. As a Religious Scientist, reason is extremely important to me. There shouldn't be any conflict between what reason tells us is the right way to live and what religion tells us. And I think philosophers have come to the same conclusions as scripture in most areas.

Bishop: I've studied world religions and philosophy, so I'm familiar with some of that perspective. And I am always open to learning. There's only one thing that's non negotiable—that you have to believe in Jesus and accept that he died for your sins in order for you to be saved.

Teri: Well, first of all, it doesn't make sense to me that belief itself would be the criteria for anything. McWilliams says in *Ain't Nobody's Business* that if I walk into a store and tell people, "There's a guy outside giving away ice cream," having faith in me means getting up and walking outside to get some ice cream. It doesn't mean believing I have special qualities because I delivered the message.

Bishop: Romans 10:9 (nkjv) makes this very clear. "**If you will confess with your mouth the Lord Jesus and believe in your heart that God raised him from the dead, you shall be saved.**"

Teri: And the second big obstacle is that I have trouble with the term "sin." I don't believe any force magnificent enough to create this universe sits around waiting to punish us for breaking rules.

Bishop: It's not about rules. Let me tell you the literal translation of "sin." It means to miss the mark. Like an archer.

Teri: Huh? That's how we define it in Religious Science.

Uh, Okay, so I can understand that "Jesus died for me" in the sense that he died willingly in order to bring us his ethical message.

Bishop: But that's not enough. Jesus died for us meaning *in our place*, as a substitutionary sacrifice for our sins.

There it was, the big one: It was the first time I had heard the term "substitutionary sacrifice," and I feared he was about to confirm my worst fears about what he believed. "*Transcend and include,*" I told myself, remembering Wilber's measuring stick that a higher truth can always include the less fully-formed versions of it.

Bishop: God provided everything man could ever want in the Garden of Eden. He told Adam and Eve they could have anything they wanted except the fruit of the tree of good and evil. Punishment for that would be death. But Adam and Eve defied him by doing the one thing he forbade. Nevertheless, God was so merciful he offered a plan of Salvation: he sent his Son to make a blood sacrifice in atonement.

Teri: What kind of a plan is that? How could you love a God who couldn't come up with a better plan than that?

Bishop: Under the circumstances, man left God no choice. He gave us free will and established the conditions for life in paradise. It was Adam who chose to defy him. God couldn't go back on his word that the consequence for defiance would be eternal damnation.

Teri: That just sounds preposterous to me. Even if it were true that some equalizing action was necessary for Adam's poor choice, it makes no sense that someone other than the guilty party would pay the price.

Bishop: That's because God required a perfect sacrifice. Man is not perfect enough to be a satisfactory atonement. So Christ had to be sacrificed in our place.

Teri: Well whose fault was it we're not perfect if God made us?

Bishop: You're missing the most important point. Jesus is really the same as God, and therefore God was willing to sacrifice *himself* for us because he loved us so much. This whole story is not about God punishing man. It's about God taking the consequences of our actions upon *himself.*

Teri: Hmm… I never heard it explained quite that way before.

Bishop: And all we have to do is accept that free gift of God's sacrifice. It's a *choice*. No strings attached.

Something about the way he emphasized "choice" rang a small bell for me. My car has a bumper sticker that says, "I'm pro choice on everything." I was surprised no one at Highview had asked me about it yet.

Teri: At least that helps me explain how you could feel good about that story. But it still sounds to me like the plan of an insecure person without much imagination.

Bishop: Well then I challenge you to think what better plan God could have implemented under the circumstances.

Teri: Uh, well. I'll take that challenge.

The full conversation took more than an hour, and we agreed to meet two more times to complete it. When we emerged from his office, his ministerial students were waiting for him, and I wondered if they had heard anything through the door. Then as I drove home I realized with a shock what had just happened: a minister had just given me a homework assignment to figure out my plan for God's life.

7

Metaphorical, Metaphysical, or Literal?

Be ye transformed
by the renewing of your mind.
Romans 12:2

Metaphysical Bible class

Before our next appointment, I attended the first session of the Metaphysical Bible class at the Celebration Center. The direction it took amazed me, and it provided exactly the tools I was going to need.

About a dozen of us sat in a circle and started by telling why we were there. Most said they had been turned off by punitive Bible interpretations they grew up with. One woman said she wanted to reconnect with the love for Jesus she had as a child that she felt was taken from her by her strict church upbringing.

We used a version of the Bible that we considered more authentic than most others because it predated them and was originally written in Aramaic, the language Jesus actually spoke. The teacher, Inge Schweiger, a stouthearted and ebullient ex-Methodist, provided a list of scripture references that paralleled the major themes of Religious Science. These included the first of three concepts that would lay the groundwork for me to be able to communicate with Bishop Thomas.

Wrath of God as a neutral force

Far and away the most important concept was that the wrath of God could be understood as a neutral force. A tenet of Religious Science is that the "Law" by which the universe runs is neutral: constructive thought in equals constructive result out. Destructive thought in equals destructive result out. I at first rebelled when the scripture Ezekiel 18:25-27 was presented as an example of how that same principle is reflected in the Bible:

> **You say the ways of the Lord are not fair. Hear now, O house of Israel; my ways are fair, but it is your ways that are not fair. If a righteous man turns away from his righteousness and commits iniquity, in the iniquity that he has committed shall he die. But if a wicked man turns away from the wickedness which he has committed and does that which is lawful and right, he shall save his soul alive.** (Lam)

No way this harsh, judgmental language reflected a neutral principle. Or could it? I had assumed for years that all that obnoxious smiting and judging in the Old Testament was just a cultural artifact of harsh times, a series of myths that had to be discarded in order to get to the good parts in the New Testament. As the possibility dawned that these obnoxious stories could be interpreted as containing a deeper truth just as they were, I felt another shift in the ground of my understanding. How much more of those obnoxious parts could be heard as neutral principle?

Parables as positive thought

The second bridging concept I learned from the class was that most of the parables could be understood as requiring careful use of our minds to "**inherit the kingdom of heaven**" with its "**peace that passes understanding.**"

We were using a 1955 text by Ervin Seale, *Learn to Live: A New Thought Interpretation of the Parables*. Seale's interpretations are based on the premise that "the kingdom of heaven" is a metaphor for the mind.

Everyone understands that the parables are stories that serve as metaphors, but Seale and many other New Thought teachers presented the metaphors as all pointing to one particular interpretation—and within the New Thought community, that interpretation is referred to as the metaphysical interpretation. (This can be confusing outside New Thought where "metaphysical" can have several other meanings.)

In this metaphysical interpretation, "**In the Beginning was the Word,**" means that before there was anything else, there was intelligence, conscious awareness; this is a proposition agreed to by many scientists, mystics, and philosophers going back to Plato. The New Thought view builds from that proposition to conclude that everything was *made out of* that conscious intelligence, and thus shares somewhat in its awareness and creative power. And thus, our "word" whether it be spoken or silent thought, is our link to that creative power. Our thinking is the primary determinant of our outcomes. Thus the informal motto of Religious Science is, "Change your thinking, change your life."

Seale was taking this concept to the point where it intersects Christian teaching. He says:

> Jesus in his teaching lets it be known that he is in this world but not of it. He is a citizen of another realm. His power, his authority, and his nourishment come from that other realm that is not distant in time and space from the realm in which other humans live… Only a relatively few attain the kingdom and those few can enter in and live in that realm after preparation and education... It is in this realm of mind that Jesus, without scepter, robe, or crown,… holds his sovereignty.

Seale also says that it is into this realm that the teaching of Jesus seeks to bring every man "as a king, ruling with authority and grace."

> While it is a paradox from an earthly point of view to make every man a king, from a spiritual point of view it is no paradox at all. For every man is inherently a king and must one day take note of his heritage, *put himself under the proper tutelage*, (emphasis added) and once more assume the throne of his life.

As I read this, I recalled Bishop's booming voice admonishing us to, "Get off the throne of your life." And I wondered if Seale's charge to put ourselves "under the proper tutelage" was a key to bridging the two ways of looking at man's relationship to God. Seale continues,

> Wisdom then, is the real king. And when it sits enthroned in a human consciousness, that human consciousness is king on earth… That you may take control of your own thought, marshal its forces, and destroy its enemies, and live in harmony with all of its surroundings, is the Bible teaching. And the parables of Jesus are illustrations to help you accomplish this task. [5]

Could it be that the only thing Bishop Thomas and I would be arguing is about is *where* that wisdom is found—in the Bible or in our hearts?

One example of Seale's approach is the parable in which the farmer burns the weeds after harvesting the wheat in Matthew 13:24-30. As a child I understood this parable as God sending people to heaven or hell when they die. In Seale's interpretation, the metaphor points to the need to cull our own minds of destructive thoughts, thus sending ourselves to heaven or hell in every moment. With this spin, many of the parables that had seemed obnoxiously punitive now became something I could relate to.

Primacy of faith

I didn't know it at the time, but within New Thought a movement was building to replace these metaphysical interpretations with a new approach to getting the "good stuff" from the Bible.[6] At the time of my class, however, this metaphysical spin on the parables was exactly what I needed to lead me to the most important bridging concept: the primacy of faith.

As I had told Bishop, I was always perplexed by the concept that faith is more important than works in traditional religion. I have secularist friends who lead exemplary lives—both in terms of personal ethics and in service to the world. So if life offers any sorts of "rewards," why shouldn't they be first in line?

But my metaphysical Bible class was about to turn this around. It reminded me that the main requirement for manifesting a desired outcome in New Thought is to focus exclusively on the constructive thought of that outcome, and then gratefully let it go as already done. I began to see a parallel with the fundamentalist insistence that man is saved by faith alone. In both systems, new realms of possibility open when you believe there is something out there that interacts with your thought. As the Bible says, "**According to your faith will it be done to you.**" (Matt. 9:29). Perhaps even my secularist friends were pursuing a form of "faith" in their ideal of Goodness. Their form got them the benefits of meaning and contribution, but not the deep extra joy of spiritual connection. They got results but missed out on the fun and comforts of seeing life as a spiritual adventure.

A bridge already there

At the end of that first night of class, we were given a chance to contemplate our goals for the class. I closed my eyes to soft music, desiring guidance about how to build a bridge. I saw a beautiful alpine meadow with something like the snow-capped Matterhorn in the background and a small stream in the foreground. Across the stream was a low, arched footbridge made of ancient stone, dating, perhaps, from the Romans. Despite its antiquity, the bridge was in perfect condition, no crack or discoloration. It was absolutely solid. There was nothing I needed to do to build or maintain it. All I needed to do was to step to the middle of it. And as I did so, deer and other creatures crept quietly from both banks to drink.

Without the influence of this class, I would not have been able to sit still for much of what Bishop Thomas would be sharing with me. He might never know it, but some of his hardest work was done for him in between our sessions together.

Where is the standard?

The populace think that your rejection of popular standards is a rejection of all standards. And the bold sensualist will use philosophy to gild his crimes. But the law of conscience is firm. If anyone imagines that this law is lax, let him keep its commandment even one day.
Ralph Waldo Emerson, *Self Reliance*

Armed with the new perspectives from my class, I told Bishop Thomas in our third meeting that I understood the overall story line of the Bible as a metaphysical metaphor.

Teri What I'm beginning to see in my class is one continuous theme running through the Bible: that our minds can interact with the mind of God.

Bishop: Well, that certainly has some truth. But as I said before, only some parts of the Bible are metaphorical, so you can't just interpret bits and pieces the way you want. You have to look at the whole thing in context. Some day I want to devote a whole session to showing you all the evidence that supports 100% authenticity for everything in the Bible. I can prove to you that the Bible is inerrant and infallible.

Teri: I'd be willing to listen, but I consider that highly unlikely. Especially since most literalists selectively exempt verses from literal interpretation – and literalists disagree among themselves what those exemptions should be.

Bishop: That's true. But study of the Bible is a lifetime commitment, and everybody is always going to be at different stages of their understanding. I am always open to hearing somebody's interpretation, as long it's fully supported by the Bible itself, and it doesn't conflict with basic doctrine.

Teri: Meaning the great commandment to love your neighbor as yourself?

Bishop: That and that you must accept Jesus to be saved.

Teri: But we've grown so much since biblical times. The authors of the Bible didn't have access to science and psychology to inform their interpretations of the divine input they received, and humans now have evolved ability to comprehend at subtler levels.

Bishop: But God hasn't changed. Malachi 3:6 (kjv) says, "**For I am the Lord, I change not.**" So I don't mind using outside sources where they're helpful. But you don't need any information outside the Bible to understand it. And I can show you testimony from countless people whose life-changing personal experience demonstrates that the Bible alone is enough.

Teri: I can believe that's true for them. And I could also show you testimony from countless other people whose life-changing experience was achieved via other sources.

Bishop: That may be, but they're on dangerous ground. Proverbs 14:12 (nasb) warns us, "**There is a way that seems right to a man, but its end is the way of death.**" Even people who refer to the Bible casually may be misguided because they have no firm yardstick for their interpretations. It's so easy to quote the Bible out of context.

Teri: That's for sure. So let me suggest some yardsticks that point to a metaphysical interpretation of the Bible.

First, the ancient metaphysical interpretation accords with what science currently knows about the universe and the mind.

Second, my understanding is that mystics in all the world's religions, the people who devote their lives to meditation, converge on a common *experience* of God whether they're Christian, Muslim, Hindu, Native American, or anything else.

And third, that common interpretation I'm talking about fully accords with Jesus' greatest commandment... "**Love the Lord your God with all your heart, with all your soul, with all your might, and with all your mind... Love your neighbor as yourself.**"

Bishop: You have me at a disadvantage in that I'm not familiar with all the research you're citing.

I was struck by the direct way he said this. It displayed a humility born of confidence that spoke more loudly than the actual facts of our conversation. Just as in our first conversation, I had the feeling he was really listening to me.

Teri: Well, I've brought one of my sources with me. My favorite philosopher, Ken Wilber, lists seven commonalities among the world's religions. I just happen to have them here in a list. May I read them to you?

Bishop: Go ahead.

Teri:

1. Spirit exists, and
2. Spirit is found within
3. Most of us don't realize this spirit within, however, because we are living in a world of sin, separation, and duality—that is, we are living in a fallen or illusory state
4. There is a way out of this fallen state of sin and illusion; there is a Path to our liberation
5. If we follow this path to its conclusion, the result is a Rebirth or Enlightenment, a direct experience of spirit within, a supreme Liberation, which
6. Marks the end of sin and suffering, and which
7. Issues forth in social action of mercy and compassion on behalf of all sentient beings.[7]

Bishop: In Christianity, there is no path man can take himself that will save him from sin. Only the sacrifice of Jesus can do that for him.

Teri: Well, yes, the world's religions mostly disagree on what the path is. But doesn't it seem significant that they all have so much in common?

Bishop: That's all interesting speculation. And as I said, I'm always open to learning. But the bottom line is that people who attempt their own interpretations are subject to temptations to pick a self-serving justification for their behaviors.

Teri: Ah. Well now I really agree with you on this one. I've been thinking that those of us who "follow our own truth" have a huge responsibility. It's easy to just accept whatever standard your culture or your holy book gives. But those who attempt a personal interpretation must subject themselves to continuous, rigorous, self-examination to weed out self-justification. Our egos are really good at concocting that, as you said. So I can see how anyone not willing to do that work might be better off following an accepted standard.

Bishop: And furthermore, another reason to believe the Bible means what it says is just to cover your bases. If you follow it and it's right, you go to heaven and avoid hell. But if you follow it and it's wrong, you haven't lost anything.

Teri: Good argument. But it puts people like me in a moral bind as we feel called by God to a metaphorical interpretation that reveals a more loving God. I would have to disobey that call and settle for a God I couldn't love with my whole heart, soul, and mind

We ended on that stalemate.

I left that evening admiring his clarity. Was I equally clear? What was my bottom line? Upon deliberation I discovered it to be that I wouldn't accept any concept of God that was smaller than the one I had. But otherwise I knew I had to stay just as open as Bishop Thomas was professing to be.

Also, I began to realize that I didn't know what I was talking about. Was I arguing from a pure Religious Science point of view that *all* roads lead to God, including the "godless mind over matter" which a mass murderer or voodoo practitioner might tap? (As my friend spiritual teacher Connee Chandler says, all roads get you there, but some take longer and go through bad neighborhoods.) Or was I arguing from the evolutionary point of view—that all roads are equal insofar as they flow with "the direction of the universe" by aligning with ever-expanding consciousness of Truth, Beauty, and Goodness?

The following Sunday, in his sermon on faith Bishop Thomas said from the pulpit, "There is nothing God can't do. And that's not metaphysical, Teri, that's supernatural. It's not mind over matter, it's faith over fact."

Mind over matter vs. faith over fact

Teri: That comment you made at the end of church last Sunday got me thinking. I've never distinguished between "mind over matter" and "faith over fact." To me they're the same.

Bishop: That's because you think everyone is basically good—that they would only use mind over matter for good ends.

Teri: I do take that for granted. Most people try to do the best they can at the time, based on their understanding.

Bishop: You've led a sheltered life. I can tell you, most people are out for themselves. And I'm not just talking about the ghetto. I'm talking about corporate boardrooms and high society. Most folks will stab their mother in the big toe to get a nickel. "Mind over matter" to most people means I use my mind to get your matter.

Teri: But there's really no difference between what's good for me and what's good for others. There's enough for everyone. And my enlightened self-interest will always include the interests of others.

Bishop: Well then you're in the tiny minority who can see it that way.

Teri: But Bishop, isn't it a losing battle to try to restrain people from doing bad? People are motivated by what makes them happy. That's why we like Joseph Campbell's advice to, "Follow your bliss." [8] Beginners may use mind over matter to get a red sports car. But eventually when that doesn't make them happy, they have to start looking deeper. So they notice what they're really looking for is excitement. But then they realize that all the other sources of excitement don't make them happy either. And eventually, all those roads lead to union with the One, with God, as the only lasting source of deep satisfaction.

Bishop: You're an idealist. It doesn't work that way in the real world. People have to make a choice to line up with God's will from the beginning. That's faith over fact.

The sun vs. the wind

I prepared myself for the next meeting by reflecting on Aesop's fable of the competition between the sun and the wind. To see who was stronger, they agree to test which one of them can force a human to remove his coat. The wind blows with all his might, but the man only wraps his coat tighter. When it is the sun's turn, it simply shines warmly and steadily, and of course, the man takes off his coat all by himself. I told myself that throughout this experience, I had to remember to be the sun. *Do not resist. Shine forth what you know for sure. And don't be so sure of what you know for sure.*

We both give ground

At the next meeting I got the impression Bishop had been imagining a similar analogy. It was clear we had both prepared by thinking of areas where we could show sympathy with the other's point of view. We were bursting with things to say, and excitement bubbled up from our mutual surprise over where the other was willing to give ground.

Bishop:

- Some ministers will quote scripture to say that women shouldn't serve in ministry, but that's a matter of interpretation, and I interpret it differently.

- Some ministers will use fear of God to manipulate people into complying, but that's not right and it doesn't work.

- Some Evangelical churches believe in speaking in tongues and baptism by water. But those are theologically controversial. Church should never be about inducing an emotional state that can't be lived by the next day.

- It's true that some of those television evangelists take advantage of people to get their money. There's a lot of hypocrisy in Christian churches. Every church has some people at the top who truly believe and many others who just pretend to.

From my side, I think I astonished him at the things I agreed to. And most of my friends would have been astonished too—shocked perhaps. The only reason I was able to make these "concessions" was because of the new light in which I was seeing the Bible in my metaphysical Bible class. Plus I was crossing my fingers behind my back about some of the terminology, thinking I could explain later after we established some common ground. The "untranslated" version in my head is shown in italics.

Teri:

- Yes, we are separated from God by sin.
  Having forgotten our Divine spark, we are prey to the ego which tells us it is safer to stay separate.

- Yes, Christ died for my sins.
  He was willing to die to bring me a message that shows how to end separation.

- Yes, we need a concrete standard to prevent someone from killing me and claiming he felt it was the right thing to do.
  When we say, "There is no right and wrong," we mean it at an abstract level, not as license for any behavior.

- Yes, the sexual revolution has gone too far and become destructive.
  On this one, I could really feel my friends throwing tomatoes at me. But I was gearing up to argue that just because sex outside of marriage frequently "misses the mark" of serving our highest good, that doesn't mean it should be illegal.

This exchange of concessions made us feel we were getting somewhere. We agreed to set a standing appointment for Thursday nights.

8

Loophole #1
Judgment, Hell, and Pagan Babies

Peggy, we've failed our children.
We can't expect the schools to do everything.
It's our job to teach them shame.
Cartoon character Hank Hill in the series *King of the Hill*

I'm wicked; he's ignorant

Something has to be faced squarely here. On the surface, the main reason people avoid discussions such as Bishop and I were having is to avoid provoking anger over strongly held beliefs. But I believe there is something deeper going on, no matter how much people deny it.

Something else explains the fact that many people resent the evangelist at their door far more than they resent the magazine salesman. Bishop says some of that resentment is really guilt—if we're in a lifestyle of cheating on a spouse or business partner, we don't want to be reminded that we are violating our own standards. And some of the resentment comes from feeling patronized; if I'm leading my life the best way I know, how dare someone else come along and tell me he or she knows better? And lastly, some of the resentment is born of fear—especially in a political climate where the other group has power to restrict our freedoms.

Yet I believe there is still something else deeper: fear of hurting and of being hurt.

The unspoken subtext in any such discussion is that only one of you can be right. If the fundamentalist is right, the other person is wicked, blind, and condemned—and maybe even worse—*unchosen* by God. If the nonfundamentalist is right, the fundamentalist is ignorant, gullible, and weak—unable to cope with ambiguity. Talk about a no-win conversation. No wonder so many of my "alternative-religion" friends feel religion has driven a wedge between them and their parents.

I remembered a time in high school I was enjoying the attentions of a boy who was a member of Campus Crusade for Christ. I remember the afternoon I stood before him outside the gym trying not to show the tears in my eyes when I realized he'd have no further use for me if I didn't convert. Now in the current scenario, I was coming to like Bishop Thomas as a person. But I figured the camaraderie we were developing might come to a quick end as soon as he realized I was not conversion material. Even worse, his statement in our first meeting that I was sent to him with something for him to learn could flip totally if he began to suspect the sender was one of those "other spirits" he'd mentioned.

And from my side, the stress of holding two realities might cause me to bolt at any time. How could I avoid thinking less of someone who took literally the story of Adam and Eve? It wasn't just that I didn't want to *show* Bishop Thomas any disrespect. I didn't want to feel it either. And thus, to avoid feeling it, I had to work like crazy to find a way to understand his perspective. I also knew I had to be prepared to release this interesting little adventure at a moment's notice.

I determined to talk to Bishop about how religion fosters judgmentalness.

The Bible forbids judgment

At the next meeting Bishop Thomas disarmed me by making my point before I could.

Bishop: Let me read you Galatians 6:1 (cev): "**If someone is trapped in sin, you should gently lead that person back to the right path. But watch out, and don't be tempted yourself.**"

Teri: That says don't get too close to a sinner because his sin will rub off on you?

Bishop: No, no. That says when you focus on someone else's sin, you're likely to just magnify that sin in yourself. So you should always keep your focus on your own behavior. A Christian can't afford to be judgmental.

Teri: What! That sounds like the psychological concept of projection.

Bishop: Something like that. Freud had some good points.

Teri: But you can't say that. That was my argument for tonight. I was all set to argue that preoccupation with others' faults is usually a projection of our own faults.

Bishop: I am always open to using psychology when it accords with scripture.

That stopped me for a couple moments as I tried to get my bearings. I felt like I was trying to swim at the point where the tides meet. I couldn't be sure which direction I'd be pulled next, but I was definitely moving.

Teri: Well… well... What about the rebuking your brother part? Who are we to do that?

Bishop: When you are based in love, and you know your brother is on a destructive course, isn't it your duty to do what you can to help?

Teri: Well, maybe. But we can never know if our perception is correct.

Bishop: That's true. That's why we have to keep going back to scripture, listen for the Holy Spirit's guidance, and remain humble about how much we know.

His words reminded me of a passage in psychiatrist Scott Peck's *Road Less Traveled* that I had been deeply struck by 20 years earlier. When I got home that evening, I pulled the book from the living room shelf. Peck was discussing the distinction between the person who takes a stand on principle and the one who ignores principle in the belief that God is on his side:

> There are two ways to confront or criticize another human being: with instinctive and spontaneous certainty that one is right, or with a belief that one is probably right arrived at through scrupulous self-doubting and self-examination. The first is the way of arrogance; it is the most common way of parents, spouses, teachers and people generally in their day-to-day affairs; it is usually unsuccessful, producing more resentment than growth and other effects that were not intended. The second way is the way of humility; it is not common, requiring as it does a genuine extension of oneself; it is more likely to be successful, and it is never, in my experience, destructive...
>
> In the arrogance of exercising power without the total self-awareness demanded by love, we are blissfully but destructively ignorant of the fact that we are playing God. …Yet there is no

> alternative except inaction and impotence. Love compels us to play God with full consciousness of the enormity of the fact that that is just what we are doing. With this consciousness the loving person assumes the responsibility of attempting to be God, and not to carelessly play God, to fulfill God's will without mistake. We arrive then, at yet another paradox: only out of the humility of love can humans dare to be God.[9]

Scott Peck died during the period of my dialogues with Bishop Thomas. I learned from his obituary that he became a Christian late in life after spending time in Eastern religions. Some Christians, however, accused him of heresy for sentences such as the last one quoted above. I found that sentence both thrilling and terrifying in its call to full responsibility.

Moral relativism isn't all bad

At most of our sessions, I led off with questions from a prepared list. But on this day, Bishop led off.

Bishop: I have a scripture for you today. 1 Corinthians 10:23 (ASV), "**All things are lawful but not all things are expedient.**"

Teri: Huh? That sounds like moral relativism. That sounds like something I would say. You don't mean *all* things are lawful.

Bishop: Yes. Christianity is not about following rules. The context of this verse is Paul telling followers that if they visit a house where forbidden food is served, meat that has been sacrificed to idols, they should go ahead and eat it rather than make their hosts feel judged by making a big deal about it.

Teri: What! That's exactly the argument I would make for moral relativism. A static set of rules can't cover all circumstances.

Bishop: Yes, but moral relativism doesn't have any standard. This scripture is counseling you to follow the spirit of the law, not the letter.

Teri: Right, exactly, serve the higher good, not the rule. That's what the sociologists call a post-conventional act, and it requires moral relativism. So I can't believe I'm hearing you right. I was all set to tell you that I am sympathetic to the fundamentalist disdain for moral relativism because it's gone too far in our postmodern culture.

Bishop: Well how can you say it's gone too far if you just let everyone set their own standards?

Teri: Okay. This is where Ken Wilber's work has really helped me. He points to work showing there is a universal standard that shows up across all cultures. And that standard is based in the fact that our growth always proceeds in a specific direction. We grow from being concerned only with ourselves, to being concerned with our families and our tribes, to being concerned with the good of everyone. The sociologists call it moving from egocentric, to ethnocentric to world centric.[10]

So regardless of what the rules are in any situation, the "higher" thing is what's good for more people, although it gets more complicated…

Bishop: It certainly does get more complicated. But if you are trying to please God, he only cares about what's in your heart.

Teri: No, you don't mean that. What about the Ten Commandments? If I break those I go to hell in your system, right?

Bishop: No. First of all, the Ten Commandments no longer apply.

Teri: What!

Bishop: Jesus fulfilled the law and brought a new covenant. He told us in Matthew 22 that it has only two commandments, "**Love the lord your God with all your heart, and with all your soul, and with all your mind. And love your neighbor as yourself.**" (Matt. 22:37-39)

Teri: Well, yeah, I can happily accept that as my prime directive but,

Bishop: And second of all, going to hell is an extremely rare case.

Teri: What! What about all those "pagan babies" the Catholic nuns had us pray for? You don't have a purgatory in your system so they're all going to hell.

Bishop: No. And this is not my system. This is God's system. No one is expected to follow the Word of God if they haven't heard it. But even people born in a deep jungle still have the opportunity to see a glimmer of God in nature. They have to take advantage of whatever light they are given.

Teri: That's not how I've heard it from other fundamentalists. And furthermore, nowadays almost everyone has had some exposure to Christianity. So that means you're saying God set up a system knowing it would send almost everyone to hell.

The loophole of how much we know

Bishop: No, because not everyone has a chance to hear the Word equally. (He turns to his laptop and looks up the scripture.) Luke 12:48 (kjv) says, "**For unto whomsoever much is given, of him shall be much required.**" So we are only responsible to the extent we have been shown the light.

Teri: I am really relieved that you leave that loophole. I have the impression that many Christians are certain everyone but themselves is going to hell.

Bishop: It's not a loophole because scripture also promises that whoever looks for truth shall find it. Matthew 24:14 (kjv) promises the world won't end until after everyone has had a chance to hear the Word. "**And this gospel of the kingdom shall be preached in all the world for a witness unto all nations; and then shall the end come.**" However, we can never know what's in another person's heart. So no Christian should go around judging who is and isn't going to hell. Everyone will have a full and fair chance to choose.

Teri: Aha! You're saying that once you're saved you can sin all you want and not go to hell?

Bishop: Yes, to some degree, but someone who is saved won't want to continue in any repetitive pattern of sin because they want to please God. 2 Corinthians 5:17 (kjv) tells us, "**If any man be in Christ, he's a new creature.**"

Teri: But what about all the people who say they're saved one day and then forget about it the next day and don't love their neighbor, which I think is probably the vast majority of people who call themselves Christians.

What it means to be saved

Bishop: They're hypocrites. You can't just say it. You have to mean it. Romans 10:9 (nkjv) says, "**If you confess with your mouth the Lord Jesus and believe in your *heart* that God has raised him from the dead, you will be saved.**"

Teri: Well okay then. But you can't tell me there aren't a lot of people who genuinely feel it in their hearts at the moment they say it, and then they forget about it the next day and just become more righteous and judgmental for being saved.

Bishop: Those people are immature in their Christianity.

Teri: So… are *they* going to hell?

Bishop: No. Some people come to salvation with strongly ingrained habits that take time to change. But if they meant it when they said it, the Holy Spirit is at work in their lives moving them to more light. Once you're saved, you would really have to get in God's face to go to hell. Confession of sin and a move to repentance is all it takes for his mercy.

Teri: Whoa, wait. What's with this confession and repentance stuff? I thought all you had to do was accept the free gift.

Bishop: To be saved, yes; that keeps you out of hell. But sin has natural consequences on earth that God's mercy can protect you from. For example, someone who has extramarital sex is likely to face physical or emotional consequences that God's mercy can alleviate if they repent. You can get an unlimited number of second chances. That's why we say, we don't want justice; the deal God offers is much better than justice.

Teri: So you're saying that everyone who is saved will get to heaven, but they may face consequences on earth for sin.

Bishop: Yes, but it's not just about consequences on this earth. Once you get to heaven, there are levels of joy that can be experienced in heaven. Matthew 16:27 says, "**For the Son of Man is going to come in his Father's glory with his angels, and then he will reward each person according to what he has done.**"

Teri: That reminds me of something a nun once told us in Catholic school. Two buckets can both be full, but the bigger one contains more. And in New Thought we think in terms of increasing our capacity for joy.

Bishop: Yes. Once you're saved you've got what we call your "fire insurance." But if you truly give yourself to God, you will want to spend the rest of your life getting closer to him. Becoming intimate. That's where the juice is. Both in this life and the next.

Teri: (After a long pause) Does anybody else know you believe these things? Wouldn't you be fired if your congregation knew these were your interpretations?

Bishop: What? What makes you ask that?

Teri: This is not what I associate with fundamentalism. The way you describe salvation isn't so bad, really. In fact, it actually reminds me of some of our precepts in New Thought. We talk about how our life transforms the moment we take responsibility for our thinking. And then we spend the rest of our lives deepening our understanding of what that means. For many of us, that process leads to sensing a flow of the Universe that we want to surrender to. *That's* where the juice is, we'd say.

Bishop: You can't just go deciding for yourself where the flow is. God's will is spelled out in the Bible.

Teri: I hear you. But I'm struck by the parallels in the way you've described salvation. It's richer and more constructive than I've heard. So I doubt that the people in your church have the same understanding you do.

Bishop: Yes they do. What makes you say that?

Teri: For one thing, whenever a visitor or Highview member gives the talk, they are frequently less... constructive than you are.

Bishop: When? Who?

Teri: Across the board.

He looked genuinely surprised at that. And then he delivered a final blow to my equilibrium by requesting something I never thought I'd hear from a clergy person.

Bishop: Would you be willing to pass me notes when you hear something you think is not constructive?

I don't know if he could tell from the incredulous look on my face that I was holding back from asking if the pope was Catholic. But instead I just said calmly, "Yes, I can do that."

Bishop: I try to maintain a high standard in who I let speak. But I also try to be open and let people learn things in their own time.

Teri: Yes, Andy and I have noticed that you are a master at what the Buddhists call "the art of allowing."

From the way his eyebrows arched, I think he got the fullness of both the compliment and the irony. And I think we may have both left that session a bit disoriented.

Moralistic therapeutic deism

I never got a clear answer to my question about the extent to which people in the Highview congregation shared the lofty understanding of salvation that Bishop Thomas conveyed to me. I got signs both ways from different individuals. I was further enlightened on this topic by an article suggesting that no matter what a preacher says, people hear it from their own levels. The piece reported a poll showing that today's teenagers who regularly attend churches that offer a high-level message of communion with God nevertheless come away with something the researchers called "moralistic therapeutic deism." MTD is belief in a person-like deity who judges right and wrong, and that the purpose of following rules is solely to make this life go better.[11] Much later, a heretical thought would cross my mind. Among my peers who report repressive religious upbringings, did some of us simply *not hear* higher messages that may have been clumsily communicated?

We are parallel opposites

Several parallels between Bishop and me were becoming apparent. Our differences in being male and female, Black and White, fundamentalist and New Ager put us on different planets of experience. But in other ways, we were mirrors for each other.

As a hard-core fundamentalist, Bishop Thomas believes man is saved only by the substitutionary sacrifice of Jesus on the cross. But he doesn't split hairs over any of the other doctrinaire disputes that fill the focus of many fundamentalists. Water baptism, prophecy, speaking in tongues: he doesn't promote them himself, but he believes they can benefit those who use them in their proper context.

Similarly, I came to him as a hard-core metaphysician and proponent of New Thought. I believe there is a power for good in the universe that I can use, and it works through my thinking. But I am not into any of the New Age extras that often come bundled with that core concept: crystals, tarot, chakras, shamanic spirituality, etc. I do believe these things can be of benefit to those who are into them—not because there's power for healing in a crystal, but because there's power in the *thought* that there's power in a crystal.

These parallels helped smooth the path for us in what was to come.

Did the devil make me do it?

Bishop: Human beings need a standard they can make choices by, and the Bible is the only perfect standard.

Teri: But reason can provide the same standard. Most of the behavior prescribed in the Bible is common sense for someone who pursues enlightened self-interest.

Bishop: No way. Human beings mostly use reason to get out of doing the right thing. They make up rationalizations to get themselves off the hook.

Teri: Well that's certainly true—except for the minority of individuals who put doing the right thing above all else.

Bishop: Even if they tell themselves that's what they're doing, there are too many forces out there pushing them to do the wrong thing: the world, the flesh, and the devil.

Teri: About this devil thing, I am extremely uncomfortable with that languaging. In New Age or humanist circles, just about everything you'd attribute to the devil, we can attribute to "ego," "shadow," or "small self." So I can see a lot of truth in what you're saying, but you should know I'm doing a translation in my head.

Bishop: But the devil is not part of ourselves. It's an outside force, and it's real.

Teri: In Religious Science we say that calling something real gives it force.

Bishop: Calling it real strengthens you to fight against it.

Teri: We say, "What you resist persists."

Bishop: We say that too. But if you're calling your ego real, you at least realize that there's a *real* force tripping you up.

How real is hell?

The next week, Bishop Thomas told me he'd been thinking about my questions on the devil and hell and had reviewed some tapes from his ministerial training.

Bishop: The devil's real all right, and so is hell.

Teri: But Bishop, no matter how bad a human being is, he or she can only commit atrocities for 80 years or so. So what justice is there in condemning someone to punishment for eternity as Revelations says? Even if you're seeking justice, that seems like overkill. (Oddly enough, this particular argument had been given to me by my Jehovah's Witness friends in the Bahamas.)

Bishop: Well, it's not outside a reasonable interpretation of scripture to say that hell isn't so much a physical place as it is a state of eternal separation from God.

As he said this, he dropped his voice, as if perhaps it was the first time he'd said it out loud. I gulped. This was more than I'd hoped for—although it wasn't quite as interesting as the interpretation of hell that my Witness friends had given me—that everlasting punishment is reserved for hypocritical clergy and politicians.

Bishop: But I'm talking permanent, total, complete separation from God. People can't begin to imagine what that's like. It is so terrible, that to call it burning in fire and brimstone doesn't begin to describe how bad it is.

Teri: Well it's easy to see how that could be true. Lots of people who believe in hell as physical torment still choose to commit suicide when they feel utterly alone and hopeless. They are risking physical pain to end mental pain.

Bishop: Whether it's actual fire or not, it's worse than any depression, much worse. And remember, the only sin that can separate us from God is unbelief—and that is our choice. When you think about it, the plan of salvation had to be something so simple that even a child could grasp it, as Jesus said, **"Let the little children come to me, and do not hinder them, for the kingdom of God belongs to such as these."** (Mk 10:14)

I noted awe in his voice. It was very much like the awe I feel when I think about participating in the evolution of the universe to ever-higher levels of consciousness.

Hell as a Sunday service

Teri: In Religious Science, the closest thing we have to a concept of hell is the state of mind we create for ourselves when we lose track of our connection to our Source, to God. It all takes place in what you call the kingdom within. Or as our founder Ernest Holmes said, "We are not punished for our sins but by them."

Bishop: That's true. I like that way of putting it. The only thing we are punished for is unbelief.

Teri: Whoa. Really? You believe that? Emphasizing faith like that always used to sound ridiculous to me. But I'm beginning to see how it fits with what I already believe. Faith is a different state of consciousness.

Bishop: Well it's more than that. And if you don't have it, you'll face the consequences not only in this life, but after you die. That's where hell comes in.

Teri: Well, what if we thought about hell this way: What if it's like a Sunday service? You know how people at a Sunday service all have very different experiences? Some are caught up in rapture sensing the presence of God, and other people look miserable, completely out of it, especially people who don't want to be there, like some of the children or men whose wives made them come?

Bishop: They're dying to go home to their chicken dinner.

Teri: Right, yes. So what if heaven is just like that? Only there's no end to it? The singing and dancing and praising just goes on and on and on, basking in the presence of God. So for people who don't love God, it would feel like hell to them.

Bishop: Well the trouble with that is, hell is definitely a separate place. The whole idea is that the faithful people don't have to get dragged down anymore by the sinners. They had their chance in life to do things God's way, but they refused.

Who believes in free will?

Teri: That's what's so hard to accept in Christianity—the idea that you only have one chance. The Religious Science belief statement says, "We believe the ultimate goal of life to be a complete emancipation from all discord of every nature, and that this goal is sure to be attained by all." (Belief statements for Religious Science and Highview are in Appendices.) And for those people who don't attain it in this life, we believe there is some form of continuing opportunity. We don't know exactly what that is. It may be something like reincarnation or perhaps our eternal nature is more like a drop of water returning to the ocean of the One Mind. But somehow you do get as many chances as you need to see the light. It just makes more sense that a loving system would be set up for continual growth and expansion of every part.

Bishop: But what if some parts *choose* not to grow? The Bible tells us everyone gets an infinite number of chances in this life. Even in the final days everyone will be given one last chance, but Revelations 16:9 says still they will **curse the name of God and refuse to**

repent. So at some point God has to cut the dead wood. What does Religious Science say about that? What about people who freely choose to turn their backs on your One Mind? Is it going to force them into oneness?

Teri: Good question. I think we'd say that the only reason people choose separateness over oneness is that they don't clearly see the alternatives. And eventually they will see the light.

Bishop: So you're saying you don't really believe in free will. Haven't you known people who were surrounded by love but refused every chance at it? Are you telling me you see no possibility that some people could live a million lifetimes, and they would still insist on doing things their own way?

Teri: Well, that's an interesting way to put it. I'll have to think about that.

I researched and meditated on this question and decided Bishop Thomas had put his finger on something. The believers in a God who is separate from us—be they Christians, Jews, or Muslims—are the only people who believe in complete free will. Eastern religions, New Thought, and most of New Age tell us everyone will return to awareness of their connection to Spirit; we have no choice. Secularists also tell us we have no choice; our choices are made by our social context or our genes.

Mounting loopholes

Bishop had just provided me with the first three loopholes in what it means to take the Bible literally. Where I assumed it required believing that everyone goes to hell who is not saved, he told me you are responsible only to the extent you have seen the light. Where I assumed it required believing in hell as a literal place of fire and brimstone, he said it could be a state of separation from God. And where I assumed that fundamentalists get their identity from judging that everyone but themselves is going to hell, he told me not only that you *must* not judge, but also that you *cannot* judge because only God knows what's in a person's heart.

These "loopholes" were more like air holes in that they created some breathing room for me within his doctrine. As such holes continued to accumulate throughout our discussions, they were going to make it increasingly possible for me to see how he could be so joyfully enthusiastic about a view of God that otherwise seemed irrational, or at best, "pre-rational" in the terminology I learned from Ken Wilber.

Call off the rescue?

I knew that I could find these loopholes taught in many mainstream churches. But the intriguing thing was that they could co-exist here with a theology that takes the Bible literally. Most of my friends assume this is impossible. They base their hope for world peace in promoting scholarship that claims to prove most Bible stories are valuable myths, not literal fact. They hope that works such as The Jesus Project[12] or Bishop Spong's *Rescuing the Bible from Fundamentalists*[13] will free people to embrace a loving God, a God that would never condone the kind of violence often done in the name of religion. And indeed, this approach is a lifeline for many people who feel something is deeply wrong with the harsh versions of Christianity they grew up with.

I took the lazy girl's approach to dipping into this research. I went to one of the most vehement critics of Christianity, atheist Ray Harris, who calls it, "an ideology based on lies and error (that) has been perhaps the single most important cause of developmental regress and arrest in the world." After extensive research on the history of the Bible, he finds evidence that undercuts the likelihood of many of its claims. Nevertheless, he concludes:

> We face an insurmountable problem; no one knows anything for certain. There has been a massive amount of work put into researching the truth of the Bible from a range of different disciplines. There is much disagreement and very little consensus. The major religions each have their own experts, and then the different Christian denominations also have their experts... There are good, independent scholars, and it is these we must rely on. But even then, these scholars are uncertain, cautious, and often very conservative in their pronouncements... No one can assert to know what really happened. [14]

That saved me a lot of work. If one of the Bible's most vehement critics couldn't know anything about it for certain, I could feel comfortable about not taking sides about what was fact and what was myth. Instead, I was getting a glimmer that perhaps there is another route to peaceful co-existence with fundamentalism. Perhaps some Christians have a way to get the "good stuff"—much of it anyway—out of the Bible just as it is. I began to feel that I was uncovering one such approach.

Too rational?

Furthermore, I was beginning to see something else that would become clearer as our dialogues progressed. Fundamentalism, at least as Bishop Thomas was presenting it, was neither pre-rational nor irrational. It was in some ways highly rational. Bishop never said to me, "Logic doesn't apply here," as I sometimes heard among New Age friends. In fact, he was quite interested in scholarship and following logical arguments. He was depending on proofs accepted by an accredited community of investigators in biblical research.* He also had an aversion to the pre-rational that I saw in several forms, such as a Palm Sunday when he passed out palm leaves but warned us, "These aren't lucky charms folks, don't go praying to them. They're just reminders." And of course, a conclusion can be "rational" without being right.

So perhaps the problem with this brand of fundamentalism was that it is *too* rational to be spiritual. Where was there space for the transrational, for that which is beyond what reason can provide?

---

* This is one of the tests for rationality suggested by Ken Wilber.

9

Loophole #2 My Intuition is Your Holy Spirit

I will put my laws in their minds and write them on their hearts. I will be their God, and they will be my people. No longer will a man teach his neighbor, or a man his brother, saying, "Know the Lord," because they will all know me, from the least of them to the greatest.
Hebrews 8:10-11

At our next meeting I explored the role of felt intuition, a concept key to New Thought.

Feeling God

Teri: I'm working on a theory that there is a commonality among people who have a felt experience of God instead of just a shared belief. Is that what's meant by a "personal relationship" with Jesus?

Bishop: No, no. Having a personal relationship means fulfilling Romans 10:9-11 (kjv): "**That if thou shall confess with thy mouth the Lord Jesus, and shall believe in thy heart that God has raised him from the dead, thou shall be saved.**" Your relationship begins the instant you make the choice to line up with the will of God.

Teri: But how does that feel?

Bishop: It doesn't matter how it feels. Some people shout and dance for joy. Others shed a tear for the release of guilt they've carried. Others feel nothing at all or maybe just a quiet sense of hope. It's about a change of mind and accepting the gift, not a feeling. And most people who continue in their commitment to follow God's will do develop a felt connection with him. But the great thing is you can have the best of both worlds. You're connected to him when you feel it, and you're connected to him when you don't feel it. You know, Teri, that few people are as emotional about their relationship with God as I am, but there are times I don't feel it, and I am so glad I don't have to depend on my feelings to know he's there. Have I told you about Irene's death?

Teri: No.

Bishop: I was very close to the wife of my brother-in-law, Deacon James. Irene had a fabulous gift for youth ministry, and I thought she would make it possible for my ministry to reach youth at a whole new level. She developed pre-eclampsia during the birth of their fifth child, and I prayed all the way to the hospital with a knowing it would be all right. When I got off the elevator at the hospital and saw the faces of all the family members looking grave, I was still sure she would be okay. And when I saw her on the respirator with all the tubes in her, I was still sure God was going to heal her. Whenever I've had that feeling before, it's always been right. But in a few days Deacon James told me she was brain dead, and they wanted to pull the plug on the respirator. I just told him that if we did that, we'd learn what God's will was. And when they did it, she died within 20 minutes.

That really shook me. I asked God why he did that. It took a long time before I could see any good come from it, though there has been much. James's second wife Tallya has been a great mother to those girls, even when the older ones rejected her. And Deacon James is much closer to God than he was. He used to struggle with alcohol, and now he's one of the most committed men in this church. But still, I don't completely understand it. But I do have faith. I know that God is always moving for a purpose.

Teri: Thank you for sharing that story with me. I think I can see why you make the point that feelings aren't important. It's funny, though, I have secular friends who also argue that a felt presence of God is unimportant, in fact dangerous. But they are coming from the opposite perspective. All they can see is that much of the world's bloodshed has always been caused by those who "feel" God is telling them what to do.

Bishop: Yes, that's why we need to stay close to scripture. A close reading would never condone aggression. "**Those who live by the sword shall die by the sword.**" (Matt. 26:52 paraphrased)

Teri: But on the other hand, the common experience of God can be what brings together people of all faiths. It certainly is a large portion of what drew Andy and me here to Highview, the passion for God we felt here. And for me the big transformation in my life is based on the way I feel the Universe interacting with me day to day. When a canceled appointment turns out for the best, when I'm puzzling over something and what I call a "workbook" example comes up giving me a chance to work it through, or when things come together in amazing ways to open a new path for me. Even in bad situations, I usually get a little calling card that says all is in divine right order.

Bishop: That's what I call being in the sovereign will of God.

Teri: Putting it that way just seems so anthropomorphic—as if God were a human king with human emotions, and we are just his subjects.

Bishop: No, no. It's so far-reaching and so omni-present, I couldn't even begin to think of God as human-like. It's much bigger than that.

The Holy Spirit as loophole

The following week I took a new tack.

Teri: In our first session you said the Bible has guidance for every situation.

Bishop: That's true

Teri: I can't believe that.

Bishop: Go ahead. Try me. Name a situation.

Teri: Well, I had a challenge recently regarding a friend who's a retired teacher who still tutors children after school at her town's library. Recently my friend was evicted from the library when a group of residents decided to renovate it and bring in a new literacy program. I wanted to stand up for her, to protest. It seemed unfair and shortsighted. But I realized I could be wrong. Maybe the new program would be better for the children. And besides, I was an outsider with no reason to have a voice. So how would the Bible answer that?

Bishop: Well in some cases you have to accept guidance from the Holy Spirit.

Teri: Aha! So everything's *not* in the Book.

Bishop: It's the Book that tells us Holy Spirit…

Teri: So that's it. That's the loophole. If people have to listen for guidance from the Holy Spirit, that implies two people might take different approaches to the same situation and both be right.

Bishop: Yes, but if they were both listening to the Holy Spirit, both of the approaches would line up with scripture. That's why you have to have a standard to measure by. So tell me, what did you do?

Teri: Well, I waited till I cooled off. Then I tried to remember to love each person involved. I went to one of the library organizers and told her how sad I was to see my friend hurting and left out by the change. And I did make a bit of a connection, because it turned out the organizer had felt similarly displaced at her church recently. Eventually she helped my friend find a new place to tutor.

Bishop: So you measured your action by a standard – the need to be loving in all situations.

Teri: I guess.

Bishop: And we have both agreed that the primary Commandment of the New Testament includes loving your neighbor as yourself.

Teri: Yes.

Bishop: So it sounds to me like you waited to hear guidance and then measured it by a standard from scripture.

Teri: Hmm. Well actually, yes. I see your point. And in fact, that approach makes a lot of sense to me. One of the things I've been puzzled over is how little there is in alternative spiritual literature about making distinctions about what one is "led" to do. Every feeling gets honored equally.

Bishop: Guidance from the Holy Spirit is not a feeling and it's not intuition. Feelings are of the flesh. And everybody has intuition; that's what gives you a sense not to go down a particular street. But the wisdom of the Holy Spirit is only available once you're saved. And the more you open to it, the fuller and richer it becomes.

Teri: Well *that* explains a lot of the trouble I've had understanding you. In my country we use "feelings" and "intuition" interchangeably, and we place a premium on learning to follow them. We think of that as hearing the voice of God directly. We don't normally make the distinction you just made. Although I'll tell you, it's clear to me that some ideas we want to think are divine are really coming from ego or some half-baked fancy. I've been surprised that there was almost no discussion in personal growth circles about how to tell the difference until Ken Wilber pointed to the distinction between "transrational"—beyond reason, and pre-rational or even irrational.

Bishop: It's easy to tell the difference. You just measure it against scripture.

Teri: Yeah, but whose interpretation of scripture?

Bishop: That's where good teaching plays a vital role in your maturity.

Finding your teacher

Teri: And how are you supposed to recognize a good teacher?

Bishop: (Pausing) That's a good question. You've got to listen to the Holy Spirit. The church I was raised in was very harsh, lots of rules, and some of the people were hateful. And my grandmother used to tell me I would go to hell if I misbehaved. I knew something was missing; it was the love. Jesus says in John 13, "**By this all men will know my disciples, if you have love for one another.**" Something in me was yearning for more. So when I was 14, I started going to another church. And I really resisted what they taught because they were knocking over the sacred cows I had grown up with. But they urged me to stick with scripture, and the closer I looked, the more I realized my grandmother's understandings were superficial. She was doing the best she could at the time. But I have more education and more exposure, so I am responsible for more. Sometimes you have to let a teacher take you as far as he or she can, say thank you, and move on.

That's why I tell people to beware getting so impressed with a teacher that you buy into the *person's* message. That's how cults develop. You can't set up a person over the Word. And one way to recognize the personality syndrome is when the teacher can't be challenged. If a teacher says, "If you don't like it, there's the door," it's time to move on. As you study and seek the light, you will be guided.

Two kinds of good

Bishop Thomas was describing a rich interplay between the Book and the Spirit. It reminded me of something I read long ago by the author famous for *Zen and the Art of Motorcycle Maintenance*, Robert Pirsig. In his second book, *Lila: An Inquiry into Morals*, Pirsig says there are two kinds of quality or good: "Static" and "Dynamic." He says we can't do without either of them. "Static quality" shows up as the patterns that hold society together; it includes cell walls, bones, burrows, houses, villages, castles, rituals, symbols, laws, and libraries, he says. "Dynamic quality," which he spells with a capital "D," brings the new and unpredictable; it includes sexual choice, symbiosis, death and regeneration, communality, communication, speculative thought, curiosity, and art. The two types of good work together to permit us to evolve: first a dynamic advance, then a static latching in; dynamic advance, static latch.[15] *

Within fundamentalism as Bishop Thomas was describing it to me, the Bible provides the set of static principles to guide behavior in most cases, while the Holy Spirit provides "Dynamic" guidance when new situations are encountered.

The kicker is that the advice of Holy Spirit must always be suspect if it contradicts the Book. But the Book says you must obey the spirit of the law, which is "Love your neighbor as yourself."

It was beginning to sound like not such a bad system.

In New Thought we think only in terms of Dynamic quality and the new. Perhaps that's because we *take it for granted* that we have fully absorbed all the basic ethical rules from static quality. But in my own case, I found it helpful to "go back to basics" when things got tough. And I didn't always remember to do so.

---

* In work that may presage that of Ken Wilber, Pirsig uses this insight to offer solutions for postmodern moral confusion. He lays out a "Metaphysics of Quality" that says the essential feature of reality is quality, value, or excellence. When we sit on a hot stove, he says, the very first thing we know is that it is a low quality situation.

Pirsig also uses the concept of "Dynamic quality" to offer a worthy answer to another question Bishop Thomas and I tangled over: how can we tell the maniac from the mystic? Pirsig identifies mysticism with Dynamic quality and says that secularists are "almost right" when they identify religious mysticism with insanity. "The two are almost the same. Both lunatics and mystics have freed themselves from the conventional static intellectual patterns of the culture. The only difference is that the lunatic has shifted over to a private static pattern of his own, whereas the mystic has abandoned all static patterns in favor of pure Dynamic quality." Lila p. 427.

10
Loophole #3
Literal Doesn't Mean What You Think

There are good and bad
interpretations of Hamlet.
Hamlet is not about the joys of
war, for example. That is a bad
interpretation; it is wrong...
That interpretation can easily
be rejected by a community of
those who have read and studied
the text—that is, by a community
of those who have entered the
interior of Hamlet, by those who
share that depth.
Ken Wilber, *A Brief History of Everything*

After the discussions in the preceding chapter, I was much relieved to learn that "All the answers are in the book," doesn't really mean all the answers are in the book, but rather that you often need divine guidance to apply what's in the book. Still, so many of the answers that *are* in the Book are so preposterous I couldn't image how any sane person could defend them. When I began uncovering the answer to this question, I was tempted to say it's because the interpreters cheat.

A judge burns his dancing daughter

My first inkling of what it means to Bishop to take the Bible literally came via a Sunday sermon on the story of Jephthah in Judges 11:1-40. Bishop Thomas read the story in which Jephthah is outcast from his family because his mother was a prostitute, so he goes out to build an independent band of warriors. When Ammonites threaten his tribe, his family begs Jephthah to come back and save the people, offering to make him a Judge. Jephthah accepts, and he tells God that if he can conquer the Ammonites, he'll sacrifice whatever first comes out of his front door when he returns home. Alas, it is his daughter who first dances out to greet him, joyously playing her tambourine. And so, the daughter must die as a burnt offering.

The congregation sat very still at the end of this story, and Bishop Thomas broke the tension by asking rhetorically, "Where in the world is he going with that?" We laughed nervously.

He then told us that Jephthah was insecure because of his low birth and early rejection. "If you are not shown love and acceptance as a child, you won't know how to show it as an adult," he said. "That's why fathers have got to take their daughters on their knee and tell them they love them so the daughters will know how a real man is supposed to treat them." But in this story, Bishop Thomas told us, Jephthah made a stupid, unconscionable vow in a bid to win back some respect by winning the battle. "Beware insecure people," said Bishop. "They will do anything to anybody to make themselves feel better… This text also tells us not to displace blame. When Jephthah sees his daughter he says, "**Oh! My daughter! You have made me miserable and wretched, because I have made a vow to the Lord that I cannot break.**" (Judges 11:35)

> Listen to that! "*You* have made me miserable…Look what *you* have done to *me*!" And all that girl did was come dancing out of the house, glad to see her daddy. Don't let your issues be your children's problem. And don't let anybody tell you you're not good enough. You're a King's kid. You got royal blood in your veins. You can be anything *God* says you can be!

The audience, which had whooped and hollered at earlier portions of the sermon, was silent now. It felt as if the theme had come too close to home for many. And I was stunned that Bishop had taken a story of superstition and savagery and used it to make sophisticated psychological points. My "literal" interpretation of this story is that it's good to burn your daughter.

This sermon made a great starting point for my next appointment with Bishop.

Learning from *bad* example

Teri: How can you call that sermon on Jephthah a literal interpretation?

Bishop: It is literal, but only when you take the whole thing in context. The Old Testament is meant for our example, not as a source of doctrine. People who try to get doctrine from the Old Testament will mess up.

Teri: Well you certainly didn't use the Jephthah story as an example for us to follow.

Bishop: Yes I did. It was a *bad* example, an example of what we shouldn't do.

Teri: You're kidding. That's cheating! That's not what anybody understands by "literal."

Bishop: The Bible is not a series of stories that each have a separate moral. It's one long story. The Old Testament portion is a record of everything the Israelites did while they were under God's covenant—but they kept breaking the covenant. So it's up to us to learn from their bad example and not make their mistakes. That's what we have to take literally.

Teri: Hmm.

Who decides what it means?

Teri: You know, according to Ken Wilber, interpretation is not merely "subjective fantasy," as the postmodernists claim. Rather, he says, the most "correct" interpretation of meaning takes the most context into account. He gives the example of interpreting *Hamlet*. The best interpretation can be reached through a community of investigators who are committed to the task and can verify each other's findings. So individuals might *choose* to create a personal interpretation that has value for them, he says, but that doesn't make it correct.[16]

Bishop: That's true. And as I've told you, I will gladly consider anyone's interpretation of the Bible if they can show me how it fits with the whole.

Depends on what you mean by "perfect"

A week later, we looked at the literal meaning of an individual word to determine the purpose of life.

Teri: It just doesn't make sense to me that life is about following rules to get to heaven.

Bishop: Didn't I already explain that to you? It's not about following rules. The purpose of life is to perfect ourselves. Matthew 5:48 says, "**Be perfect, therefore, as your heavenly Father is perfect.**"

Teri: Right.

Bishop: (Surprised) You agree?

Teri: Well, yes, but it depends on what you mean by "perfect." I think of the purpose of life as expressing divine qualities, being the eyes and hands of Spirit here in material form, expanding my awareness of my connection to all life. Doing that requires me to always learn and grow to be better at giving and receiving love, and at enjoying and appreciating this wonderful world God created for us.

Bishop: That's pretty good, that's a start. But what is that answer grounded in? My hope for you, Teri, is that you can move toward finding your answers in scripture. It's the only authoritative source for what God wants from us. The scriptures set the standard and define the *kind* of love that you must give and receive. Keep in mind that the definition of love, for example, is not open for anyone's private interpretation. Some people think love is just a mushy feel-good thing, but it makes demands.

Teri: Tough love?

Bishop: Yes, but always for our own good.

Teri: Well, I'm willing to do any homework assignments you give me in studying the Bible. But it just seems I find the answers packaged more efficiently from other sources.

The following week, I got the best possible opportunity to begin fulfilling Bishop's request that I look more closely at the Bible. Andy and I attended a conference of the Global New Thought Alliance, an affiliation of New Thought churches. Speakers from around the country gathered at a hotel in nearby McLean, Virginia. We were drawn by one speaker we had heard rave reviews of, Dr. Rocco Errico. Dr. Errico is considered by many the world's leading authority on the Aramaic version of the Bible that is used by Eastern Christian churches from Armenia to India. Dr. Errico makes the case that Jesus spoke Aramaic, and that an Aramaic, "Peshitta" text of the Bible is the original, and it predates the Greek translations from which all western Bibles are translated.[17] Along with George Lamsa, who translated the Peshitta into English, Dr. Errico has spent a lifetime putting the Bible into its original cultural context. To an untrained eye like mine, the differences were minor, but they took on significance as Dr. Errico spoke.

He was indeed an engaging and inspiring speaker. He told us, for example, that the Aramaic word "gamala" has three meanings: camel, rope, and beam. Therefore when Jesus used it in Matthew 19:24 he meant, "**It is easier for a *rope* to go through the eye of a needle than it is for a rich man to go to heaven,**" and not the more commonly accepted translation I had heard as a child, "It is easier for a camel..." And of course, this shifted the meaning significantly.

Several of Dr. Errico's translations pointed to a rich view of God more inspiring to New Thought ears than traditional translations. But one point in particular made me sit up straight and grab for my notepad.

The term "perfect" he said, has the sense in Aramaic of a circle, something that is full, all encompassing. Therefore a more accurate translation of Matthew 5:48 is not "Be perfect..." but "**Be all encompassing, therefore, as your heavenly Father is all encompassing.**"

I was stunned at the linkage to the Wilber concept that the highest system *transcends and includes* all those below it. On the break, I bought one of Dr. Errico's books, *Aramaic Light on the Gospel of John*, and I told him I wanted to use it in a dialogue I was having with a fundamentalist Bishop.[18] "Good luck," he said ruefully. "The fundamentalists in the South have branded me as the devil's helper."

Undaunted, I dashed home to my computer and did a little of what I'd told myself I never wanted to get into—cross referencing scripture. I looked up "perfect," and what I found made me eager for my next meeting with Bishop.

Teri: I learned something this week. In the Aramaic language spoken by Jesus, "perfect" means "all encompassing." So to me the passage you cited last week says that our goal is to keep growing our minds and our hearts to make room for everything. We can handle the good along with the bad in life without losing the peace that comes from knowing who we truly are. So we're ready for anything. We can transcend and include everything, content with it all, but also eager to make it all better.

Bishop: Well that's pretty interesting. A lot of people think "perfect" means a state of sinless perfection, and of course, that's impossible for man. But the Bible was not only written in Aramaic; in fact most of the New Testament was written in common or "koine" Greek. And if you researched further you'd learn that "perfect" in the Greek has more meaning than you've discovered. For example, it can also mean "mature." A mature Christian is more like Christ.

Teri: Yes, exactly. That's what I was trying to say.

Bishop: I'd like to have one of those Aramaic translations. I try to cross reference from several different versions. And it's not just about translations. After you look up a word in a particular passage, you should look to see how that word is used in other passages as well.

Teri: Actually, I did that. How about this: 1 Corinthians 13:10 says, **"But when the perfect comes, the partial will come to an end."** Doesn't that show "perfect" means whole?

Bishop: Well, well, I think you may be learning something. And this is a good example of the necessity of a proper word study. Context and a good Greek expository dictionary are real helpful as you study a passage of scripture. Let's look at the context of that verse. (He opens the Bible on his desk and finds that his *New International Version* does not use the word "partial" in the passage I just cited.)

I wish I had my NASB with me (New American Standard Bible); that's a word-for-word translation, whereas NIV is thought-for-thought. Where did you get that citation?

Teri: I used the online concordance at Crosswalk.com. I don't remember which version. Probably I just used the default version.

Bishop: (He turns to his laptop and looks up the passage on Crosswalk. The *Holman Christian Standard Bible* comes up by default. He finds the passage and begins reading from 1 Cor. 13:8-13.)

> **"Love never ends. But as for prophecies, they will come to an end; as for languages, they will cease; as for knowledge, it will come to an end. For we know in part, and we prophesy in part. But when the perfect comes, the partial will come to an end. When I was a child, I spoke like a child, I thought like a child, I reasoned like a child. When I became a man, I put aside childish things. For now we see indistinctly, as in a mirror, but then face to face. Now I know in part, but then I will know fully, as I am fully known. Now these three remain: faith, hope, and love. But the greatest of these is love."**

Isn't that a beautiful passage?

Teri: It sure is.

You can't get there from here

After this dialogue, I began to imagine that Bishop and I separately were each out in the woods after long hikes alone. A heavy fog surrounded us as we tried to find each other via our cell phones:

Teri: *Where are you?*

Bishop: *I'm standing on a plateau with three tall trees and a rock formation shaped like a dove. Where are you?*

Teri: *That's funny, I'm standing on a plateau with three trees and a rock formation shaped like a dove.*

Bishop: *Well you can't be on the same hill as me, because the only way up here is the way I came.*

Teri: *And I know you're not on my hill, because you started from the south, and the only path up here from the south goes through impenetrable thorns.*

Bishop: *Yikes!*

Teri: *What happened?*

Bishop: *Somebody just bumped into me.*

Teri: *Me too! Who do you think it could be?*

Bishop: *Beats me. What a coincidence, heh?*

11

Praise for Whom?

In your metaphysics you have
denied personality to the Deity,
yet when the devout motions
of the soul come, yield to them
heart and life, though they
should clothe God with shape
and color. Leave your theory, as
Joseph his coat in the hand of
the harlot, and flee.
Ralph Waldo Emerson, *Self Reliance*

A year before I came to Highview, firefighters in Oregon sparked an urban legend as they used helicopters to scoop up seawater and dump it on a forest fire. A faked press report on the Web said that one helicopter accidentally scooped up an offshore diver who was then dropped on the fire.

As I struggled to get oriented at Highview, I kept thinking about that diver. One moment I had been swimming among the pretty fish at Celebration Center of Religious Science. Then all went dark for a while, and then I found myself in freefall with flames all around me. *Where the heck am I, and how did I get here?* Curiously though, I had a soft landing, and the forest I landed in seemed not too badly scarred by the flames—inviting, really.

The one familiar landmark at Highview was the "praise and worship" music that Andy and I had been attracted to in the Bahamas. After a few months of attending Sunday services at Highview, we became more comfortable with participating actively: our arms raised, voices lifted, hearts joyful. Bishop said we were fulfilling Psalms 150:1-6. "**Praise him with loud cymbals, praise him with a mighty song.**" And a mighty song it was. Occasionally, the intensity peaked as someone writhed and stomped when "overtaken by the Spirit." At first this seemed too out-of-control. But then it began to seem sacred. I was impressed at the way the white-gloved ushers stood close to a person experiencing such a release, carefully guarding that the worshiper not hurt self or neighbor. There was something quite magnificent in the contrast between the out-of-control release and the in-control zone of safety created lovingly by the ushers. Contrasts such as this were part of what kept Highview appealing.

Bishop Thomas always insisted that the purpose of praising God was not for us to get an emotional high. "God wants it, and God deserves it," he told us frequently. "It doesn't matter if you feel like doing it. If you've got a backache or headache, he still deserves the praise. '**Let everything that has breath praise the Lord,**'" he said, quoting verse 6. "But if it doesn't affect the way you treat your neighbor the rest of the week, then you're just going through the motions."

This made a certain sense if I translated "God" as The Universe, seeing praise as something that lubricated the whole. I came to love it. Songs stayed in our heads during the week, and occasionally Andy or I would break out into a chorus at home. It had the effect of accentuating my gratitude for life and, yes, lowering my resistance to the concept of a personal God.

Personal or impersonal: it is as you will

Getting away from "worship" to a personal God was a major attraction for many of us in New Thought. On the surface, seeing God as a personal or impersonal force is one of the greatest differences between Western and Eastern-influenced religion. But when you look closer, the line is not so sharp.[19] Some of the clearest thinking I'd seen on the apparent paradox between a personal and impersonal God came from one of the fathers of New Thought, Judge Thomas Troward. In his 1904 *Edinburgh Lectures on Mental Science* he grappled with the paradox.

> The attributing of an impossible individuality to the Universal Mind is one of the two grand errors which we find sapping the foundations of religion and philosophy. The other consists in rushing to the opposite extreme and denying the quality of personal intelligence to the Universal Mind.[20]

Troward maintained that God was essentially an impersonal force, "Universal Mind," that is both the source of human consciousness and the law through which our thought outpictures. Therefore, if I think of God as a loving *personal* force, He really, *really is* one to me.

> It becomes, therefore, the most important of all considerations with what character we invest the Universal Mind;... for it will infallibly bear to us exactly that character which we impress

> upon it; in other words it will be to us exactly what we believe it to be…
>
> The initial step then, consists in determining to picture the Universal Mind as the ideal of all we could wish it to be—both to ourselves and to others, together with the endeavor to reproduce this ideal, however imperfectly, in our own life.[21]

This still made a lot of sense to me, but I was no longer certain it was the whole picture. All I knew for sure was that something out there seemed to be interacting with me. And it seemed to have a darned good sense of humor.

Giving it "praise" began to feel natural.

12
Loophole #4
Smiting, Fighting, and Wrath in a Good Cause

Ram says over and over again, "Unless you honor Shiva, you cannot come to me." That is, until you have fully embraced chaos—chaos!—you cannot go through the door. If you want to be a preserver of love and beauty, you've got to be able to look at the destruction of love and beauty and say, "Yeah, right. And that, too."
Ram Dass, *Paths to God: Living the Bhagavad Gita*

My understanding was growing that for some fundamentalists, taking the Bible "literally," still leaves plenty of room for interpretations that are almost identical to the interpretations of those who start from a wider base. But I couldn't imagine how my fundamentalist friends could see a loving God in the Old Testament with all its smiting, fighting, and wrath. The answers I came to didn't make me completely comfortable with a wrathful God, but they did vastly increase my respect for those who can believe in such a God and yet refrain from judging others themselves.

Smiting: God makes quail come out of Israelites' noses

In a Sunday sermon, Bishop Thomas interpreted Numbers 11:18-21, in which the Israelites are sick of wandering in the desert, eating the manna that God has provided, and they long for the days of slavery in Egypt, where at least they had plenty to eat. God promises to send so much quail they will have it, "**until it comes out of your nostrils and you loathe it.**" Moses doubts that God can supply enough for the 600,000 of them, and so after God sends the meat, he sends a plague.

This struck me as so abominable that nothing of value could be taken from the story. And indeed, Bishop told us it is "a difficult text" until we look more closely. And then we notice that God did not send the plague because the people asked for meat, but rather because they did not have faith that God could provide it. So once again, it came back to the primacy of faith.

I was beginning to see the pattern—and the parallel with New Thought. In New Thought, it doesn't mater how hard I work for something; no lasting good can come about unless I focus on the harmonious "reality" beyond appearances. To do that I use affirmative prayer to focus on a positive outcome, I follow guidance as best I can hear it, and I surrender to knowing those steps are enough. This began to seem to me pretty similar to what Bishop called having faith and being obedient.

Wrath and holiness

On another Sunday a visiting speaker preached on 2 Samuel 6:6, a story in which the Israelites are carrying the Ark of the Covenant on a cart across the desert. The Ark starts to tip, and a man reaches out to steady it. God strikes the man dead because he told King David that no one was to touch the Ark but the priest.

I couldn't wait to talk to Bishop about this one.

Teri: How can you trust a God who loses his temper like that?

Bishop: God didn't lose his temper. He gave David specific instructions on how to carry the ark, and David ignored them. So God didn't kill that man, David did through his careless leadership. Leadership is a sacred trust; a large part of the Old Testament is the story of God developing leadership among his people so they could bring forth the plan of salvation for the whole world. That's the reason they had his special protection.

And furthermore, you have to understand that the Ark symbolized the presence of God. It's his holiness. It's so vast, so magnificent, so glorious, you can't mess with his holiness. Because his holiness is our holiness too. We are magnificent because we are his creatures. That's what this story is saying.

Teri: Well that's nice. That's a nice interpretation. But I don't believe that's what anyone else is hearing in that story.

Bishop: That's just because you haven't been around here long enough. Everyone else has grown up going to Bible study and understanding the deeper meaning in these stories.

Teri: I have trouble believing that.

Bishop: Go ahead ask them. Ask around in the congregation.

What about the children?

Teri: I might do that. But what about children in the audience? I am certain there was at least one child who heard that story and concluded that if his father's trophy ever fell off the wall, and he tried to catch it, his father might strike him dead, and would be justified in doing so.

Bishop: Well look what a wonderful teaching opportunity that is. Everyone knows I preach that you should never discipline a child in anger. That father should bring that child to my office and we could have a nice chat to explain the story… What? You have a funny look on your face. What? …Say something.

Teri: I'm speechless… That is so idealistic. You called me an idealist. The child wouldn't have the awareness to ask the question, and the parents wouldn't have the courage to come to you if they weren't sure themselves.

Bishop: You just haven't been around here long enough. A good church encourages questions.

Teri: Uh… Let's just say I have trouble believing that. People are intimidated by the pastor no matter how much they love him or her.

Bishop: You say that because you're comparing us to all those other world religions. In Buddhism and Hinduism and all those, you have to keep striving for perfection. You have to go through all those deaths and rebirths trying to learn lessons. But when you're saved, you're perfect now. There's nothing else you have to do. So you have nothing to be afraid of. Your holiness is complete, right here, right now. And that is so magnificent, so freeing, so empowering, that if you really understood it, you'd never do anything to defile it. …Now your eyes are really bulging. What? Tell me.

Teri: (Exhaling audibly) Okaaay. What we have here is a reality gap. You are using the exact same terms to explain your view of God that I would use to explain mine. Only yours is upside down, inside out. So there's just nowhere for me to go.

If you believe humans are perfect once saved, why do you focus so much on avoiding sin? Why don't you talk more about the ways we can extend the love and healing and compassion of Jesus?

Bishop: Because we can't extend love when we don't feel good about ourselves. And we can't feel good about ourselves when we know we're sinning.

Teri: So you're saying you talk about sin to promote self-esteem?

Bishop: You could say that.

Teri: *Help me Lord.* Let me try this: If the Bible is intended as guidance for everyone, why is it so easy to misinterpret it?

Bishop: Well that's easy. It's because God wants us to devote a lifetime to studying it, always getting more and more intimate with him. If the meaning were plain on the surface, someone of higher intellect could zip through it and tell everyone else he had all the answers. But the Bible is so rich and deep, that there's an equal challenge for someone with no education. If he or she studies with the intention of becoming closer to God, the Holy Spirit will slowly reveal deeper and deeper meanings. It's a great equalizer, for we are all equal in the sight of God.

Teri: Okay, two points. I didn't think you'd be able to answer that one. But I also suspect that you could find beauty and meaning in the phone book.

Bishop: Oh, I doubt that.

At the time, his response about studying the Bible over a lifetime just seemed like a convenient answer. But the more I thought about it, the more I would come to see it as a key to why so many of our values were alike. In fact, this insight would become a cornerstone of a vision for mending many religious disputes. Truth is indeed timeless. But we are all at different levels of maturity in our grasp of it.

13
Loophole #5
God Doesn't Change, but His Methods Do

God is Change.
Octavia Butler, *Parable of the Sower*
in the apocalyptic novel series
Earthseed: The Book of the Living

God is a verb.
William P. Young, *The Shack*

I am that I am.
Exodus 3:14 (kjv)

Fighting wars for God

Next up was the warlike nature of God in the Old Testament. My small exposure to the Muslim point of view since 9/11 gave me a chance to see history through new eyes. It was time to ask Bishop about all those wars to kill idolaters.

Teri: Many non-Christians around the world fear Christians because of the warlike nature God encourages in the Old Testament.

Bishop: What are you talking about? There is nothing in the Bible that authorizes war unless it's necessary to prevent being conquered yourself. You have to understand that at the time of the Old Testament, wars of conquest were common, everyone had to fight for territory.

Teri: But it's more than self-preservation they were fighting for. You just mentioned in a sermon recently, Joshua 6, in which God not only tells the Israelites to take a city, but also commands them to kill every man, woman, and child—even their beasts.

Bishop: That was a special case. God wanted to preserve the lineage of Abraham so Jesus would be born of King David. As I told you, God was preparing one people to bring salvation to the entire world. And at that time, enemy bands plundered villages and raped the women every chance they got. So God couldn't let that happen. There is no other reason God would call a nation to eliminate a conquered people. He wouldn't need to do that in these times.

Teri: But you told me God never changes.

Bishop: God never changes, but his methods change.

Teri: Ahh!

The age of grace

Bishop: Those wars were in a different dispensation of time. In each era God uses methods appropriate to the level humans are at. Remember, his only motive is to bring us closer to him. So there is one school of Bible study that looks at the seven eras or "dispensations" of God's methods over time, and how he keeps adjusting them based on our reactions. It's not an exact science, but it tells us that at the time of the battle of Jericho, for example, the Israelites were under the dispensation of Law—under the Ten Commandments. Now we are in the dispensation of Grace.

Teri: Whoa. That sounds something like that Spiral Dynamics theory I told you I'm interested in. Tell me the seven eras. (He listed them as I took notes.)

Bishop:

1. *Innocence*—before the fall of Adam and Eve
2. *Consciousness*—before the flood
3. *Human government*—until man showed he couldn't govern himself ending at the Tower of Babel
4. *Promise*—from the call of Abraham
5. *Law*—God gives Moses the Ten Commandments
6. *Grace*—following Jesus' death, the period we're in now
7. *Kingdom Age*—when Jesus comes again, leading to *Eternal State*—a new heaven and a new earth*

---

* Later in our story, I encounter a similar seven-point synthesis of the Bible in Brian McLaren's *The Story We Find Ourselves In*, an encounter in the Galapagos Islands between a secular naturalist and a Jamaican preacher-turned tour guide. I am so enchanted by McLaren's version that I get Bishop's permission to develop a play around it for Highview.

Today we're in the dispensation of Grace. And the only way we are called to bring people to Jesus is through their free choice to accept the plan of salvation.

Teri: What about all the conquering by Christians since the death of Jesus? Burning down temples, the Crusades, or Spain ejecting Jews and Muslims the same year they sent Columbus to conquer the rest of the world?

Bishop: Just because people declare wars in the name of Christianity doesn't mean they're really Christian. All of that was based on superficial interpretations—or it was excuses for man's greed and power.

Teri: So again my question is, what's to keep God from continuing to call for wars of conquest today?

Bishop: God only moves forward. Why would he go backward to using a method that didn't even work the first time to keep his people faithful?

For the first time, I felt him becoming irritated by my questions. He stood up, picked up his Bible, and paced as he continued.

Bishop: I don't know why anyone would go looking to take things out of context like that to make God look warlike. The whole story of the Old Testament is one of infinite love, mercy, and promises kept, despite all the times the Israelites failed to keep their covenant. Romans 12:21 tells us, "**Do not be overcome by evil, but overcome evil with good.**" How can anybody think God would condone war except to protect the innocents? I think some of the people who would do that are just trying to distract attention from their own failings.

Teri: Okay. I get it, I get it.

He actually kept talking for another five minutes. Such are the hazards of getting a preacher on a topic dear to him. But the frustration he expressed was telling to me. Something was perfectly obvious to him that I was not able to hear the way he meant it. This sense of not being able to reach each other occurred frequently in our dialogues. But it made those moments when we were in sync seem all the more valuable.

This particular conversation added to my store of "loopholes" explaining how peaceful, loving people could embrace a "literal" translation of a book full of war stories. It reinforced my understanding that one could believe the stories in the Bible literally took place, but still believe that the lessons to be taken from them are open to interpretation. And it added the "loophole" that God may not change *but his methods do*.

This loophole—along with Bishop's seven "dispensations"—echoed a key concept I was encountering in Ken Wilber's work: humans develop through levels. Wilber builds on the "Spiral Dynamics" ideas of Don Beck and Chris Cowan (based on the work of developmental psychologist Clare Graves). Their research claims that we all move through predictable stages of growth—both as individuals and as societies. And as we do, the world looks different to us. For example, we see the need for war differently; when we were hunter-gatherer tribes, it was more necessary to fight for territory, just as Bishop had said. Bishop's "Age of Grace" echoed to me the post-conventional group of levels in which we no longer feel bound by the rules of our group.

Probably I was stretching the comparison. But Bishop's acknowledgment of different eras was one more factor that helped me respect his adherence to an "unchanging" standard.

Spiral to heaven

I'm going to digress here to flesh out this key idea of Spiral Dynamics (SD) and the way it color codes levels of development. I discussed it only briefly with Bishop that day, but it was beginning to "color" everything we experienced together—like the fact that some things just can't be communicated across levels. In fact, I started seeing the stages of growth everywhere I looked. (To get back to the story, skip to the end of this chapter.)

Spiral Dynamics maps the levels of development in what we *value*: from survival to magical safety, to power, *etc*., as shown in the following table.

Developmental Stages			
Kohlberg's stages[22]	**Spiral Dynamics Color/Value** [23*]	**Wilber**	**In Societies and History**
Pre-Conventional	Beige: SurvivalSense Automatic/ Instinctive	Instinctual	Foraging Clans
	Purple: KinSpirits Animistic/ Tribalistic	Magical	Ethnic Tribes
	Red: PowerGods Egocentric/ Exploitative	Impulsive	Feudal Empires
Conventional	Blue: TruthForce Absolutist/Saintly	Rules and Roles	Ancient Nations
Post-Conventional	Orange: StriveDrive Materialistic/ Achiever	Achiever/ Rationalist	Corporate States
	Green: Humanbond Relativistic/ Sociocentric	Pluralist/ Sensitive Self	Value Communities
	Yellow: FlexFlow Systemic/ Integrative	Integral	Informational Integral Commons

As shown in the first column, the levels in Spiral Dynamics are a more detailed breakdown in the stages I mentioned earlier that sociologists call pre-conventional, conventional, and post-conventional. One aspect of this model especially intrigued me. It maps our levels as proceeding not in a straight line, but in a spiral pattern that loops back and forth as we cycle from a focus on the individual to a focus on community. That aspect fascinated me, given that my own life seemed to be a lurching between the value of individual expression and the value of working for the good of the group.

* (Color names are unrelated to the popular use of color names in politics; Wilber uses a different color scheme based on the spectrum.)

My life on a chart

Indeed, I thought I could see my life on this chart. I remember as a young child my *purple* "magic" phase of building altars to Mary to protect me, while my sister helps me remember my *red* power phase of fighting with her over toys. My years in Catholic school fit the bill for my *blue* phase: roles and rules, absolute truth, trying to be saintly. All that officially ended the day that I told the pastor I wouldn't be returning to Sunday school because we teens were forming our own group to discuss social issues. That was surely the start of my post-conventional phase. It was also the start of my *orange* rationalism and focus on personal achievement.

As to my *green* stage of pluralism and universalism, I could say it started in college in the 70s, but it was only my head that opened to the perspectives of people not like me—by gender, race, religion, and sexuality, *etc*. My heart didn't open to people not like me until I took the set of personal growth workshops I described in Chapter 3. Before that time I would have told you that I honored all people equally—or probably I would have said based on their merit. But now I was looking in the eyes of strangers, loaning money I wouldn't necessarily get back, and feeling awe while standing in a circle at Celebration Center singing, "We Are the World." My mother said with tears, "I've got my daughter back." I always wondered what she meant by that.

At Celebration Center, I got a glimpse of levels that felt still higher than green. But I eventually felt that something was missing. We could meditate and vision together quite magnificent possibilities for our group and for the world. But follow-through was often lacking. Spiral Dynamics helped me diagnose the problem: We had *transcended* our orange rationalism and blue structure, but we hadn't *included* them adequately to always be effective in the world. And although we talked a lot about personal empowerment, we didn't have access to the red level's willingness to use power effectively in conflict. An ideal was birthed in me of finding a way to integrate the best of each of the levels.

How blue is Highview?

Highview intrigued me for its focus on the elements I had been missing. According to the Spiral Dynamics theory, churches like Highview sit in the middle of the map as solidly blue: absolute truth, rules and roles, saintliness, and a theology based on believing a particular version of a story. The major contribution to civilization of blue is that it brings under control the self-centered power drives from the lower *red* level—whether those drives are expressing in a 2 year-old child, a street gang, or a primitive culture (including parts of ours). This blue stage is absolutely vital for development. As soon as I understood that,

I saw that Highview was doing a great job of reaching people at the red level and offering them a path up to blue *and beyond.*

But as the next several chapters will show, Highview began to look much more complex. I was seeing explicit attempts to integrate power, structure, rational processes, and compassion to achieve good for "God's Kingdom." True, as with Celebration Center, the outcome didn't always live up to the vision. But each of the values I had been missing was explicitly called upon at Highview when things went awry.

In my mind, the question began to evolve: which of these environments is better positioned to include the whole spiral of values—Highview by reaching *out* to embrace a broader world with compassion, or Celebration Center by reaching *back* to reclaim power, structure, and reason?

Temptations at each level

My view of this question was shaped by two refinements to Spiral Dynamics offered by Ken Wilber. The first is that aspects of ourselves grow through the levels at varying rates. So a person can be at a medium level of awareness *spiritually* but be more developed mentally, emotionally, or ethically than someone with a "higher" perception of spiritual reality. That could explain why I got a dizzying feeling on first visiting Highview—I was sensing a mixing of levels that violated my preconceptions of what was possible.

The second refinement to the theory that shaped my view is that each level of development has a healthy and an unhealthy form of expression. Most of us pride ourselves on the healthy form of our own level while we disparage the unhealthy form of all the other levels.

The unhealthy form of the blue's roles and rules is a temptation to rigidity, judgmentalism, and use of shame for control. These were the only aspects of traditional religion that most of my friends could perceive.

Above blue's rules and roles is the *orange* of rationality and personal achievement. Its temptation is to disregard non-scientific values.

Above orange comes the *green* of pluralism and relativism, the set of values common in universities today. Green pluralism values all cultures and belief systems; everything and everyone is Okay. The twin temptations at green are contradictory: one is to fail to make any distinctions between good and bad, and the other is to decide that the only bad system is one that does make distinctions between good and bad. In other words, green is *sure* that any *other* group that's sure of something must be wrong.

This is an ironic contradiction in green that leads to extremes of political correctness. When these extremes are mixed with "red" narcissism, Wilber calls the result "mean green." It is a force that is creating huge tension among groups in society and is blocking people at green from moving to the next higher *yellow* level. At yellow, we begin to see the value of all other levels, and we desire to integrate them.

And what is the temptation of *yellow*? To start ranking everything and everyone by levels.

"Mean green" unleashes red

This idea of unhealthy levels started to explain a lot of things that were bothering me. For example, it explained why most of my peers have nothing but disdain for traditional religion, no matter how much good it may do. In his novel, *Boomeritis*, Wilber notes the undermining of the good work done by "blue" (roles and rules) churches. He cites Clifton Taulber's account of the contribution of the African American church during segregation. Those churches were the major force for upliftment in America during periods when other opportunities were not open to Black people. But when the green relativists began trashing any form of blue hierarchy in the 60s, the effect on many churches was not to "raise" them to the green standard of universal harmony. Instead it robbed them of the respect in which society held them and thus gave one more excuse to red "outlaws" to reject the church's hand up. "Using green to dissolve blue" does not produce more green, says Wilber. Instead it exposes more red anarchy from below. And while the effect is notable throughout society, it has particularly strong consequences in the Black community where young people who reject church may see fewer other paths up. No wonder traditional religion sees relativism as the enemy!

You are here

Spiral Dynamics presents a powerful call for each level of development to appreciate the contribution of the others. And that call clarified the conflicts I was feeling in my whole adventure at Highview. After years in an orange-green environment, I was committed to reason and pluralism. But knowing that I could never see the whole picture had sapped my energy for making distinctions and taking action. Now I was re-discovering the lost values of blue roles/rules and red willingness to use power. I wanted to integrate blue "saintliness" with orange desire for achievement and green respect for all—and then use those qualities for the good of the whole system. It felt like someone pointed to a map that said, "You are here." And that "here" was attempting to move to the "yellow" level at which one integrates the strengths of all the other levels. (There are higher levels than yellow, but apparently I'm not at them. One of the tests is that the levels below you make perfect sense, but the ones beyond you seem fuzzy or threatening.)

But what if I *wasn't* really at yellow but somewhere far below? And how could I know? I latched on to Wilber's concept that higher levels "transcend and include" the levels below them. Watching myself squarely, I could report that I was not rejecting the "orange-green-yellow" friendships and values I had just spent decades honing. I might not be transcending them, but I was including them. So by that standard, I must be growing instead of regressing. Of course, if I was wrong about that, I would be post-9/11's worst nightmare: the vanguard of a pendulum swing *backward* to red/blue fundamentalism instead of forward to a yellow integration of something new.

Part of a trend?

If I was moving backward, I was not alone. Many young people with "green" parents are turning in droves to the bluest churches they can find, according to Colleen Carroll's, *The New Faithful; Why Young Adults are Embracing Christian Orthodoxy.* Among the factors she cites that draw young people to orthodox Christianity are "authentic community, the challenge to live a moral life geared toward serving others, and a genuine connection to a transcendent God." Carroll quotes 31-year-old seminary professor Melody Knowles, "Today's postmodern young adults are not as concerned with having a purely rational modern faith. Instead they are 'rebelling' by embracing traditional worship," Knowles says. "It's sexy and exotic. The previous generation wimped out, and you want a challenge. It's kind of idealistic." Carroll notes both the constructive and the potentially negative aspects of this trend. She says that these young people, "face tough choices and severe ridicule when embracing orthodoxy. They also face the danger of becoming defensive, judgmental, and isolated from a world that mocks their deepest values." [24]

Were these young people moving *forward* by rejecting "mean green" extremes but still bringing healthy respect and compassion for all people to their new orthodoxy? Or were they only moving *backward* by rejecting pluralism altogether and retreating to the blue "temptations"?

For myself, sampling a different level felt like having one foot on the boat and the other on the dock. And that uncomfortable feeling was going to get much worse before it got better. But so far I was resisting the temptation to jump ship in one direction or the other. In my best moments I liked to think Andy and I might be on a Jungian "hero's journey"—visiting a strange land to bring back to our tribe the gift of forgotten traditional values.

But so far, none of our friends were seeing it that way.

Pushed to our limits

Another intriguing aspect of the Spiral Dynamics model is the claim that the only thing that makes us let go of one level and move to the next is a problem that can't be solved at the current level. In that sense, Bishop Thomas and I seemed to have become each other's problem. Certainly we were pushing each other to our limits.

Of course, there was one more explanation for everything I was seeing that didn't occur to me at the time—that something might be missing from the theory.

I explained Spiral Dynamics to Bishop as best I could during our discussion of war in the Bible. His reaction was one I was becoming used to.

Bishop: Well there's no need to go chasing down a bunch of unproven theories when it's right here in the Bible.

As to the wrath of God, I thought we had gone as far as we could go on the topic. But several months later I was given reason to doubt that we had covered any ground at all.

14

Learning to Love the Wrath of God

You can avoid reality. But you cannot avoid the consequences of avoiding reality.
Ayn Rand

Bahamas Revival

In November, Andy and I made one of our regular fall trips to the Bahamas, and our two worlds began to merge. While other tourists were at the pink sand beach, we were rocking out at a tent revival overlooking neighboring islands across the turquoise bay. The singing, shouting and praising were punctuated by the fact that some teenagers had packed themselves into a red trailer van behind the stage. As they danced to the music, the van bounced cheerily to the beat. The last song was a raucous rendition of the Beatles "Do You Love Me," using the words,

Do you *love* Jesus,
Do you love him?
Do you *love* Jesus
Do you love him?
Nowwwwww that yooooou've been sa…aa…aa…aaved!

It was both ridiculous and wonderful. It felt like the pieces of our experience were melding into a joyful gumbo.

Backsliding into the wrath of God

When we returned from the Bahamas, I purchased the tapes of the Highview sermons that I had missed. I planned to listen to them in my car on the way to work. But what I heard on one of them Monday morning nearly caused me to drive off the road.

In a sermon titled, "Failure to Listen to God," Bishop Thomas said a lot of great things about wanting an alive relationship with God that transcends the Sunday-only experience. But then his tone shifted.

> One factor that holds back our faith is the lack of understanding of what God is like. Some of us have concocted our own view of God. I'm going to tell you, I have been ministering to some folks, some really interesting people, and you would be surprised how many people don't really understand what God is like.

I turned up the volume.

> How many of you know that God is a God of love? Oh yes, he *loves* all of us; all of us want to know the warm and fuzzy side of God. We like it when God is just dropping little dainties in answer to our prayers. But you need to know *all* of his character. How many of you also know that he is a God who will judge; he is a consuming fire; he does not play.

He said this building into his full-out, freight train, old-fashioned preacher style ending several minutes later with the full-bore shout:

> It's a dangerous thing to fall into the hands of an angry God!

And there it was, all my worst preconceptions about using fear to control behavior. In high school rhetoric class, we had studied the classic sermon by 19th century preacher Jonathan Edwards, "Sinners in the Hands of an Angry God." It includes the classic line, "God holds you over the pit of hell, much as one holds a spider, or some loathsome insect over the fire, abhors you, and is dreadfully provoked."

"This is as bad as it gets," I thought. We were back to square one.

"I never said that"

The next Thursday, I arrived for our appointment with dread.

Teri: I bought the tapes of your sermons we missed, and I'm upset and confused. Did you just store all that up till Andy and I were out of town?

Bishop: What? Why?

Teri: All that stuff about the wrath of God. You told me you would never use fear of God for control. I took that as a promise.

Bishop: I wouldn't and I didn't. You know, I think you're prejudiced. You so much expect to hear negative things from me that you imagine them where they don't exist.

Teri: I admit I am prejudiced. But this has happened before in cases where I heard harshness and you claimed there was none. Only this time I've got it on tape.

Bishop: Well you bring that tape in next time, and we'll clear this up. You probably just took something out of context.

Over the next week, I listened to the tape repeatedly. It was a sweet-and-sour mix of uplifting points along with some that made me shiver. I had learned by now how to translate or filter language that would have made most of my friends faint; "The wages of sin is still death. But even though you were stinking sinners worthy of death, he made a way for you. That ought to make you shout. That ought to make you want to live holy." "*Yeah, yeah, I know what you mean.*" But this was different. Way harsher than anything I had heard him say before.

What the wrath of God does *not* mean

I arrived at our next appointment with my tape player and placed it on Bishop's desk between us. I played the part about it being a dangerous thing to fall into the hands of an angry God.

Bishop: That? Oh yeah, I said that. You've taken it out of context though. If somebody just heard me say that, they'd think I was one of those fear preachers. But rewind a few paragraphs and you'll hear me say that God has made provisions for all who recognize their wrong and turn from it. The slate is wiped clean. Then I talk about the glory that God has prepared for us, how the Holy Spirit can enrich your life in a way that will blow your mind. And all you have to do is accept the gift. That's the uniqueness of Christianity.

Teri: You did say all that; you said it beautifully, Pastor. But if someone didn't listen very carefully, what they'd remember is the loudest part, which is that line about God being angry.

Bishop: Well I do get caught up sometimes when I'm preaching which is why I don't like to listen to my own tapes. But as I've said before, everybody else here understands that. Everyone else places the intensity in context. But the fact is that I would be neglecting my job if I didn't let people know about the rough side of God. That is just information they need to know. If they think they can go around thinking only happy thoughts and meanwhile they're lying and cheating and acting cruel with no thought to how it affects anybody else, they're going to have a surprise coming.

Teri: Well, yes, maybe. But here's the chain of events I fear. Many people don't place that kind of talk in context. They hear it, and they make choices solely out of fear that they wouldn't otherwise have made. Or when disasters befall them, they are wracked with guilt that they've offended God. And then other people judge them as deserving the wrath of God and feel justified in neglecting their plight and even condemning them for it. And it all adds up to a society of scared, stunted people in isolated groups.

Bishop: Now Teri be fair. Nobody's going to jump to those conclusions if they hear a balanced gospel. You have heard me preach the opposite of every one of those scenarios. You've heard me say that motivation through fear doesn't work and is counter-productive. You've heard me preach that holding on to guilt makes no sense because Jesus' death absolved us of all sin. And we've had many conversations that should make it absolutely clear a Christian has no business judging anybody else and in fact must continue to love and forgive even the most wicked sinner. Isn't that the truth?

Teri: Yes, it is.

Bishop: So where do you get these ideas?

Teri: Everywhere. When hurricane Katrina hit, some preachers said it was because of the wickedness of New Orleans. And just this week Pat Robertson said that a town in Pennsylvania that voted out Intelligent Design in science classes should not expect God's help if there were a disaster in their area.[25]

Bishop: That kind of talk does not reflect the God we embrace. That kind of superficial interpretation makes sincere Christians look foolish to the rest of the world. And furthermore, God specifically promised Noah after the great flood that he would never again curse the earth no matter how wicked man was.

Teri: I need to hear you say something like that every once in a while. You confuse me because you're like the opposite of a hypocrite. Hypocrites say all the right words but do all the wrong things. But from my point of view, you say all the wrong things on this topic but do all the right things. You talk about an angry God but behave in a compassionate way.

Bishop: If that was a compliment, thank you. And I think you need to continue your study so you can absorb the message in a more complete way—the nice part along with the rough part. As a minister of the gospel I am responsible to preach the *whole* counsel of God. Not to tickle your ears, but to liberate you to live for a Holy God that loves you too much to simply be fair. So he offers his grace and mercy in place of his justice. Yet since it's a gift you must be a taker. It's really all about choice, Teri.

Teri: It doesn't feel like a choice when he's standing there with a stick.

Facing the rough side of God

Bishop: You seem to be confused about a couple of things. First of all, anyone who is saved doesn't have to face the wrath of God. In fact, God is more than fair with us. He often *protects us* from the consequences of our acts. Think about all the times you did or thought the wrong thing and didn't meet the consequences. No, the wrath of God is faced solely by those who have utterly rejected God, after every opportunity to see the light.

Teri: Well, I'm glad to hear that. But still, when I hear it that way, I cringe for some of the finest people who ever lived, people who stood up to tyrannical, pompous, church authorities and refused to accept their dogma.

Bishop: No Teri, wrath is not for them. God directs wrath at those who cause grievous harm to themselves and others. Please understand that God is angry with unrepentant wrongdoers all the time—just as you and I are. The difference is that he, as God, reserves that right to hold the perpetrators accountable. We don't have that right. So we must learn to let him be God. He is sovereign, and as one of my friends would say, he really doesn't need our help being God.

God is not a role model

Teri: But what kind of a role model is that? Good parents would never wrathfully punish even the most unrepentantly evil child—though they might turn him out of the house and call the cops. If God can be said to have a personality, it must be way better than human personality. So what kind of role model is that?

Bishop: God is not the role model, Jesus is.

Teri: Aaaah. I get it. That must be why the early church let itself be ripped apart by disputes over the trinity. It solves the paradox that there seems to be a part of God that loves and a part that enforces.

Bishop: Jesus is both fully human and fully divine. That's the core of Christianity.

Teri: You know, the model of Universal Mind in Religious Science also separates out three aspects of God. First there's a loving consciousness that creates with its thought—a power that we can share in with our thought—second, there is a neutral "Law" through which thought passes to be manifested, and then third, there is everything that is created. We think of all of that as adding up to God.

Bishop: That's some pretty far out speculation. And I would suggest to you that Christianity offers a better deal; the tiniest little thought of repentance is enough to get *all* of God's grace and mercy.

Teri: We say, "The Universe is biased on the side of healing."

Bishop: If you mean God, he certainly is.

Teri: So if God reserves wrath for the totally unrepentant, really bad guys, why don't we see the really bad guys swallowed up today?

Bishop: We can never judge from the outside what is going on in someone's life. But God has set up a system such that everyone feels the consequences of their acts.

Teri: Well we certainly believe that in Religious Science. Every thought has consequences. So let's see if we agree about the nature of those consequences.

Bishop: All right then.

Another loophole: wrath as consequences

Teri: It's clearly not a literal tit for tat system because good things happen to bad people and bad things happen to good people.

Bishop: That's right. Matthew 5:45 says, "**He causes his sun to rise on the evil and the good, and sends rain on the righteous and the unrighteous.**"

Teri: Okay, yes. But at the same time, our acts do have natural consequences that almost always reward what any reasonable person would call virtue and punish evil. So if I choose to do something that hurts myself or someone else, in almost all cases I'm going to get an unpleasant consequence from that. If I'm boastful, people will avoid me; if I do a lot of drugs, I may lose my ability to take pleasure in other ways, that kind of thing.

Bishop: Yes, what goes around comes around. But that's only "natural" in the sense that God set it up that way. Galatians 6:7 (kjv) tells us, "**Be not deceived; God is not mocked: for whatsoever a man soweth, that shall he also reap.**"

Teri: Okay, fine. But the really interesting point to me is that this effect becomes much richer and deeper for people who are *on to the game*, either because they have traditional faith or because they otherwise believe that their every thought and word has consequences. And that's because it's their *thought* that has the consequences, not the act. So if I spend my life sacrificing for others, but I feel superior or put upon, I don't get any benefits from that. Once I realize that I can change my thinking, my whole experience of life opens up—even if my behavior is the same.

Bishop: God cares about your motivation.

Teri: Exactly. In New Thought we picture it as the working of a neutral force, and that seems to get us pretty much the same results it gets you. In fact, my study with you has caused me to go back over the work of the founders of New Thought. And I've been amazed how much a lot of it lines up with the Christian concept of the wrath of God. I must have ignored all that part in my early studies. But for example—and you'll like this—Thomas Troward quotes scripture to support our belief that the image we have of the Universe actually affects how it interacts with us. "**With the pure thou will**

show thyself pure, and with the forward thou wilt show thyself forward." (Ps. 18:26 and 2 Sam. 22:27 kjv).

Bishop: That's true, and scripture also says, "**According to your faith will it be done to you**" (Matt. 9:29). And Solomon says in Proverbs 23:7, "**As a man thinks in his heart so is he.**" (nkjv)

Teri: Oh wow, those are our absolute favorite scriptures. So the way I see it is that for most of us, if we don't realize the power of our thoughts, we get consequences that make life a kind of hell, even if our deeds are good and all our material needs are cared for.

Bishop: Yes, God uses consequences to chastise us for our correction, as we've discussed, and that's a good thing, it's a benefit to us. Hebrews 12:11 tells us, "**No discipline seems pleasant at the time, but painful. Later on, however, it produces a harvest of righteousness and peace for those who have been trained by it.**" He completely restores us back to fellowship with him when the corrective measure brings us to a proper response to life.

Teri: I've seen that idea working in my life. But when you say it that way, it sounds so heavy. It's so much more inspiring to me to think of life as a joyous opportunity to learn and grow, interacting with a set of laws that provide just the environment we need for each lesson. Or as my first Religious Science minister, Rev. Noel McInnes, says, "We have freedom of choice but not freedom of consequence."

Bishop: You are so sensitive to how things are said. You can't just view life from rose- colored glasses. Life on either side of the fence is full of all sorts of challenges—some good, and, whether we like it or not, some are very ugly. But it's true we don't have freedom of consequence. Take AIDS for example. People mostly get AIDS from homosexual sex, sex with prostitutes, or IV drug use. So AIDS is a "natural" consequence of behaviors the Bible warns us against. As you would say, Teri, the Universe provides natural consequences for breaking its laws.

Teri: (We both smile at his use of "the Universe") Exactly—though I have to add the caveat that of course innocent spouses get AIDS, and monogamous homosexual couples do not. So it's never a one-for-one relationship with any disease or accident. It's much subtler than that. It relates to each person's state of mind, including unconscious thoughts.

Bishop: Like if a man is unfaithful to his wife, his prayers may not be answered.

Teri: Okay, let's go with that. The way I'd put that is that if our energy is tied up in something that requires hiding, we're not emitting the kind of open vibration that would draw to us rich, juicy new adventures.

Bishop: Hmm. Interesting, but I'll stick with the way the scriptures put it.

Correcting father or neutral force?

Teri: But that's my point. As soon as you use scriptural language that personifies that effect and say that the consequences come because God is chastising me, to me that makes all of life a brutal trap; it makes me powerless. Although, I'll tell you, New Agers can fall into the opposite trap. If I believe I created my illness through my thoughts, that can make me feel guilty.

In fact, I'm beginning to wonder if we're seeing the same phenomenon but naming it differently. Take those natural disasters for instance. There are some in New Thought who say that if we all raised our consciousness high enough, there wouldn't be so many disasters, or at least they wouldn't harm populations. I'm not sure I go with that, but it's a positive way of saying that belief is all-powerful. I can see it as the flip side of saying that we have disasters *because* God is displeased by a lack of faith—though I expect my friends at Celebration Center would resist the comparison.

Bishop: And so would most Christians.

Teri: But whichever terminology you use, the God I know is much more subtle and sophisticated than to wipe out a town for the sins of a few. Within any disaster, each person can have a different experience. Some people will be rescued in coincidences that feel to them like miracles, and some will experience their finest hour rescuing others. Many will die horribly, but some, even among those, will die with a sense of peace, knowing they are spiritually safe no matter what. For each person, the nature of their experience will be deeply colored by how they see life. Those with faith have potential for a much richer experience, even in death.

Bishop: Yes, yes. Your problem is you're thinking that to "chasten" means to punish. But it's like a parent correcting a child for the child's own benefit. It's an act of love. And it comes from knowing what's best in the long run. He called us, "**My little children.**" (John 13:33 nkjv) Can you hear the tenderness in that?

A squirt gun in the face from the Holy Spirit

Teri: I hate the word "chastisement," but I can relate to the idea if I think of it in a purely positive sense—as getting opportunities to grow.

I had a sweet example once. I took a workshop that featured the importance of generosity, and we were all supposed to bring something we valued to give away. The day before the workshop I went Christmas shopping, and I was attracted to a beautiful tree ornament, a dove of white and gold frosted glass. It was more money than I'd usually pay, and I sensed immediately I should bring it as my gift the next day. But as I stood in line to buy it, I started to think that I wanted to keep it. It was just like one of those cartoon conversations between the little devil and angel on my shoulder. I even thought that if I kept it for myself, it would always remind me of the value of giving. I knew how lame that was, and it began to feel urgent that I make up my mind to give it or keep it before the cashier rang me up. But when I got to the cashier she said, "Do you want another one? The doves are two-for-one."

I wouldn't expect anyone else to understand this, but tears came to my eyes. I felt I had just been "chastened," to use your word, in the most loving and gentle of ways. So in that sense, I can relate to "chastening" as a positive thing.

Bishop: That's a fine example of how sweet guidance can be when we listen carefully.

Teri: In New Thought we sometimes say, "Better to listen to the squirt gun than wait for the Universe to pull out the two-by-four."

Bishop: Exactly.

Final reckoning

Teri: I will confess something that's bothered me, though—those few situations in which someone does not face natural consequences in this lifetime, for example the warlord or corporate executive who gets away with his plundering and enjoys living well.

Bishop: If he hasn't been saved, he's going to be eternally separated from God. And that's a free choice. Again Teri, everyone will ultimately reap what they have sown. He may get by, and get over, but he will not get away.

Teri: Okay, that's the Christian answer. Mine is that my consciousness lives on in some form—either it's reincarnation with karma or its something subtler, more like a drop of water returning to the ocean of consciousness, and the whole ocean is benefiting from the experience of each individual. Not for punishment but for growth toward perfection.

Bishop: Again, I'll stick with the scripture on this one.

After this conversation, I went home and looked again at Troward's *Edinburgh Lectures on Mental Science* from 1904. His biblical references were even more pointed than I remembered. But I winced at an attitude my new Christian friends could see as patronizing. Referring to Jesus, Troward says,

> The greatest Teacher of Mental Science the world has ever known has laid down sufficiently plain rules for our guidance… He bids his unlearned audience picture to themselves the Universal Mind as a benign Father, tenderly compassionate of all and… exercising a special and peculiar care over those who recognize its willingness to do so... Prayer was to be made to the unseen Being, not with doubt or fear, but with the absolute assurance of a certain answer, and no limit was to be set to its power or willingness to work for us. But to those who did not thus realize it, the Great Mind is necessarily the adversary who casts them into prison until they have paid the utmost farthing. Such teaching was not a narrow anthropomorphism but the adaptation to the intellectual capacity of the unlettered multitude…

The next part shocked me. How could I not have seen it before? Saying, "I do not wish to dogmatize," Troward says that the more we discipline our human minds to interact constructively with Universal Mind, "the more current objections to the gospel narrative lose their force…"

> We shall grasp something of the meaning of Christ as "The Son of God"—the concentration of the Universal Spirit into a Personality (as being a pattern for) the individuality of each human who affords the necessary thought conditions. It is as such an external manifestation of the divine ideal that the

> Christ of the Gospels is set before us.
>
> It is for this reason that St. John puts the question of Christ manifest in the flesh as the criterion of the whole matter: **The Spirit of God is known by this: Every prophecy which declares that Jesus Christ is come in the flesh is from God. And every prophecy which does not declare that Jesus Christ has come in the flesh is not from God.** (1 John 4:2-3 Lam)[26]

If the leading thinker in New Thought had been able to make his peace with the core of fundamentalist ideology, shouldn't I be able to do the same?

Why are these people smiling?

Something else had me perplexed. The overall ambience at Highview was usually very upbeat. With all the talk about sin and wrath and unworthiness, why were these people smiling? Even in Sunday sermons when Bishop was chastising the congregation for something, a look around the room often caught more broad grins than frowns.

Just for fun, I looked up Jonathan Edwards, the hellfire preacher I had studied in high school who called us "loathsome spiders." I was surprised to find JonathanEdwards.com, an upbeat site with a tribute to the preacher's "God-entranced vision" on the anniversary of his 300th birthday.

> His vision of God and Christian living are unsurpassed in grandeur, gravity, and gladness… The aim of every speaker will be Edwards-for-today, not just the Edwards-of-old. His vision is more relevant for our day than most of what is fashionable. We need his message badly. Not his dress. Not all of his language. Not even all his views. But the weight of glory that he felt, and the depth of biblical truth that he knew, and the radiance of the Redeemer that he saw, and the glorious "harmony of all things" in Christ — these we need.

A teasing line at the bottom of the page quoted 1 Corinthians 16:13 (nasb), "**Act like men; be strong.**" [27]

Mulling all of this over, it occurred to me that there is a sense in which the best of the Fundamentalist Christians are tougher than us tenderfoot secularists and New Agers. Being compared to a "loathsome spider" saps our self-esteem. So anyone who can conceive of God as wrathful and still have self-esteem that is not based on judging others, obviously has some wellspring of strength. I don't know how they do it, but I am faced with the fact that some Christians do.

I felt another little ironic twist when I came across this advice by Ken Wilber.

> Choose your teachers carefully. If you want encouragement, soft smiles, ego stroking… find yourself a Nice Guy or a Good Girl and hold their hand on the sweet path of stress reduction and egoic comfort. But if you want enlightenment, if you want to wake up, if you want to get fried in the fire of passionate Infinity, then, I promise you: find yourself a Rude Boy or a Nasty Girl…they live as compassion—real compassion, not idiot compassion—and real compassion uses a sword more often than a sweet. They deeply offend the ego… tear you into approximately 1,000 pieces… so that Infinity can reassemble you, Freedom can replace imprisonment; Fullness can outshine fear. If you can stand the rudeness, stay in the fire, you will burn clean as Infinity and radiate as the stars.[28]

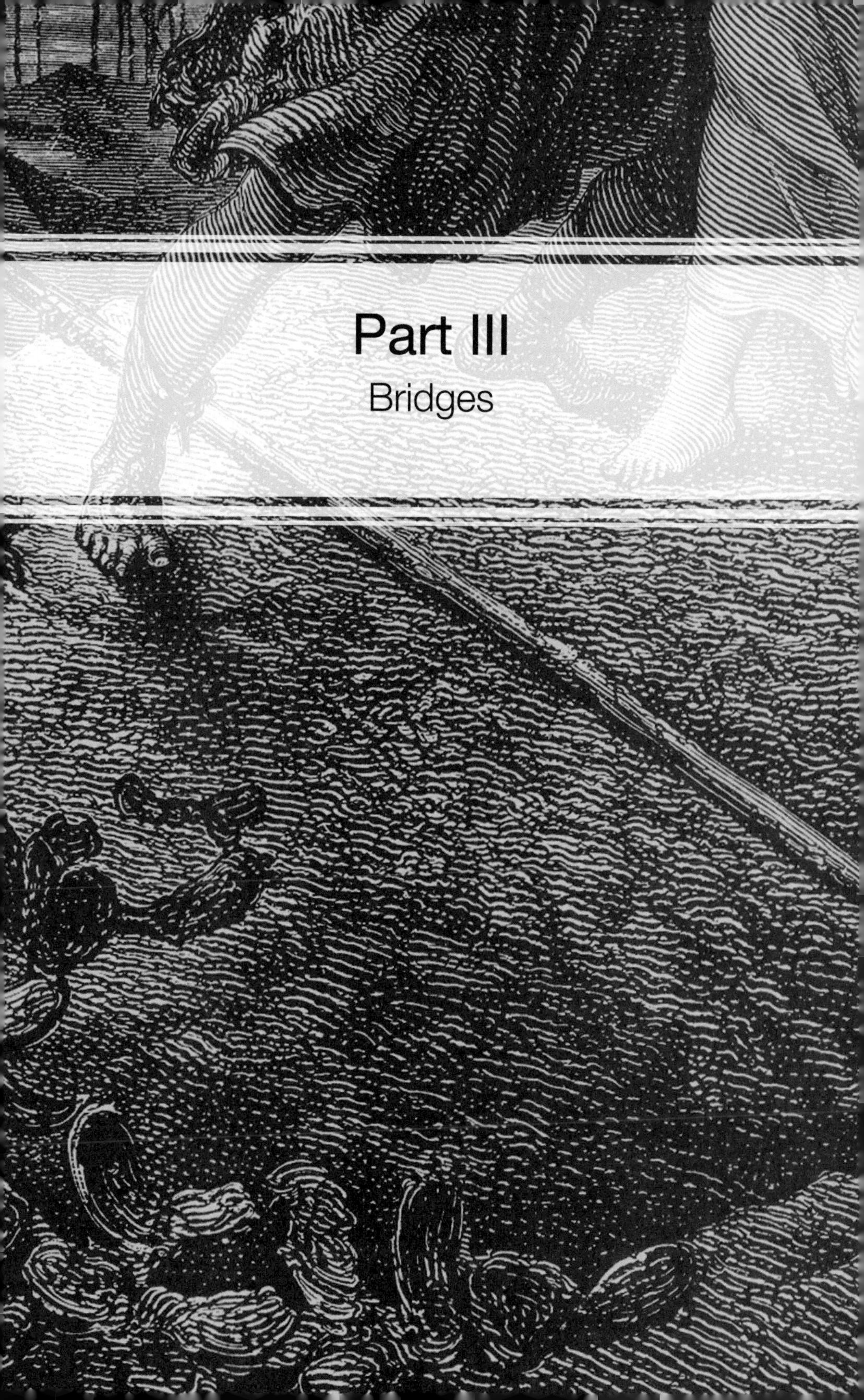

Part III

Bridges

15

Science vs. Religion 1: Evolution

God operates through what
we call the law of evolution
or unfoldment... There is an
unfolding principle within
us which is ever carrying us
forward to greater and greater
expressions of freedom, love, joy
and life.
Ernest Holmes, *Can we Talk to God*

Great are the works of the Lord;
they are studied by all who delight in them.
Psalms 111:2 (nasb)

One reason I was attracted to a church with the name "Religious Science" was that it makes sense to me that there should never have to be any conflict between religion and science. I wanted to find out how science fits in Highview's "literal" interpretation of the Bible.

Teri: I believe that science and religion are different ways of knowing reality. Science tells us about what we can measure from the outside, and religion tells us about what we can know from the inside. They should never contradict each other.

Bishop: We can understand the natural, but we can never totally understand the supernatural.

Teri: In one sense, yes. But in a bigger sense, in New Thought, there isn't really anything *super*natural, because *everything* is supernatural;

that is, everything is obeying rules beyond those that our physical tools can measure.

Bishop: God's law.

Teri: Yes, but it's all one system. In other words, as we see it, what we might perceive as miracles don't break the laws of physics, they work with them in some exquisite way that makes them look like miracles. I get three miracles a week when I'm paying attention—though my secularist friends would call them coincidences. So if science ever *could* figure everything out, it will be all due to one set of rules. We've already seen hints of this in quantum physics—like the fact that one particle can influence another at a distance. That doesn't actually prove anything about prayer, but it suggests…

Bishop: So,…you believe in… evolution?

In the flash of that nanosecond, the gulf between us inflated to such cosmic width we could barely see across it. And our bridging materials suddenly seemed like matchsticks.

"*Transcend and include,*" I told myself, "*I don't think I can include this one.*"

Teri: Uh, well, to me it gives much more glory to God to believe that creation happened via evolution than via a series of supernatural acts. We believe in New Thought that Conscious Intelligence came first. How astonishing is it if that intelligence was able to think into existence the Big Bang and a set of principles that would inevitably lead from it to stars, planets, and life?[29] The intelligence behind *that* takes my breath away more than a "magic wand" kind of creation.

Bishop: Magic wand? Oh, Teri, it's so much vaster and more powerful than that…

Teri: I don't mean to be disrespectful, but I can't buy a God who just said, "Poof, there are zebras." That would be far less impressive than working through a series of natural laws that Source created to make it possible for life to expand infinitely.

I had done lots of popular science reading about evolution. The arguments challenging it had become much more sophisticated in recent years. Still, it seemed clear to me that each of the new and reasonable-sounding arguments against evolution were well refuted in works such as those of leading theorist Richard Dawkins. I had read his classic defense of evolution, *The Blind Watchmaker*.[30] The main arguments went through my head, and I considered asking for a separate session with Bishop Thomas just to cover them. My worst fear was that he would simply say, "If the Bible says creation took six days, then it was six days."

It was he who broke the silence.

Bishop: Well, I have some colleagues who believe the description of the six days of creation in the Bible doesn't all refer to *earth* days.

He was trying to throw me a line, which I appreciated, but it wasn't enough. If he was going to deny scientific fact, it would be extremely difficult for me to respect anything else about his belief system.

Teri: Are you saying that if the Bible contradicts plain scientific fact, you will believe the Bible instead?

Bishop: There's no reason for it to come to that. The Bible has been thoroughly researched by generations of historians, archeologists, and scientists. Everything we know about the Bible is well backed up by science. I'd be eager to go over all that material with you.

I was relieved to hear that we could have a fact-based conversation, and I decided the details could wait; so I changed the topic. And then a few things happened in the intervening period. Several news items brought to my attention the fact that some of the challenges to evolution were coming from sophisticated scientists, some of whom were being fired for expressing their views. I also came to realize how strongly attached I was to my belief in evolution. My whole sense of reality was grounded in it.

Why everybody who doesn't believe in evolution isn't necessarily an idiot

First the *Washington Post* ran a long piece on Phillip Johnson, a respected, secularist legal scholar whose life turned around when he read *Blind Watchmaker* and saw holes in its arguments. He wrote *Darwin on Trial*, which argues that evidence for evolution is weak in key places, but because scientists have no other theory, they have lowered their standards of evidence in this case. About the same time, I learned that one of the largest and most sophisticated, Bible-based churches in the Washington area, McLean Bible, was running a seminar on disproofs of evolution. Many members there have advanced degrees and high-power Washington jobs. And then one Saturday morning, Andy came home from one of his yard sale runs with the book, *The Case for Creationism*, which he left on our living room coffee table. I circled it for several days before peeking inside. The new arguments for intelligent design did sound much more sophisticated.[31] [32]

These events made me realize that it isn't just little backwater churches that question evolution. Evolution's defenders say the challengers oversimplify complex issues and quote scientists out of context to make evolution look shaky where it is *not*. Richard Dawkins has said, "It is absolutely safe to say that if you meet somebody who claims not to believe in evolution, that person is ignorant, stupid, or insane (or wicked, but I'd rather not consider that)." [33]

The scientific community was adding to the tension by reacting to challenges with indignation and possibly intimidation. I poked around in Internet chat rooms and found that challenges to evolution are often met with hostility and personal attacks. Of course, that's the nature of the Internet, but I was not able to find sites where rational discussion was taking place. I also learned that respected scientists are risking their reputations to question evolution—in 2004 the editor of a scientific journal published at the Smithsonian lost his associateship when he included an article on Intelligent Design. The editor holds two doctorates in evolutionary biology, and the article was approved in the standard process of peer review.[34] Someone who holds two doctorates in evolutionary biology is obviously not ignorant or stupid. The likelihood of insanity is small, which leaves only "wicked" from Dawkins' list of causes for challenging evolution. Could there be another option?

Genius aliens

Awareness of this tension softened me up for the next time Bishop Thomas and I discussed evolution. Next time we met, we both had studied up.

Bishop: First of all, even at the simplest level, life is so complex that the chance for it to come about by accident is ridiculously small. The famous mathematical astrophysicist, Sir Fred Hoyle, recently argued that the probability this could have happened even once in the entire history of the universe is roughly equivalent to the probability that a tornado sweeping through a junkyard would assemble a Boeing 747.

Teri: I've heard that. And the funny thing is, Hoyle is an atheist, so he concluded that the gene code for life must have been devised by genius aliens.

Bishop: (Scoffing) Well who does he think created those aliens?

Teri: He says we can't know that. (More scoffing from Bishop)

You've put your finger on one of the creationist's best arguments. But there is an answer to it. Dawkins and other evolution supporters say that evolution has had an unimaginably huge amount of time to work—four billion years. Their computer simulations show that the time available *is* enough for random mutations to build on each other for even the most complex organs. In the case of the eye, for example, the first step is photosensitivity in a tiny sea plant that turns it toward the sun. From there nature shows every intermediate level of sophistication from the eye of the worm that burrows toward light, all the way up to the eye of the mammal with its astonishing acuity. It *sounds* unbelievable, but most scientists believe that it *has been shown* how each one of these steps could have built on the others.

Bishop: *Could* have. No proof. Look, Teri, I am open to the fact that we see small changes happening within species today. But there is no evidence that one species can change into another. Where are all the missing links between species?

Teri: Scientists say they've found lots of missing links, and they find more all the time. But we can never find them all, for heaven's sake. It's a miracle we have any fossil record, considering that flesh and flowers had to withstand eons in nature's crock-pot.

Bishop: In other words, you take it on faith that those links exist.

Teri: That's not what I'm saying. We have enough evidence to make a reasonable assumption. And remember, when I argue for evolution, I'm not arguing against God. I believe God set the evolutionary process in motion.

Bishop: You say there's enough evidence that species evolve. But what about the origin of life itself—the very first living thing. Where did that come from? You have absolutely no evidence for that.

Despite much media-induced misunderstanding on this point, not a single living molecule has ever yet been made from nonliving chemicals in the laboratory, despite all the many costly experiments attempting to do so.

Teri: That's true.

Bishop: Yet evolutionists imagine that what cannot be accomplished by trained scientists with costly equipment in artificially controlled environments somehow occurred by blind chance a billion years ago. Some unknown process operating in an unknown liquid mixture beneath an unknown type of atmosphere somehow generated unknown primitive life forms from unknown chemicals, and that's how life began! That seems to take a lot more faith then even I can muster.

Teri: I know they don't have any proof on that particular piece of the puzzle. But the overall case is strong. And again, the part I want to focus on is how beautifully evolution can support belief in God.

Bishop: If there were adequate scientific proof that evolution is true, then we would have to believe it and know that our interpretation was wrong. But the evidence just isn't there.

Evolution is really three theories

Shortly after this discussion, a friend referred me to an article with the fascinating spin that evolution is really three theories:

1. That life *began by chance*, which has no proof,
2. That *evolution happens now*, which is well proven,
3. That the mechanism of evolution is *random* mutation of DNA, which is only partially proven (meaning random rather than influenced by an unknown factor).[35]

The author suggested that people can believe in the second of these "theories" while still questioning the others. It's not a package deal, as most people assume.

As if to punctuate this point, the *Washington Post* ran a piece on competing theories on the origin of life—the first of the three points above. Some researchers believe life originated in tidal pools while others see stronger evidence that it began around deep ocean vents. The article quoted origin of life researcher George Cody saying, "No one knows anything about the origin of life." [36]

This shook something loose for me. I had never really focused on the fact that the origin of life is a question separate from the rest of evolutionary theory. But it is, in fact, a very different type of question. When scientists encounter a mystery they can't solve, they assume there is a "natural" explanation, and in most cases it makes sense to leave it at that. If, for example, we didn't know how caterpillars became moths, no modern person would assume God interrupted natural law when we weren't looking (although the facts behind this particular natural event are astounding enough to make scientists fall to their knees). But over my years of popular science reading, I came to believe there are three questions in science that have a unique quality to them: the origin of the universe, the origin of life, and the origin of consciousness—the beginning of stars, genes, and minds.

These three questions share two special qualities: first, science will probably never be able to prove an answer to any of them, and second, the answers are intensely entwined with the meaning of life—or lack thereof. But now I began to see that most "moderns" *take it on faith* that there *is* a natural answer—so much so, that we are not open to saying, "We don't know how life began, and we'll never know, though we will never stop working to develop theories that are more and more plausible." That would be an honest answer. Why doesn't science just say that? Instead, secularist friends often end conversations on these topics with, "There's no point in even asking those questions."

All the scientific evidence and plain facts in the world...

The last brick in my sense of the breadth of disbelief in evolution came in a spam email I received from an unknown source. It promoted a book by a Turkish Muslim who is a leading opponent of evolution.

> Message text written by "Demir Baser"
> The Religion of Darwinism By Harun Yahya
>
> The goal of Darwinism is to get people to reject the obvious fact of Creation, which is clearly evident and assured, and to believe in the myth embodied in the theory of evolution. Darwinism and the theory of evolution are incredible and illogical beliefs; they are like the proposition that black is a chance byproduct of the changes that white undergoes over time. But over the past 150 years, countless individuals have adopted these ideas passionately, and nothing can convince them to give them up. *All the scientific evidence and plain facts in the world* haven't been able to free them from this spell's influence. It is as if they've been bewitched to believe that it is raining when the sun is out.

I was flabbergasted by the turn-about in the thinking; it was an exact mirror of arguments that evolutionists make about creationists. In other words, both sides are equally convinced that the *facts* are on their side. It became apparent that Richard Dawkins left out at least one cause for disbelief in evolution: being so blinded by a pre-existing view that we can only perceive facts that support our view. I began to suspect this condition applies equally to most people on both sides of this debate. In fact, Ken Wilber's Integral Theory tells me that some truths simply *cannot* be seen until one reaches a particular level of development. But it's also true that a person at a given level will not see truths from earlier levels that the person failed to *include* as he or she grew.

Poof genes!

I asked myself the tough question: does this blindness apply to me? I have no difficulty believing that some "first cause" thought the universe into being without use of a physical mechanism. So why am I so positive it didn't also "think" life into being without a physical mechanism? And perhaps it thought human consciousness into being as well. That would be three separate creation events instead of one: Poof stars! Poof genes! Poof minds that can think about themselves and God.

Ugh. I hated the idea. It felt so much less elegant than the concept of continuous, moment-to-moment creation via evolution—the view expressed so beautifully by Ernest Holmes:

> Plato said everything is made up of divine ideas… He meant the thoughts of God: "In the beginning was the Word." God thought Creation into existence and is still thinking it into existence in you and in me. The creative Energy and Intelligence that speaks the planets into their spheres of rotation and revolution is the same Intelligence that digests our food and enables us to read the morning paper.[37]

A revelation

And then I had a revelation. Just for a moment I considered what it would be like for me if evolution were ever disproved. The tectonic plates of my worldview heaved, and I tumbled into a terrifying crevasse of implications.

Suddenly I saw how much my values and self-image are rooted in belief in evolution. I am thrilled by a sense of an ever-expanding and evolving universe. Since childhood I consumed science fiction and marveled at the idea of continual exploration, continual expansion for the human race. Light years of distance and billions of years ahead of us.

For most of us in the New Thought movement, God is "Consciousness unfolding." Evolution provides the metaphor and the imperative for us to grow, change, diversify, and seek our highest expression as part of that unfolding. We see ourselves as "riding the wave" at the leading edge of a magnificent, expanding crest of consciousness. In fact, that particular image of wave riding is one of the most inspiring motivators for many of us in New Thought.

For my secularist friends, proof of an intentional intelligence behind creation might threaten them with the feeling that the material world is unpredictable. But for me and my New Thought brethren, nearly the opposite is true. Belief that we are integrated into that intentional intelligence gives us some control. If all this magnificent life around me was just the product of a series of arbitrary waves of a magic wand by a God separate from me, then I didn't see how we as humans could really participate in it. Life became a flat, pre-ordained thing. Not to mention the fact that I'd have to question everything else I'd ever believed. Unthinkable. Impossible.

No, there is *nothing you could ever say or discover* that would make me disbelieve in evolution—unless you replaced it with another explanation that had similar implications and that still let me *ride that wave.*

Oh my God, Teri. Listen to yourself. Do you realize what you just thought? So that's why creationists fight so hard. That's why they seem so unreasonable. They probably feel just like you do! Both sides are blind to some of the other's facts because their worldviews are equally threatened. There may be no one with a truly open mind on this question.

At our next meeting, I confessed to these feelings.

Teri: Pastor, I want to admit something to you. In my mind I was accusing you of being unable to see both sides of this debate. But the truth is, I've realized that the concept of evolution is so central to my sense of myself that I can't even talk about God without using the word "evolve." I didn't even bother to look at the facts on your side before because I can't imagine giving up my view.

Bishop: You could if you realized there is something better to replace it.

Teri: It would be hard to top the vision that I have. The way Ernest Holmes explained it, after studying all philosophies and religions, is that evolution is the other half of involution. Divine intelligence existed before the universe began. It *in*volves or incarnates itself in every life form, expressing itself more perfectly as every form *e*volves.

Bishop: Jesus was the only incarnation of the divine.

Teri: We think of him as the most perfect incarnation. Christ consciousness—which we believe was also attained by Buddha and other spiritual masters—is the last step, the top of the ladder. From one-celled creatures up through man we become more aware, reaching toward Christ consciousness.

Bishop: What would be the purpose of all that?

Teri: Holmes said, and it feels right to me, that the purpose of all evolution is to produce beings who can consciously cooperate with Life so God can fully express. It is the awakening of the soul to recognition of its unity with its source. It's a way for God to know himself through us.[38]

Bishop: God doesn't need evolution to serve his purposes. He promises in Revelations a new earth without suffering and a joy without measure for those who follow him.

Teri: A vision of final perfection just seems static to me. Remember when we talked about becoming perfect as the purpose of life? It's the *becoming* that's exciting to me.

I will admit, however, this whole discussion has left me with a couple of nagging questions about evolution. But I *have faith* that they'll be answered as soon as I do more research.

One of the questions that started to nag me was this: If I believed in an initial creation event, did I really believe that event was unintentional—something like a hiccup from the original consciousness, or like a baby flailing its arms? "*Whoops... wow, look what I did.*" If not, if the original event was *intended* to create life that could "know its source," then was there anything else life was *intended* to do? Was there a right way to evolve? I thought about the purpose of life I learned in Catholic school: "to know, love, and serve God." It was beginning to sound like not such a bad fit to the story of creation that I believed.

Riding the wave

A few days after we discussed evolution, Bishop and I were finishing another difficult dialogue session at which a visitor from the Celebration Center was present. We were deadlocked; the energy was blocked. The question hung in the air as to why we were pursuing this difficult venture of trying to understand each other. The three of us looked at each other for a moment before Bishop spoke.

"Well, I'm just riding this wave to see where it goes."

It struck me like a gong sounding that he was using my cherished analogy of riding a wave. And when the gong's ringing stopped, there came a whisper. Bishop's understanding of creation led him to the same sense of exhilaration and responsibility about life that evolution did for me. *That* was the key thing. Facts are important and must be openly debated, and both sides could go a long way to turn down the heat on this issue. But it seems to be a grievous mistake to let facts tear us apart while an underlying truth is calling us all.

16

Science vs. Religion 2: *What the Bleep Do We Know?*

When I was growing up, it was thought that Christianity had to be integrated with scientific thinking, or else it would not be acceptable. It was feared that, torn between science and Christianity, students would give up Christianity. It never occurred to anyone that they might just give up on science.
Tony Campolo, *Adventures in Missing the Point*

At this point, Andy and I were attending service at Highview every Sunday, and we were returning to the Celebration Center of Religious Science for special events. I began to yearn for some crossover between the two communities.

Just about this time, an underground movie that had been gathering rave reviews from New Agers hit the East Coast. According to the buzz, the film showed the cutting-edge science that proves that our thoughts change reality. *What the Bleep do We Know?* was as eagerly awaited by many in New Age and New Thought as *The Passion of the Christ* would be by Christians a few months later. I organized a group from the Celebration Center to go to *What the Bleep* and have a discussion afterwards. And then I invited Bishop Thomas to join us.

"Are you sure this is a good idea?" Andy asked me.

"Absolutely not," was my reply.

I didn't foresee that my own reactions to the film would be as much out-of-step as Bishop's would.

Coming together for a cult movie

Forty-two people from the Center signed up, though a few said they would not be comfortable coming to the discussion knowing that Bishop Thomas would be there. I arrived first at the theater, and Bishop Thomas and his wife Cindy arrived last. They sat in front of Andy and me.

The movie tells the story of a woman who has lost interest in life because her fiancé jilted her. She regains her spark in a breakthrough moment that shows her she can change her thoughts about her past. The next morning, we see her in a reverie drawing a heart on her hand as a symbol that she has hope of loving life and herself. We also see her visualizing unlimited paths ahead that are available for her to create with her choices.

This simple plot is backed up by interviews with scientists and mystics and by a series of wild animation sequences. The best scenes show that thoughts can be physically addictive: our bodies become addicted to the chemicals released by various mental states. Happiness breeds more happiness; anger or depression breed more anger or depression until we act intentionally to break the cycle.

The experts also discuss the "observer" in our heads—science cannot locate it in our brains, they tell us. But mystics report that there is only one observer or "witness" which is common to us all. And in that sense, this observer is God; we are all part of God; we *are* God. And thus, our thoughts can change reality outside our bodies as well as inside.

Cutting edge science?

It was the science behind this second thesis that started to bother me. I *believe* the thesis. But the science here seemed poorly explained and documented. One scene seemed especially suspect, but it elicited murmurs of delight from the audience: water molecules changed shape when angry or loving words were spoken to them. (A check of the Internet later revealed that no one had been able to replicate this experiment.)

Religion is an "ugly superstition"

Sitting in the darkened theater, I found myself increasingly uncomfortable over something else as well. I saw no love in the movie *between* people. What good was changing your reality without that?

And then came the worst moment, an expert identified as a "mystic" said, "Any religion that says we as tiny human beings can sin and displease God is an ugly superstition that blasphemes God." I sank down in my seat and started hoping Bishop Thomas and his wife wouldn't walk out. Apparently, interfaith understanding was not one of the realities the moviemakers were trying to create.

At the end as we all walked out together, Bishop pronounced the movie, "interesting," which brought to mind a friend's young daughter who says adults use "interesting" when they don't want to say something was a disaster.

Mixed reactions

We drove to Celebration Center and arranged the chairs in a circle. I was perplexed to hear that most of my friends were ecstatic about the movie. Reactions included, "Wow—Inspiring—Uplifting—Fascinating—Best movie I ever saw—Can't wait to buy it—Need to see it several more times to understand the science."

A few people said they had personal spiritual experiences during the movie. "I actually felt my consciousness uniting with those around me in the theater," said one. "It shows us we are all one at the sub-atomic level and we are one in the heavens," said another. I agreed with him, but I didn't feel those points were supported in the movie.

Only one person said something negative. Rev. Harriet's husband called it "scientific psychobabble crap… all head and no heart," he said. "I wasn't convinced by the lead character's transformation; she barely even smiled. And the depiction of the observer consciousness had none of the warmth of a personal relationship with Spirit."

I agreed that the ending left me "cold" because the heroine did not reach out in love to anyone else as a result of her transformation. Several people responded emphatically that *loving yourself is the first step before you can love others.* True, I thought. But most of us had been at this for decades. Why were we still excited by the first step?

Clearly I had "seen" a different movie than most of my friends.

The bishop responds

When it first came around the circle for the Thomases to share a one-word impression, Bishop said "confirming" and his wife chose the masterfully ambiguous word, "searching."

We began discussing the ideas, and Bishop T listened a while before speaking. Starting with his areas of agreement, he said the movie confirms Christian belief that science can't answer the important questions, and the portrayal of addictive thoughts confirms the scripture that, "**Whatever a man sows, that he will also reap.**" Otherwise, he said, the movie completely contradicts Bible teaching that man is inherently sinful and can only be saved by accepting God's plan of redemption as the Bible teaches. Several people looked down or away when he said this.

"And the only way our thoughts change reality outside our bodies is through prayer that is aligned with the will of God," he said. Then he finished with the point that the movie ignored the important question of what happens to us when we die and face judgment for what we've done in this life.

This led to a flurry of discussion on reincarnation and the concept that there is ultimately no right and wrong. One fellow stole the show by pronouncing that if his wife butchered him in his sleep, he'd know that the two of them had a karmic, pre-life agreement that such an act would be for their mutual spiritual growth.

Sensing way more trouble than we could get ourselves out of in one evening, I tried to steer the conversation back to commonalities. I said that one of the most fascinating aspects of my regular dialogue with Bishop Thomas is that even though he limits himself to the Bible as his sole standard, when it comes to choices he would actually make or counsel others to make, I had yet to hear anything different from what I might come to drawing on a much wider range of sources—which points to the fact that God speaks to us all.

The tone grew warmer with lots of laughter. Bishop Thomas several times asked someone's name, got up to shake his or her hand, and then remembered to use the name later in conversation. One of the best laughs was when someone said half jokingly that there are no evil people "except for Republicans." Bishop Thomas, who is normally careful not to apply any political labels to himself, stood up and pretended to walk out saying, "That does it, I'm outta here." Everyone laughed. His undefended good-naturedness under fire took my breath away. The term "authentic" came to mind. Also the term "Christ-like."

A meeting point in "Christ consciousness"

Then Ed Preston, my buddy the interfaith chaplain, said something that shifted the tone. He said the meeting point between our two ways of looking at the world is in our desire to emulate "Christ consciousness." He said his personal goal to is bring the Christ consciousness into himself and express it in the world. Rev. Harriet added that one way to grow toward Christ consciousness is to use meditation to inquire, "Who am I?" and thus to determine firsthand who the witness really is. These comments caused Bishop T to rise to his feet and deliver a sermonette that went something like this:

"I can tell you who the witness is. Christian theology tells us it's our connection with God. Oh, I feel like preaching now (laughter). And we need not just to imitate Christ in our outer lives, but to bring him into who we are. St. Paul says we must take on the "**mind of Christ**" until Christ is "**formed in us.**"

His choice of words hit the perfect note: we cheered and leapt to our feet in what felt like discovery of a meeting point. Rev. Harriet then asked Bishop Thomas to give the closing prayer, and he said simply, "Heavenly Father we thank you for the sharing that has brought us together tonight. In Jesus' name, amen."

In the surprised silence that followed, he created the final laugh of the evening saying, "I know y'all think Baptist preachers pray too long."

It was the perfect close to an evening that coincidentally was the anniversary of 9/11.

Afterwards

Something else took place that night that colored all my future discussions with Bishop Thomas: he came away with a strongly positive impression of the people at the Center. "Those are some fine folks," he would say again and again. "Except for that hypocrite who wouldn't mind if his wife killed him," he teased. "Just let me steal his car and see how well he remembers there is no right and wrong.

"But I don't blame those people for being turned off by Bible interpretations that are superficial and miss the beauty of the message," he said. "They can run around getting ideas from science, humanism, and all the world's religions, and some of those ideas will line up with the Bible. But I like to work smarter, not harder. For me the movie had the opposite of its intended effect. It reconfirmed that science will never answer the important questions about God."

I didn't necessarily agree with him on that last point. But the exact relationship of science and religion was one of several things that I was feeling less and less compelled to fully understand.

17

Loophole #6
Wicked and Evil Isn't That Bad

Some men see pleasure as essentially good, and some men see pleasure as essentially bad. Others, knowing it can be both, teach that it is all bad, for they know that men are so powerfully drawn to it, that only by restraining them as much as possible is there any chance of them attaining the middle ground.
Aristotle's *Ethics*

The joint movie discussion at Celebration Center had a ripple effect that continued to influence my discussions with Bishop Thomas.

Bishop: I just can't believe those friends of yours say there is no right and wrong. Do they read the newspapers?

Teri: Actually, some of them don't so they can keep their thoughts elevated. We believe that what you give attention to expands.

Bishop: Well no wonder you all don't realize how wicked and evil most people are.

Teri: We don't deny that people do terrible things to each other. Part of the reason to stop reading a newspaper is that when you have a vision of how good we *could* all make our lives, it's all the more heartbreaking to see the choices people make.

Bishop: You've got that right.

Teri: And bad news can get you in a cycle of reactive, defeatist thinking.

Bishop: That's why you need to teach people about evil, so they can stay strong to fight it.

Born good or bad?

Teri: Most of my people would disagree and say it's important to remember that we are born "perfect, whole, and complete," but society teaches us the idea of right and wrong. In fact, some point to the Bible and the fact that the tree Eve ate from in the Garden of Eden is called the tree of the *knowledge* of good and evil. So it was the knowledge of good and evil that caused her downfall.

Bishop: That's ridiculous. Children have to be taught morality or their natural impulse is to steal a cookie and look you right in the eye and tell you it wasn't them.

Teri: I don't have children, so I'm no authority on this. But I'm inclined to agree with you. You're probably sick of hearing me mention Ken Wilber, but he really clarified my thinking on this. He says we get two thing mixed up. On one hand, it's true that the *spiritual* aspect of ourselves is perfect at birth.

Bishop: Our soul.

Teri: Right. But our personalities are born at the bottom rung of ethical development. Remember the stages I mentioned before: from egocentric to ethnocentric to world centric? That's "egocentric" where we only care about ourselves. We need to *grow into* the higher levels of caring about others—first our family, then our "tribe" and eventually the world. You can't skip stages.

In fact Wilber uses the rather colorful language that we're all born Nazis. "Every time anyone anywhere has sex, they're generating a fresh supply of Nazis," he says.

Bishop: That's just another way of saying the devil is always working in us.

Teri: I'm beginning to see how those two ways of looking at it line up.

Two kinds of atheists

Teri: Another thing I'm beginning to see is how *intention* is the key for both our ways of looking at life. I'm thinking that the real dividing line between people is not good people versus bad, but those who do and do not have an explicit intention to serve the highest good.

Bishop: Atheists.

Teri: No, It doesn't have to do with religious belief. That's the whole point. In fact, some atheists live by higher moral standards than the average, life-long, churchgoer because the atheists have *chosen* their belief after careful study and are very committed to it. I love it when Emerson said, "If anyone believes the path of Self Reliance is easy, let him try it for just one day."

Bishop: I could show you plenty of atheists in prison who can't wait for a chance to slit your throat.

Teri: Okay, yes. So there are really two kinds of atheists depending on whether they have an explicit intention to serve the highest good or not. And it's extremely important to me that you be able to recognize the difference. It drives secular humanists crazy that religious people just lump together as wicked and evil everyone with different beliefs.

Bishop: But intention is not enough; good works alone won't get you into heaven without faith in God.

Teri: I'm not talking about how God judges; we've been over that, and you've really shifted my thinking to see that the only way to "peace that surpasses understanding" is via something that can be called "faith." What I'm talking about now is how *you* judge, your ability to honor the efforts of non-Christians who go to great lengths to do what they think is right.

Bishop: But they might do great harm pursuing what they think is right. Proverbs 14:12 says, "**There is a way that seems right to a man, but in the end it leads to death.**"

Teri: That's probably true, but it's still not my point. I'm talking about loving people of different beliefs and honoring their *intentions*.

Bishop: Oh well, *that's* easy. You know I love everybody, even if their intentions aren't so honorable.

Teri: (Sighing) Yes, Pastor, I believe you do. And perhaps this is all so obvious to you that the distinction I'm trying to make isn't even on your radar screen. But it would help me if you could stay aware that I'm sensitive to having Christians call my friends wicked and evil.

Reinforcements

At this point I was yearning for some help in expressing myself, and I wanted to get an outside view on these discussions. So one night I brought two licensed practitioners of Religious Science, Ed Preston and Laurie Bolster. They are friends I respect for both their intelligence and their spiritual groundedness. Ed is the interfaith chaplain who had counseled me between my first and second sessions with Bishop Thomas. Laurie has a doctorate in education and has been an assistant editor for the *Journal of Transpersonal Psychology*, an academic journal in topics that overlap psychology and spirituality. She is normally a thoughtful person who chooses her words well. But I could tell she was wary about this meeting because of past experiences with fundamentalist Christians.

Figs and toy soldiers on the Bible

As we settled in to Bishop's office, I made introductions and then set some props on his desk: A Bible, a basket of figs, and a set of toy soldiers. I placed a few of the figs and a few of the soldiers on the Bible.

Teri: Let's say this Bible represents the interpretation of Christianity that Bishop Thomas has been sharing with me. The figs are the benefits of relationship with God, and the soldiers are the obstacles to a relationship with God that I associated with fundamentalist beliefs when I first came to Highview: shame, judgment, hypocrisy, and undue money focus. In our dialogues I've been working to see how many soldiers I can clear away so we can talk about the good stuff—the figs.

Judgment and *hypocrisy* were the first to go. Bishop has convinced me that he is every bit as committed to non-judgment as we are in New Thought. And based on my personal observation, he walks his talk and discourages anything that smacks of a false face. (I removed two soldiers from the Bible.)

As to *money focus,* from what I've seen of the church budget, the pastor's salary is well within reason, which is how I personally measure that. (I removed another soldier)

And the question of *shame* isn't clear yet in my own mind. I like very much the way we strive to hold each other accountable here at Highview. But that means treading the razor's edge between being honest and blaming or shaming. (I took one more soldier off the top of the Bible and leaned it up against the book's edge.)

So that leaves us pretty much ready to deal with the figs—the sweet and juicy benefits of a relationship with God. And that's why I invited you, Laurie and Ed; you can help me speak for my view of those benefits because you share them, and you live them. I've called you in as reinforcements.

Bishop: Well I'm delighted to have you all here. What did you want to talk about?

Laurie: Teri's been telling us that your version of a literal Bible interpretation is more constructive than we might expect. And I don't want to give any offense, but there are just so many unreasonable things in the Bible, I just can't imagine how anyone could try to live their life by it.

Bishop: Like what, for instance?

Laurie: (Hesitating) Oh I don't know… Like the command in Leviticus that if a man lies with a sheep you have to kill the man *and* the sheep.

Bishop: Oh yes, Teri and I have been over some of that. First of all, some of those rules were for health reasons at the time. But more important, as I keep telling Teri, the Old Testament is not meant as a source of doctrine.

Laurie: But what about the New Testament?

Ed jumped in as if he were trying to head us off from getting to too sensitive a topic too soon.

Ed: This is just terrific. My son is an Evangelical Christian, and our differences used to be a source of family tension. But we had the same kind of dialogue over a period of several months. It took us about 20 sessions, but we got to where we realized how similar our values were. Except of course, for that one word "only"; as in, Jesus is the *only* way to salvation.

Bishop: That's right.

Ed: And that experience has been extremely helpful in my work as a hospital chaplain at Alexandria hospital. But it creates an asymmetrical relationship, because I can respect the views of people in any other religion, but often they can't respect mine.

Bishop: Well I will say I was very impressed with the people I met at your Center the night you all invited me for that movie discussion. You all seemed very committed to God. I would trust those folks with the keys to my car. I'd trust them with my firstborn. But you all have a very idealistic view. You have to realize that most people out there are wicked and evil.

Laurie: (Sitting abruptly forward in her chair) That's sad!

Bishop: It sure is.

Laurie: No, I mean it's sad that you think that. With all the people struggling to do the best they know, and you just lump them all together as wicked and evil?

Bishop: No, wait, (he looks confused). Being wicked and evil isn't that bad.

The conversation came to a halt as we stared at each other, minds atilt. "A moment of epiphany," Laurie would call it later.

Bishop: What I mean is, there are no degrees of sin in God's eyes. So when I say most people are wicked and evil, that includes the average person in their self-centered, everyday pettiness right alongside with murderers, rapists, and those who commit every manner of evil with no concern for others.

Laurie: But most people do the best they can.

Bishop: If you look in the heart of even the nicest person you know, I guarantee you'll find selfishness, jealousy, judgment. A lot of us don't act on these things, but they're there for all of us.

Teri: And, Bishop, you're so used to calling that "wicked and evil" in everyday speech it doesn't seem like such a big deal. But it's shocking to us. We wouldn't use the term at all, but if we did we'd reserve it for some really atrocious crime.

Bishop: I see.

Teri: This reminds me of the time my sister Tina and I traveled Europe together in college. A woman overheard us squabbling about the next day's touring. "You two must have had a big fight today, huh?" she asked. "Why?" Tina replied defensively. We were unaware how much our natural tone with each other was stuck at the level of 12-year-olds fighting over which TV channel to watch. "That's just the way we talk," Tina explained.

Bishop: (Laughing) Well we do say "wicked and evil" from time to time around here.

Laurie: So that means you're judging people all the time.

Bishop: Not if we remember that we are all sinners and God loves every one of us. We love because we know we are loved.

Laurie: Hmm.

I'm God; you're God

Laurie strummed her fingers on her chair, pressure building. She was about to demonstrate that we could be just as surprised as Bishop had been by the effect of our concepts when they are taken out of a commonly understood context.

Bishop: So Laurie, what do you believe?

Laurie looked cornered. I made cautionary hand signs she didn't see. She launched in full speed to the bottom line.

Laurie: You keep talking about God like he's separate from us. Everything is God. It's all one. I'm God, you're God, this chair is God. There is no separation between us. Everything is one. There is no right and wrong..."

Bishop: (Practically out of his seat) No right and wrong!!! What if I steal your car? I'm going out there right now!

Laurie: You better not!

Bishop: Well why shouldn't I!

Laurie: How can anything that came from God be wrong?

The tone got intense, but never unfriendly, until finally Bishop paused and spoke quietly, as if he had just discovered that his guests were aliens.

Bishop: So then, you're pantheists.

Laurie got an "Oh, what have I done" look on her face, concerned that she had prematurely exposed me as a heretic who would be cast out from the congregation. In fact I had intended to make the same points eventually, after laying more groundwork of common understanding. She tried to break the awkward pause by joking:

Laurie That's it, I'm not saying another word until I've gone to ministerial school and learned to express myself properly.

Laurie had just realized that her words symbolized something entirely different to Bishop than they did to her. Someone committed to New Thought may take years to appreciate the full meaning of "I am God," and they will then more likely express it as, "I am God expressing." On first hearing, this can seem like nothing but arrogance and blasphemy. In fact, considering how Bishop must have felt about it, he was controlling himself pretty well.

It was now clearer than ever to me that my challenge was finding as much common ground as possible so Bishop and I could focus on the real differences in our worldviews. Laurie just nudged the project schedule up by several weeks.

And now it was Ed who tried to bring us back from the gulf yawning between us.

Ed: Well, technically we're not pantheists, we're panentheists.

The "en" in "panentheist" is God

Bishop: I'm not familiar with that distinction. And by the looks on their faces, I'd guess that Teri and Laurie aren't that sure either. So please enlighten us.

Ed: Pantheists believe that the life force we call God is in everything: trees, rocks, people, etcetera, and that's it. They don't see more to God than that. So nature worshipers are pantheists, along with eco-feminists, neo-pagans, and many people who put themselves under the general term "New Age."

Teri: And generally the pantheists don't place a high value on reason.

Ed: Right. The founders of New Thought, on the other hand, were very committed to reason. Along with many of the philosophers going back to Plato, they looked to the time before the universe began and reasoned that before there was anything physical there was simply awareness: call it Cosmic Consciousness, Universal Mind, the Absolute, or just God. At some point a movement in that consciousness caused the Big Bang.

Bishop I'll tell you what that movement was, it was God saying, "**Let there be light,**" (Genesis 1:3).

Ed: Right, exactly. But the way we think of it is that everything created in that moment was an expression of God. There wasn't anything else around to build out of, so the stars and planets are made of God. And those stars and planets have been developing in such a way as to bring forth life, and then consciousness, and finally man—a form so conscious, it could look back to know its source. It could know it came from God. That's the purpose of the whole show: for God to know itself.

Bishop: Well, you've got to be careful….

Ed: So Religious Scientists are really pan*en*theists, and that little "en" is crucial. Unlike the nature worshiping pantheists, we know there's more to God than just the physical universe. We see our limited human minds as a localized expression of the Mind of God. Everything exciting takes shape out of the interaction between our minds and that "Universal Mind," which, of course, is God. Once we know that, we can see ourselves as the hands and eyes of God here on earth. It's an exhilarating open-ended possibility. But it's also a humbling and challenging responsibility.

Teri: As an old friend of mine used to say, "God needs me to taste the pizza."

Bishop: Well that's not exactly true. God has no needs whatsoever. We Christians believe, as the Bible teaches, that everything he created already existed in his divinity. And he created everything he did to bring Him glory.

Ed: I could be comfortable saying we are here to *express* the glory of God.

Bishop: To become perfect…

Teri: To speak the truth as we see it…

Bishop: There's only one truth, and you see it when you look right there (pointing to the Bible).

Ed: (Fingering the green toy soldiers on the Bible) I've been looking at these little guys, and I notice this guy here holds a minesweeper. He's sweeping it over the Bible, so he seems to be picking up on-the-ground guidance from it. But this guy over here has an antenna on his helmet. I was in Signal Corp in the Army, so I can identify with him. He's picking up signals from the base camp. That's like divine guidance that's not in the Bible.

Bishop: From the Holy Spirit.

Ed: Well I can tell you from my days in the Army, we need both kinds of intelligence all the time.

Bishop: Yes we do. But if you're listening right, the Holy Spirit will never disagree with the Bible. That's our base camp.

18

Co-Creation or Surrender?

There are two ways (to unite with God): One is to expand your ego to infinity, and the other is to reduce it to nothing, the former by knowledge, and the latter by devotion.
The Knower says: "I am God – the Universal Truth."
The devotee says: "I am nothing, O God, You are everything."
In both cases, the ego-sense disappears.
Swami Ramdas

After this conversation I was a little nervous that Bishop's impression of my beliefs could derail our dialogues prematurely. I was aware that Christians trace New Age thinking back to the Gnostic heresies, and that plenty of people have been burned at the stake for the kind of ideas my friends and I just expressed. So I was prepared for Bishop to grill me at our next meeting, but he didn't bring the topic up. Near the end of our session, I raised it myself.

Teri: Aren't you going to warn me against heresy?

Bishop: That's not my approach. People are free to believe whatever they want, so I won't comment unless somebody asks me. 1 Peter 3:15 (nkjv) says we only witness to those who ask. **"Sanctify the Lord God in your hearts, and always be ready to give a defense to everyone who asks you a reason for the hope that is in you, with meekness and fear."**

Teri: Fear?

Bishop: A proper interpretation is "gentleness and respect."

Teri: Oh. Okay then. But I'd like to explain what we mean about being one with God or co-creators with God.

Bishop: Only God creates. That would have been my answer to Ed when he said everything has God in it because there was nothing else for God to create from. So God is not in that desk. Things created are things that come from nothing. They are separate from God.

Teri: Looking at it that way makes me feel cut-off, insignificant.

Bishop: On the contrary, the biblical approach is more palatable to me because it takes the burden off of me to try to make life perfect. I wouldn't want to be God because I know myself. And God is so much more capable.

Teri: The way we think of it is that it makes me responsible to give shape to the energy I'm given. Every time I have a new thought, or write a poem, or extend love, I am co-creating with God something that never existed before.

Bishop: You couldn't do any of those things without God.

Teri: That's true. But there's also a sense in which God couldn't do any of those things without me. (His eyebrows went up, but he didn't say anything.)

Here's an example of what I mean when I say my thinking creates my reality. A friend and I were caught in a snowstorm driving to a personal growth workshop in Baltimore—what should have been a one-hour trip took ten hours. But my friend had with her ten hours of tapes by Ram Dass—he is a spiritual teacher I had wanted to study. His words on that trip helped me deal with my mother's approaching death at the time. It was just what I needed. So for me, that snowstorm was a gift. And that kind of gift happens regularly when I keep an eye out for it.

Bishop: Well, I strongly agree that the way we think about something can turn it into a blessing. You know how much I like to quote Romans 12: 2, "**Be transformed by the renewing of your mind.**"

Teri: Yes, that's our favorite scripture, too. My secularist friends would say that coincidence of those tapes being available was just a case of me making lemons into lemonade. But I think you and I would both say there's something richer going on.

Bishop: Romans 8:28 (kjv) says, "**All things work together for good for them that love God.**"

Teri: Yes, yes. In New Thought we call it the law of attraction. We say that all thought is energy, and whatever energy pattern I put out with my thoughts draws to me people and situations with patterns that are similar. It's kind of like our explanation for how God could be paying attention to the needs of billions of people all at once. He just created a system that could take care of everything on autopilot.

Bishop: I'll stick with the way the Bible puts it.

Teri: Hmm. Okay. So when I say, "I co-created that storm," I mean two things. The first is that I'm responsible for how I *respond* to it, but there's more to it. And this is where I'll be getting a little radical on you. The second meaning of co-creation is feeling that I am one with God. So in that sense, God and I together created the perfect circumstance for my growth; we always do. I already agreed to the storm; it was partly my idea at a spiritual level. It's as if I sat on the committee that decided to send it. So I know it has a hidden gift. When I hold that attitude, that faith, it can work *backwards in time* to put in place whatever I need for it to be a blessing. I believe we'll eventually learn that the laws of physics allow that.

Bishop: It sounds to me like a lot of fancy words for saying you surrendered to God's will.

Teri: No, no. I mean yes. I mean, well kind of. Just before Andy and I stopped going regularly to Celebration Center, the movement in Religious Science was shifting to using the traditional terminology of surrendering to God's will. I was very uncomfortable with that, and I've been struggling with it ever since. I've been asking myself whether there is really any difference between saying I surrender and saying I co-create. It feels like there is, but I can't put my finger on it yet.

Bishop: You're still seeking something.

Teri: I guess. The traditional way of putting it makes me feel like life happens *to* me, without my input, like I'm a victim or a slave. The co-creation language makes me feel like life happens "*through* me or *as* me" as some of our teachers say.

Bishop: God works through me when I do his will.

Teri: It may just be a matter of perspective. You see your relationship to God as 100% surrender to a sovereign Lord. You bow before him in praise saying, "I am nothing, Oh God, you are everything." You seek to have your own will or ego disappear into God's.

Bishop: Well, not exactly, but finish your point.

Teri: When I say I am a co-creator, it feels like I move a step beyond God acting *through* me. He acts *as* me. But I'm still surrendering to knowing that the "bigger half" of this team knows more than I do. It's just that instead of picturing myself bowing down, I'm reaching up. In fact, I see God and me skipping off into the future arm-in-arm, seeing what adventure we can co-create next.

Bishop: (Pausing) Well you're right that I've never heard anything quite like that. I've got two problems with all that. The first is that Christians don't really say, "Oh God, I am nothing." It's true we were nothing before He elevated us. But why accentuate the negative when it's past? God doesn't encourage us to say what we're not; he tells me I am "**more than a conqueror.**" (Ro. 8:37) He tells me "**I can do all things through Christ who strengthens me.**" (Phil 4:13 nkjv)

Teri: Well that's cool. I don't think all churches present it that way.

Bishop: And as to your being one with God, besides the fact that that's impossible, I wouldn't want God's job. He is so much smarter and stronger than we are. As a friend of mine says, "Let God be God." I have enough of a job just being a human being.

Teri: I'm with you, but I think there's a paradox. My local portion of God's mind can't see the big picture from where I'm standing. That's why I need to stay open to divine guidance. But I *can* see the perspective *from* where I'm standing better than anybody. I see it *for* God in a sense.

Bishop: You've got to be careful with that…

Teri: I know it sounds arrogant. And I readily acknowledge the danger of arrogance in saying I'm one with God. That's one reason I'm grateful for being here at Highview. You've opened me to the opposite kind of relationship to God through devotion. You've taught me the value of passionate praise. It feels like the flip side of my "equals" relationship with God. It balances my feeling of being *one* with Him with the feeling that I can also bow down in awe of him.

But both approaches to God have their dangers. Too much bowing down can make you feel worthless.

Bishop: If you truly understood the scriptures, that would never happen.

What's the plan?

Teri: I'm looking forward to understanding how that is, since my generation is full of people who felt disempowered by being told they were worthless sinners, born in original sin. But I also know that I face the trap of arrogance when I call myself a co-creator. It's just that I'd rather risk arrogance than feel like a robot whose only value is to obey orders from God's predestined plan. I can't get excited about the idea of "a plan." I need to believe in possibilities.

Bishop: Where did you get the idea there's a predestined plan for your life?

Teri: Isn't that the whole point of surrendering, to hear God's plan for your life?

Bishop: I can tell you God's plan for your life. Jeremiah 29-11 says, "**For I know the plans I have for you, declares the Lord, plans to prosper you and not to harm you, plans to give you hope and a future.**" That's the plan. It's the plan of a loving father who provides everything for his children, including free choice in how to use the gifts. How many possibilities are embedded in that? He wants us to move from A to Z, but in between are a million ways to go. It's a kaleidoscope of possibilities.

Teri: That's the plan? When you put it that way, it doesn't sound so bad.

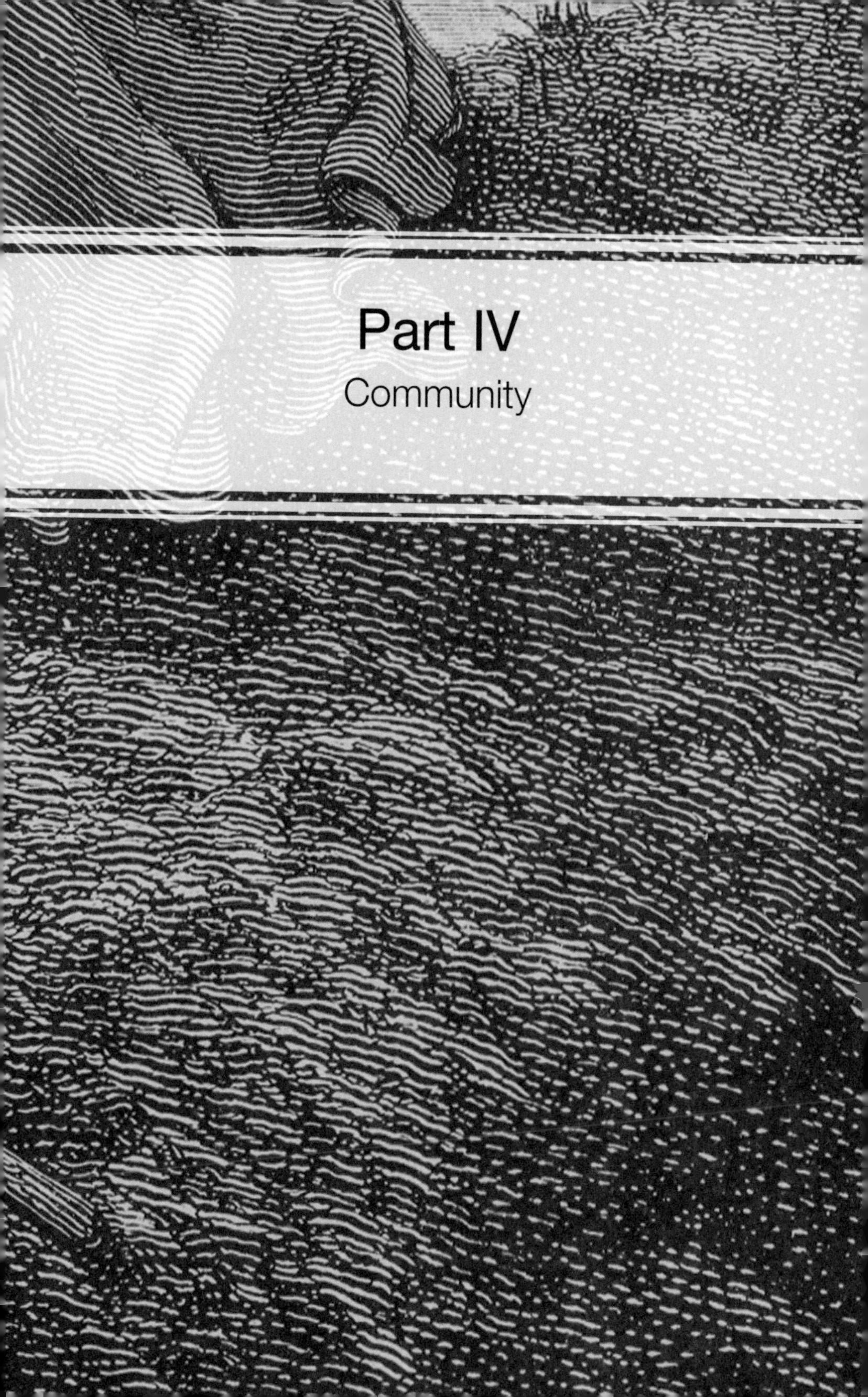

Part IV

Community

19

Behind the Scenes at Highview

I can do all things through
Christ who strengthens me.
Philippians 4:13 (nkjv)

Bishop Thomas had asked me to "ask around the congregation" to confirm some of the things he was telling me. And while I wasn't comfortable doing that directly until much later in the story, I did begin to participate in a few events outside of Sunday services. I started at the new preschool.

Excellence in action

Highview was in the midst of purchasing a larger church building, and prior to taking occupancy they leased space there to get started with the "Mark of Excellence" preschool that Bishop Thomas envisioned as part of his "total man ministry." The preschool is directed by Olga Lloyde, whom I found to be one of the most warm, engaging, adventuresome, and purposeful people I know. Being a single mom has not stood in her way of leading a rich life and being a major player in the Highview ministry. She has a plan to travel the world and settle in Vermont by the time she's 40. So far, all of her plans have borne fruit.

For one thing, Olga fully expresses the excellence in action that I had been yearning for back at Celebration Center. When Andy and I were first attracted to Religious Science, action got equal emphasis with consciousness via the slogan, "Treat and move your feet," a refinement on the Christian saying, "God helps those who help themselves." But in recent years, the slogan more frequently heard at the Center was, "There is nothing you have to do." If we attuned our consciousness, right action would flow from us effortlessly. Just remove the blocks and the good stuff will happen.

Highview, on the other hand, was about action. Bishop Thomas said, "People are always saying, 'I'm waiting for the Lord to tell me what to do.' I tell them, 'He's already told you; it's right there in the scriptures, so just go do it.'"

As director of the preschool, Olga single-handedly made happen the licensing, insurance, procedure manuals, curriculum development, hiring, etc. At about the same time, Celebration Center held a 6-month visioning for a preschool it wanted to open. The team developed a vision of a place in which children would be completely free to know their spiritual nature and thus discover their full potential. But the Center hasn't actually opened a school as of this writing. Olga meanwhile simply took her vision from the Bible: "A place where children live the scripture, **I can do all things through Christ who strengthens me**." (Phil 4:13 nkjv)

I confess that I'm taking a single example out of context, something that may say more about me than about my postmodern, New Age, and New Thought brethren. But I believe there is truth all around. Perhaps the school at the Center will be more enduring and effective once it is established. Or perhaps the mere act of working together to create the vision at Celebration Center was a transformative process for both the visioners and the community. Furthermore, I believe that some people's job on earth is to get things done while others serve by "holding the consciousness," as we say in New Thought. And in fact, things *do* get done at Celebration Center, often in ways that just seem to come together, well, *effortlessly*.

Nevertheless, I was fascinated one day when I saw Olga's personal day planner open on her desk. Across the top of each page she had five, hand-drawn symbols, one for each area of life: work, family, community, spirituality, and health. She said it reminded her to accomplish something in each category every day. Tears came to my eyes. *For this is my sheep of effective action which was lost to me and now is found.*

Setting boundaries

Olga helped me retrieve another missing piece. One day a boy was sent to her desk because he was hitting other children in his class. I know nothing about children and nothing about education; I just watched. Olga talked to the boy quietly, hugged him, and gave him a series of instructions.

"Sit by me. Put your shoes on. Don't throw the shoes. Go get them. Don't run. Stop. Turn around and say, 'Yes Miss Olga.' Don't run. Sit back down here. Look at me."

It was like dog training, but with lots of love. It went on for about 15 minutes, the instructions alternating with Olga looking him in the eye, giving him a hug, and having him play with a toy at her feet while she continued her paper work.

Then he crept up behind her, and I was a little concerned that he was going to try to tip her chair.

"Miss Olga, do you like Power Rangers?" he asked.

"Yes I do," she said.

"Would you come to my house every day and watch Power Rangers with me?"

I felt I had just learned something about raising children. This kid was desperate for structure (and probably attention). It struck me that my peer group had felt so oppressed by the structure many of us grew up with that we had rejected it altogether. It was good to have it back in an appropriate dose.

A salvation story

I picked up another missing piece sitting at the preschool's front desk. One day while I was watching the phones, one of the fathers we'll call Ronald arrived to pick up his children. My husband tells me this big fellow looks like boxer Mike Tyson. He planted himself at my desk and started telling his life story with all the energy of a St. Bernard who's just enjoyed a romp in a river of love and is now joyfully shaking off the droplets onto everyone in sight.

"When I was growing up I liked Bible study, but then I fell away from it and started to run with a bad crowd," he said. "I got into trouble, and I tell you, I been shot, stabbed, you name it. Ended up in prison. And everybody respected me there cause I'm big, you know; I was kind of a ring leader. Anybody needed anything they had to come to me.

"Then one night the fellow who runs the prison Bible study comes to me and says he wants to talk. He sits me down and tells me I'm wasting my life. The Lord gave me leadership skills, and I should be using them for him instead of for trouble, he says.

"I told him I'd think about it. A couple hours later I'm alone in my cell and something comes over me. All of a sudden I can see all the time I've wasted and all the people I've hurt. And Teri, I just started to cry. I cried and cried. I cried so hard the snot about bust outta my chest. So I got down on my knees and I told the Lord I was sorry, and that I wanted to come back to him.

"The next day I went to the guy in charge of the Bible study, and I told him I wanted to start coming. But he said he had just been transferred to another prison, so if I wanted to be in Bible study, I'd have to take over as the leader. And so I did.

"And now I got me a wonderful wife and two beautiful children. And I want my kids to do better than I did. So that's why I bring them here to this preschool, even though it's half way across town. And I'm studying at night to get my high school equivalency so I won't always be driving a delivery truck. Oh and also, I'm on good terms with my Mom again. She pretty much ignored my brother and me when we was growing up, and I was always mad at her. But now I just love her. And that's another reason I want to do right by my kids."

I don't think Ronald saw the tears in my eyes as he bounded off to scoop up his little ones. I had heard so many stories about the ways "salvation" can erect barriers between people that I lost sight of the ways it can heal them and bring them together.

Going to the big boy room

For another look behind the scenes, I dropped in one Saturday morning on the monthly leadership session that Bishop Thomas requires for everyone who runs a ministry or special project. I arrived late, and when I entered the room the atmosphere was tense. Someone had just been used publicly as an example of bad teamwork. I wasn't sure what had happened, but it seemed to do with someone making accusations via a widely spread email. Bishop was speaking.

"When we've got an issue with somebody, we go to that person directly. Anything else is being a coward and a chump. And when we've made a mistake, we need to be willing to take responsibility for it and make amends."

He strode up and down the aisle of the sanctuary.

"If you want to do something important for the kingdom, you can't be taking offense at everything somebody says to you. You've got to be able to look them in the eye and say, Yes I did it, or No I didn't without getting distracted by your need to look good. When you're a leader, you can't let your measuring stick be what other people think of you. Sometimes you have to be able to step into the Big Boy room—that's where you square your shoulders and say what needs to be said."

The group of about two dozen men and women hung on his every word.

"I know how difficult it is when you feel personally attacked. Last year I got called on the carpet by the other bishops in PCIF.* We organized an event for them here and they wanted to know where all the money went. I felt as though my ethics were being challenged. I knew it was time to step into the Big Boy room. So at their next meeting I came prepared to give an accounting of every dime. I told them flat out, 'I know you saw a lot of people at that event, but the expenses ate up all the income. If anybody's got any ideas of how to turn more profit next year, we'll be happy to talk to them."

Maybe I'd been too long in an environment where conflict was always smoothed over and everything was made *nice*. Maybe I was starved for some good old-fashioned 'masculine' virtues of courage and accountability. But I started to see the word "integrity" floating in huge letters over Bishop's head, and a tear filled the corner of my eye. Over time, I would see at Highview even better examples in which someone told a raw truth with courage and compassion.

This was another piece of what I had been missing when I came to Highview. When I was first attracted to personal growth work, I perceived it as calling forth this type of honesty, directness, and accountability. Over the years, the emphasis

* PCIF is Praise Covenant Interdenominational Fellowship, an East Coast affiliation of independent Bible-based churches.

seemed to shift to merely holding a vision of our good. We worked so hard not to judge that we never called ourselves, or each other, to account. How powerful could it be to integrate the two approaches: vision and action, non-judgment and accountability, compassion and raw truth?

Throughout my time at Highview, Bishop Thomas would keep telling me that a literal interpretation of the Bible had "all that and a bag of chips"—one of his favorite phrases. The words he used to describe his theology frequently made no sense to me. But the truth he embodied spoke for itself.

20

Living for Heaven or Earth?

As anyone who knows anything
about the unknowable clearly
knows... God is both One and
Many, at the same time, now.
Tom Robbins's wacky novel, *Villa Incognito*

At this point, I was convinced that the version of fundamentalism Bishop Thomas and his congregation followed did not fit my prejudices of being a haven for judgment, shame, hypocrisy, or undue money focus. The question now was, what about all the positive benefits of a liberal or interfaith approach to God? It was time to start the second part of my investigation.

Teri: Where I come from, we place a high value on knowing ourselves and expressing our uniqueness. So we celebrate and foster our differences, whether that means solving a problem in a new way, or expressing an unpopular opinion, or just wearing purple.

Bishop: I'm excited about new things and variety. You can wear purple as much as you want as long as it doesn't distract you from doing God's work.

And there it was, the quality of single-mindedness I was to encounter again and again at Highview. Drinking alcohol distracts from focus on God. Wearing sexy clothes distracts from focus on God. Halloween lore distracts the children from the truths they are learning about God. There was never anything frivolous going on at Highview, no wasted motion. Previously I would have considered all this as narrow-minded. And perhaps some of it was. But I was beginning to meditate on what the term "narrow minded" really means.

Narrow-minded vs. single-minded

If narrow-minded means choosing to live within a narrow sphere of conduct, especially with regard to anything bordering on "vice," then Highview fit the bill. And choosing not to participate in popular culture certainly left them with a narrower sphere of reference. But most of the people I know surround themselves with others of similar interests, which can seem narrow to those outside their sphere.

On the other hand, if narrow-minded means being unable or unwilling to consider another point of view, Bishop Thomas was certainly showing himself to be very much the opposite—not that he was necessarily accepting a single word I said, but he did seem to be considering them.

Another hallmark of narrow-mindedness is what you can laugh at. My husband and I are hams and frequently push the envelope in a group. Highview had a talent show coming up, and we decided to see if our antics could be accepted there.

Andy drops his pants in church

A series of commercials for the Jamaican beer Red Stripe had caught our attention. In them, a formally dressed Jamaican host interacts with a clueless White tourist. In one commercial, the tourist watches the Jamaican dance rhythmically to reggae, and he tries his pathetic best to pick up the beat. The tourist's rhythm improves after he accepts a beer from his host. The tag line is, "Red Stripe and reggae. Teaching our White friends to dance for over 40 years."

Andy and I thought that was hysterical. But the next commercial was even better. The Jamaican says, "If your friend has been drinking too much to drive, take his keys." When the clueless tourist refuses to hand over his keys, the Jamaican says, "If he won't give you his keys, take his pants…May I have your pants, please." The tourist takes off his trousers and hands them to the Jamaican who removes the car keys before handing the pants back while giving the audience a knowing look.

Andy and I rewrote these commercials to express our experience at Highview. After outlining the idea to the talent show's director, Joy Ramen, we thought it would be wise to get explicit permission from Bishop Thomas. We warned him that it might be a bit risqué, but before fully hearing us out he said, "I'm sure anything you and Joy agree to do will be fine."

In our version of the first commercial, Andy and I came on stage to solemn Gregorian chant in the prayerful pose of the Catholics we were raised as. Then one of the Highview elders, Deacon Marino, came on dancing and arm waving to lively gospel music. Andy and I picked up his beat, awkwardly at first, and then moving into full-out praise mode. The deacon's tagline was, "Highview, teaching our White friends to praise for over 100 years." The crowd loved it.

The second skit featured one of the ushers holding a collection basket and saying, "If a member won't give you his tithe, take his pants." Then she turns to Andy, dressed in tropical shirt, and says, "May I have your pants, please." Andy dropped his trousers to reveal boxer shorts with pink pigs on them. The audience squealed with delight as the usher removed a dollar from the pants pocket. Then we passed the basket around the room asking for "your money or your pants."

The next day at Sunday service, the church was all abuzz about the performance. Eunesa Bennet, the smart and sassy choir director and minister-in-training said loudly, "I can't believe a man dropped his pants in church and I wasn't there to see it."

And Andy and I couldn't believe how much leeway there was for out-of-the-box personal expression. We expected to find that only in settings that exalt the individual. Although of course, the expression in this case was all in the service of "doing God's work."

Ascending and descending paths to God

As I tried to sort out the distinction between narrow-minded and single-minded, once again one of Ken Wilber's "maps" proved helpful. He talks about yearning for the "Ascended God" of heaven or the "Descended God" of earth.

Most people in alternative spiritual circles associate the Eastern and alternative religions with personal freedom; they associate restrictive puritanicalism with the Western monotheistic religions: Christianity, Judaism, and Islam. Ken Wilber illuminates a more striking distinction that cuts across East and West: what he calls the Ascended God and the Descended God. This distinction is brilliantly laid out in his major work, *Sex, Ecology, and Spirituality*. He summarizes it in *A Brief History of Everything.*[39]

> The God of the ascenders was otherworldly to the core—my kingdom is not of this world. It was puritanical, usually monastic and ascetic, and it saw the body, the flesh, and especially sex as archetypal sins. It was purely transcendental, and always pessimistic about finding happiness in this world… and thus true salvation, true liberation, could not be found in this body, on this earth, in this lifetime… no matter what lip service was given to the Goodness of God's creation.... Always for the mere Ascenders, Descent is the devil. In both the East and the West…You find this from early Judaism to virtually all forms of Gnosticism to early Buddhism and most forms of Christianity and Islam.

Wilber calls this path of ascent "the path of wisdom" because it sees that behind all the forms there lies "the One, the good, the unqualifiable Emptiness, against which all forms are seen to be illusory, fleeting, impermanent… Wisdom is the return of the Many to the One," he says.

He then describes the earthy "Descended God" and its array of strange-bedfellow followers.

> The path of descent, on the other hand, is *the path of compassion*. It sees that the One actually manifests as the Many, and so all forms are to be treated equally with kindness, compassion, mercy. … it found its glory in the celebration of diversity. Not greater oneness, but greater variety was the goal of this God.
>
> Salvation in the modern world—whether offered by politics, or science, or revivals of earth religion, or Marxism, or industrialization, or consumerism, or retribalism, or sexuality, or horticultural revivals, or earth goddess embrace, or ecophilosophies, you name it—salvation can be found only on this earth, only in manifestation, only in the world of Form, only in pure *immanence*… There is no higher truth, no Ascending current, nothing *transcendental* whatsoever. In fact, anything "higher" or "transcendental" is now the devil, is now the great enemy, is now the destroyer of the earthbound, sensory-drenched God and Goddess… it is a religion of great compassion, little wisdom.

One striking aspect of this model is how both camps see the other as evil. This mutual demonizing creates a vicious cycle that we explore in chapter 36. Law & Politics: Seeking a Way *Beyond.*

Both ends toward the middle

On the surface, New Thought and Fundamentalist Christianity appear to be at opposite extremes of this spectrum, with fundamentalists as Ascenders—value is not of this world; it is found only in God—and those in New Thought as Descenders—value is only in the here-and-now as expressed through human beings. But looking more closely, the truth is more complex. Indeed, I came to see that a large part of what drew me to both the Center and Highview was their attempts to balance the two currents. Except "balance" is the wrong word, because any midpoint between these currents would be fluid, more like surfing a wave or walking a tightrope.

I was attracted to Religious Science because its very name bespeaks a confluence of these currents: humans are one with God, and thus whatever makes humans happy makes God happy—as long as happiness is defined as the "true happiness" that Aristotle, the Dalai Lama, and current psychological research[40] all claim aligns with virtue, meaning, and inner peace.

But in any congregation, the weight of these various factors shifts over time. When Rev. Harriet first came to Celebration Center, we had been in a long period of "descended" focus on creating what you want on earth. And thus, many of us were fascinated with Rev. Harriet's asceticism. Besides meditating several hours a day and avoiding alcohol, she spoke of the value of sexual abstinence as a way of focusing all one's energies on becoming closer to God. These were strange concepts in a setting devoted to "prosperity consciousness" and the belief that, "It's all good; it's all God." Strange but intriguing.

Highview, on the other hand, favored praise songs with lyrics like, "Forget about yourself and worship him." But it also aspired to promote excellence in every aspect of its members' lives. One Sunday Bishop Thomas preached on the parable of the ten virgins, five of whom miss a wedding feast because they failed to fill their lamps with oil (Matt. 25:1). "This story is usually interpreted to mean we must be prepared for the End Times," Bishop said. "And that's a valid interpretation. But this story also tells us to live our lives fully now." He built to a powerful chant:

I'm going to get my life in order now!
I'm going to get my education now!
I'm going to get some counseling now!
I'm going to take care of my body now!
I'm going to stop complaining now!
I'm going to forgive you now!
I'm going to love you now!
Because I want to be ready. Ready to receive my breakthrough. Ready to walk in his favor. Ready to be trusted by a God who wants to exalt me now!

New Agers as ambassadors

It was as if the two communities started at opposite ends of the spectrum but were drawn to aspects of the other's pole. In fact, it occurred to me that those of us in New Thought are perfectly positioned to serve as ambassadors between the ascenders and descenders. We can see the beauty in both. We value the personal empowerment and sensuality of the descenders equally with the surrender to a spiritual force. What might be possible if instead of attacking Bible-based religion, as so many humanists do, we instead acknowledged its contributions? Instead of getting caught up in arguments, what if we asked questions: "How does the Divine show up in your life? What do you love about your relationship with Jesus? How does it make you a better person?"

I even began a fantasy that others like myself would begin joining fundamentalist congregations—loving and staying open to anything the experience might teach us. Who knows where that might lead? Of course, such an experiment would require people of extraordinary maturity with solid self-esteem. If anyone tells us we are going to hell, we'd need to be able to stay grounded in love. Or we might just take Ed's advice to me in my second meeting with Bishop. "Just smile and say, 'Oh pastor, what am I going to do with you?'"

I wanted to explore these overlapping currents with Bishop Thomas.

Pie in the sky, by-and-by

Teri: I want to talk about how folks at Highview are mostly living for heaven while folks at Celebration Center are mostly living for this life on earth.

Bishop: We're not mostly living for heaven; that's pie in the sky, by-and-by. We're living for God, both now and later. But you better be prepared for eternity, cause it's going to last a whole lot longer than this life.

Teri: Okay. So I guess the real point is that we'd say that whatever brings the most genuine fulfillment in this life will also please God and will serve in whatever comes after. So, in addition to feeling spiritual communion, I'm talking about maintaining health, good relationships, and a satisfying work life that lets you contribute and express your talents.

Bishop: You're partly right. God wants us to have those things, and the Bible provides guidance for developing them. 3 John 1:2 (nasb) says, "**Beloved, I pray that in all respects you may prosper and be in good health, just as your soul prospers.**" That's why my vision of a "total man ministry" includes providing job training, financial counseling, parent training, whatever serves people in achieving excellence.

Prosperity consciousness and the new televangelists

Teri: In New Thought we use the term "prosperity consciousness," for the idea that we live in an abundant universe and everything we desire can be available. We like to quote the scripture from Luke 12:32 (nkjv), "**Do not fear, little flock, for it is your Father's good pleasure to give you the kingdom.**"

Bishop: That's true, insofar as God wants every man to have his basic needs filled. But after that, material possessions risk being a distraction.

Teri: It's certainly possible to become overly focused on those things. But there shouldn't have to be a conflict. We should be able to appreciate all the material and sensual delights of this life and still be devoted to God.

Bishop: Matthew 6:33 says it all. "**Seek first his kingdom and his righteousness, and all these things will be given to you as well.**"

Teri: But isn't part of seeking the kingdom to express excellence in everything we do?

Bishop: Absolutely, with a sense of divine priority and divine purpose.

Teri: That focus on abundance and excellence attracts people to a spiritual life—"catch more flies with honey," as they say. The successful televangelists now are integrating Christianity with this positive, here-and-now approach.

Bishop: I think some of those evangelists are doing good work, and I wouldn't want to judge any one of them because I haven't followed any that closely. But I also have to wonder about some of those large congregations and where all their money goes. I think some of those congregations are large because they're swollen.

Teri: Swollen?

Bishop: You know, with pus.

Teri: Oh.

Bishop: It's not a healthy thing to be telling people they can just think whatever happy thoughts they want and not fulfill responsibilities to their communities and to glorify God.

Teri: No question, filling responsibilities is part of the picture. So what do you mean by "glorify God?"

Bishop: That's a good question. You tell me your answer first.

Teri: Christians use the phrase so much, I've been meditating on what it means. The philosophers tell us that all values can be grouped as Truth, Beauty, and Goodness. I've been thinking that it feels to me like I glorify God when I express those qualities.

Bishop: Well yes, that's true. But you can't just define for yourself what Truth, Beauty, and Goodness are. That would make them relative. You've got to have a standard. They are whatever God says they are.

A clash of values at Christmas

This conversation added more paradoxes to the armful I was already holding. The strain of holding two realities was keeping me awake nights, and an incident before Christmas nearly pushed me over the edge.

Andy and I attended a cocktail party at the home of former Celebration Center members Mat and Del Kirsten. The Kirstens are devoted and successful practitioners of prosperity consciousness. They carved out a business for themselves as independent homebuilders that permitted them to retire early. Their own home at the time was a showplace reminiscent of an executive retreat center in the Colorado Rockies: exposed beams, magnificent stone fireplaces, and a large lot landscaped with ponds nestled among boulders.

Mat and Dell are purists in the concept that man co-creates with God, and they left the Center about the same time we stopped going regularly, which was when Rev. Harriet started talking about "surrendering to God's plan for your life." It's important also to note that while Mat was at the Center, he was one of the most generous contributors of both his money and his time to the community. "Keep it flowing out if you want it to flow in," he'd say.

At the party, Andy said something to Mat about the miracle of Christmas. Mat replied, "You know what I think typifies the miracle of Christmas? On the reality show "Survivors," the winners were taken to a private island, and they were each given an opportunity to drive a Lamborghini sports car on a private track with no obstacles and no speed limits. What a metaphor, heh?"

We knew that Mat meant this metaphor to include opportunities of all kinds, not just material. But we had become so acclimatized to the spartan environment at Highview, that we were stunned by the materialist flavor of this particular example.

The following day, I was helping out at Highview's preschool when I got a double dose of that contrast. I asked Olga what her plans were for Christmas. "We don't do anything special, and we don't exchange gifts," she said of herself and her 10 year-old son Amos. "I'm always uncomfortable at Christmas gatherings that focus on presents. I don't really get what the purpose of presents is; how can they bring you closer to Jesus? And Amos is well trained, he can go into a toy store and admire all the nice things, but he knows they're not for him. We'll just spend the day together, probably make something for each other."

This felt like more contrast than I could handle. I loved and admired both Olga and Mat. They both express excellence in form, but their attitudes toward material success were poles apart. Ascended and Descended. Both truths were beautiful. I thought I knew how to honor diversity, but this experience was forcing me to a whole new level. The pull on my heart, however, was from the ascended direction. With opportunities to spend Christmas Eve with friends from both communities, Andy and I decided to join the family of Ronald, the fellow whose salvation story is told in the previous chapter.

21

Fundamentalists as Positive Thinkers

Wouldn't it be wonderful if a group of people somewhere were for something and against nothing?
Ernest Holmes

Andy and I continued to enjoy Sunday services at Highview for the upbeat inspiration and warm community. Some Sundays, we did not feel engaged when sermons focused on overcoming temptations of sex and drugs or of maintaining faith when the rent is due. But other Sundays were terrific for us when some tidbit within a message seemed perfectly targeted for us.

They do call it "Good News"

On one such Sunday, a visiting speaker set an upbeat tone by speaking from a Religious Scientist's favorite scripture, Philippians 4:8, "**Whatsoever things are true, whatsoever things are honest, whatsoever things are just, whatsoever things are pure, whatsoever things are lovely, whatsoever things are of good report; if there be any virtue, and if there be any praise, think on these things.**"

Bishop Thomas followed up with a spin on positive thinking that was uncannily well timed for me.

"Tomorrow morning at 10 a.m. some of you are going to face some storms," Bishop said. "And you need storm insurance for your minds. I'm going to use a military term here: You need to 'garrison' your minds (and as he said that he twirled his finger around his head), so that nothing will get through that can disturb the peace of God that surpasses all understanding." Then he had us all practice twirling our index finger around our head while saying, "garrison." It was a total hoot with lots of laughing and shouting and high-fiving. And it was just what I needed.

Good news from the pulpit heads off bad news from the doctor

Unknown to Bishop I had a doctor's appointment the next morning at 9:30 to find out if I had breast cancer. It was just about 10 a.m. when my doctor was telling me I did. My husband stood behind the doctor twirling his finger around his head, and I smiled.

The coincidence of the timing is something I knew my secularist friends could explain. "*No-brainer,*" I imagined one saying. *"It was a sure bet that somebody in that congregation had something important happening the next morning, and it just happened to be you."*

As it turned out, I had the mildest form of breast cancer, and it was caught early enough to put me in the 97% survival category. In fact, my radiation appointments quickly turned into a blessing because they put me right around the corner from the new Highview location. I was nudged by this circumstance to make double duty of the drive out to the suburbs by helping out at the new preschool after each appointment. And it was there that I met Olga, the director mentioned in the previous chapter. Getting to know her and some of the other people involved with the preschool was a major blessing that rounded out my view of this brand of Christianity.

A couple more "coincidences"

I want to divert just a bit more here to cover two more of those "no-brainer" coincidences that happened surrounding my breast cancer diagnosis. The first is that I was pretty sure the doctor would tell me that my mammogram results showed cancer because of something that happened the week before. I had one of those medical appointments at which technicians keep telling you they need to take more images, and they call the doctor between each one. I left shaken and with half a thought that I'd like a sign what the news was.

The next day, I was at a New Thought convention, and I dropped in on a workshop given by my friend and respected spiritual counselor, Connee Chandler. Connee's topic was "Seeing Beneath the Surface," and she began it with a piece of music that I had introduced her to three years earlier when I played the piece at a Celebration Center function.

Life is eternal
And love is immortal
And death is only a horizon.
And a horizon is nothing
But the limit of our sight.

Connee didn't know how I had encountered the song. She didn't know that I was trying on clothes at a Macys when I heard a compelling tune over the sound system and was instantly transfixed. I stood with a new pair of black stretch jeans around my ankles straining to hear the words. As soon as I got home, I searched the words on the Internet to find out what the song was so I could buy it. It was the song Carly Simon composed when she learned she had breast cancer. Hearing the song now for the first time in years under these circumstances, I figured I had my sign: Yes I had cancer, and yes, everything was in divine right order.

Not my will?

The second coincidence happened when I arrived at Fairfax hospital for my first radiation appointment. I determined to make good use of any time spent in the waiting room by reading a book that a friend said had much strengthened her during her bout with cancer, *Making Miracles* by Paul Pearsall.[41] That friend, Pam Wright, had died of lung cancer. But she told me this particular book made more sense to her than all the other New Age books friends had recommended.

As I arrived for my first appointment, I figured I was in better shape than most of the patients, so I set my intention that if I could be of service to anyone else in the waiting room, I would gladly be available. My backside had not yet touched the waiting room sofa when a woman wearing a scarf over her bald head made a beeline for me and started talking without introduction.

"My daughter had to take off work again to drive me here," she said. "Her office is two hours away. I've tried to tell her I could get here by myself, but she doesn't listen. She's wearing herself out looking after me."

Just then the daughter arrived from the parking lot. "Your mom tells me she's worried about all the driving you've had to do," I ventured cautiously.

"Oh Mom, you know this is where I want to be," she said. "I don't care about the time off. I like being able to be with you."

"Are you sure?"

"You bet I'm sure," the daughter said, hugging her mom.

I was extremely pleased at that tiny chance to be of service, and I was eager to see what my next "assignment" might bring. But after that incident, no one else spoke to me in the waiting room, and I was free to read my book.

It was the story of a health expert who had suffered the most devastating kind of cancer and cancer treatment imaginable. And yet he survived. But more important to me, since I was feeling comfortable about being in that 97% survival group, was the book's overall message. It was halfway between alternative spirituality and a traditional religious message. And thus, it was perfectly targeted to the spot on the bridge where I was standing. Pearsall didn't talk about "God" in any traditional terms. But he did say that for himself and the other survivor patients he encountered, their most successful prayer had been, "Not my way but *the* way be done."

My way, Thy way, The way. *The* way seemed to point to a force outside ourselves, but one that was not tied to a human-like personality. It was one more pointer toward common ground, or perhaps rather toward a midpoint between my New Thought concept of being a co-creator and the Christian concept of surrender to God's will. This was another case of walking a tightrope. "By the time you have the faith to move mountains, you realize the mountains are already in their right place," one saying goes. In a similar vein, spiritual teacher Andrew Cohen says that enlightenment is being able to hold the paradox of knowing that everything is already in divine right order while simultaneously being compelled to make everything better.[42] I wasn't yet able to even clearly articulate the question this raised for me before Bishop Thomas provided an answer in a sermon I didn't hear.

Speak Life: a sermon that tips the balance

Teri: I've been glad to hear you say that the New Testament replaces much of the harshness of the Old Testament law with the grace available through Jesus. In New Thought it's extremely important to keep a positive focus. But even the teachings of Jesus include some oppressiveness that puts fear back in our relationship with God.

Bishop: Like what?

Teri: Like that story where Jesus can't get any fruit from a fig tree, so he curses it and it dies. I wouldn't want to be around anybody who lost his temper like that.

Bishop: No, Jesus wasn't angry; I thought I explained that.

Teri: Huh? When?

Bishop: Last Sunday, when I spoke about that story.

Teri: We weren't there last Sunday. We went to a special event at Celebration Center.

Bishop: (Confused) You weren't there? You just happened to be thinking of that story? Teri, you have got to get the tape of that sermon.

I got the tape and took it with me on our annual vacation to my sister's walnut orchard in Northern California. I needed a break to sort things out, and the orchard would be the perfect place. My sister Tina and her husband Tom manage the orchard to make a little extra income on top of her job at the local newspaper. Andy and I love to walk in the orchard, especially the old part with its stately rows of wide, gnarled trunks. Standing in their shaded spaces and looking up through the high, arching branches feels like being in a natural cathedral.

On our second morning, I wandered to the center of the orchard, a special place where the old trees meet the new, and where a couple of peach and apple trees that pre-date the orchard still give fruit. The wellhead is there, the source for the irrigation system, and spillage from it creates a green, mossy carpet. You can look in all directions without seeing any houses. It's easy to imagine being in the Garden of Eden.

Pondering in the Garden of Eden

I sat and asked myself to just forget all my ideas and beliefs and instead focus on my experience of how life actually happens to me. I'd been repeating for years the New Thought concept that my thoughts draw experiences to me through "the law of attraction." But did that really stack up to my experience?

I began to construct a metaphor that my life feels like I'm wandering through an orchard on a treasure hunt. And as I stay continually alert for signs of where the treasure is, golden fruits are dropped in my path drawing me in this direction or that. Or brambles appear on the path, and I have to decide whether to cut through them or turn in another direction. Sometimes I arrive at a tree that appeared heavily fruited from the distance, and it actually is barren—but it has put me within sight of the next tree that does have fruit.

Tentatively, I came to the conclusion that it feels less like my own specific intentions are creating a path for me and more like success comes from my *belief* that treasure is all around me, my *alertness* for signs of that treasure, and my *willingness to switch paths* when I see something new—"bending beats," Andy and I call it, using the metaphor from jazz. And, yes, it also feels like something "out there" is interacting with me in this hunt. Religious Scientists will debate all day whether there really is something "out there" or if rather our own thoughts get reflected back to us in a way that makes it seem so. For me the sense of "out thereness" was becoming more prominent. I could almost imagine little cherub voices chuckling behind the trees at my attempts to catch them out in the open as they darted about placing fruits and brambles.

A tape that turns things around

I returned to "the bunk house," the little converted garage we stay in on the orchard's edge. Remembering the tape I'd brought, I popped it into a player and settled into a rocking chair to listen. As you read the summary below, imagine the sermon quickly building to freight train speed and volume with the audience whooping and hollering in the background and generally having a much better time than most folks are allowed to have in church. The title was "See Something and Say Something."

See something and say something

"Jesus had just driven the money changers out of the temple, and he was hungry. He had done God's work, and now he had a need, and he knew God would fulfill that need. So he saw a fig tree off in the distance and he moved toward it.

"So first off you've got to *see* your possibilities. God is constantly surrounding you with the answer to your needs, but most of the time we don't see it or we don't take the effort to move toward it because we judge it beforehand. 'Oh that will never work out. I'm not smart enough for that job. Somebody else will get there first.'

"And when Jesus arrived at the tree and there was no fruit, he had no reason to be discouraged, because fig trees were plentiful in Palestine, and he knew that there would be a fruit-bearing tree nearby. You see, sometimes God brings us part way to our good, one step at a time. But we get impatient. We want him to meet our needs our way. We don't see that he might have something better planned for us around the corner. That's why you need to talk to other people when you're discouraged. And don't talk to negative people, talk to people who've come through themselves and can tell you how God provided for them. (Bishop referred to several older people in the congregation by name.)

"Next off, Jesus says something to the barren fig tree. And this part of the text is difficult, y'all. Some people think Jesus cursed the tree because he was angry. No, Jesus wasn't angry. I had to ask Holy Spirit to help me see this clearly. Sometimes you have to go deep to understand a situation that looks bad on the outside. And I got so excited when Holy Spirit spoke to me on this one.

"Jesus wasn't angry, no. Jesus was recognizing a bad situation for what it was. That tree wasn't doing what it was supposed to do. It was unproductive. So he dealt with it harshly. How many of you have unproductive situations in your life? You can't always be nice to those situations. Sometimes you have to deal harshly with them...

You've got to deal harshly with your addictions

You've got to deal harshly with your temptations

You've got to deal harshly with your dysfunctional family situations

You've got to deal harshly with your anger

You've got to deal harshly with your depression

You can't go around being sissified with anything that comes between you and your God.

"You've got to *see* it, and then you've got to *say* something to it. And what you say to it has got to be positive if you want to claim your blessings. Proverbs

18:21 says, **'Death and Life are in the power of the tongue: and they that love it shall eat the fruit of the tree.'** You've got to say:

I AM healed!
I HAVE a loving family.
I AM prosperous
I AM at peace with my God.

And as you *say* it, you've got to *believe* it. And then *do* that which reflects your belief."

The tape ended, and I sat stunned at the similarities to my morning musings. The metaphor was not of life as a straight-and-narrow, pre-ordained path. Rather it bespoke a journey of discovery that was elevated to adventure by divine guidance. The story integrated the positive, here-and-now, outlook of New Thought with the Christian gumption to make distinctions and take action. It even ended with affirmations that were similar to the "spiritual mind treatment" form of prayer used in Religious Science. And furthermore, this "tough love" version of Jesus filled in the piece I had felt to be missing in my personal experience of New Thought. Yes, hold only the highest vision in your consciousness, but then *act* to make it happen. Or as we say in Religious Science, "Treat and move your feet," which includes making difficult decisions.

And then the truly radical aspect of the sermon hit me. In this interpretation, we weren't supposed to identify with the fig tree. We were supposed to identify with Jesus.

That was the missing link. When we truly identify with Jesus, with God, then "my way" and 'Thy way" become the same. "Ascended" and "descended" have an opportunity to meet.

A metaphor come-to-life seals the deal

Shaken, I walked outside where I found Tom surveying a sunny, open area of the orchard. "Tom, what happened to the big, old trees that were here last year?" I asked.

"We had to take them out," he said. "They were beautiful, but they weren't bearing nuts, and they had a fungus that could have spread to other trees. I've ordered some new trees to replace them."

I sucked in my breath and couldn't speak. Bishop's metaphor had come to life before my eyes. And in that moment I knew that I wanted to join Highview.

I still didn't believe that the Bible is the *only* source of wisdom, and I was no closer to being comfortable with the traditional salvation statement. When Andy requested to join Highview early on, no one had asked him if he was already saved. I hoped I could squeak in just as unobtrusively.

22

If You Can't Beat 'em...

I wonder if I can trust you.
But then, uncertainty is part of
life's fascination, isn't it?
Dr Frankenstein speaking to his new assistant in
The Revenge of Frankenstein, Jimmy Sangster

Belonging precedes believing for many
people today. And if you agree with
that, your life is going to get a whole
lot more complicated.
Brian McLaren, *More Ready Than You Think*

Teri becomes a fundamentalist—with a caveat

I returned from California eager to tell Bishop Thomas of my decision. I sat on the church steps at dusk on a mild October evening, just a year after Andy and I had first come to Highview and 6 months into my dialogues with Bishop.

He drove up harried from traffic and burdened with briefcases from a presentation about Highview's new building. After years of planning, they were about to move to a larger church farther out in the suburbs of Fairfax. Preparing to leave the home of 100 years was bringing out strains in the congregation.

"Sit down on the steps, for a moment," I said. "I have what I hope you will think is good news."

"Oh I could sure use that today," he said.

"I would like to join Highview, if you'll have me. I want to support the work of this ministry, I want the wonderful people here to be my spiritual family, and I want you as my pastor. It was the fig tree sermon that did it."

"That's terrific news. That's great. I really needed that."

"But I have a condition, and you might want to think about taking me. I don't want to give up my membership in Celebration Center. I will still also consider myself a Religious Scientist, and I still believe there are many paths to God. And, uh, if you haven't figured it out by now, you should know I can be trouble."

"That's all right. We can work with all that. You should know too, though, that I'm not perfect by any means. I make mistakes, and you may have to forgive me from time to time."

"Sounds like a good deal to me," I said.

And that was it. Now my husband and I, as far as we knew, were the world's only New Age Fundamentalists.

Prophecy of a paradigm shift

Deciding to join Highview released in me a reservoir of interest in helping out. The new building meant seats to fill and a mortgage to pay. So my inclination was to jump right in and offer to redo the website, which was very traditional and outdated. But would I be treading in dangerous waters? It was one thing for me to come to a richer understanding of this church's mission. It was another for me to express that understanding on the Highview website. Could I hold back from mixing in my own views? Should I?

The Universe put a trumpet to my ear to give me the answer.

The Sunday after I joined, a visiting minister gave the sermon. Just before his message, Bishop noted in his announcements that my husband Andy was offering a GED class. At the end of the sermon, the visitor paused, looked at Andy seated near the back, and said, "You sir, would you come up here please. And the woman next to you, I presume that's your wife."

The two of us walked up to the altar and stood before him. "Holy Spirit is laying it on my heart to tell everyone that these two people are going to change things around here," he said. "They are going to bring about a paradigm shift and open up possibilities that you have never dreamed of. And they are going to be instrumental in paying off the new mortgage."

We returned to our seats amidst a buzz in the crowd. The service continued as usual, and extra numbers of people came up to us afterwards for hugs and to tell us they believed we were indeed sent to Highview for divine purposes. My cheeks have never been so red.

Usually Andy and I chat eagerly during the drive home from church. We exchange insights about the service and any interesting conversations we've had. But this time, we were half way home before we dared even steal a glance at each other.

This was scary. I knew I had just been handed an unfair advantage in my dealings with other members of the congregation; no matter what radical thing I did, I could not be dismissed out-of-hand. And it would be a sacred trust not to misuse that advantage. I laughed silently to myself to realize that I felt as if Mat's vision from "Survivors" had come true for me: I was being offered a chance to drive a high-end sports car on a racetrack all to myself with no speed limits. I had been invited—no, *commanded*—to do whatever I felt was right in this strange situation.

Another "no-brainer"

I've mentioned our Unitarian friends, all of whom have strong ethics but are what Ken Wilber calls "flatlanders" in that they reduce or flatten psychological or spiritual experience to its measurable material content. Shortly after the "prophecy" episode described above, we had dinner with one such friend, Bill Cressey, who teaches a college course on the mind. When we told him about the prophecy he said, "Well that's a no-brainer. Anybody looking around the church and seeing you two as the only White people could have predicted you'd shift the paradigm. There's nothing unusual in a visitor picking up on that."

And perhaps Bill was right. It even occurred to me later that the visiting minister hadn't said that Andy and I would shift the paradigm for the *good.*

Taking prophecy with a grain of salt

Rain was falling during my next meeting with Bishop. I started by asking what he had told the visiting speaker about Andy and me prior to Sunday's service.

Bishop: Not a thing. I've never met him before. And unfortunately, I didn't even have a chance to greet him before the service.

Teri: You're kidding. I was certainly surprised by his prophecy. It seemed awfully coincidental, given some of our conversations. But I believe in taking things like that with a grain of salt.

Bishop: Yes, there are all kinds of possible sources or explanations for a prophecy like that.

Teri: Yes, exactly.

Bishop: Though on the other hand, I wouldn't discount such things entirely.

Teri: They're just one factor to consider.

Bishop: Yes, that's it. One factor.

Teri: So I guess it will be my job to say or do whatever I feel guided to do, and your job to filter through it to judge if there's anything of use for you.

Bishop: That's exactly what I was thinking.

Teri: Okay. So what I came to tell you tonight is that I'd like to volunteer to redo the church website. And I'm thinking to do some things that are nontraditional, out of the box.

Bishop: That would be great. We really need that.

Teri: In fact, I have one idea drafted up I'd like to show you.

Taking the "High View" in the church website

I opened my laptop and showed him a page called "Ten Reasons Not to Come to This Church." It was a partly satirical and partly straightforward way of telling people what they could expect and what I saw as the church's values. I had used the same idea successfully for my Bahamian client at *myharbourisland.com*. This page started with items like:

Don't come to this church if

- You prefer a quiet, contemplative service to electric, all-out, arm-waving, passionate praise of God.
- Your job and possessions provide all the sense of identity you need.

And it ended with things like:
Do come if

- You're ready to move beyond questing for *self*-fulfillment.
- Once you've heard the voice inside that calls you to a juicier life and a peace that surpasses understanding, you're the kind of person who won't let anything get in your way of claiming it.

Bishop: (looking it over) Whoa… whoa… this is scary.

Teri: I'm sorry. I know it's a little radical. It's the result of a lot of time I spent trying to clarify the qualities I experience here. But maybe it's not appropriate.

Bishop: No, no. I want to use this just the way it is. This is exactly what I would have written if I'd had the time and focus to think it through.

Mop bucket attitude

On our way out of that meeting, we passed through the small basement of the aging church. A leak had let in enough rain to create a deep puddle in the middle of the floor. Several people were standing around waiting for class to begin, and someone said that the member who has a shopvac would be over in an hour. But that wasn't soon enough for Bishop Thomas. He went to the utility closet to get a mop bucket and waded in to the mess in his business suit and dress shoes.

I stood transfixed. Bishop had often said he wanted members to have an "MBA," that is, a "Mop Bucket Attitude," toward doing the work of the ministry. Suddenly I knew what I wanted to put on the home page of the new Web site, a picture of him with that bucket.

The following week when I proposed the idea to Bishop, ready to make a pitch for it, he cut me off saying, "Let's do it."

This was too easy. Way, way, too easy. Like a sports car on an unlimited track.

And when the website came out with a photo of the Bishop holding a mop on the home page, several members of the congregation were indeed concerned. Only one person, however, had the courage to express those concerns to me directly. A woman who has been an active volunteer her whole life, cautioned me that it might be considered inappropriate to show a bishop, "and especially a Black bishop," in a menial role. Indeed, she had doubts about the appropriateness of a church engaging in any form of self-promotion.

I did my best to share with her my vision of why I saw it as appropriate to make visible Highview's "niche," and I think I convinced her. Mostly I was very grateful and impressed that she had spoken out, thus giving me a chance to explain.

Plan or possibilities?

The last piece to be created for the Website was the banner with the church mission statement. Highview's vision statement, created by Bishop Thomas, is "Providing world class ministry deserving of an awesome God."

What I love about that statement is how it calls for excellence in form on earth while pointing to the magnificence of the formless in heaven; a mix of ascended/descended. But on the other hand, it doesn't really say much to a visitor curious about Highview's focus. And just as I was having that thought,

I received an email out of the blue from a church marketing firm; it cautioned against mission statements that focus on what a church *does* rather than on the effect it has on the world.

So I started playing with a tagline for the Website that would take advantage of the name Highview, the name itself having been one of the beacons that drew me there.

Maybe something like "providing a high view of God's possibilities for your life."

At this point, Bishop Thomas and I had not much discussed one of the important points I took from his fig tree sermon: the distinction that still felt important to me between leading a life of possibilities and merely following "God's plan for your life." So I was extremely curious to see how Bishop would react to my proposal.

"Hmm," he said, looking at a mockup of the banner. "'Providing a high view of God's possibilities for your life.' This is good. Let's see, should that be God's plan, purpose, or possibilities? Everybody is talking "purpose" now with *The Purpose Driven Life.* Let's go with 'possibilities.'"

"*Yes!*"

And he finished rewriting to integrate my draft with the mission statement:

"World class ministry providing a high view of your possibilities in an awesome God."

23

A Dialogue with C.S. Lewis

What often happens when we face
this stripping away of our models is
that we will give up this and that, and
instead grab onto that and this. It's too
uncomfortable not to have anything to
cling to, and so we substitute a new set
of attachments for the old ones. We give
up family, we give up social forms—and
we start clinging instead to spiritual
leaders and spiritual forms.
Uh-uh. It's all gotta go.
Big clearance, everything must go.
Ram Dass: *Paths to God, Living the Bhagavad-Gita*

"The Challenge of Religious Pluralism"

It's an irony of the Washington area that one of the largest Christian churches is headed by someone who was raised Jewish. Pastor Lon Solomon turned to Jesus after spending his college years selling LSD and dabbling in Buddhist meditation. Today his church, Mclean Bible in Northern Virginia, makes it a priority to bring the Christian message to secular Washington. And thus they run a series of radio ads with the tag line, "Not a sermon, just a thought."

Is Christianity the most coherent belief system?

In April 2005 I heard an advertisement for a seminar at McLean Bible on "The Challenge of Religious Pluralism." *Challenge? Uh oh,* I thought. *How can they be against pluralism?*

The workshop featured Dr. Ravi Zacharias from the C.S. Lewis Institute in Atlanta. This was prior to all the publicity surrounding release of the film version of *The Lion, The Witch, and the Wardrobe* from Lewis's *Chronicles of Narnia*, so I was not familiar with Lewis as the most famous apologist for Christianity, ("apologist" meaning one who explains). Dr. Zacharias is respected around the world as a top presenter for the institute that bears Lewis's name. One of the subtopics for this seminar was to be, "Why Christianity is the Most Coherent Belief System."

I decided to go for two reasons. The first was to see what the alternative spiritual community was "up against" from this organization. Would they brand us as wicked and evil and urge people to redouble their efforts to convert us? The second reason was that I felt I should give traditional Christianity a full and fair chance to "come and get me." A few things Bishop Thomas was telling me still didn't make sense to me. Perhaps the perspective of this expert would strike me differently.

A worthy opponent

The seminar was held in the 2,000 seat auditorium of McLean Bible, and the room was over half full. I was surprised at how nervous I was entering the sleek new facility. Although I was now completely comfortable at Highview, I had all my original fears about other orthodox Christian churches. So I felt like I was there in disguise. And I knew that if there was a Q&A session, any question I asked would blow my cover.

The speaker's opening statement only increased my anxiety. It is easy to identify "superficial similarities" among religions and philosophies, he said. The real test of a religion's value is in how it *differs* from the others. He told us that he had debated a famous atheist about this over many years. And finally, Dr. Zacharias claimed, the atheist admitted on his deathbed that logic alone cannot fully explain the ethics that all humans hold in common. In fact, Dr. Zacharias claimed, many modern atheists are so steeped in the ethic of Christianity that they cannot recognize its unique imprint on their attitudes.

I was both heartened and dismayed at what I heard that day. I was heartened because Dr. Zacharias was a magnificent speaker who struck me as a truly good and wise man. Instead of being a rabble-rouser, he was a man with a passion for God and a passion for reason. His points were beautifully argued, and he said that whenever he debates someone, he always moves to embrace them afterward, if they will allow it. I trusted this man—just as I had come to trust Bishop Thomas. If the ship were sinking, I would trust either man to assign the lifeboats.

Dr. Zacharias said that every religion or philosophy must answer questions about our origin, meaning, morality, and destiny. He said the answers to all four of these questions must be coherent and consistent, and that only Christianity fulfills this demand.

I had never heard anyone approach religion that way, and the discussion fascinated me. However, his arguments fell far short of convincing me. He made several interesting points about Hinduism, Buddhism, and Islam as they compare to Christianity. But I was dismayed that he did not touch upon the area of greatest interest to me—the apparent fact that mystics of the entire world's religions, those people who spend their lives in meditation and devotion to God, tell a similar description of their *experience* of God. I submitted a written question about that, but he received hundreds of questions and had time to answer only a few.

He did say one thing, though, that struck a personal chord for me; he said that Eastern religions are about *union* with God, while Christianity is about *communion* with God. And thus, only Christianity offers the joy of relationship with God since you can't be in relationship to something you've merged with. My reaction was to think that I wanted both types of relationship with God.

One other thing struck me as curious. Dr. Zacharias talked about the sacredness of marriage and said that his own marriage was a central source of strength in his life. Frequently, he said, the Institute sends out mixed-gender teams to conferences around the world. In order to forestall improprieties among members of the team, they follow a set of behaviors including a curfew. In fact, Dr. Zacharias told us, one member of the team once overcame temptation on a lovely evening in Paris by locking himself in his hotel room and throwing the key over the balcony to the interior court. Only in the morning did the fellow call the concierge to retrieve the key.

Imagine that.*

And finally, as Dr. Zacharias was finishing his talk, one more curiosity. He said that he had been invited to speak at a Mormon gathering in Utah. A murmur went through the crowd that felt to me like fear. The tension seemed to be relieved when he said he had made his acceptance conditional on a promise that there would be no discussion of the criteria for salvation. It occurred to me that while I lump most Christians together, people *within* Christianity see themselves in a hierarchy. And evidently the Mormons were near the bottom. Probably right next to my friends the Jehovah's Witnesses.

On my way out of the workshop, I stopped in the church bookstore thinking I might buy something by Dr. Zacharias or by C.S. Lewis. Instead I found myself

* A couple of female members of the focus group for the draft of this book reacted negatively to the story of a man locking himself in his hotel room to avoid temptation. "It's immature, and thus it undercuts the credibility of Dr. Zacharias for telling it," they both said. I asked, "Which is immature, that a man would *feel* a temptation or that he would go to extreme lengths to resist it?" Neither woman was able to answer that question.

strongly attracted to books by an author named Brian McLaren who apparently had started a movement called the "Emergent Church." But the bookstore line was too long, so I came home empty-handed. This proved to be a near miss in encountering work that would shape the outcome of my time with Bishop Thomas. Buying the books that day might have cut short some of the fun.

Surprised by Joy

Really, a young atheist cannot
guard his faith too carefully.
Dangers lie in wait for him on every side.
C.S. Lewis, *Surprised by Joy*

Two weeks later, Andy and I invited to dinner a friend who is a Christian Scientist. She brought me a book by C.S. Lewis, *Surprised by Joy: The Story of My Early Life.*[43] It looked interesting.

Have you ever had the experience when reading a book that the life being described is so much like your own, that your palms begin to sweat as you turn the page because it feels like you're about to learn what will happen to *you* next? That's how I felt while reading *Surprised by Joy*. It starts out by describing the childhood experiences Lewis had of "glimpses of joy." These were mystical experiences like my own childhood sense of the Virgin Mary described in Chapter 2. And these were exactly the types of mystical experiences I hadn't had a chance to ask about at the religious pluralism seminar a few weeks prior. Later I would learn that *Surprised by Joy* is one of Lewis's lesser-known works because both its mysticism and its heavy dose of philosophy make it less suited to a popular audience. But to me, of course, it was perfect (or, as Lewis himself said of a tutor who required pupils to prove everything they said, "Some boys would not have liked it, but to me it was red beef and strong beer.")

Lewis tells the story of his spiritual journey in five steps. The first three steps include the Christianity of his childhood, the atheistic "realism" of his adolescence, then the belief in an impersonal force called the "Absolute" that he absorbed from his study of philosophy at Oxford University. His conversion is then completed in two final steps after he is wounded in Word War 1: in the first of these steps he feels drawn by something bigger than himself to believe in a personal God. And finally, as a last step, he returns to Christianity. I placed myself somewhere between his step three and four—struggling with the paradox that whatever runs the universe seems to have a nature that is both impersonal and personal.

Throughout Lewis's account of this journey, I basked in his clear writing, his self-deprecating humor, and his love of truth—no matter how painful. I felt like I was having a mind meld with this Irish scholar who died in 1963.

Here was a person smarter and better educated than I, someone from a time and place where little boys spent summers reading Longfellow and Greek Tragedies in their mothers' gardens. Lewis had passed through almost every philosophical view that I had, and one by one, he had been forced to cast them aside by reason or by experience. When he made fun of his philosophic period, it felt like he was making fun of me.

> There were in those days all sorts of blankets, insulators, and insurances which enabled one to get all the conveniences of Theism without believing in God.

Ouch, I said as I read that. Then he related how each of those "insulators" fell away.

First to fall, he said, was his "chronological snobbery." This was his term for the assumption that new beliefs are better than old ones, and thus anything scientific was better than traditional religion. His call to reconsider that reaction sounded like Wilber's call to "transcend and *include*" the values at each level of our growth. And furthermore, Lewis's intellectual friends replaced their traditional religious beliefs with a group of philosophies they loosely termed the "New Look." This sounded a bit too much like my New Thought.

Next, Lewis described an experience that paralleled my recent rereading of my favorite New Thought authors; I was finding in them more personalness about God than I had seen in earlier readings. I was surprised to see that my New Thought hero Thomas Troward had referred to "the question of Christ manifest in the flesh as the criterion of the whole matter." Ernest Holmes filled the second half of his "Science of Mind" text with biblical references; why had I previously read only the first half of that book? And recently I had noticed that even my beloved Emerson, the man who sneered at "mouldered old religion," had also written this: "In your metaphysics you have denied personality to the Deity, yet when the devout motions of the soul come, yield to them heart and life, though they should clothe God with shape and color. Leave your theory, as Joseph his coat in the hand of the harlot, and flee."

Apparently, I had seen only what I wanted to see. And Lewis rubbed it in.

> All the books were beginning to turn against me. Indeed, I must have been blind as a bat not to have seen, long before, the ludicrous contradiction between my theory of life and my actual experiences as a reader. George McDonald had done more to me than any writer; of course, it was a pity he had that bee in his bonnet about Christianity. He was good *in spite of it...*

> I thought—I didn't of course *say;* words would have revealed the nonsense—that Christianity itself was very sensible 'apart from its Christianity.'

Ouch. Too close to home. But it got worse.

> The natural step would have been to inquire a little more closely whether the Christians were, after all, wrong. But I did not take it. I thought I could explain their superiority without that hypothesis… I thought that 'the Christian myth' conveyed to unphilosophic minds as much of the truth… as they were capable of grasping, and that even that much put them above the irreligious… The implication—that something which I and most other undergraduates could master without extraordinary pains would have been too hard for Plato, Dante, Hooker, and Pascal—did not yet strike me as absurd. I hope this is because I never looked it squarely in the face.

Ugh! Please. Make him stop.

But he did not stop. Instead he talked about how two of his best friends, both solid atheists, had "betrayed" him by converting to Christianity. I did not know anyone who had converted; my oldest and most respected friends were still Religious Scientists. But there was that nagging coincidence that the two most interesting new friends Andy and I had made in the last 5 years were both fundamentalists—Bishop Thomas himself, and my client the baker and Jehovah's Witness in the Bahamas. Both were people of extraordinary vitality and integrity, heads of their congregations, and in long-term marriages. And of course, there was the small additional coincidence that they were both Black. It crossed my mind that the Bahamas experience was a sort of John-the-Baptist preparation for me to encounter Highview and Bishop Thomas.

Lewis continued:

> Realism had been abandoned; the New Look was somewhat damaged; and chronological snobbery was seriously shaken. All over the board my pieces were in the most disadvantageous positions. Soon I could no longer cherish even the illusion that the initiative lay with me. My Adversary began to make his Final Moves… equivalent, perhaps, to the loss of one's last remaining bishop.

I slammed the book shut. I took a walk to get my bearings.

It was not just the logic trail Lewis was tracing that paralleled my own journey. It was also and more powerfully the mounting evidence that for me, too, it might be an "illusion that the initiative lay with me." (More of the events that created this sense of being led are described in the chapter 33. Evangelism: Good News and Bad.)

Okay, so maybe Lewis had thought carefully about *most* of the conceptions of God I was attracted to. But there did seem to be critical differences. For one thing, the personal experiences he or his friends had with anything like New Thought had all been negative. Some of his friends became lost in despair, confusing "connection with the One Mind" with the occult. Whereas for my friends and myself, New Thought had been a strongly positive influence in our lives.

And furthermore, there was no indication that Lewis had ever been exposed to the evolutionary perspective that so strongly called to me. He wasn't aware of the concept that we are all Spirit expressing. I opened the book again to take a small peek.

> I thought the business of us finite and half unreal souls was to multiply the consciousness of Spirit by seeing the world from different positions while yet remaining qualitatively the same as Spirit; to be tied to a particular time and place and set of circumstances, yet there to will and think as Spirit itself does… The way to recover… this universal vision was daily and hourly to remember our true nature, to reascend or return into that Spirit which… we still were.

There it was: something very close to my evolutionary perspective. Lewis had been attracted to it, too. I was breathing shallowly now. And apparently, so was Lewis.

> The fox… was now running in the open, bedraggled and weary, hounds barely a field behind.

And then Lewis dropped the final axe. He described his move to belief in a personal God.

> I was to be allowed to play at philosophy no longer. It might, as I say, still be true that my "Spirit" differed in some way from "the God of popular religion." My Adversary waived the point. It sank into utter unimportance. He would not argue about it. He only said, "I am the Lord"; "I am that I am"; "I am."

I started to cry. It was like moving from Lewis's step three to step four (from an impersonal God to a personal God). Except it was more like picking up the stepping-stone of God as an impersonal force and carrying it with me to step four. I faced up to the fact that I had been experiencing the personal nature of God, and that hanging back from it only built walls between me and other believers. More important, my sense of having the *best* concept of God fell away, and along with it went any last shred of feeling superior to those who held traditional beliefs.

God, okay. But what about Jesus?

At this point in his story, Lewis's conversion was "to theism pure and simple, not to Christianity." But the last chapter in *Surprised by Joy* is about his conversion to orthodox Christianity. What would happen to me when I read the last chapter? Would I continue to follow in the author's footsteps? The first few lines pulled me in.

> The question was no longer to find the one simply true religion among a thousand religions simply false. It was, rather, 'Where has religion reached its true maturity? Where if anywhere, have the hints of all Paganism been fulfilled?' With the irreligious I was no longer concerned… As against them, the whole mass of those who had worshiped—all who had danced and sung and sacrificed and trembled and adored—were clearly right. But the intellect and the conscience, as well as the orgy and the ritual must be our guide... Where was the thing full grown? There were really only two answers possible: either in Hinduism or in Christianity.

I sucked in my breath. But I also felt that if I were ever to come all the way to seeing Christianity as the *only* true religion, there was a very good chance that it would happen as I read the next couple of paragraphs.

> I was by now too experienced in literary criticism to regard the Gospels as myths. They had not the mythical taste. And yet the very matter which they set down in their artless, historical fashion…was precisely the matter of the great myths. If ever a myth had become fact, had been incarnated, it would be just like this. And nothing else in all literature was just like this. Myths were like it in one way. Histories were like it in another. But nothing was simply like it. And no person was like the Person it depicted; as real, as recognizable, through all that depth of time, as Plato's (description of) Socrates…, yet also numinous, lit by a light from beyond the world, a god. But if a god—we are no longer polytheists—then not a god, but God. Here and here only in all time the myth must have become

> fact; the Word, flesh; God, Man. This is not "a religion," nor "a philosophy." It is the summing up and actuality of them all.

I gazed in wonder over the edge of this cliff. The view of Jesus it gave was compelling, challenging. It started me on a journey of reconsidering the statement by Science of Mind founder Ernest Holmes, "Christianity may be the best religion for Western man." I used to think Holmes only said that to make his own philosophy palatable to the masses. But now I had evidence that he meant it. Perhaps there was something unique about Jesus—and thus, about Christianity. For me, at least, my personality fits the profile of "western man"—in that I am entranced by reason and by effective action. And I was feeling more at home in Christianity, or at least in a form of it that set clear boundaries and then maintained them through boundless love. I was more at home on this tightrope of "right action" than I was on the meditation cushion of felt oneness—although I suspect that treading the tightrope would be easier if I spent more time sitting in the silence.

As I studied Lewis further, I learned that the call to right action was indeed a main factor in his conversion. He said it may be true that we are all "vantage points for Spirit" who need only to "remember our true nature…"

> But I now felt I had better try to do it. …An attempt at complete virtue must be made.

From that day forward, my appreciation of Jesus became richer, as hinted at in my Afterwords chapter. But that day, as I gazed over the cliff of the uniqueness of Jesus in *Surprised by Joy*, I did not fall. At least, that is, I did not suddenly see that Jesus is the *only* way to heaven, or that reciting a specific belief statement is the *only* way to Jesus. I felt like I had let the fundamentalist's God take his best shot at me, and he hadn't chosen to hit *there*.

As I closed *Surprised by Joy*, I felt both inspired and relieved; I felt "safe" about not having to be "saved" in the most strict, dogmatic sense. It looked as if I wouldn't have to eat that hat, after having Bishop Thomas feed me so many other hats (with more to come). But I was also a bit saddened because I assumed this meant there would always be a barrier between me and my Highview brethren. Someday, somebody was going to ask me straight on, "Have you accepted Jesus as your personal Lord and Savior?" And I was either going to have to tap dance, mumble, or take my remaining hats and go.

24

Salvation: World's Biggest Loophole?

I noticed that those who said the prayer the first time they were invited to almost never were seen again in church. Those who resisted or argued or just weren't ready continued coming back to church and asking questions. The first group seemed to "get saved" without staying saved, and the second group seemed to stay saved without ever getting saved.
Brian McLaren, *More Ready Than You Realize*

My confrontation with salvation came almost immediately after the experience with C.S. Lewis. But it took a completely different turn from what I expected.

Salvation as transcending good and evil

Bishop Thomas had explained to me that individual congregations of fundamentalists may pursue this or that doctrine, but they agree about one "fundamental" belief: Your life changes irrevocably the moment you "Confess Jesus as your Lord and Savior." And from then on, the Holy Spirit is working in you, and you can't go to hell—whether hell is described as a literal place or as eternal separation from God.

The whole concept of being saved was foreign to me. On the surface it sounds preposterous to modern ears. But as I thought about it, I saw the contradiction in my own rejection of it. Which part of the equation was I more upset about: that some people "go to hell" or that others don't, no matter what they do—that there *was* justice in the traditional sense or that there *wasn't*? Most of my friends will say that there really is no distinction between good and evil and no final judge. But when I bring up this aspect of salvation, they sputter something like, "You mean they believe you could torture a child and get away with it? That's crazy." In other words, my friends are suddenly more repulsed by the idea that someone is getting away with something than that anyone is being punished.

I came to see that all belief systems address justice, a way to fit the punishment to the crime. Catholics have purgatory, Eastern religions have reincarnation, New Thought has immediate consequences of our thoughts. And Bishop Thomas had given me the fundamentalist equalizer when he said that saved people who please God in this life will have richer rewards in heaven than those who don't.

So working from the assumption that all belief systems contain some truth, I dug to find a way to hear the salvation belief as something I could relate to. When I found it, I was stunned at how much it lined up with my own experience. I decided to try a trick question, mildly uncomfortable with remembering that those were the stock-in-trade of the Pharisees.

Teri: Is God's will always that which is in the highest and best interests of all?

Bishop: Yes.

Teri: So if I say I align myself with the highest and best interest of all, that's the same as aligning myself with God's will?

Bishop: Yes, but you can never know what's in the best interest of all.

Teri: I get that. So the best I can do is be guided by the wisdom of scripture—which I believe is repeated among the world's great religious and ethical teachings—use my reason to balance what that seems to say against the standard of the Great Commandment, "Love the Lord your God with your whole heart, and love your neighbor as yourself," and then watch for signs that I can interpret as guidance.

Bishop: Yes, that's it.

Teri: Well that rings true for me. And as I do that, a whole new world begins to open to me: coincidences provide guidance, resources fall into place when I need them, and a calm sense settles in that the big picture is going to take care of itself.

Bishop: Yes, you become indwelled by the Holy Spirit who provides counsel at a whole different level from that which is available to those who aren't saved.

I had the sense I might be approaching the world's biggest loophole.

From software copying to abortion

Teri: I want to make sure I'm understanding you about salvation. No matter what sins a person commits after being saved, that person is still going to heaven?

Bishop: That's the great thing people don't understand. Christ died for our sins, past, present, and to come.

Teri: So I could sin as much as I want?

Bishop: Yes, but you wouldn't want to as a practice. Once you are saved, your whole focus changes; knowing what God has done for you, all you want to do is please him. You don't think so much about things that used to tempt you. And when you do miss the mark, you are grieved and so is God, until confession and true repentance takes place.

Teri: So in that sense you could say a saved person has transcended good and evil?

Bishop: No, not at all. A saved person has been justified by God's grace and given the gift of salvation on the basis of their faith.

Teri: Okay, let me try a slightly different angle. Let's just say hypothetically for sake of argument that I am saved. I've got two sins active in my life, what might be considered a small one and a big one. The small one is that I occasionally copy software. I believe it's wrong, but I occasionally do it anyway. And in Religious Science we'd say that the mere fact that I do consider it wrong means there are consequences for me—because whatever I think outpictures.

Bishop: Yes, God cares about your motive, what's in your heart. There are a few gray areas where scripture doesn't give specific instructions. And in those we have to interpret the best we can, as we are lead by the Holy Spirit. And it could happen the other way—I could interpret something is not a sin and thus have no consequences. But for others the same action might convict them.

Teri: But only in the gray areas, right?

Bishop: That's right.

Teri: So let me ask about the greater sin I referred to, something on which I'm sure you'd say scripture is clear. In my twenties I had an abortion. At the time, I didn't believe abortion was morally wrong. So I was surprised when my body and emotions told me otherwise. Nevertheless, I stand by my choice, and I would make it again in the same circumstances, although I would do everything I could to prevent the circumstances.

So in that sense, it's different from the software sin. For the abortion I can say to God, "I'm sorry I felt I had to do it. And I regret any consequences it might have had for a plan you were working at the time. But in the same circumstances, I would do it again today. And in that sense, I'm not sorry. I need you to work with me on this one."

Bishop: Well you're right that one is scripturally clear. (His tone was concerned and cautious.) You have to be careful with that. God is not mocked.

Teri: But you've told us we should be buds with God. And for me to feel a close personal relationship, it has to be more like equals. So I can say, "I know this is a tough one, I take responsibility for the call." Isn't that why the Old Testament closes out with that great statement in Hosea, "**The day is coming when you will call me husband, you will no longer call me Master**"?

Bishop: We can be close, God and I, but never peers. He's sovereign. People want to have things their own way. All I can do is keep pointing to his way. (He gestures like a football coach waving toward the goal posts.)

Teri: Nevertheless, in this belief system, I wouldn't go to hell for it if I were already saved?

Bishop: It's extremely difficult to get to hell. The only thing you can do is reject his offer of salvation.

Teri: So I'm not going to hell?

Bishop: Every act has consequences, you can't escape the consequences.

Teri: Yes. I accept that. And I'm willing to accept the consequences of this act.

At our next meeting, I followed up:

Teri: So putting together your two statements: first that an act can have different consequences according to your belief about it and, second, that we are only held accountable to the extent we have been exposed to the Light. Doesn't that mean people who have not been exposed are not accountable for acts they don't believe to be sinful, for example, abortion?

Bishop: It's not that easy. Because God finds ways to speak to us unless we have completely dulled ourselves to his voice. I challenge you to find me a woman who has had an abortion and not felt some wrongness about it at some level. You can't go against God's will without feeling some tension. And life is one of God's highest priorities.

I didn't tell Bishop Thomas this, but he had hit a nerve. Despite not having a *belief* that abortion was wrong in my twenties, when I got the news that I was pregnant, I was devastated. And then for the two nights after the abortion, I had vivid nightmares, except that it felt more as if I was taken to another realm where I could experience how my body, and perhaps my soul, were reacting. I heard wails of anguish, alarm, disbelief. As if my very cells cried out, "Where is it? Where is it? I sensed a frantic searching in the dark. A great bear claw scooping out my insides. And then an ashen, barren landscape. Stark silence. Utter aloneness. Giving up. After two nights, this dark angel departed as abruptly as it had come upon me, and I was fine, never to be haunted again. I got the point though, that abortion is not a morally neutral choice. At least not at the biological and emotional levels of what's real for me.

So perhaps I had my two nights of hell.

The sticky question of whether Teri is saved

Throughout our discussions, I had been working from a stance that my life experience in turning to spirituality was equivalent to being saved. I figured I would eventually propose to Bishop Thomas that I should be able to "test out" of salvation without partaking in the specific ritual of coming to the altar to say, "I accept Jesus Christ as my Lord and Savior."

Indeed, I would be happy to say those words but for two things. The first is that I'd need to be translating a bit it my mind. My discussions with Bishop led me to see a perfect parallel between the traditional salvation statement and the words that come naturally to me: "I align myself with the highest and best for myself and all others. I have no way of ever being sure what that is. So I am guided by the teachings of Jesus (which are reflected in other religions and philosophy) and by the voice of the Holy Spirit (as the highest thought I can access in any situation)."

And furthermore I didn't feel it was right for me to participate in the traditional ritual while having those parentheses in my mind along with two more big caveats. The implied words "only" and "substitutionary." As in "Jesus is my *only* savior because of his *substitutionary* suffering in my place." And of course those two words are key to orthodox Christians, even though most people who accept Jesus formally at the altar may not actually say them.

So given all this, it came as a shock to me when I won this battle without a fight. It came in the middle of the preceding dialogue about abortion.

Bishop: You started off this discussion saying, "Hypothetically, if I were saved." No hypothetical about it. From everything you've shared with me, I believe you are saved.

Teri: You do?

Bishop: There's just one part of it you don't get yet. I'm not sure what's in your way.

Teri: So… my experience in the way that I came to the light is parallel?

Bishop: Based on how you've presented your beliefs to me and how I've seen you behave, I believe it is. You can be saved and not call yourself a Christian.

Teri: What?

Bishop: No, no, I see that gleam in your eye. I'm not saying this is one of your loopholes. I'm just saying there are people who have accepted the truth of the Gospels, but they have such negative associations with Christianity because of past experience that they would not be comfortable joining a church or calling themselves religious or even Christians. Personally, I am not religious, either; I have a relationship with God—although if you look at the definition of "religious," James 1:27 says to be "religious" means to help widows and orphans. But of course, that's not how people mean it.

Teri: That sure sounds like a loophole to me.

Bishop: No it doesn't.

Teri: Does to me.

Bishop: No, there are no loopholes in salvation. I am not saying you can create your own version of the truth. The truth has to come through the scriptures.

Teri: Except for those people who are never exposed to scripture, right?

Bishop: That's right. But that's not a loophole either. That's just a part of God's plan until the time that everyone has had a chance to hear the Word.

Teri: So... what did you mean when you said there's one part I don't get?

Bishop: This can't be just an intellectual exercise for you, Teri. You need to move beyond seeing God as just "the Universe." And for that you need to study the Bible more closely so your understanding can evolve. If you have an honest desire to know God, to the degree you've accepted what you've been taught, God holds you accountable.

For just a moment, I felt a glimmer of fear, until he continued.

Bishop: And from there, the rest is up to you in your prayer life. Matthew 5:6 says, "**Blessed are those who hunger and thirst for righteousness, for they will be filled.**"

Part V

Consciousness

25

Who Needs Psychology?

Self-esteem is best understood
as a spiritual attainment, that is,
as a victory in the evolution of
consciousness.
Nathaniel Branden, *The Six Pillars of Self-Esteem*

To get closer to Buddha (or Jesus)
it helps to get closer to Freud.
Ken Wilber, *A Brief History of Everything*

"Freud had some good points. I'm not opposed to using psychology when it accords with scripture."

When Bishop Thomas made this point early in our dialogues, it was so inside-out from my way of thinking that I was speechless. "*That's funny, I'm not opposed to using scripture when it accords with psychology*," I thought.

We had several discussions about psychology, self-esteem, and guilt.

Teri: My world is so drenched in psychology that I was stunned when you said you only rarely meet people who need help from it. Psychology helps us all become aware of feelings we repress or hide from ourselves—which psychologists call our "shadow." Without awareness of those feelings, the shadow influences everything we do, so we're not really free.

Bishop: I understand that. I gave a sermon once suggesting that repression is a type of bondage itself.

Teri: But repression comes from ignoring feelings, and you keep saying feelings aren't important. Let's say, for example, I am angry at my pastor, but it is unacceptable to admit that to myself because I see myself as a loyal member of the flock. So I repress that anger and experience it as tension or a headache or as anger at someone else, perhaps even the neighboring church.

Bishop: No, Teri, I've never said that feelings aren't important. We should be aware of our feelings; it's just that we shouldn't base decisions on them without comparing them to an outside standard. And didn't you tell me that many New Age people try to think only happy thoughts?

Teri: Uh, well, yes. I know some people who lead very successful lives by focusing exclusively on desired outcomes. Though for myself, I've felt uncomfortable about the extremes of that. I think it's more valuable to admit to myself when I'm scared, angry, or disappointed. Then I can work on shifting to something else.

A little repression is a good thing

Bishop: On the other hand, there are some feelings you should repress, like sexual attractions to somebody other than your spouse—although a Christian wouldn't even think of it as repression but as temperance or self-discipline, which is a fruit of relationship with the Holy Spirit.

Teri: I think psychologists use the term "sublimation" for those. You acknowledge the feeling and then shift the energy to something higher. Like making your own marriage better.

Bishop: I actually prefer the term "sacrifice" because it's got some bite. Sacrifice means giving up something you hold dear *willingly.* Romans 8:18 says, "**I urge you, brothers, in view of God's mercy, to offer your bodies as *living* sacrifices, holy and pleasing to God.**" He calls this our "**spiritual act of worship**."

Sacrifice vs. boundary setting

Teri: Sacrifice has such negative connotations. For many of my friends who left traditional religion, a central issue is their sense that Christianity pressured them to sacrifice their own needs. Wives putting up with demanding husbands, mothers giving up careers for their children, adult children controlled by belittling parents.

Bishop: The Bible doesn't ask you to do any of that.

Teri: Well a lot of people grow up believing it does. Consciousness raising in the 70s helped many people break free of these traps. Assertiveness training taught us to draw lines between being in service to others and being a doormat. You can't deny the value of all that.

Bishop: That's fine. But you could have gotten those same benefits from the Bible in a more reliable way.

Teri: I have trouble believing that. Let's take an example: what about people who have alcoholic parents who have made their lives miserable, and now the aging parents need care?

Bishop: It's true we have an obligation to care for our parents. Scripture is clear on that. But we could subjectively decide in some circumstances that we could fill that obligation in another way, such as by paying for their care.

Teri: So you're saying the principle is prescribed, but not the specifics?

Bishop: That's it. In the specifics you're guided by the Holy Spirit.

Teri: My mom used to say, "We must love everyone, but some folks are best loved from a distance."

Bishop: That's true. But there are also plenty of times that genuine sacrifice *is* required. You can't just go off and play rock and roll while your kids need a roof over their heads. The term *sacrifice* implies that somebody wins while somebody else loses.

Teri: Aha, win-lose. Psychology tells us that every sacrifice has something in it for us, some payoff—even if it's just that we get to feel righteous. Acknowledging our motives to get those payoffs protects us from the victim attitude that tries to guilt-trip the one we sacrifice for. "They ruined my life and they never appreciated what I did for them."

Bishop: In genuine sacrifice, if your motive for sacrifice is love of God, you would never think that way.

Teri: Well how about this: I've also heard sacrifice defined as "to make sacred," to lift our thinking about something to a level that focuses on the love in the act.

Bishop: I like that, but I still like the word "sacrifice" better.

When personal growth isn't enough

Bishop: If psychology helps you know your motives so you can do the right thing, that's good. But if it gives you excuses to do whatever you feel like without regard to others, that's bad.

Teri: Psychology created the whole personal growth movement. It led me to seeing my good as tied to that of others.

Bishop: No. Personal growth is just focused on self. Spiritual growth focuses on what God wants, and that always includes the good of other people.

Teri: But when I'm fully aware of my connection to others, my good will be aligned with theirs.

Bishop: No. Most people don't see it that way.

Teri: That's what the whole assertiveness training thing was about in the 70s: finding win-win situations so I could align my good with something good for those around me.

Bishop: Lots of people learned those techniques just so they could *look* good. I saw that all the time when I was in the corporate world. People smooth as silk on the outside. They took every class in so-called "personal growth" skills, and all it did was make them more effective at getting their own way.

Teri: Well, I have to admit I have seen that syndrome. I used to teach a class in communication skills for women. We talked about the difference between *assertiveness*, which is win-win, and *aggressiveness,* which is only focused on getting your own way. One time I had two students react in opposite ways. One woman started to cry. She said she had been afraid that she'd have to give up her values to be successful. But now she was seeing that assertiveness could be part of her spiritual growth. I agreed with her. Then at the end of the day, another woman wrote on her evaluation that she was disappointed that the day wasn't focused on success. To her success meant getting her way at any cost.

Bishop: It's all about motivation.

Teri: We call it intention. And I believe people can get *drawn into* an intention to lead a win-win life via therapy or a personal growth program. It's a first step.

Bishop: That first step isn't going anywhere if the program doesn't seek to honor God.

Self-esteem from the inside out

Teri: I want to talk about another benefit of psychology: self-esteem. I hear you talking about humility and obedience, but not about self-esteem.

Bishop: Humility and obedience are part of self-esteem. Obedience just means lining up with the will of God, and humility is being willing to admit you don't know everything—having what we call "a teachable spirit."

Teri: I like that definition of humility. The Buddhists encourage us to keep a "beginners mind."

Bishop: But the only genuine source of self esteem is knowing you're a child of God, a king's kid, and then accepting and embracing what the king says about his kids: This whole world was created for you. And God loved you so much he was willing to die for you. Knowing that, you can't feel good about yourself if you're just looking out for yourself.

This conversation sent me back to the work of the father of the self-esteem movement, Nathaniel Branden. Branden says self-esteem comes from two sources: internal and external. Internal is what we do to create a good reputation with ourselves, how we live up to our values. External is the feedback we get from the world. Branden is appalled that much of the current work on self-esteem focuses only on external sources. In other words, he says, the current work ignores the inescapable need all of us have to measure ourselves against a standard—preferably our own standard.[44]

There it was again, the concept of a standard. The worldview Bishop Thomas was sharing with me took self-esteem from internal sources. "Do good things and remember that you did them." Many of my peers at the "green" pluralist level of Spiral Dynamics sought to provide people with self-esteem primarily from external sources. Interestingly, according to Branden, research shows that people are born with different levels of need for external validation. Some people can survive a horrendous childhood with self-esteem intact. Others with supportive parents continue to need validation throughout life. [45]

I began to take a fresh look at the therapy culture around me. Most of it did huge good. But some of it seemed to go too far in the direction of protecting individuals from outside threats to self-esteem without challenging them to build internal strengths. Within my own social circle I saw the following:

- A 30-year-old science professor tells his mother he won't be coming to visit her this year because his therapist says he needs to heal from his parents' divorce 20 years ago.
- A 50-year-old massage therapist tells her minister that she can't help out with community activities because she needs to put all her energy into healing wounds from childhood sexual abuse.
- A 50-year-old friend of mine tells me that her therapist has rejected my request to join one of their therapy sessions. I wanted to work out some tensions that have mounted between us as I supported her through a series of personal challenges the last several years. The therapist says my friend needs to break free of controlling influences like me.

These examples may represent extremes, or they may be well-deserved reactions in their particular circumstances. But they feel like contraction and protection rather than expansion to build better relationships. I could see how such examples could give some people a bad impression of "psychology" as being self-centered.

I talked to the massage therapist mentioned above. She is a friend and someone devoted to both spiritual and personal growth. "How would your life look different if your past didn't have so much power over you," I asked. Her answer was immediate. "I'd be more available to my community. I'd take more of a leadership role in helping others in my abuse survivors group, which I have begun doing. And I would help out at my local food bank, which I've been telling myself I want to do for years. In fact, I think I will call them tomorrow."

Ah, that's the ideal, I thought. Healing and strengthening ourselves while also being available to the world around us.

Is it a sin to feel guilty?

One of the repressed feelings that holds people back from their potential is guilt. My secular friends and my spiritual friends are in complete agreement that guilt is destructive. Most of them blame guilt on traditional religious teachings. How would Bishop Thomas respond to that?

Teri: Another accomplishment of the awareness that comes from psychology is to free us from guilt.

Bishop: No Christian should ever feel guilty. That's the whole point of accepting salvation. Jesus' death on the cross completely freed you from all sins past, present, and *future*. Fretting over sin and guilt just distracts you from God.

Teri: Well yeah, but guilt comes from comparing ourselves to some outside standard.

Bishop: No. If you've done something that you know is wrong, you naturally feel guilt and you want to confess. Confession just means acknowledging you've done something wrong.

Teri: "Missed the mark," as you've said.

Bishop: That's right. In fact it really is just agreeing with God about what he has said regarding how we should act. Wow, you might call it recognizing a higher thought, hey?

Teri: Hmm.

Bishop: And after you agree with God, then you repent, which is to turn away from that dysfunctional condition. From then on, there's no more point in feeling guilt.

Teri: I like those definitions. In New Thought we put a lot of effort into releasing guilt—without always noting the distinction you just made about first acknowledging that we have missed the mark.

Bishop: That's crucial. But hanging on to guilt and letting it eat at you is destructive. It shows a lack of faith that Jesus freed you from sin. In fact, if you let guilt eat you up, that's a sin.

It's a sin to feel too much guilt. I shook my head and groaned at the prospect of an endless loop: feeling guilty about feeling guilty. And then I realized that we in New Thought have our own version of this loop. We work hard to see and create the best outcome for everything. But when we forget to do that, we sometimes end up feeling bad about feeling bad. Rev. Noel Mcinnes made up a satirical song for us at Celebration Center. It built to the refrain:

I feel grateful, that I feel angry, that I'm ashamed, that I'm guilty.

Those of us in alternative religions could do some looping of our own.

Putting it together

Our dialogues on psychology clarified something I already knew: Both Christians and those in the alternative religions find ways of avoiding unpleasant realities. To keep ourselves on our chosen paths, hard-core Christians rely primarily on the "masculine" virtues of strength and will. Jesus saved you, so now you're on the honor system. There's no point in denying or hiding your weaknesses, everybody's a sinner, so quit worrying about it and get on with leading a constructive life. On the other hand, my peer group pioneered using the "feminine" virtue of surrender along with a form of non-judgment that says nothing is really wrong. Sometimes Christians go overboard with their strength into being bullies. And sometimes my peers and I go overboard with our non-judgment into being enablers or pushovers. Wouldn't it be wonderful if we could tap the best of each other's strengths?

26

Spiritual Practice, Spiritual Bypass

We can deceive ourselves into thinking we are developing spirituality when instead we are strengthening our egocentricity through spiritual techniques.
Trungpa Rinpoche, *Cutting Through Spiritual Materialism*

Be still, and know that I am God
Psalm 46:10

"Raising consciousness" is the goal in much of New Age and New Thought. Psychology is supposed to raise awareness of our inner states while meditation makes us aware of higher realities. My preconception was that orthodox Christianity gives meaning for this life but does not raise consciousness to higher spiritual realities. But a powerful sermon one day confirmed my sense that Bishop Thomas was tuned in to something *beyond*. To my surprise, he pointed to a source of guidance beyond the Bible.

Into the Holy of Holies

In the sermon, he talked about moving toward the "Holy of Holies." The Bible gives us an image of this in the temple's inner tabernacle, he said. Salvation through Jesus lets us move through the outer gate of the temple and into the courtyard where we stand washed clean. But standing in the courtyard, we are still guided by natural light, "Where we have to be proving stuff—we're still listening to people's opinions." From there, he said, we must move into the inner court where we are affected by the lamp stand, which is light from the Word in the Bible. Then we don't have to depend on other people; we can feed ourselves on the Word of God.

His voice started rising toward its trademark crescendo (audio excerpt at BishopandSeeker.com/audio.htm).

"I look over to my left and I see the altar of incense. And I can go to the Lord for myself. I can pray for myself. How many know that I've come closer? I've come out of natural light into Word light.

"But I still need to come a little closer.

"Because now I need to go beyond the veil, into the Holy of Holies, where the presence of the Lord really is. Where I don't need natural light; I don't need Word light; you don't have to explain anything to me. Now I'm in the presence of the living God where there is a fire and a smoke that cannot be explained.

"Come a little closer. Get in his presence. Where the presence of the Lord is, there's no need for explanation. Just believe what he says and *do it!*"

Bishop's words had gone from a roar to a hoarse whisper, and several in the audience were weeping. Then he warned that on this journey, we must avoid many sources of deception, especially self-deception, "fancy footwork" that sounds good but is hollow.

And what is the remedy for deception? He doesn't give the answer I expect—checking feelings against the Bible. The answer leaves a bit more room, and it puts a glowing smile on my face. He quotes John 10:4-5. "**My sheep hear my voice, and a stranger they will not follow.**" That sounded to me like knowing the truth for ourselves.

At our next meeting, I asked about this sermon.

Teri: I was very moved by that message. But tell me, how are Christians supposed to come to this place of just knowing they're in God's presence?

Bishop: It's a long process of developing a relationship with God. Because you've been in close touch with him over a long period, you come to a gut understanding. It's just an intuition; those who can rely on it the best are those who have moved through the stages of spiritual maturity. You're not in a good position to count on it until you've taken a mature walk. You have a history with God. You've not just read his Word, you've let it play itself out in your life. So you've seen how things go when you follow the Word, and you've seen what happens when you deviate from it.

At this point I felt we'd come full circle; in our first meeting he told me that feelings cannot be trusted but also that he trusted Andy and me because of a good feeling in his heart. Finally I understood the contradiction.

Meditation vs. contemplation

This conversation also let me see in a new light previous discussion we'd had about spiritual practice. We talked about that while he was trying to finish his dissertation for his Doctorate in Ministries along with his full schedule of pastoring and traveling as bishop to 12 other churches across Virginia.

Teri: So what's your dissertation topic?

Bishop: The churches I serve are mostly in rural areas. Regular church attendance is not as much of a habit there as in urban areas. So I'm calling it, "A Value Added Proposition." It's about what rural churches can do to add value to people's lives so they *want* to come to church.

Teri: My favorite philosopher Ken Wilber says religion has two jobs: translation and transformation. "Translation" means explaining this life: why we are here and how we should live. Whereas "transformation" means lifting our consciousness to be more in tune with ultimate reality—with God.

Bishop: Those two jobs are what I call the horizontal and vertical axes of the cross. And a good church has to do both.

Teri: Uh, yeah.

Bishop: And too many churches focus only on one or the other.

Teri: That's what some of my people say.

Bishop: So how do your people think we can bring our minds closer to God?

Teri: Well I told you about our five-step method of affirmative prayer in Religious Science. That always has a powerful and immediate impact on me. In addition, we stress the value of meditation for raising consciousness.

Bishop: We meditate. When I can get out to the golf course I meditate on the glory of God. I meditate on the scriptures every day. Lots of people in Bible-based churches don't really read the scriptures, or they read it all the way through, a chapter at a time. And that's good. But after that you've got to go back and meditate on individual passages. I especially do that if there's a passage that doesn't make sense to me. Or if I'm having a problem in my life and need an answer.

Teri: That's what we call "contemplation."

Bishop: So what do you mean by meditation?

Teri: There are various techniques. In some you clear your mind and just concentrate on your breathing. Or you might start with a question like, "Who am I?" But the main idea is to turn off all distractions and notice the natural sense of connection with all things. It's the *awareness of that connectio*n that opens a flow of knowing what to do next.

Bishop: But how do you know it's God you're listening to and not other spirits?

My stomach tightened at a question that seemed almost superstitious. In time, however, I would come to see wisdom in it.

Is it dangerous to still your mind?

Teri: Well first of all, as we've discussed, we don't think of any other voices as spirits outside us but rather as our own egos or shadows. But I think that boils down to the same thing, so your question is important to me.

The first part of the answer is that we're supposed to notice *all* the voices—notice all thoughts and then let them go. That sensitizes us to the fact that our minds are full of chatter—voices that say we're better than anyone else along with the voices that say we're not as good. If I were to use your terms, I'd say it's easier to fight the devil once you can recognize his voice. And when you finally turn off all that chatter it's like going to the desert and really hearing silence for the first time—only it's not just silence, its pure awareness. It feels like the presence of God.

Bishop: But how can you know for sure when you're hearing divine guidance if you don't have an outside standard to measure it by?

Identifying voices

Teri: I've been thinking about this. One answer is that we just know. I liked what you said about building certainty over a lifetime of practice.

I'd like to tell you a story. There was a period before Andy found Religious Science for us when a woman we knew was channeling—speaking on behalf of spirit entities. She said her guides had a message for me, that I was destined to be a leader and do much good. And she said I was supposed to receive the rest of the message via automatic writing—I was supposed to sit quietly with a pen in my hand and see what my hand was moved to write. I was highly skeptical, but I tried it.

And indeed, without my conscious control, I wrote out predictions of doing good works and instructions of people to avoid—friends of mine. The whole thing freaked me out, especially the warning part. How was I to judge whether this was something I should pay attention to? Who do you ask about something like this?

Bishop: You ask your pastor. I'd have told you to run like the wind.

Teri: Well I didn't have a pastor at the time. But a girlfriend of mine had been getting constructive advice from a woman who billed herself as an "intuitive counselor." So I figured seeing her would be like consulting with an expert. I made an appointment with this counselor. Her small office in a high-rise building was very peaceful, like a meditation room, painted in coral and white. And what she told me was exactly what I needed to hear.

After meditating quietly for 20 minutes, she said she couldn't say for sure if I was contacting spirits or just expressing a part of my subconscious. But, and this is the part I'll never forget, she said, "You know Teri, if they are spirits, that means they're just dead people. They're no smarter or more well-intentioned than they were when they were alive. And there's no reason to think they know any more now than they did when they were alive; you have the same access to divine wisdom they do. So why would you pay attention to them?"

It was such straightforward common sense; I practically slapped my forehead in recognition. And it immunized me permanently against any attraction to the occult. And then this counselor said something else that stayed with me. "Thoughts are vibrations in consciousness. And the way you can tell if a thought is coming from a high place or a low place is by the quality of its vibration. A thought from a high source makes you feel more loving and open. It lifts your sternum. A thought from a low source contains fear. Always go with the higher thought, and you'll be on the right road."

"Go with the higher thought," became my personal motto. And that prepared me for Religious Science and its emphasis on raising consciousness.

Bishop: Well that's a great story. Though of course you know what I think about where wisdom is found. Still I like what she said about fear. In fact, you could have gotten that same advice by just opening your Bible without paying a counselor.

Teri: What do you mean?

Bishop: (Turning to his laptop) 1 John 4:18 says, "**There is no fear in love. But perfect love drives out fear, because fear has to do with punishment. The one who fears is not made perfect in love.**"

Teri: You're kidding me. That's in the Bible?

Bishop: Sure is.

Teri: But that's my whole point. That's everything I've been trying to tell you.

Bishop: Well, I already knew that.

Teri: You're confusing me. I need time to think.

This was one of many times throughout our dialogues that I imagined myself as one of those pesky little cartoon characters. I circled the feet of Bishop Thomas, shadow boxing frenetically—left hook, right hook, karate kick—while he stood there in the middle, calmly munching an apple—and waiting for me to exhaust myself.

One body length at a time

The following week, we talked about meditation again.

Bishop: I still don't understand how you know you're hearing genuine divine guidance when you meditate or "raise consciousness."

Teri: Oh yes. The best answer I've found is that we never know for sure. Remember I mentioned Ram Dass, the psychologist-turned-spiritual teacher who helped bring Hinduism to the West? He says our ego is present in every decision, so we can only proceed "one body length at a time." He says the best we can do is set our intention to know the truth, study sacred works, meditate, and listen as clearly as we can. Then we take a step, fall flat on our faces, pull ourselves up, take another step, and fall again.[46]

Bishop: That sounds to me like the cycle of sin and repentance.

Teri: Hmm.

Being spiritual and being a jerk

Bishop: Well let me ask you this (he said this in a way that was absolutely genuine and interested): Do you find that people who meditate your way are better people? Because I know some people who meditate on the scriptures every day, and they have a special glow about them. I want to be around them; I want to be more like them. That should be the proof, shouldn't it?

Teri: Yes…(thinking). That's true for some of the meditators I know—especially the well-known teachers like Ram Dass or the Dalai Lama. And I think everyone I know who meditates a lot would say it makes him or her calmer, more at peace, more easily able to know what they should do next. Although some of them become so detached they don't do much in the world.

Bishop: We call that being so heavenly minded that you're no earthly good.

Teri: Yes, some people in alternative spirituality have begun to say that too. I just saw a piece in a Buddhist magazine asking why meditators haven't developed a compassionate strategy for helping to free Tibet. And the magazine *What is Enlightenment* has been saying that the traditional meditation practices were developed within the context of a spiritual discipline: Buddhist, Christian, Jewish, or Muslim for the Sufis. Taken out of context, the practices can lull Westerners into apathy.

Bishop: We have that problem in Christianity, too.

Teri: We call it "spiritual bypass" when you attain a high level of spiritual awareness but are still backward in other areas: physical, moral, psychological. So you can be attuned to the oneness of all life and still be a jerk, as Ken Wilber puts it. In fact, the thinking now is that meditation can hinder moral development if it's not tied to a set of moral teachings.[47]

Bishop: That makes sense.

Teri: When I'm tuned in to what you call "the glory of the kingdom," I can be less inclined to extend myself to my neighbor and more vulnerable to believing that everything would be blissful if it weren't for certain others—*those* religious people, *those* right wingers. They're the problem. Why can't they just respect everybody like I do?

The solution is to continue to develop the other sides of ourselves in addition to raising consciousness. Wilber's folks call it "integral" development.

Bishop: That's what's so great about the scriptures—all of that is in there. It's one-stop shopping. That's what I call integral.

After this discussion, I came to the humbling realization that another point Bishop had started us out with, the need for a standard, was proving to have validity both in my own experience and in the work of authorities I trusted. In fact, I suspect it was the Judeo-Christian standard I was raised with that caused me to balk when the pendulum in my peer group swung too far from the best of the values I learned as a child.

This is not to say that I was coming to see the Bible as the sole and ultimate authority, but that there was value in *an* authority. Progress in raising consciousness is important, but it is not a complete spiritual system if I am still messing up my own life or the lives of those around me. For that I need an objective yardstick. I found one in the universal stages of growth identified by developmental psychologists: the path from looking out for myself, to looking out for my tribe, to looking out for all people—the "world centric level"—and then perhaps beyond to what Wilber calls the "kosmic centric" level of looking out for all consciousness throughout the universe. This progression provides a general moral compass.

This core concept of ethics is found in the world's religious traditions as the golden rule, "Love thy neighbor as thyself." The Bible, for example, conveys the world centric level in a scripture Bishop mentioned often, "**There is neither Jew nor Greek, slave nor free, male nor female, for you are all one in Christ Jesus.**" (Gal. 3:28) Was there a parallel also to be made between serving the next higher level of all consciousness and serving "the kingdom of God," as my Christian friends so quaintly put it?

Not "just" a myth

The rich body of religious historical material is dismissed by many as simply myth. Regardless of the extent to which that charge may be true, religious historian Karen Armstrong warns against stripping our religions of anything smelling of myth. Most religions achieve intuitive insight by integrating myth with disciplines for mental focus, she says. And it is only in this context that the value of myth can be fully appreciated or tapped.

> Without a cult or mystical practice, the myths of religion would make no sense. They would remain abstract and seem incredible, in rather the same way as a musical score remains

> opaque to most of us and needs to be interpreted instrumentally before we can appreciate its beauty.[48]

And thus Armstrong cautions against the modern urge to nail down what is and is not myth. She calls myth:

> An ancient form of psychology… Bringing to light the obscure regions of the subconscious realm, which are not accessible to purely rational investigation, but which have a profound effect upon our experience and behavior. Because of the dearth of myth in our modern society, we have had to evolve the science of psychoanalysis to help us deal with our inner world.[49]

27

Expelled from Bible Study

Why do you doubt your senses?
"Because," said Scrooge, "a
little thing affects them. A slight
disorder of the stomach makes
them cheats. You may be an
undigested bit of beef, a blot
of mustard, a crumb of cheese,
a fragment of an underdone
potato. There's more of gravy
than of grave about you,
whatever you are!"
Charles Dickens, *A Christmas Carol*

The magnetism which all
original action exerts is
explained when we inquire the
reason of self-trust.
Who is the Trustee?
Ralph Waldo Emerson, *Self Reliance*

At a point late in our dialogues, Bishop Thomas announced one Sunday that he was going to start a new session at Wednesday night Bible study. "This is the advanced course. This is for those of you who are sick and tired of a superficial relationship with God and want to know him up close and personal. It will not be for the squeamish, so don't come if you're not prepared to move up to the next level."

I decided to go, even though my one other experience at Highview's Bible study had not gone so well. Shortly after I began meeting with Bishop Thomas,

Andy and I went to a Bible study to see what it was like. We were a little surprised at the setup: Pastor talked from the front of the church with Power Point slides in a relaxed, teacher-like mode—very different from his more priest-like mode on Sundays.

Asking God to show some ID

Andy and I were used to Celebration Center classes at which everyone sat in a circle and shared their personal experiences on a topic. In fact, at the Metaphysical Bible class I had taken back at Celebration Center, some nights we went a whole evening without quoting the Bible itself, just people's experience of it: something like, "I had a dream that my house was on fire, and this huge Bible was blocking me from getting out…"

But there were no personal stories at Highview's Bible study that first night I went, and only a few people asked questions. Despite my intention to keep a low profile, I couldn't help myself; I raised my hand. "Pastor, you just told us that Abraham was faithful because he was willing even to kill his own son when God asked him to. What I want to know is, how did Abraham *know* it was God who was asking him?"

A hushed alertness fell on the audience, as if Oliver Twist had asked the orphanage master for *more* porridge.

"Well, Teri, in those days, God spoke to the prophets audibly; they could actually hear him. But today we just know because we have studied God's Word so closely that we can recognize his voice in our hearts."

"I think if it had been me, I would have asked to see some ID."

The group laughed, and Bishop Thomas said, "Teri, what are you doing here? Haven't I given you Thursday night all to yourself? Isn't that enough?"

The group laughed again, and so did I, but I didn't come back to Bible study. And now, a year later, I figured it was time to try it again.

Second try

This time I knew everybody and exchanged hugs as folks arrived. We were in our spacious new location now in Fairfax, a building we bought from Fairfax Community Church. That predominantly White congregation had grown and moved to a beautiful new building: a park-like setting, sweeping modern lines, full multi-media setup, and even a coffee shop in the lobby. Their easygoing pastor, Rod Stafford, hit it off immediately with Bishop Thomas. On the week of the move, the two churches held a joint service, their rock band worship style making a curious blend with our high-energy gospel. Pastor Stafford joked about the surprise of learning that a Black church was first to bid on their building in this mostly White neighborhood. I sensed he was tempted to throw political correctness to the winds but checked himself, asking, "Guess who's coming…

(to Fairfax) to sing later?" The two congregations developed a bond, with Fairfax Community graciously playing big brother to Highview and inviting Bishop Thomas when they needed a guest speaker.

So now we sat in padded pews for Bible class and watched our Power Point slides from a built-in projection system in our new sanctuary. The title slide was already up when Bishop Thomas bounded into the room that Wednesday night. His mood was buoyant; he joked with people about bringing them presents from his recent trip to Africa. And then he spied me.

"Oh no, Teri's here. What are *you* doing here? Now I have to be on my Ps and Qs all evening." It was good-natured, and everybody laughed, including me. I promised myself I wouldn't ask any questions.

He began a high-energy presentation that mixed humor, inspiration, and embodied example. "One of the best proofs that the Bible is from God is right inside the text: '**There is a way that seems right to a man, but in the end it leads to death.**'"

Now you tell me, who else but God could get away with saying something like that? You tell me, if anybody else tried to say that, what would you call that person?"

"A prophet?" said a man in the front now.

"Actually, the word I was thinking of is 'prick,'" Bishop said. Then he imitated a man cussing under his breath, "Arrogant prick. Who do you think you are telling me what's right for me?"

The audience laughed nervously. He continued covering his bullet points about following the Bible rather than personal experience. "You can have dreams, schemes, visions, all kinds of stuff and not know where it's coming from," he said. "It might be from God or it might not. People call me, they say, (he imitates voice of a fuss-budget church lady) '*Paaastor*, I had a *dream* last night. My basement flooded and my little doggie couldn't get out. Does it *mean* something?'" Everybody laughed in recognition. "How do I know if it means something? Maybe it does, and maybe it doesn't. If you want real meaning, deep meaning, you meditate on a scripture you don't understand. Give it over to the Holy Spirit. He'll show you some meaning that will change your life and set you up for the bounties God has prepared for you.

"Do not rely on your own little private experience. What do I always tell you: 'If you don't stand for something'…" He paused to let the audience finish the sentence.

"You'll fall for anything," they called out.

I couldn't help myself; my hand went up.

"Oh no. What is it, Teri?"

"Pastor, you've been telling us not to rely on experience. But I've been sitting here looking at the title on every one of your slides, and I'm wondering how that fits in."

He turned around to look at his own slide projected on the front wall. In letters two feet high its title said,

EXPERIENCE GOD

For the first time that I can remember, he looked confused. But it lasted only a moment.

"Well, yes, experience God. And the way you experience God is through his Word, just as you would experience anyone else by being in conversation with him. And the more you engage him that way, the more you develop the spiritual muscle that lets you distinguish his voice in the Holy Spirit."

"Let me give you an example," he continued. "I was once driving home tired from a long day when I got the feeling I should stop to visit a friend in the hospital. So I made a U-turn, and when I got there I found my friend's son alone in the waiting room. He said his father was dying, and he was longing for someone to be there with them. So in that case, the feeling I got was the prompting of the Holy Spirit; and I knew that because it lined up the scriptures that call us to visit the sick."

I decided to hold my follow-up question to my private session with Bishop the next night.

One voice, two answers

Teri: Pastor, your example with the hospital was an easy one because everybody agrees it's a good thing to visit the sick. So I've been trying to think of examples that are not so obvious. And one is a time when I planned to visit a friend in the hospital, but my day got full and I was trying to get several other things done. I noticed that I *didn't* have a feeling that I needed to visit her that particular day, and so I didn't go to the hospital. And when I tried to call her that night, I found out she had been released from the hospital that morning. So in that case, wouldn't you say Spirit told me it was Okay to go against the scripture to visit the sick?

Bishop: Oh no. If you look closely at scripture, there are plenty of places it calls us to fulfill our responsibilities. So if you had other commitments you had to honor, not going to the hospital was perfectly in line with scripture.

Teri: So you're saying a message *to go* would be supported by scripture, and a message *not to go* would also be supported by scripture?

Bishop: That's right. It depends on the situation.

Discovering the new

Teri: Okay, I get how that could be. But shouldn't I also be able to get divine guidance to tell me something beyond what I already understand to be in the scripture? For example, in this case, suppose I just wanted an evening to myself. Couldn't I assume the lack of a feeling to go was a message from Spirit that I could safely *ignore* scriptural guidance to visit the sick in this case?

Bishop: You can do that. But you take a chance of being wrong.

Teri: Doesn't that way of looking at it discourage us from discovering anything new? You have said that our understanding of scripture should continually grow. So doesn't it make sense that Spirit would be our first alert to the need to grow?

Bishop: Well. If *all you have* is a feeling, you should go with that. But don't go running away with that with your rose colored glasses. Because people will take the tiniest opening and use it to justify every weakness and self-centeredness. Some people feel conflict with the Word, so they think the Word is wrong. When really, they're missing the invitation to dig deeper.

I liked that answer. At about this time, I saw the cartoon movie *Shrek*, and my image of myself with Bishop Thomas shifted. Now Bishop was the green giant Shrek, and I was the lovable but foolhardy Donkey—always getting us into trouble, but keeping life interesting. Funny though, I had a similar image about my relationship with God.

28

Prayer vs. Raising Consciousness

As soon as man is at one with God, he will not beg.
Ralph Waldo Emerson, *Self Reliance*

At this point, I no longer thought the way of my peers was "better" than orthodox Christianity. To reach the spiritual goals we all held in common, Bishop Thomas and his flock didn't need anything from New Thought—with one possible exception.

Bishop: The best way to "raise consciousness," as you say, is through prayer.

Teri: Ah. Well. This is something I've been waiting to talk about. I used to think we in New Thought had all these theological issues figured out much better than the traditional religions, but you are making me realize I was wrong; most everything we have an answer for is just a parallel concept with a different spin on it to something in traditional religion. But there's one thing we have in Religious Science that I think I could share as a gift here at Highview, and that's our technique of affirmative prayer.

Bishop: The Bible tells us everything we need to know about prayer. Jesus specifically taught us how to pray in Mathew 6:9, the model prayer that starts with recognition of divine authority, "*Our Father.*" And prayer is fleshed out in some related scriptures.

Teri: That may be, but I think Religious Science puts it together in a package that's especially powerful. We don't use prayer to ask for things, we use it to shift our own consciousness, to change our minds.

Bishop: We enjoy the best of both methods. For example Romans 12:2 tells us to **"be transformed by the renewing of our minds."**

Spiritual mind treatment

Teri: Yes, exactly, though, of course, we believe that our minds intermesh with the mind of God. That's why we call our prayer method "Spiritual Mind Treatment." We treat our minds in a spiritual way to affect conditions in our lives. The method has five steps.

Bishop: Well first of all, we've already discussed the fact that we are separate from God, so our minds can connect to his, but they don't "mesh." And second, I've spent years trying to get away from formulas for prayer; you can't put it in a box. 1 Thessalonians 5:17 (nkjv) tells us to **"pray without ceasing."** Prayer is about a living relationship with God moment-to-moment. It can't just be 911 "gimme" prayer when you want something.

Teri: I'm with you on that, absolutely. Unity, our sister church, has a song that goes, "Our thoughts are prayers, and we are always praying." So we have to be conscious of every thought. You can't be praying for health one moment and spend the rest of the day thinking, "I'll never recover."

Bishop: That would be showing a lack of faith.

Teri: Right. So when a condition in my life is causing discomfort, the solution begins in me changing my thinking about it, elevating my view of it to a higher level. And affirmative prayer helps me do that.

Bishop: You mean affirmations? That's what some of those prosperity preachers use.

Teri: What people call an affirmation is the middle step in our process, but we nest it in a spiritual context. Before we begin a treatment, we prepare by becoming clear on what we seek—a purpose statement for the prayer. Most people get stuck thinking about what they *don't* want; "Lord please don't let my boss yell at me again today." We work to turn that around to something affirmative like, "I have a constructive relationship with my boss." That shift can be very difficult for beginners. Our practitioners are trained to guide people through it.

Bishop: It would be better to just seek to know God's will for you in the situation.

Teri: That just seems so passive, like we have no responsibility.

Bishop: It's not passive to seek God's will.

Teri: I struggle with that idea. I found a beautiful answer from Ernest Holmes when Andy and I were planning our wedding and prayed for good weather. Holmes's suggested treatment says,

> "I have no fear of any kind of weather since I know that I am at one with all. I love clouds, the rain, and sunshine. I am one with heat and with cold. I love the heat of the desert and the dampness of the ocean. I feel physically complete and harmonious with every climate.... I know and feel my freedom. In this freedom I rejoice." [50]

Bishop: That sounds to me like a prayer of surrender.

Teri: Well, maybe it's an aggressive form of surrender. For me, treatments like that always work: either the weather improves, or I don't care. And we did have beautiful weather for our wedding.

Bishop: That makes some sense. But I still don't like steps. Prayer should be spontaneous and casual, like a child talking to his father. You don't use a technique to communicate with someone you love.

Teri: I do when things aren't flowing right. When you and I have a tough topic to cover, I think ahead about the right way to say things. In fact, I'd like to come back to this topic when I can bring Ed Preston with me. He's a licensed practitioner of Religious Science, and he can explain this better than I can.

Ed makes it easy

Ed did join us at our next meeting. We arrived with me carrying a copy of *USA Today* with a cover story reporting that a person's concept of God is the best predictor of that person's values and politics. Across the top of the page were four versions of an image of God's hand reaching toward the hand of man. The images were each named for a common attitude toward God—they proceeded across the page as A, B, C, D: "Authoritarian," "Benevolent," "Critical," and "Distant." The researchers had placed participants into the categories based on responses to survey questions. I was pretty sure that if Bishop had taken the survey, the researchers would have labeled his view of God as "Authoritarian."

Teri: Pastor, do me a favor. Take a look at the four images at the top of this page and tell me which one best represents your image of God.

(Bishop Thomas looked at the images for a moment, and then he looked at me quizzically before pointing to "Benevolent.")

Bishop: That's all you want me to do? Wait; I've been waiting for a moment like this.

He twirled around to his desk, reached over and slapped his palm on a big, red, "Easy" button, a recent promotion from an office supply store. "That was easy," said a recorded voice. Ed merely chuckled, but I rose from my seat for a fit of stomping laughter.

Teri: I knew it! Sorry, Pastor. I'm guessing the researchers might have placed you in a different category.

(Recovering myself and sitting down) So. Ed, so far I've told Bishop Thomas a little about spiritual mind treatment, but he's uncomfortable with the idea of steps in prayer. I'm hoping you can give us your perspective.

Ed: Let me put the steps on your flip chart, if I may. (He moved to a flip chart in Bishop's office and wrote out the steps.)

Steps of Treatment

1. *Recognition*—of God
2. *Connection*—with God*
3. *Realization*—that the conditions we desire are already available in consciousness
4. *Thanksgiving*—that it's already done
5. *Release*—letting go and being ready to receive

Ed: In the first two steps we recognize that God is right here, right now, and that we are connected to him. I like to compare that to the beginning of the *Our Father*. "**Our Father, who art it heaven, hallowed be thy name. Thy kingdom come, thy will be done, on earth as it is in heaven.**"

Bishop: That acknowledges that God is all-powerful and that we can partake of that power now on earth.

Ed: Right.

* The second step is actually "Unification" with God. As an interfaith chaplain, Ed used the version more appropriate to those who believe God is separate from creation.

Bishop: (Looking at the flip chart) Your "realization" step sounds like it comes from Mark 11:24, "**Whatever you ask for in prayer, believe that you have received it, and it will be yours.**"

Ed: Yes, exactly! We really focus on the part that says, "you *have* received it," not "you *will* receive it." So we express the condition we seek in the present tense. For example, "My boss and I treat each other with respect, and I enjoy contributing my best work."

Bishop: I've got trouble with that. That verse of Mark is taken out of context by all those prosperity preachers. It just sets people up for disappointment when they think God hasn't answered their prayer. They don't realize that God answers all prayers, but the answer can be "Yes," "No," or "Not now." We can't know what the best outcome of a situation is.

Dealing with blocks

Ed: Yes, and it's also possible that God has been saying "yes" all along, but we have been thinking "prayers" in conflict with the thing we are praying for overtly. When prayer doesn't seem to be working, we ask what has blocked us from being ready to receive. We may have to become a new person to receive a new condition.

Bishop: Yes, for example, a woman is looking for a good husband, but her life and finances are in disarray.

Ed: Or she still has resentments toward her father that are messing up every relationship. We seek to uncover those things that are blocking her from receiving.

Bishop: So at least we can lead people away from projecting their failures and blaming them on God.

Ed: Or on their partners.

Bishop: I would take it a step further and ask what is your motive for requesting something? James 4:3 addresses prayer that is inappropriate. "**When you ask, you do not receive, because you ask with wrong motives, that you may spend what you get on your pleasures.**"

Ed: When people come to us with a specific, materialistic request, we call that outlining—telling God exactly how to fulfill your request. That's okay for beginners, but practitioners often work with them to find out what's behind their desire. For example when a client says he or she wants a red sports car, I ask them to imagine having a red sports car. They may describe a sense of release, of the wind in their hair, of freedom. So I'll say, "Let's pray for those things instead." Once they recognize what experience they're seeking, they realize there are vastly more ways that God can bring those gifts. God is infinite and we are finite. So there's no way we can imagine the amazing ways he can answer prayer.

Bishop: Preach it Ed! Good stuff. I like all that, but I haven't heard you talk about repentance and forgiveness. Where do they fit in your prayer life?

Repentance is taking responsibility

Teri: There's some controversy about that in Religious Science.

Ed: What are you talking about?

Teri: The way I first understood it, we're supposed to look at our own role in creating a situation—take responsibility. You could consider that as repentance. But many people in New Thought say it's better to look only at the desired result of prayer, not at any aspect of the problem.

Ed: Well they're wrong.

Teri: I am coming to see this as one of the key things I became uncomfortable with in New Thought. We can be so concerned about creating guilt in ourselves or others that we avoid making distinctions that would compel us to act to change a situation. I know several people who have created rich, harmonious lives by focusing *exclusively* on desired conditions. But for me it feels like denial, like something is missing.

Ed: I'll tell you where that missing thing shows up—when treatment fails, as it often does for many people at Celebration Center. Then your only option for making progress is to look at ways you may be blocking your good. Often that means taking responsibility for how you contribute to a problem.

Teri: And when we do look at how we contribute to a problem, we often become aware of a need to release a judgment against someone else.

Bishop: Mark 11:25 (nkjv) says, "**And whenever you stand up to pray, if you have anything against anyone, forgive him.**"

Ed: Yes, that's it! And we go farther; we forgive ourselves, too. Often it's guilt that holds us back. "I failed the last six times; I don't deserve it," that kind of thing. If you go to a good therapist, he or she will help you uncover those feelings. We just build it into our prayer.

Bishop: Hmm.

Thanksgiving

Ed: Then after you've affirmed the condition you are seeking to create, there are two final steps: giving thanks and releasing.

Bishop: Your thanksgiving step is from Philippians 4:6 (nkjv). "**With thanksgiving let your requests be made known to God.**"

Ed: Yes, we express gratitude to know it is already done in the mind of God.

Release

Ed: Then the last step is release. Let it go and let God do it. We don't fret about it in the meantime.

Bishop: That sounds like Mark 4:26, "**This is what the kingdom of God is like. A man scatters seed on the ground. Night and day, whether he sleeps or gets up, the seed sprouts and grows, though he does not know how.**"

Ed: Yes, we're not supposed to be digging up the seed each day to see if it's growing yet. We've released it into what we call "the Law." We let it go and know that it is done. But it's about more than just releasing it to God, we're also releasing any doubts or habits that held us back from receiving it.

Bishop: That's it! That's the way we are taught to pray. The "*Our Father*" ends with the same idea, "For Thine is the kingdom and the power and the glory, forever and ever." When you know *that's* true, you turn everything over to him completely. Ed, I'm going to ask you to come preach for us some Sunday (we all laugh).

Teri: Then after we pray, we keep a sharp eye out for opportunities; "Treat and move your feet," we say.

Bishop: How about, "Say your prayer and do your share."

Teri: I like it!

The one-step

Bishop: I can see some value in all this, but I still don't like the fact that it's based in steps. That's too rigid and dogmatic. In an emergency we just say, "God I need your help now!"

Teri: Well, there's nothing magic about the steps; some versions use seven steps and some just use three. I even had a minister once, Rev. Rita McInnes, who said that in an emergency, you could just say, "Oh hell, all's well!" (Bishop puckers up his face but doesn't say anything.)

Teri: I know that sounds blasphemous. You have to translate it. In English, "Oh what the hell," is what someone says when they give up fighting something. It's another way of saying, "I surrender," but with an extra emotional charge to get you over the hump.

Bishop: I'll stick with my version on this one.

Knowing what to affirm

Bishop: As I said before, the best prayer seeks to learn God's will. There may be a purpose for a difficult situation, something that will benefit the "higher good" if you surrender to it. What we mean by "affirmative prayer" is that as you mature, you no longer make requests: you affirm what is.

Teri: That's one of my favorite paradoxes: "By the time we have the faith to move mountains, we know the mountains are already in their right place."

Bishop: Yes, for example, when I am praying for someone with cancer, I ask for healing. But when God chooses not to heal, I pray to know that we are in his will, that everything he brings us is for good, and that he knows best in all things.

Ed: (With a tear coming to his eye) Oh wow. That's my experience as a hospital chaplain. I agree with that 100%. I usually never agree with anything more than 99.9%, but I agree with that 100%.

Bishop: So tell me this. How do you know that the thing you're affirming in your prayers is in the will of God?

Ed: That's the purpose of the first two steps of treatment. If I remember God is right here right now, and I connect with him, once I have that feeling of being connected, I can trust what comes to me.

Bishop: So you base your trust solely on how you *feel* about your connection to God?

Ed: Yes. I'll give you an example. In New Thought, we don't encourage people to read works that are "channeled"—which means supposedly they are inspired by some kind of spirit. But a couple years ago I took a look at one of those books—I forget the name, Teri?

Teri: Seth?... Ramtha?

Ed: No, no. The one in three volumes.

Teri: Abraham?

Ed: No, no. The one that purports to be a retelling of the Bible.

Teri: *Course in Miracles.*

Ed: That's it. I read that several years ago when it was first popular, and I got nothing out of it. But then recently I decided to look at it after doing the first two steps of treatment. I remembered that God is present and I connected with him, then I opened the book. And I was amazed that it seemed completely different to me. In fact, I read it side-by-side with the Bible, and I found myself seeing the same message in the *Course* as I saw in the Bible.

Bishop: I'd be curious to borrow a copy of that someday. We don't deny that inspiration can come in different forms. But the Bible is the only absolute truth. It's the only thing you can trust 100% as the standard for testing everything else.

So I can see why your steps seem like a nice package for what you're trying to do, but only because they're based in the Bible. In fact, I sometimes get frustrated when I see some of these New Age gurus on TV promoting ideas that they've really just taken from the Bible and repackaged. I suppose it's just good business sense on their part. But if people understood the scriptures, they wouldn't need all that fancy packaging.

As we left, Ed and Bishop Thomas both said they'd be eager to meet again. Once Ed and I were outside the building, Ed told me he felt better than he had all week. He and I spent years working together on various committees at the Center, so I was not surprised that he shed a tear in this meeting. He's a cantankerous softie who can be scrapping about the budget one moment and crying the next moment if someone says something beautiful. But what he said next about Bishop Thomas took me completely aback.

"That man's energy reminds me of the Dalai Lama... with an edge."

29

Hawaiian Repentance and the Three Faces of God

In Christianity, God is not a static thing—not even a person—but a dynamic, pulsating activity, a life, almost a kind of drama. Almost, if you will not think me irreverent, a kind of dance. The union between the Father and Son is such a live concrete thing that this union itself is also a person... Each one of us has got to enter that pattern, take his place in that dance.
C. S. Lewis, *Mere Christianity*

Just a few weeks after this discussion on prayer, I was exposed to yet-another philosophy that gave a wild new twist to both "repentance" and the nature of God as personal or impersonal. It brought me one step closer to reconciling the contradictions that pulled me.

It was the latest thing among my New Thought brethren: a Hawaiian spiritual practice that seemed to be an ancient form of ancestral worship "updated" by a psychologist in a way that reflected both Christianity and Buddhism. I suspect Bishop would see it as one of those "New Age gurus repackaging ideas from the Bible," but it was the most intriguing mix I'd ever encountered.

Repenting for everything

Working with the criminally mentally ill at Hawaii State Hospital, Dr. Ihaleakala Hew Len claimed to have cut the average patient stay by *taking on his patient's sins and repenting for them.* He used an updated version of the ancient Hawaiian healing practice of Ho'oponopono. He never met with patients; he only sat in his office, occasionally observing them through his window onto the yard. He assumed that whatever was in them that provoked their crimes was also in him. So he repented of that thing in himself by saying continually to the Divine, "I'm sorry. Forgive me. I love you. Thank you." That's it, nothing more.

New Thought avoids the concept of repentance as negative, focusing instead on the new condition we want to create. Bishop Thomas recast repentance for me as turning away from a negative condition—plus agreeing that God is right about what serves us. Now I was encountering a man who repented for the sins of the world—and my New Thought friends were enthusiastic about his practice. Everything seemed to be turning around.

In fact, one of the "stars" of *The Secret,* Joe Vitale, became so enthused about Dr. Len's work, he coauthored a book with Dr. Len in which Vitale recanted some of his own previous teachings.

In *Zero Limits*, Vitale says, "Too many people, myself included, were visualizing and affirming in order to manipulate the world... You're better off letting go and letting the Divine operate *through* you... Miracles tend to happen. You live in a constant state of amazement, wonder, and gratitude."[51]

Consciousness in a chair

Andy and I had stopped going to the many seminars and workshops we still heard about through friends at the Celebration Center, but this one drew us. It was sponsored by a staff member of the Senator from Hawaii and held at a small hotel just off the grounds of the U.S. Capitol. Dr. Len wore a Hawaiian shirt tucked in to khaki pants and a baseball cap over his silver hair. With a kindly face but a no-nonsense manner, he told the 40 of us that in order to receive inspiration from the Divine, we must clear ourselves of "memories" and return to the void, the emptiness that is our touch-point with infinity, the mind of God. To do that, we should say, "I love You" silently in every waking moment. Just those three words—although those words were understood to include the thought, "I'm sorry for whatever memory (thought) I have formed that blocks the flow from You. Whatever it is, please transform it."

As in Religious Science, Dr. Len told us that our thoughts are 100% responsible for our experience of the world—which I now recognized as the "ascended" idea from Hinduism, Plato, and the Gnostics that the physical world is an illusion. He spoke from the extreme end of this idea, implying that intentional effort is unnecessary to solve any problem. We don't have to consciously extend ourselves because the Divine will move our steps in whatever direction is necessary. That part made me nervous.

But Dr. Len went further, in a way that suggested to me that he was onto something about how God could be both personal and impersonal. He read us a beautiful Hawaiian prayer about minds in continuum with rainbows. He said we could attune ourselves to our connections with every atom of creation to the point of communicating with inanimate objects. "Ask your chair how it feels about you sitting on it," he suggested. Was there some form of primitive consciousness in my chair? Religious Science says yes, the Mind of God is in everything. Dr. Len's claim fed my growing suspicion that there is something profound in the idea of a trinity—more than one aspect of God.

The Three Faces of God

It took Andy and me several days to figure out why we were disoriented by this odd but strangely appealing teaching. It seemed to pull everything together. It distilled all the religious practices we had ever encountered into just saying three little words: "I love You." It put "repentance" in an attractive new light by saving us from the burden of identifying *which* thoughts cause us trouble.

Furthermore, Dr. Len's approach seemed to honor God as both personal and impersonal—a force that worked automatically and one that I could communicate with. Did this point to there being something key in the Christian insistence on the Trinity: God as Father, Son, and Holy Spirit? Biologist Rupert Sheldrake called the Trinity "the unique contribution of Christianity." But some version of a trinity kept emerging everywhere I looked. The Buddhists saw it as Spirit, Form, and Ground of Being. Religious Science calls it Intelligence, Matter, and Law. And from Ken Wilber it was God as the three persons of the grammatical structure in all languages—first person, second person, third person: I, you, it.[52] He calls these the "Three Faces of God" saying each is important. I played with putting all these ideas together.

- *God as first person:* "I" co-create everything via my thoughts about it;
- *God as second person*: "You," beloved God beyond myself, do what I cannot do for myself—identify which thoughts cause my errors and transmute them into blessings;
- *God as third person*: "It," the presence of Divine life exists in every rainbow, waterfall, and chair.

We never followed up with the people in the Hawaiian seminar. But I was left intrigued that there might be a way for me to have all three kinds of relationship with God.

In *Zero Limits*, Dr. Len tells Joe Vitale not to worry about recanting his former books. "Your books are like stepping-stones. People are at various steps along the path. Your books speak to them where they are."

Part VI

Flesh

30
Gender Roles: What are We Really Talking about Here?

Four decades after the sexual revolution, nothing has worked out the way it was supposed to... most curious of all, that women would move from playing with Barbie to denouncing Barbie to remaking themselves as Barbie.
Maureen Dowd, *Are Men Necessary?*

From friends and the media I knew many horror stories of how traditional religion subjugates women. I was eager to hear Bishop's view of the relationships between the sexes.

A manly church

Highview has more men active in the congregation than the average church, partly because Bishop Thomas goes out of his way to set a masculine tone. "Lock and load today's message," he might say, "for tomorrow we fight." This came as a shock after 15 years at Celebration Center where language was either gender-neutral or tilted to the feminine: Mothers Day sermons usually acclaimed the feminine virtues, and Fathers Day sermons acclaimed men who integrated the feminine virtues.

My husband Andy and I could be role models for a postmodern marriage. We work in comparable jobs earning comparable salaries. We share housework and we make decisions together. When things get tense, we use communication techniques we've worked hard to learn.

We learned these techniques and the attitudes behind them from books and workshops such as John Gray's *Men are from Mars, Women are from Venus.*[53] In the wake of the sexual revolution, this body of work made it acceptable again to believe that men and women have different needs. Then, ex-Baptist preacher

Harville Hendrix took that lesson to a new level for us; his *Getting the Love You Want* showed how the differences between partners could serve as a map to personal and spiritual growth for each of them. For example, frequently one partner yearns for more closeness while the other yearns for more independence. When each gives the other some of what he or she wants, they both grow. They both become more whole.[54]

Early on I realized that these techniques and attitudes had potential to produce something that far exceeded the promised results of happier marriages. Their real benefit was in increased awareness, "higher consciousness." You had to let go of your narrow view of yourself and identify with someone else. It was a step toward universal consciousness, Christ consciousness.

Along the way, Andy and I learned that some of the "old ways" smoothed the waters in gender relations. In fact, we wrote a book together called *The Husband's Manual,* which suggests that couples find their own ways to honor their gender differences.

My husband learns how to have a submissive wife

So I was extremely curious what Andy would hear when he went to a men's revival at Highview on "Taking Leadership in Your Family." He came back reporting that there was nothing domineering about how men were encouraged to treat their wives. As evidence, he brought home a handout, *25 Ways to Spiritually Lead Your Wife* by Dennis Rainey. It included items like these.

- Pray daily with her.
- Discover her top three needs, and over the next 12 months go all out to meet them.
- Have a family time at least one night a week.
- Catch your kids doing something right.
- Inspect what you expect from your children.
- Ask your children for forgiveness when you fail them.
- Persevere and don't quit.

I went over the full list carefully several times, looking for evidence of male domination. I know some of my feminist sisters could find it. But I suspected most wives would be thrilled to have their husbands carry it out faithfully. It was time to talk to Pastor again.

Are men superior to women?

Teri: I am not a knee-jerk feminist; I believe some aspects of feminism go too far and have negative consequences. However, I personally have benefited hugely from the opening of roles for women. And if those roles weren't open, I'd probably be one of those women in earlier times who opted out, lived outside of town, and got burned at the stake as a witch or a heretic. So I want to find out if you'd be one of the people gathering the kindling.

Bishop: Okay, I got ya.

Teri: So I'm going to ask you straight out. Do you think men are superior to women?

Bishop: The Bible teaches no such thing. In fact here is what the Bible teaches: Galatians 3:28 (kjv), "**There is neither Jew nor Greek, slave nor free, male nor female, for you are all one in Christ Jesus.**"

Teri: Well that's cool. So what's up with this submissiveness thing?

Bishop: Every enterprise needs a leader, and God has ordained that a man be the leader of his family. Ephesians 5:22-24 tells us, "**Wives, submit to your husbands as to the Lord. For the husband is the head of the wife as Christ is the head of the church, his body, of which he is the Savior. Now as the church submits to Christ, so also wives should submit to their husbands in everything.**" People stop there and they don't read the next verse. "**Husbands, love your wives, just as Christ loved the church and gave himself up for her.**"

Do you realize how much love Christ had for the church, for the people? He gave his life for them. A man based in biblical principles should be willing to give his life to be sure his wife and family have everything they need.

Teri: That may be the ideal. But from everything I've read and heard from friends, it rarely worked out that way in traditional marriages. All I hear are horror stories of oppressed women who believed they had to keep silent no matter how bad their husbands acted. And for that matter, oppressed men, too, who felt they had to live up to the role of always being strong.

Unequally yoked

Bishop: First of all, that's a case of the squeaky wheel getting the grease. You don't hear so much about the successful marriages. And second, the failures are not the fault of biblical principles, but rather the failure of people to live up to them. If those husbands were going to Bible study every week, and applying biblical principles, they'd know what it takes to be a real man and the head of a successful family. And how much more successful are today's marriages without that discipline?

Teri: I think the statistics show that divorce rates have nearly doubled over the last 30 years, and marriage rates are still falling.[55]

Bishop: That's why it's important for a Christian to marry a committed Christian. 2 Corinthians 6:14 (nkjv) tells us not to be "**unequally yoked together with unbelievers.**" It's important to know that when things go wrong, you and your spouse will both be playing by the same rules.

Teri: But two people could be committed to the same values without being Christian—or even religious.

Bishop: Of course it doesn't guarantee success if both spouses are Christian. You may find someone who is not saved who may appear to offer everything you want. And there are plenty of professed Christians I wouldn't trust—being saved doesn't stop us from sinning. But because the scriptures are clear on this point, I would counsel saved people to go out of their way to find someone with the same values. Then when the chips are down and they come to me for counseling, I can point to a scripture that offers guidance and know they'll both respect it as an unbiased authority on the matter at hand. Otherwise, what handle do you have?

I do understand that marriages break up. But we want to give them every possible chance going in. You commit to following God's plan. And God's plan puts the man in the lead, not as a matter of value or worth but to promote function and order.

So what are we really talking about here?

Teri: I'm not denying there are inherent gender differences. But they can vary extremely from one couple to another. It seems to me that each couple has to work out for itself how to balance them.

Bishop: I have no problem with that.

Teri: So what are we really talking about here with the man being the head of the wife?

Bishop: Why don't you ask around some of the women?

Teri: I might do that.

The frying pan option for wives

Bishop: Look, I know that women are frequently more mature at the time of marriage than their husbands are. That's why I counsel patience and forgiveness for wives. I tell them, "I know he just blew the rent check on some crazy scheme. I know he let you down the last ten times. I know it sometimes seems he hasn't got sense to come in out of the rain. But how is he going to learn if you don't give him a chance and treat him with respect?"

But just between you and me, Teri, I'll tell you there are times in marriage counseling when I want to tell the woman to wait till that joker goes to sleep and wop him upside the head with a frying pan.

I laughed. This might be a fundamentalist perspective that a feminist could love.

I ride the women's bus to "Pantsland" and return with a pink T-shirt

For the first year at Highview, I had not attended any activities beyond Sunday service. But now I felt it was time to put my toe in and get to know people. The Women's Ministry held a monthly gathering at a member's home. I decided not only to go, but to take the church bus rather than driving alone. "In for a penny, in for a pound," as my grandfather used to say.

I was extremely impressed that this small church owned a bus, two actually. Highview uses the bus to pick up people for Sunday service, to take groups from the morning service to afternoon services at sister churches—sometimes an hour or more away, and for special events including a trip to Disneyland with a nearby revival. The transportation minister, Minister Pfizer, is a sweet man approaching retirement from the cleaning company he owns. He cheerily dropped us off and then waited outside for 3 hours till all the stragglers were accounted for.

On the ride over, I sat next to Martha, devoted mother of two small children who are both autistic. Her young husband has heart trouble and an arm damaged by a car accident. Martha is going to cooking school at night with a plan to sell pastries for a little extra income. One day at church she set aside two of her best creations for Andy and me: perfectly pear-shaped tarts enclosing candied pears.

On the bus that night she told me what was on her mind. "I'm worried about the influences my kids get on TV," she said. "Their favorite show used to be Teletubbies, and I thought that was safe. But then I heard how the homosexuals were implanting messages in that show. It's so hard to keep my kids safe."

Oh dear. Maybe I was making a mistake trying to get to know people. Martha didn't realize that I thought her concerns were groundless, prejudiced. But despite our different worldviews on this subject, I couldn't help but love this dear woman. So maybe there was no mistake.

For everything, there is a season

The meeting was at the home of one of the foundational families of the church. The Marinos have nine grown children plus many grandchildren, and Senior Deacon Marino is a carpenter and contractor who built the expansion on the original church and several expansions on his suburban home. The house has that wonderful, rambling, added-on quality that comes from growing as the family grows.

After cake and ice cream and opening prayer, the women separated into two groups: the single women moved to the front room to discuss chastity, and the married women stayed in the extended dining room to discuss keeping our husbands happy. I have traveled overseas and visited villages with language and customs much different from mine, but this was the most out-of-my-element I have ever felt. I felt as if I were glowing nuclear green, but no one paid particular attention to me.

The pastor's wife and another woman led off with a list of ways to please your husband. They were mostly the kinds of things that feminists had scoffed at or condemned as oppressive: looking nice when he comes home, having his dinner ready, showing interest in whatever he talks about. (The male side of this equation was covered in a recent sermon when Bishop Thomas got us laughing hysterically with this advice for men: "You can't just come home at night and say, 'Honey, it's right here and it's hot!' No. You got to call that woman up in the daytime. Say *real* sweet, 'I *love* my little chili pepper." Brothers, you got to set that thing up in the *daytime.* And whatever you say, it better be *real* and *meaningful.*")

As backdrop to our discussion, we heard bursts of laughter and dance music coming from the chastity discussion in the front room.

Of course the main item on the list of ways to please your man was by giving him the lead in decisions. A woman who was particularly competent and active in the church raised her hand. "It's really hard for me because I have more education and make more money than my husband," she said. "And with my first husband, I kept wearing the pants, and he always felt threatened; it was a total disaster. So in my new marriage I'm trying to remember not to take over. If his job is to pay the bills and he doesn't do it on time, I find myself slipping on that pants leg—saying something to him or doing the bills myself. So I say to myself, 'Whoa girl, you're slipping into pantsland. Don't do it. He'll never learn if I go behind him, and we'll both lose respect for each other. Stay away from pantsland.'"

One of the older women spoke up. "That's right as far as it goes. But don't feel you can't speak to your husband about these things. Just don't nag him when you do. Be constructive. First Peter tells us that if we are submissive to our husbands as Jesus was submissive on the cross, our good example will help others come to the Word. That means the best way to help your husband be more Christ like is for you to be more Christ like as an example. And today when it can take two incomes to run a family, it can also help to remember Ecclesiastes 3:1, "**There is a time for everything, and a season for every activity under heaven,**" she said. "In our early twenties is the time for a woman to have a career if she wants. Then you marry and devote yourself entirely to your family until your children are grown, and if you also have to work to support the family during those years, you're going to be working a double shift. Then finally when the children leave, you and your husband get to enjoy each other again."

Another young woman said, "It was really hard for me in our early years. My husband ran around a lot, drank too much. Some months we didn't have money for food, and if I got angry and yelled at him, he hit me. It's better now, but when I think back on those times, sometimes it's hard to show him the kind of respect I want to."

The older woman who had spoken earlier said, "I want to be clear, we are not talking about putting up with infidelity or physical abuse. Maybe some of you younger women would choose to put up with that, but I wouldn't stand for it."

Throughout this discussion, I felt like I was in a time warp to 1950. It was as if none of the psychological insights or feminist awakenings of the last half-century had happened. I was disoriented. But I couldn't say for sure that I disagreed with a single thing that had been said.

At the end of the evening, we were asked to buy T-shirts to support the women's ministry. They were pink with embroidery that said, "Hand picked for the harvest." I bought one and wear it regularly. The curious looks I get from friends are a perfect souvenir of the evening.

Tie goes to the man

To supplement the impressions I took from that evening with the Highview Women's Ministry, I asked a couple of fundamentalist women outside of Highview about their role as wives. Each one started by telling me that the man must be the head of the house, but then she had trouble answering my request for a specific example of what that meant. I heard that couples should talk things out, have an explicit family and financial plan that decisions can be measured against, etc. And when I asked if a woman should be silent no matter what foolish decision her husband was about to make, I was quoted scripture for good communication skills: Proverbs 25:11, "**A word spoken at the right time is like golden apples on a silver tray,**" and Colossians 4:6 "**Your speech**

should always be gracious, seasoned with salt, so that you may know how you should answer each person." (hcsb)

In fact, one woman seemed perturbed when I noted that her scripture-based advice sounded like common sense that a secular marriage counselor might offer. "It's not so common today," she said. "You've got feminists keeping separate bank accounts and taking the attitude that they don't have to consult with their husbands on anything."

"So give me an actual example of how the man should be the head of the house," I asked. And when she faltered, I suggested a case in which the man and woman each got good job offers in different cities. "Well, if you're based on God's Word, money won't be the deciding factor," she said. "You'll talk about the long-term good of your family."

"Okay," I replied, "So let's say that after talking all that out he wants to move and you want to stay. Would you say that in a deadlock, tie goes to the husband?"

"It should never come to a deadlock if you're honoring each other," she said.

"But if it does?"

"Well then, yes, a tie goes to the husband," she said.

These experiences caused me to rethink my assumption that the biblical approach was unaffected by the feminist movement. If I were asking the same questions in 1950, the answers would be different. There would likely be no acknowledgment of spouse abuse and infidelity. And there would have been no ready answers for women with careers who make more money or get job offers in different cities. Even in proclaiming submissiveness for women, the fundamentalists seemed to be taking for granted a level of equality. Could it be that the feminist pendulum, necessary as it was, had swung too far, and now both traditionalists and moderns were re-establishing the middle? Could it be that the two groups maintained their animosity from the early days of the feminist movement, even though their new positions were actually quite close?

Thou shalt not nag

A factor in my own marriage made me think the traditionalists were on to something. All my work on my communication skills had taught me to recognize a tendency to nag my husband. Sometimes it was very subtle, and sometimes it was via innocent comments that I could predict he would hear as nagging. And yet knowing this was a problem didn't seem to be enough for me to always stop myself.

I knew the skills. I knew that, "Are you going to put more salt in that soup?" is less effective than, "Would you be a dear and set aside some soup for me before you season it?" Just as I know that, "Did you tell him you'd have to charge him extra?" is less constructive than, "Were you content with the deal you negotiated?" And I know that silence is frequently my most appropriate response. Sometimes there simply is no right way to say "You need to get in the right lane if you're going to make that next exit."

So why did I find it required continuous effort to do it the way that I know works best? And wasn't this kind of negative, controlling, mother-like communication one of the greatest complaints men have always had about their wives? I briefly wondered if the devil made me do it. Psychology says it's "shadow" anger from some other unresolved conflict. But I realized that whether I called it devil or shadow, my response needed to be the same: continual *awareness*. Perhaps the awareness itself was the real prize; being married is just something that pushes us to acquire it. And perhaps staying alert to follow scripture has the same effect.

Marriage as a bicycle built for two

Our picture of gender roles rounded out when Andy and I went to a weekend couples retreat sponsored by Highview. One of the women who organized the event testified passionately from the front of the hotel meeting room where we gathered. "My marriage is a bicycle built for two," she said. "Wherever he's going, I'm going. If he goes off in the tall weeds, I'm going with him. The only time I get in front to steer is when he asks me to."

Bishop Thomas stood and said, "I want to caution the brothers. When you're steering this bicycle built-for-two, be sure you pull over frequently and rest in the shade with your wife so the two of you can share your ideas and plans and dreams. And be sure to listen to your wife, appreciate her wisdom. You don't want to be peddling down the highway full speed ahead while your wife is peddling behind you, crying her eyes out because she *knows* you made the wrong turn at the last exit."

Andy and I exchanged a smile. To me this sounded less like a return to the past and more like finding a new balance. Women have proven themselves in the boardroom, the academy, and the racecourse. There can be no turning back in knowing what we are capable of. Perhaps now we are truly free to choose what serves both us and our families.

A shifting midpoint?

In her book reviewing the state of gender differences, *Are Men Necessary*, left-leaning *New York Times* columnist Maureen Dowd catalogues changing attitudes. She quotes the *New Republic's* Ruth Franklin that some early feminists were "consumed by primary doubts about their own personhood: 'I want status, I want self-respect. I want people to think that what I'm doing is important.'"[56]

In contrast, Dowd cites current polls showing that the percentage of women who keep their own last names upon marriage continues to drop, and that 68%

of women polled would "ditch work if they could afford to." Dowd then quotes clinical psychologist and mother of three Daphne de Marneffe, who agues that it is in staying home and taking care of children that an identity is forged, not forsaken.

Dowd concludes, "You can make the case that women are not going backward. We're moving ahead, at home and at work—and in more elastic combinations of the two. We're just moving in less predictable and programmatic ways. We can be rescued or choose not to be. We can be alpha moms or beta career girls."

Of course, no matter how much the midpoint on women's roles may look the same for secularists and believers, it stems from a different source. The secular woman does what seems best for herself and her family. The woman pursuing spirituality, whether fundamentalist, New Age, or anything in between, does it to become closer to God.

Women in the church: thou shalt not be unruly

If Bishop Thomas was seeking a balance regarding women's roles in marriage, he was walking a tightrope regarding their roles in the church. He is somewhat unusual among fundamentalists in that he encourages women to become ministers if that is their calling. In a Sunday sermon he told us, "The scripture that advises women to be "**silent**" in church, 1 Corinthians 14:35, can be interpreted to mean women should not be unruly—not engage in disputations or correcting their husbands during the service." He told us that before Christianity, women were not allowed in the Jewish temple to worship because the pagan worship included sex orgies. But Jesus brought equality; women were permitted to worship equally for the first time. And so rules were needed to keep women or men from taking advantage of the new freedom.

This difference with other orthodox churches became apparent when a young woman minister returned from a mission to the Dominican Republic organized by another church. She reported one Sunday what it had been like. "Their church is all White, and I got to see how they do things differently," she said. "They're pretty conservative; they don't believe in women being ministers, so that was hard to get used to. And their music is more subdued than ours. I had a great experience, but I am glad to be *home*."

From what she said, I was glad to be home at Highview, too.

Keeping doctrine off the table

But while Bishop's interpretation says that women may be ministers, he draws a line that they should not be placed in positions of authority over men, and they should not be pastors. "There is no scriptural authority for women as pastors," he says.

So imagine his dilemma upon being elected Bishop in a network of independent churches, Praise Covenant Interdenominational Fellowship (PCIF).

As Bishop of Virginia, he became responsible for supporting a dozen churches, and most of the churches that applied to join PCIF were pastored by women.

"To make something like this work, you have to keep doctrine off the table," he said. "So isn't it interesting that the first new member churches under my watch are pastored by women? I'll have to pray for guidance on how to handle that."

31

The Bible vs. Free Love: Why We All Left Church?

On an episode of Oprah, teenage girls say they feel ashamed that they can't say no to sex. Counselor Dr. Robin Smith tells them, "You're trying to fill a hole in yourselves. But instead of filling it with something that will build your self-esteem, you're filling it with refuse from boys: they throw away their semen in you; they throw away their insecurities in you. They walk away all pumped up, and you walk away feeling like trash."
The audience applauds wildly.
Oprah says, "What we need, is a revolution."
Oprah, March 13, 2006

Teri: I came of age in the "free love" 70s when there was no outside reason not to have sex on a first date. It was a valuable experiment, an experiment that humanity needed to do. Although in my view, it pretty much failed. Despite all the talk of overcoming oppression and having honest, open, mature relationships, I think most of us learned that negative consequences are almost inevitable. If it's not disease or pregnancy, it's deceit and heartbreak. I had a girlfriend who killed herself at 35 when one guy too many dumped her. And then there are the social consequences of children raised by single parents.

Bishop: That's all because sex outside of marriage is displeasing to God. The term is fornication, and it's condemned numerous places in the Bible.

Teri: I'm not going to argue with you because I think it's plain for anyone willing to look that promiscuity mostly doesn't serve the highest good of all involved, which is my definition of sin or "missing the mark." However, that's not always true. Sex outside marriage can be harmless when the parties aren't lying to themselves or each other. And I defend my own right and the right of others to judge when to take that risk.

Bishop: Well then you'd have to face the consequences. And people's judgment regarding sex is notoriously bad.

Teri: That's true, but at least the consequences are usually not as bad as rushing to marry someone too young just to have sex—which is what I think people in prior generations often did. Then children suffer from parents who are poorly matched.

Bishop: Even in that case, if you follow God's will, he will make a way for you. And the flip side is that when you have too much sexual experience, it can get in the way when you finally do get married. That's why we insist upon premarital counseling for all members. In secular society, marriage is one of the few things that require licensing and no training. So we fill that gap.

Teri: Yes, okay, there may be something to that. You know, I'll be honest with you. I thought about this a lot as soon as I started coming to Highview and saw how much emphasis is placed on chastity. I was single until I was 36, so I had a lot of years to deal with dating. I'd like to think that if I had it to do over, I wouldn't let myself get into situations that were clearly inappropriate at the time–times when I slept with someone I didn't even like all that much because I was lonely or experimenting with freedom, or just too polite to say no. But there were also cases when I dated someone for months or years whom I really cared about. We were experimenting with making a life together. And frankly, even if I believed that it would be better to abstain from sex before marriage in all cases, I just can't imagine it being practical in today's lifestyle.

Bishop: Well that's what's wrong with today's lifestyle. As I've said before, Proverbs 14:12 says "**There is a way which seems right to a man, but in the end it leads to death.**" That doesn't have to mean physical death. Heartbreak is a kind of death.

Teri: But I'm talking about stuff like single people having their own apartments, having the resources to go out and travel, the media's image of sex as cool. Unless you brought back the whole oppressive social apparatus of chaperones and public shame, I don't believe it would be possible for single people to even attempt celibacy.

Bishop: Well, first of all, if people spent more time focused on their divine purpose they wouldn't have so much idle time on their hands. And as I've cited you before, Phillipians 4:13 (nkjv) "**I can do all things through Christ who strengthens me.**" God really does supply the strength and capacity to do what he commands. If you don't embrace that truth, he could just seem to be a cosmic killjoy. But on the contrary, the Bible says in 1Timothy 6:17 (kjv), "**Charge them that are rich in this world, that they be not high-minded, nor trust in uncertain riches, but in the living God, who giveth us richly all things to enjoy.**"

Teri: What I don't understand is why fundamentalists pay so much attention to sex compared to sins that always hurt someone else: theft, rape, murder. It's almost like you consider consensual sex to be worse than those acts.

Bishop: They're not worse, but they're a serious obstacle to your union with God. There's a parallel in sexual intercourse with the intimacy of worship. The priest goes alone into the Holy of Holies to meet with God. The exclusivity is key to it. Scripture suggests that each time you have sex with a person you become one with that person. So can you see the problem with that? 1 Corinthians 6:15 says, "**Do you not know that your bodies are members of Christ himself? Shall I then take the members of Christ and unite them with a prostitute? Never!**"

This discussion caused me to feel a need for reinforcements. I invited a woman from my Metaphysical Bible Class, Gail Renwick, to join my next discussion with Pastor Thomas. Gail is an open-hearted ray of sunshine who told us in class that as a child, she had a love for Jesus that she felt was stolen from her by her strict religious upbringing. I also invited Laurie Bolster, the friend from Celebration Center who had caused Bishop Thomas to say, "Wicked and evil isn't that bad."

It's in there!

To our amazement, Gail came out like a tiger in our meeting. Laurie and I laughed, whooped, or put our hands over our faces and tried to get an occasional point in edgewise while Gail and Pastor Thomas alternately stood, stomped, got down on their knees to scoot over in each other's faces, and *testified*. Our one-hour appointment grew to 2.5 hours.

Gail started off slowly enough telling how her upbringing in a Christian church left her hungering for a broader view of God. So she sought out spiritual books, and she said that when she found *Science of Mind*, the primary text of Religious Science, she cried and kissed the book.

Pastor Thomas impressed me afresh by taking out a pen and asking Gail what she found in the text that made her want to kiss it. Then he took notes as she listed the things she learned: that she was completely responsible for the outcomes in her life, and that she could rely directly on divine guidance as her heart came into alignment with the All that is God.

Gail said one of the primary things that drove her away from her first church was being made to feel ashamed of her sexual attractions. She said she was attracted to a man in her congregation who was engaged. Laurie and I got a bit nervous as Gail's story became more explicit. "I used to sit in church and long for him," she said. "I could imagine putting my hands all over his body."

"Uh, Gail. Why don't you tell Pastor Thomas more about the book?" I suggested.

Gail returned to listing ways that Christianity made her feel restricted, becoming more animated and forceful with each remembered incident. And for each point she made, Pastor Thomas countered that she had been exposed to an "erroneous teaching" of the Bible. He said that for each restorative idea for which she had "spent all that money on all those other books," that he could show her the same positive interpretation in scripture. "It's in there, it's in there," he said.

"Well then, you are only proving my point that the truth is available from many sources," Gail countered.

"Ah yes, but the Bible is the only source you can count on for the whole truth and nothing but the truth."

We ended on that standoff. As we got up to leave, Pastor suggested that Gail could become even more connected to God by reading the Bible for herself, and she replied by asking if he'd be willing to read *Science of Mind*. He said he'd be glad to because it might give him some sermon ideas. So she offered to write up a little summary for him to save him from reading the whole book.

So far, she hasn't finalized that project. But then, Religious Science is notoriously difficult to summarize.

Is this why everybody left the church?

After that evening with Gail, I wondered how many people had left the church of their upbringing because of issues around sex. Historically, sexual passion was one of the first themes that challenged the rationalism of the early Enlightenment. Rousseau kicked off the romantic period in the 1700s with themes of the struggle of the individual against social norms, the value of emotions, and the goodness of human nature. But it was his glorifying of sexual love in *Julie and the New Heloise* that first brought wide public attention to the Romantic Movement. We hadn't freed ourselves from the dictates of the medieval church for a life guided by reason alone, we wanted unfettered emotion as well. (Some would say this is where the real trouble started). Certainly in my own case, it was unwillingness to list sex as a sin in the confessional that finally drove me away from Catholicism. For how many others was this the defining issue? *This is the 21st century, and we want sex.*

Through much of my Highview experience, I had felt like I had one foot on the dock of modernity and one foot on the boat to *somewhere else*. One Sunday, the issue of sex came together with many of the other issues I had been pondering. The boat pulled away; I fell in the water; and I was forced to choose which way to swim.

Tested: what if it were the bishop's own family?

It was at a Sunday service a year after I joined Highview, and the atmosphere around the altar call seemed especially intense. Altar calls normally happen in two parts: first a call for anyone who wants to accept Jesus as Savior and then a call for anyone already saved who wants a renewed connection and prayer support.

The speaker, Minister Pfizer, had done a clever riff on the topic, "Being sure your buts are in the right place." He said our "buts" were in the wrong place if we said, "Yes God, I want to do your will, but…" Lots of laughter and high-fiving among the audience about double entendres on "butts."

When Pfizer was done speaking, Bishop Thomas took over to do the altar call. "We all know 'but' is a conjunction," he said, "And whenever you hear a conjunction, the second part is usually more important than the first part. For example, if someone says, 'You're a nice person but...' it's the second half of that sentence you better pay attention to. And God is like that; he doesn't care about anything that's gone before, he only cares where you're at now. So if there's anyone who'd like to get their conjunctions straightened out, come up here now."

Only a handful of people came up, and Bishop began to call people by name. "Come up here Brother so-and-so." Softly the choir sang a tune from Bishop TD Jakes' "Hemotion" CD.

It doesn't matter where you've been
It doesn't matter what you've done…
And it's because of what he's done...you can start all over again.

One man who came up to the altar had just learned that his brain tumor had recurred. Bishop had the man's wife place her hand on her husband's head while the rest of us prayed for him. Tears ran down the wife's face. People gathered around to embrace them both.

"It doesn't matter where you've been..."

Then Bishop called another brother to come up to the front. "He has taken a serious fall from righteousness. Some of you know about it, and the rest of you don't need to. We pray for him and we pray for his wife as he moves forward into reconciliation with God. He was a deacon; we're going to put him back as a deacon-in-training as he strengthens himself. We love him and we are with him."

"It doesn't matter what you've done..."

And then Bishop called his 19 year-old daughter to come up.

"It's time. I've been waiting till Spirit told me it was right. Come up here Bernadette." His beautiful daughter came up with tears on her face, looked him in the eye, and then buried her face in his chest as he put his arm around her.

"Some of you already know," he said. "I know there's been plenty of whispers. It's time to come out with it. She is pregnant. She has sinned and there's no excusing it. Not hormones or a society with no support for virtue can excuse it. But God is willing to forgive her, and I expect all of you to do the same. She's still going to have to face the consequences. My wife and I aren't going to raise grandchildren. But we love her, and we stand by her. She won't be standing up here in the choir while she's pregnant. That's just not right. But as soon as the baby has come, she will take her place again, and I expect all of you to love her and support her."

"You can start all over again."

The altar call broke up with lots of tears, hugging, and exchange of phone numbers from those offering support to each individual who had been prayed over. Bishop chose an upbeat song to close with, one of the congregation's favorites. And the tone shifted to jubilant.

Patriarchy reconsidered

I was stunned in more ways than I could name. Had I just participated in something that was manipulative, patriarchal, and abusive? Or authentic, courageous, and restorative?

I have an undergraduate degree from U.C. Berkeley in Communications that included propaganda studies. I recognize lighting, voice tones, and hypnotic music as means of inducing a receptive state. Back in my days taking intensive personal growth workshops, I gave silent and grateful assent to use of those techniques because they made possible a priceless expansion in my perspective. But occasionally, 24 hours after such an episode, I felt manipulated and changed my mind about whatever I'd been convinced of at the time—usually a method for bringing in more recruits. I came to realize that I could count on my ability to see clearly 24 hours following such an intensive session.

On this day, my heart filled to overflowing with a sense that something here was right. In fact, more than right, perfect—authentic, loving, an ideal way to do community. Looking at it within its own frame of reference, I saw first that Pastor Thomas had not flinched from applying the same standard in his own family as he applied elsewhere, despite the potential for public embarrassment to himself: No sending the daughter quietly away or making up a story of blame and excuses.

And second I saw members of the congregation willing to be held accountable publicly for living up to their stated intentions. Hadn't I appreciated the same opportunity during the period of my "transformation" in personal growth groups? I had departed those groups because my values were not identical to theirs—just as my values now were not identical with those of Highview; if I were unmarried, I would not necessarily intend to be celibate. But could I imagine subjecting myself to public accountability for something I did value, like speaking only kind words of others? Hadn't I longed for more willingness to confront difficult issues directly in my previous congregation? And what if the "sin" involved had been spouse abuse or theft within the congregation? Wouldn't it be good to have a forum for settling disputes that was wholly voluntary before somebody had to call outside authorities?

Intellectually, I knew this exercise in public accountability flew in the face of much of the 20th century. But 24 hours later my awed feeling about it hadn't changed. In fact, one important element became clearer. The event had been conducted with extraordinary finesse and integrity. Both the goal and the result, as far as I could see, were reconciliation and restoration. It felt like a perfect balance between promoting the good of the group while still honoring the dignity of the individual.

The catch, of course, was that this particular public reconciliation had been directed by someone of extraordinary wisdom and integrity. For each leader like him, there may be a thousand others of lesser skill, maturity, or character in whose hands such a scene would be a disaster, something that would create shame, fear, and resentment—exactly the feelings that had driven so many of my generation away from church. This form of reconciliation was a high wire act, with no room for missteps. And furthermore, I was participating in this event as a mature person fully at choice about walking out. What effect might this have on children who had seen less of the world or on those whose upbringing in a church never gave them a true opportunity to choose it?

As I weighed whether I could give my full blessing, the voice in my head that got the last word was the slightly taunting one from my days in Religious Science. "Remember, you get to choose. And whatever you choose is how it will be for you."

I might never buy the whole package of this intensive form of Christianity that I was being allowed to witness from the inside. But I could see the beauty and value in it, and I was ashamed of judgments I had made based on other people's opinions of it. There was an unsullied idealism here that went beyond the stereotype of fundamentalism. The stereotype tells us that the lures of fundamentalism are structure, certainty, and predictability—and those factors were certainly present here. But the larger lure I saw here was love: mature and responsible. Truth, Beauty, and Goodness had been rejoined.

I swam away from the dock of postmodernism and toward the boat of who-knows-what's next, tugging my "buts" behind me.

One year later

Of course, in a philosopher's definition, a situation doesn't have "Goodness" unless it's agreeable to all parties.* I got some evidence on the goodness of this situation a year later.

The Bishop's daughter moved in with her parents, despite what he had said about how she'd have to support herself. The Bishop's wife eagerly took to her new role as grandmother, beamingly carrying the baby girl to Sunday service in the cutest little dresses. One day we were at a housewarming party for another family in the congregation. I overheard the baby's grandmother talk about how much Bishop Thomas loved the new baby.

"All of us women make sure the baby is fed and dry. But then sometimes we let her cry. He can't stand it; he'll pick that baby up, walk her around and talk to her. We all say, 'It's okay if she cries a little.' But he can't stand to see a child unhappy."

A few months after that, the baby's mother testified at a celebration honoring the ten year anniversary of Bishop Thomas as pastor of Highview. "Sometimes people ask me why I'm still not married," she told the crowd. "I tell them it's because I'm still looking for someone who's as good a man as my father."

---

* Here's a whole other book crammed into a footnote. Ken Wilber defines Beauty, Goodness, and Truth as the full possible range of experience from the first, second, and third person perspectives. "I" alone measure beauty, "you" and I together measure the goodness of our voluntary interactions, and "they" as neutral outside parties measure scientific truth.

32

Homosexuality Revisited

You can love all humanity,
but you can't hang out with six
billion people.
DJ Chris Stevens on *Northern Exposure*

Over the year that Bishop Thomas and I were meeting regularly, we came back again and again to the topic of homosexuality. Sometimes it felt like we were making progress toward understanding each other; other times we moved backward, and the frustration on both sides was palpable. We came to appreciate that the topic carries so much emotion because it encapsulates competing perspectives on the purpose of life. And this difference spills over and fuels much of the conflict worldwide between those who take their holy books literally and those who do not.

Avoiding pointless strategies

To keep us focused, I conceded immediately that promiscuous behavior usually has negative consequences for self and others whether the sex is straight or gay. I knew I would have my hands full just focusing on gay couples in a monogamous, committed relationship.

I also realized early on that it's irrelevant to argue about anything in the Old Testament. My offbeat guide Peter McWilliams argues in *Nobody's Business* that most Old Testament references to homosexuality are to homosexual rape, prostitution, or orgies. Most notably in the story of Sodom and Gomorrah, a good argument can be made that it is the inhospitality to strangers that the city is punished for, not the homosexual act itself. But defenders of homosexuality waste a lot of breath with this line of argument; Bishop made it clear early on that most fundamentalists conclude that the Old Testament is not intended as a source of doctrine for today. "It sets the context or story line of the entire Bible, and it is a source of promises and examples," he said. "But its covenant of laws is fulfilled and replaced by the law of love and reign of grace in the New

Testament." So for those seeking to defend homosexuality via the Bible, the critical passages are in the New Testament.

Looking just at the New Testament, it is certainly worth noting that Jesus never mentions homosexuality. The closest he came is a single reference to "sexual immorality" that is recorded in both Matthew 15:19 and Mark 7:21-22.* In fact, some postmodern and feminist theologians argue that the essential message of Jesus was one of liberation for oppressed groups such as women, slaves, the poor, and homosexuals. They find this expressed in Luke 4:18 (hcsb), **"He has sent me to proclaim freedom to the captives and recovery of sight to the blind, to set free the oppressed."** [57] Fundamentalists counter that being homosexual does not confer "oppressed" status because it depends on a set of *behaviors* that are chosen.

So the core of the biblical argument against homosexuality comes not from the Old Testament, nor from Jesus, but from the letters of Paul in the New Testament. It does no good to argue that Paul was homophobic and misogynistic—or simply a reflection of his time. Not only is this irrelevant to someone who takes the Bible as the literal Word of God, but also Paul says so much else that is extraordinarily wise and compassionate, that his overall character appears soundly within the Christian ethic.

The solution is elsewhere

No. These arguments sometimes appeal to fundamentalists and evangelicals who have positive relationships with gay people in their own lives. But much of the world is moving in the opposite direction, with more people—Christians, Muslim, Jews, and even Hindus—drawn to literal interpretations of their holy books that leave no loopholes for homosexuality. If we seek to ease the tension around this cultural conflict, the solution lies elsewhere. But before I became convinced there was a better route to take, Bishop and I had to work our way through all the basic arguments.

All the basic arguments: biblical loopholes

Teri: How can fundamentalists place so much emphasis on homosexuality when Jesus never even mentioned it?

Bishop: You can't just read the red letters (words of Jesus). Remember that the entire Bible is the inspired Word of God. In particular, Romans 1:24-31 places homosexuality in a context as being both a cause and a result of God's disfavor. Let me read you the entire passage. Paul is describing people who are ungrateful to God:

---

* Peter McWilliams points out that both these references by Jesus use the Greek term *porneia* defined in *Strong's Hebrew-Greek Dictionary* as "harlotry (including adultery and incest); idolatry:—fornication."

> **"Therefore God gave them over in the sinful desires of their hearts to sexual impurity for the degrading of their bodies with one another. They exchanged the truth of God for a lie, and worshiped and served created things rather than the Creator—who is forever praised. Amen. Because of this, God gave them over to shameful lusts. Even their women exchanged natural relations for unnatural ones. In the same way the men also abandoned natural relations with women and were inflamed with lust for one another. Men committed indecent acts with other men, and received in themselves the due penalty for their perversion. Furthermore, since they did not think it worthwhile to retain the knowledge of God, he gave them over to a depraved mind, to do what ought not to be done. They have become filled with every kind of wickedness, evil, greed and depravity. They are full of envy, murder, strife, deceit and malice. They are gossips, slanderers, God-haters, insolent, arrogant and boastful; they invent ways of doing evil; they disobey their parents; they are senseless, faithless, heartless, ruthless. Although they know God's righteous decree that those who do such things deserve death, they not only continue to do these very things but also approve of those who practice them."**

Teri: I've got lots of problems with that passage. First of all, it lumps together all kinds of evil. If homosexuality came packaged with those behaviors, I'd have no trouble with Christians emphasizing it. But the only trait homosexuality frequently comes packaged with is good taste in draperies. The homosexuals I know lead lives that are otherwise just like everybody else's.

Bishop: Nevertheless, the homosexual act itself is clearly displeasing to God.

Teri: And how about the "deserve death" part. Does that mean anyone who's "disobedient to parents" deserves to die too?

Bishop: Of course not. This passage is a cumulative list of acts by those who have utterly thumbed their noses at God, their fellow humans, and all that is good. A homosexual who dies unsaved will not go to heaven, just like any other unsaved person. But that doesn't necessarily mean he or she fits in this list.

Teri: Okay, here's my best shot at a biblical argument. It really sounds to me like Paul is talking about heterosexuals who engage in homosexuality for thrills because their lives are empty. For them, homosexuality would be unnatural and not serve their highest good. But people who are born homosexual never "exchanged" natural sexual intercourse for something else. So it sounds to me like they're not covered by this passage—if you want to be literal about it.

Bishop: You may have a point there. But the Bible always considers any act of homosexuality as unnatural in any scenario. There are plenty of references in the Old Testament that make it clear that homosexuality is displeasing to God, period.

Teri: But I thought you said the Old Testament rules no longer apply.

Bishop: We no longer have to follow the rules that were based on cultural circumstances at the time. But this is not one of those situations. The Old Testament makes it clear that all homosexual acts are displeasing to God.

Scapegoating

Teri Okay. Let's just assume for a moment that homosexuality "misses the mark" and is always sin. All the attention that Christians place on condemning it sure looks like scapegoating since it's the one temptation the majority don't have to contend with. It looks like a blatant attempt to distract attention from their own shortcomings.

Bishop: Anyone who stays close to the Word won't focus on someone else's sin. Homosexuality is just one sin among many that I preach about—though there are some reasons it's an important case.

Teri: How can you say that when other sins that the majority *is* tempted to commit cause so much harm? Like extramarital affairs: look at the harm they cause to the family, yet they don't get anywhere near as much attention from Christians.

Bishop: They do in my ministry. But the difference is that people who have sex outside of marriage pretty much know they're wrong. Many homosexuals, however, claim there's nothing wrong with their lifestyle.

Changing what you're born with

Teri: You do realize that homosexuality is something you're born with; it's in your DNA.

Bishop: That may be true. But that doesn't mean you can't change it. Prayer can change anything.

Teri: I believe that. But there are plenty of things people pray for and don't get. Plus, why should a gay person want to change?

Bishop: Because it displeases God. And when you're saved, you want to do everything you can to please him. Not to please me; it's God that's out to do the changing, not me.

This was a juicy hint of something to come I didn't pick up on at the time.

Who determines the highest good?

Teri: So why would homosexuality displease God, since it's a condition he created in people?

Bishop: I never said he created it. If anything he allows it. There are many conditions we are born with that we need to overcome. Pedophilia, for example, is supposed to be something you're born with, and that doesn't make it any less wrong.

Teri: But pedophilia has victims. It hurts people. Consensual sex among adults does not.

Bishop: That's equally true for consensual sex among single heterosexuals, but God calls it fornication and condemns it as sin. It's wrong if God says it's wrong. He's sovereign. The nature of man and sin is that sin distorts Gods original plan for man. That's why the redemptive plan of God is so significant and unique.

Teri: Isn't God's will always in our highest and best interest?

Bishop: Yes. God is not a cosmic killjoy; he wants what's best for us. And he knows what's best for us, even if we don't agree.

Teri: Okay, so, I am friends with several gay couples. In every case, their relationships benefit themselves, their families, and their communities. They shoulder all the responsibilities of a committed relationship: they care for children or elderly parents; they support each other in being better people. Without their partnerships they would be less happy and less effective members of society. How could God possibly want that stopped? Where is the harm?

Bishop: We aren't always wise enough to see what's in our best interest, and we certainly can't see the big picture of God's plan for us.

Teri: I admit that is often true. That's why I've come to see that it's not enough for me to hold an intention to serve the highest good. I have to hold myself open to divine guidance about what that is, and I have to be rigorous about what qualifies as divine guidance. You've really helped me clarify my thinking about the need to compare what feels right against the time-tested wisdom in the Bible—and other traditional sources. But if the Bible says the sky is pink, and everyone can see the sky is blue, something's wrong with the interpretation.

Bishop: I would agree with that statement. However, if we follow the course of life based on what seems right in our own eyes alone, our end would be as Solomon predicts in Proverbs 14:12. "**There is a way that seems right to a man, but in the end it leads to death.**" We can't know what good God might have had in store for those couples you're describing if they resisted those relationships. I have faith that he would make a way for them.

Look at the example of Abraham and Sarah in Genesis. God promised them they would have a son who would bring forth a great nation. But when Abraham got old, Sarah got impatient and told Abraham to father a son with her maidservant. That union produced Ishmael, and Ishmael fathered the line of nations that produced Mohammed. So when Sarah finally did give birth to Isaac, the rivalry between Isaac and Ishmael caused tragedy all down through to the present day rivalry with Muslims.

Teri: Hmm. Okay. That story helps me see how faith could lead you to avoid an action that appears to be in your best interest. I can even say that I would take the same stance as you if I believed that the Bible is inerrant about the highest good of all. But can you at least see my point that to all human appearances, these committed gay relationships I'm describing benefit the individuals, their families, and their communities?

Bishop: Not at all, there are lots of negative consequences to those relationships. For example, there are… health consequences.

Teri: You mean AIDS. There's no more risk of AIDS for a monogamous gay couple than for a straight couple.

Bishop: Not just AIDS. What they do. (He dropped his voice a bit.) Using body parts in ways they weren't intended. That can't help but have consequences.

Teri: (I blushed, and this threw me for a moment.) Uh, well, I understand there are things in the Bible that relate to health information that wasn't known at the time. But once we have knowledge about those things we can take appropriate measures. Then it becomes a health question, not a spiritual one.

Bishop: But the real point is that it's the will of God that sex is reserved for married men and women. Marriage is the most important institution God gave us. It's the foundation of a stable society.

Teri: I completely agree. But that argument drives my friends and me crazy because it seems so irrelevant. Homosexuality is not contagious, right, we've agreed to that? So what possible harm to marriage is there in having gay couples live peacefully together? Show me one straight marriage that's ever been harmed.

Bishop: (Pausing for a moment to think) Children growing up need the influence of both genders so they get exposed to a balanced role model. That is really a problem in the Black community with all the single-parent families. I understand that most Black male prisoners were raised by single moms.

Teri: No question: the *ideal* situation is a strong role model from both genders. But plenty of children with heterosexual parents get terrible role models. I personally know of one case in which the homosexual grandparents have to protect the children from abuse by the heterosexual parents.

Bishop: Well, people with borderline tendencies can get tired of their spouses and think they'd be happier with someone of their own sex.

Teri: Ah, but that's the same whether the attraction is straight or gay. That's about fidelity and divorce. I really want to keep that discussion separate.

Round two: fitting the role

Each time Bishop and I discussed this topic; we repeated some of the same points and added a few new ones, as if both of us were trying to sharpen our arguments.

Bishop: The main reason Christians put so much emphasis on avoiding homosexuality is that gender difference is at the very core of what God intended for human beings. Genesis tells us "**God made them male and female…. a man will leave his father and mother and be united to his wife, and they will become one flesh**" (Gen. 5:2, 2:24). Only a man and a woman are physically suited to become one flesh;

the two cannot become one if they are of the same gender. When we reject that, we are fundamentally rejecting his plan of creation.

Teri: Okay. I can see how that makes sense to you. The idea of completing each other is a beautiful aspect of the story of Adam and Eve. In fact, it's so beautiful, that I can't see how God would limit it to heterosexuals. Doesn't the Bible say, "**It is not good for man to be alone?**"

Bishop: That's Genesis.

Teri: *All* humans benefit emotionally, psychological, spiritually, and just in terms of safety from a committed relationship with one other person. Plus most homosexual couples have a gender-style difference in their personalities. So they can complement and complete each other in ways other than physical.

Bishop: The Bible says, "**The two will become one flesh.**" (Mk 10:8) That's God's plan.

Teri: So are you saying that people born without clear sexual differentiation are outside God's plan?

Bishop: Absolutely not. No matter how you are born, he can make a way for you if you turn to him. You see Teri, as a result of sin, much of God's original intent for mankind has become distorted. That's why his plan of salvation is so necessary.

Teri: I, too, believe God can make a way no matter what. But there's something fundamentally different about sexual orientation; it's about who you love and—more than that—who you are. If a little boy wants to take cooking class or a little girl plays with dump trucks, there are still parents who will discourage those interests. The children get forced into roles that aren't natural for them and never achieve their full potential.

Bishop: They can express their full potential however they want—just as long as they don't have sex with the same gender.

Teri: Then you are asking them to be celibate—or worse, to have sex with someone they're not attracted to. How miserable would that be for both partners? For example I have one gay friend who is a successful professional woman; she says she had sex with men a few times and it was like going bowling—not obnoxious, but not something she'd be interested in doing often. Would you really want some man to try to make a successful marriage with her?

Bishop: As long as it's not me. (We both laugh). But look, some married couples fall out of love and end up having sex with someone they're not attracted to. So I don't know how God would resolve that. Sin has distorted so many things. It might be that the person's attraction shifts or they receive the grace to abstain. God will not give us greater challenges than we can bear. 1 Corinthians 10:13 says, "**No temptation has seized you except what is common to man. And God is faithful; he will not let you be tempted beyond what you can bear. But when you are tempted, he will also provide a way out so that you can stand up under it.**"

Teri: If it were true that gays are supposed to repress all of their sexuality, it would mean that God places far higher demands on them than on straight people. He would be asking them to reject the persons they naturally fall in love with. I did some research and found those scriptures that say that the lifestyle best suited for a total commitment to God is celibacy, but that teaching is only for "**anyone who can accept it**" (Matt. 19:12 and 1 Cor. 7 1-9). When monks and nuns follow a call to celibacy they are highly revered. So asking a gay person to forego all sex with the same gender is asking for the same level of commitment. That's way more than you say God asks of any straight person.

Bishop: No. It's not asking any more of gays than it is of a straight person who thinks he or she married the wrong partner or who wants multiple partners. I've had plenty of men sit right here in my office and tell me they think it's natural for men to have multiple partners. Just because it *feels* natural doesn't make it right.

Teri: Okay, yes; just because a desire is "natural" doesn't mean it serves us to follow it. And as I've said, I think postmodernism has done a terrible job of making that distinction between what we "feel" attracted to and what serves us. That's why it's a better distinction to seek what makes us truly happy and fulfilled at the deepest levels.

Bishop: No, you've got it backwards. It's not about seeking what makes you fulfilled. It's about seeking what honors God. He is our creator and designer, and he has promised that if we seek his will we get fulfillment in our lives and "**a peace that surpasses understanding.**" (Phil 4:7 paraphrased)

Teri: Right. So, haven't we just said the same thing? I'm saying that when we're doing that which brings deepest fulfillment we are also honoring God.

Bishop: No, you've put the cart before the horse. You've got to seek him first. *Then* you get the joy that comes from being in right relationship with God.

This was one of many standoff points at which we backed off to regroup. Then at another session, I mentioned to Bishop that my Religious Science congregation was looking to hire a new minister, and some of the candidates might be gay.

Round 3: feeling uncomfortable around gays

Bishop: Would everybody at your Center be willing to vote for a gay minister?

Teri: For most people it's completely irrelevant. But I'm sure we have a couple people who would be reluctant to have a gay minister.

Bishop: Well now that is really interesting to me. Tell me about that. How could that be if they don't follow the Bible?

Teri: It may be a simple matter of wanting someone who will appeal to the widest possible audience to bring in new members. Or it may be that they have some of the same prejudices that other people have.

Bishop: Why, why do they have those prejudices?

Teri: I don't know. Some people just grew up with them, and changing their spiritual beliefs didn't change that.

Bishop: I would really like to talk to those people.

This conversation must have started something cooking in his mind, because a few weeks later he was more aggressive on the topic.

Bishop: You keep asking me where the harm is in gay relationships. A lot of people are very uncomfortable being around gays. I am not homophobic, but it is a very common thing, and not just among Christians. The sex act for homosexuals is unnatural, and most people don't want images of it being imposed on their minds.

Teri: Oh boy… Okay, yes, a lot of people are uncomfortable. I could even go so far as to say it may be natural to feel uncomfortable—but only in the same sense some children feel uncomfortable around people with physical handicaps. There's probably something in our animal instinct that wants to avoid genes that don't seem to promote the evolution of the human race. That's why we have to teach children to see through that reaction. It's a matter of education and exposure.

Bishop: No, no, no. Being physically handicapped is completely different from being gay. We don't feel uncomfortable just because gays are different. It's a strong inborn knowing that their behavior is morally wrong. And by the way, please understand that it's not the perfect will of God that anyone be born either handicapped or gay.

Teri: Well then let me ask you this. Exactly what tips off this uncomfortable feeling you're talking about? Is it the way some gays talk and walk? Because those things are not going to change just because they swear off having sex. They could be completely celibate, and they will still get called names and beaten up in the street.

Bishop: Those are not Christians that beat people up. A real Christian would never do that.

Teri: Oh yes they would. They may be bad Christians, but many of them use the Bible as the excuse for their violence. You never hear of anybody beating someone up in the name of Buddha. It's Christianity and Islam that provide good excuses.

Bishop: People that profess Christianity are not always those who possess the love of Christ. A biblical perspective calls such people hypocrites.

Teri: I understand. But even without violence, when people look down on gays, you get a self-fulfilling prophecy. Gay children feel ashamed of who they are, so they deny their feelings or hide them. And that leads to behaviors that really *are* unhealthy, which is how you get the ugly underside of gay behavior when it's been blocked from healthy expression. In fact, I'll admit to you that I've also had a couple gay friends who got pulled into that stuff—extreme promiscuity and dominance/submission stuff. And I have no trouble making the judgment that it doesn't serve them in expressing their highest potential. So if you ask me, Christians should want to *require* homosexuals to get married, not prohibit it.

Bishop: (Scoffing) You're kidding.

Teri: Well yeah, mostly. But that's also why it's so important for preachers to watch what they say in the pulpit. If you're going to be quoting Leviticus that God swallowed up homosexuals in Old Testament times, you better spend ten more sentences explaining that it's just like any other sin and Christians are supposed to love them just like anyone else. Otherwise, what people remember in the middle of the week is a feeling that gays deserve to be swallowed up.

Bishop: That's not true in a good church. Compassion is a central message of Christianity. Anybody who doesn't understand that isn't listening very hard and isn't studying their Bible. Of course we love sinners; we're all sinners.

Teri: Pastor, I know that's true for you. You do seem to love everybody, even when you're angry or disappointed. I think everyone here at Highview feels that from you. And perhaps that makes it hard for you to see how someone could absorb the part of the Christian message about sin and not absorb the part about love and compassion.

Bishop: Well that doesn't happen where there's a properly balanced Christian message. As I've said to you before, for every true expression of a religious belief there is also a counterfeit.

Round 4: a shift—not for me to judge

At this point I was getting discouraged. I hadn't expected to change Bishop's mind. But I had developed some understanding and sympathy for his position, and I didn't feel like he had done the same for mine. If anything, he seemed to be more defensive about it than when we started. So I was surprised at a shift in his tone the next time this topic came up.

Bishop: I've been trying to see this from your perspective. I can understand that you have friends who seem like good people. So you must feel like I did when the church I went to as a teenager challenged the sacred cows I had grown up with.

Teri: I appreciate your trying to see it from my perspective. You certainly have caused me to rethink some of the "sacred cow" principles I've spent my whole life building. But I think this one is different. In this case, I think the parallel is more with the childhood church you left. You said the reason you left was that the lack of love there didn't stack up with the scriptures you were studying.

Bishop: That's right.

Teri: The reason I can't buy this particular Bible principle is that from everything I can see, it takes love out of the world without putting anything back in. And I'm really sorry that we seem to be deadlocked here because there's nothing I would like more than to find that anyone who rigorously pursues truth with both an open mind and an open heart as we have done will come to the same deepest values. I've been amazed how true that's been in every other issue you and I have pursued—I could either share your values or understand them. Even with abortion it's easy for me to see why you oppose it.

But this issue seems to get to the heart of our difference about the nature of life. We both agree that we are here to give glory to God—as you put it—or in the terms I'm still more comfortable with, to serve the highest good of all by expanding Truth, Beauty, and Goodness. We even agree that doing so puts us on a path of unlimited adventure. But you see the way to serve your purpose as following a path that's been laid out for you, and I see it as helping to carve that path.

Bishop: That's true. And I think I can see why this issue bothers you. In fact, if I were God, I might change some stuff.

Teri: What!

Bishop: Well maybe I don't see any rational reason why two women who want to live together as a couple shouldn't do so.

Teri: Really. Did I hear that right?

Bishop: Yes, I figured you'd want to write that one down. (We laugh as I in fact grab for my notepad.) It's just not up to me to set the standard. It's only up to me to study the Word and meditate on it until I understand it to the best of my ability.

Teri: So you're saying there could be cases in which you don't yet comprehend the reason God judges something to be wrong. You may feel sympathy in a different direction.

Bishop: That could be. But it's not up to me to judge. The Bible teaching will always make sense when I go deep enough. And even when it doesn't yet make sense to me, I trust that the God of all creation knows what's best for his creatures—what is for the best and highest good of all, as you would say. So I'm comfortable with him calling the shots, not me. Isaiah 55:8 teaches us that **"his thoughts and ways are not as ours are."** But then, since he is creator, he has that prerogative.

Teri: It means a lot to me to hear you say you might do things differently if you were God. I didn't really believe you before when you said you were willing to substitute what you see in the Bible for your own best view of the truth. I figured you were just using the Bible as an excuse for your own prejudices.

Bishop: Well, then I should say that I can feel some empathy for how difficult it could be for some people to deal with homosexual temptation. And if I feel it, I suspect God feels it much more. Look at Paul. God surely loved him deeply, but Paul had some kind of "thorn in the flesh" that he asked God to take away three times. We don't know what that thorn was. It could have been… something similar. But look at the fabulous results Paul got in his life. I just trust that God knew what he was doing by leaving him with the temptation.

Teri: Throughout this whole conversation, there's been a part of me that just wanted to say, "Please don't hurt my friends." And I can be more confident that you don't intend to hurt them when you show some empathy.

Bishop: Well then, I should also add that you're right that if you take the human distrust of gays and mix it with shallow biblical interpretations, it brings out all sorts of hatefulness in people. But the solution to that is more faithfulness to the Bible, not less—along with a balanced understanding of its timeless principles.

The more I thought about it afterwards, the more impressed I was with Bishop's admission that he didn't necessarily see the rationale for this particular rule. It's one thing to follow a rule blindly. But if you're going to yoke yourself to a set standard, how much extra courage and strength would it take to handle some uncertainty about it? I absolutely did not agree with his stance, but my admiration for him rose to a new level. And I assumed that if more fundamentalists took such a stance, it would be easier for the rest of us to believe they truly do "love the sinner" even while they "hate the sin."

Seducing children

But I was to get an even bigger surprise the next time homosexuality came up.

Bishop: I've been thinking over the social harm homosexuals can do. I had a situation once myself growing up. My mom and dad were both gone, and this older man took an interest in me. He bought me things and took me places when there was no other man around to pay attention to me. Then he wanted to get physical. He told me he needed my help with his "medical condition." Luckily, I knew enough to get out of there, and I ran like the wind. I don't want young kids exposed to that.

Teri: Oh wow. I really appreciate your telling me that. That's an immoral, illegal, reprehensible thing to do. Nobody wants that. That's why it totally makes sense to have laws against seducing minors, straight or gay.

Bishop: It's not just minors though. People can be vulnerable at any age if they're unsure of themselves. They could get sucked into the homosexual lifestyle even though it wasn't their original orientation.

Teri: I'm sure that happens. Straight people with low self-esteem get themselves into sicko relationships with the opposite sex, too. But people who aren't really gay will eventually realize it and pull themselves out of that situation. We can't protect children forever.

Bishop: I don't know about that.

This discussion gave me a new appreciation for the force with which Bishop sometimes instructed the ushers to sweep the building during church service. "Make sure there is no 'funny business' going on in other rooms," he commanded.

Salvation and homosexuality

For a while, I thought I saw a loophole in salvation.

Teri: You've told me salvation is a free gift, no strings. So homosexuals who are saved will go to heaven no matter what their behavior is, right?

Bishop: That's not necessarily true. Only as long as there is repentance. Where there is repentance there is always forgiveness and restoration. It's just like any other sin in that regard.

Teri: But wait. You told me in our discussion about salvation that a person doesn't have to accept any particular doctrine in order to be saved. If they have truly given their lives to God, they will begin a lifelong study that will continually deepen their understanding.

Bishop: That's right.

Teri: And you told me that a person doesn't have to repent of sin *in order* to be saved, that repentance can come after as a natural process of guidance from the Holy Spirit.

Bishop: Yes. Repentance comes as a result of salvation.

Teri: So doesn't that say that a person could come to God with a 100% intention to please him but not immediately see a need to stop or repent of homosexual behavior?

Bishop: No. You're trying to twist things around. You're looking for loopholes where there are none. The Bible is completely clear that homosexuality is a sin, and if someone who claimed to be saved did not repent of homosexual behavior and try to change it, that would indicate they were not sincere when they accepted salvation.

Teri: Hmm (stymied). Well, but there could be a time lag, right? It might take a while for the person's understanding to develop.

Bishop: That could be. But the key to true repentance is found in accepting what God says about what pleases and displeases him and moving towards and away from that the moment you are made aware of it.

Teri: Okay. But you also told me that it's not up to you or anyone else to judge who is and is not sincere about choosing salvation. You completely changed my attitude about salvation when you described it that way.

Bishop: That's true. But scripture tells us, "**You will know them by their fruits.**" (Matt. 7:20 nasb) I am not a fruit inspector, as I've said. That's God's job. But if someone in my congregation who professed to be saved continued in a homosexual lifestyle, they would not be left to business as usual—no more so than they would be with any sinful practice. Any person who truly understands the magnificence of the free gift of salvation will turn away from anything that displeases God—even though the temptation may come again and again. As God told Paul, "**My Grace is sufficient for you, for my power is made perfect in weakness.**" **Therefore**, Paul said, "**I will boast all the more gladly about my weaknesses, so that Christ's power may rest on me.**" (2 Cor. 12:9)

I was disappointed that I couldn't mend a disconnect I felt between the open way Bishop Thomas described salvation and the strict tone he took with it in this case. My husband, Andy, helped me out.

"It just doesn't seem to be consistent," I complained one night over dinner. Frequently after my Thursday night appointment with Bishop, Andy and I strolled to Pasha, our favorite Middle Eastern Café, where he helped me sort through the important points we'd covered.

Fingering his glass of merlot, Andy said, "Well Teri, are all of your beliefs consistent?"

"Oh… You can't compare… Well, maybe sometimes I… But in my case... Uh, okay."

I got his point. Nobody's beliefs are wholly consistent.

Who is welcome in a congregation?

I was still getting over this disappointment when something in the news brought a surprise from another angle. In the fall of 2005 the press reported that a Methodist pastor barred a practicing homosexual from joining his congregation. The Methodist Judicial Council backed him up by ruling that pastors have the discretion to bar individuals from membership. (That ruling was later contested by an assembly of Methodist bishops).[58] I wondered what Bishop Thomas would say about this.

Bishop: Excluding someone is not biblical. The problem is that they have strayed from a literal interpretation. Matthew 18:15-17 is the passage usually cited to justify ousting someone from membership. "**If your brother sins against you, go and show him his fault, just between the two of you. If he listens to you, you have won your brother over. But if he will not listen, take one or two others along, so that every matter may be established by the testimony of two or three witnesses. If he refuses to listen to them, tell it to the church; and if he refuses to listen even to the church, treat him as you would a pagan or a tax collector.**"

Teri: (Laughing) Tax collector? That sounds pretty clear.

Bishop: But does it say exclude them? No. How are we supposed to treat a tax collector or a pagan, which just means a nonbeliever? We are supposed to embrace them to keep open the way for them to come to the Lord. So no way does that say they should be ousted. But it does suggest that restoration is the key and that a member of the congregation that won't correct their ways should not be left to business as usual: whether that means someone has a chat with him or her over coffee, or offers counseling, or—yes, Teri—as you've witnessed, I might call attention to their behavior in public. That's because joining a committed community of believers implies that you seek correction. Proverbs 12:1 tells us, "**Whoever loves discipline loves knowledge, but he who hates correction is stupid**."

Teri: I can respect that, as long as people are free to leave the community. But what if the person is a disruption in the congregation? Then would you oust them?

Bishop: Some of my fellow pastors will use 1 Corinthians 5:6 (nkjv) to justify asking someone to leave: "**A little leaven will leaven the whole lump,**" which in context means one person can corrupt the others. In fact, in that scripture Paul is writing about a man in the congregation at Corinth who is having sex with his father's wife while the congregation looks the other way. And some translations of Paul's advice to the congregation say, "**Deliver him to Satan for destruction of the flesh, that the spirit may be saved in the day of the Lord Jesus.**" (1 Cor. 5:5 nasb) Now, what that means I have no idea.

(I burst out laughing.) Why are you laughing like that?

Teri: I never thought I'd hear you say that you don't know what a scripture means.

Bishop: Some scriptures take a lifetime of devotion to fully understand.

Teri: I'll bet that particular one was used to justify torturing heretics in the inquisition.

Bishop: Maybe it was. But if so, the inquisitors obviously had it wrong because the whole point of that scripture is to save the spirit, and killing somebody wouldn't do that. If you look at the NIV translation, it's clearer that it just has something to do with getting the attention of a sinner in the congregation to correct bad behavior and reconcile him to God and the congregation. And in the case we were discussing, Paul later instructs them in 2 Corinthians to treat the same man as a brother. So, obviously, he corrected his behavior and the corrective measures were not continued indefinitely.

Teri: Well, I think you just gave me another loophole that it's okay not to understand a scripture. That's a good one.

But back to my point: what would you do if someone here were a disruption in the congregation, perhaps because the person had some different beliefs and was vocal about them? It could be me for example. So far no one here has asked me about my beliefs. But if it ever comes up, I'll share them.

Bishop: Stirring up questions is good. Of course, if someone's only motive were to be disruptive, then I would just ask the ushers to escort them out. But normally, before I would even consider asking someone to leave, I would first try all kinds of counseling and would work with the person. And if they were still a disruptive influence, I'd take them aside and ask, "Hey, are you sure you want to be here?" Quite frankly, Teri, motive is everything.

Teri: So you're saying that homosexuals who have some level of intention to avoid same-sex relations should be welcome in any congregation?

Bishop: Yes, and as for those who do not believe homosexual acts are sinful, I assume they simply wouldn't be comfortable in a place that takes the Bible literally. So they would not choose to come in the first place—though they would be welcome.

If they did stay, though, we'd love them. (He dropped his voice again to add cautiously) You probably won't believe this, but there are a couple of homosexuals here in the congregation who are under my care. They realize that the practice is sinful, and they desire to honor God with their lives by changing their behavior.

Teri: Actually, I'm not surprised. And I know that being under your care means getting the very best of everything you know how to give. But if any of the gays in the congregation ask my opinion, I'll tell them I think they're perfect as they are.

Bishop: And if you were God, Teri, I'd tell them to listen to you.

Teri: Ouch! (grabbing my stomach)You got me. I take your point. Though as you know, there's a level at which I feel I *am* one with God.

Bishop: Well there's your problem right there.

Shifting public attitudes

I wondered how much the attitudes of my new Christian friends were shaped by lack of exposure to solid, middle-class homosexuals leading lives that were ordinary or better. Research shows that heterosexuals tend to hold favorable attitudes if they know two or more gay people, if those people are close friends or immediate family members, and if there has been open discussion about the friend or relative's sexual orientation.[59] In the early 70s, the beginning of "gay liberation," about two-thirds of the U.S. public felt that homosexuality was wrong (and 60% felt that it was "disgusting"). Those percentages decreased for about 20 years as many gays "came out" to family and friends, television added gay-themed shows, and "Gay Pride Days" exposed heterosexuals to the gays among them. By the early 90s polls showed that the number of Americans who believed same-sex relations were morally wrong was down to about half.

However, since the mid 90s, the decline in unfavorable opinions has stalled or backtracked. I suspect some of this reversal is due to the fact that *more* exposure to homosexuals has not necessarily been *better* exposure. I started to wonder what it would take to raise the public dialogue to a new level of sophistication—one that could honor the genuine values of both sides.

An audacious experiment in fellowship

Teri: It's such a shame that there is so much ill will over this issue among people who want the best for everyone. It's tearing up churches, families, the whole society.

Bishop: Yes it is. Again, Teri, sin has a way of doing just that.

Teri: I've been thinking about an experiment. Instead of segregating ourselves by what we believe on this issue, wouldn't it be wonderful if we mixed it up more? Imagine what it would be like if mature gay couples joined and were active, contributing members in fundamentalist churches?

Bishop: Oh I can't see that happening. Since the homosexual lifestyle is not compatible with biblical teaching, why would they want to do that? What's the point?

Teri: You're right, of course. The whole point of coming together is to encourage each other's growth in shared values, so it would be awkward to integrate someone with different values. Although you've integrated Andy and me beautifully.

Bishop: All the homosexuals I have known have come to me already knowing it's wrong. I guess it would be interesting to work with a gay person who is dedicated to God—not just someone who is out to justify their behavior—who could show me how they can believe it's all right—given what's in the scriptures.

Teri: That's what it would take: gays willing to remain open to divine guidance on this topic—which is what I have tried to do. I just feel that if people in fundamentalist churches knew some of the gay couples I know, they wouldn't necessarily change their minds about the interpretation of scripture, but they would have a huge advantage in learning to love the *people*. And that goes both ways. If my friends knew people like you, they would see that belief in homosexual acts as sin doesn't necessarily come packaged with the hateful or immature attitudes they assume it always does.

Bishop: You may be right about that. But it just doesn't make sense to me that a gay person would come here while believing gay sex is not a sin. I fully expect that if they accepted Jesus and opened themselves to do God's will, the Holy Spirit would convict them and show them gay sex is wrong as promised in John 16:8-9. If that didn't happen, I would have some doubts about whether they were sincere about being saved.

Teri: You know, Pastor, you said that before, only then you said that if a saved homosexual didn't come to see gay sex is wrong, you'd be *sure* he or she wasn't sincere about salvation. You've softened just a bit on that.

Bishop: I never soften. (We laugh.) But like I've said before, I am not the fruit inspector. And I guess I have shifted some since being exposed to you and some other people like McLaren. (We meet Evangelical reformer Brian McLaren in the chapter *McLaren Completes the Bridge*). I might not handle some things as publicly as I have in the past. Yet I'm glad we can always count on the Holy Spirit to reveal our sin to us where we've denied it. It's just not up to me to judge his methods or his timing.

A Black man befriends the Klan

Bringing gays into fundamentalist churches sounds preposterous, but during these discussions I learned of an extraordinary example of the power of adversaries getting to know each other. Daryl Davis is a black musician based in Washington whose exuberant piano playing has been compared to that of Jerry Lee Lewis. Davis made it his life mission to understand members of the Ku Klux Klan. He set up interviews with Klan leaders around the country for his book, *Klan Destine Relationships*, and only upon his arrival at the interviews did his subjects learn he was Black.[60] Under extremely dangerous conditions, he worked earnestly to understand, asking questions like, "Why do you consider multiracial children to be inferior?" These questions elicited not only blatant prejudice and misinformation, but also genuine concerns by working class Whites that affirmative action cut into their fair share of the pie, and that they would lose their jobs if they even expressed their concerns.

Many of the Klansmen Davis met this way were so taken aback, and then moved by his willingness to dialogue with them, that they eventually surrendered their Klan membership and presented their robes to Davis. Several became his friends. Davis has received numerous peace awards for his work, but he has also been criticized by both sides. Some Klan members who cooperated with him received threats from other Klansmen. And some reviewers condemned Davis for writing a book that puts a human face on the Klan.

I personally was so moved and astonished by his book that I invited Davis to dinner where Andy and I found him to be warm, forthright, and absolutely genuine. We liked him a lot. He is just a simple guy, no big theories or spiritual path; he gave up being a deacon at his church because he found it too dogmatic. But he had a quality of undefendedness that raised the bar on my sense of what's possible for human beings. It was as if he were an X-Man—a mutant from the future with extra powers, or perhaps like someone from another realm. His approach wasn't exactly to "turn the other cheek"; it was to offer to buy the guy a cup of coffee. When I asked Daryl the secret of his success he said, "You have to start by listening to your adversaries. Once you find any common ground, it becomes easier to tackle the major differences."

Give me 10,000 more like Daryl, strategically placed around the globe, and I'll give you world peace in 10 years, I thought—at least, insofar as it's possible to attain peace in *this* realm.

One more trick

I thought there was nothing more Bishop Thomas and I could accomplish on this issue without the presence of some mature gay couples with a passion for God. But the universe had one more trick up its sleeve, and it was a doozie.

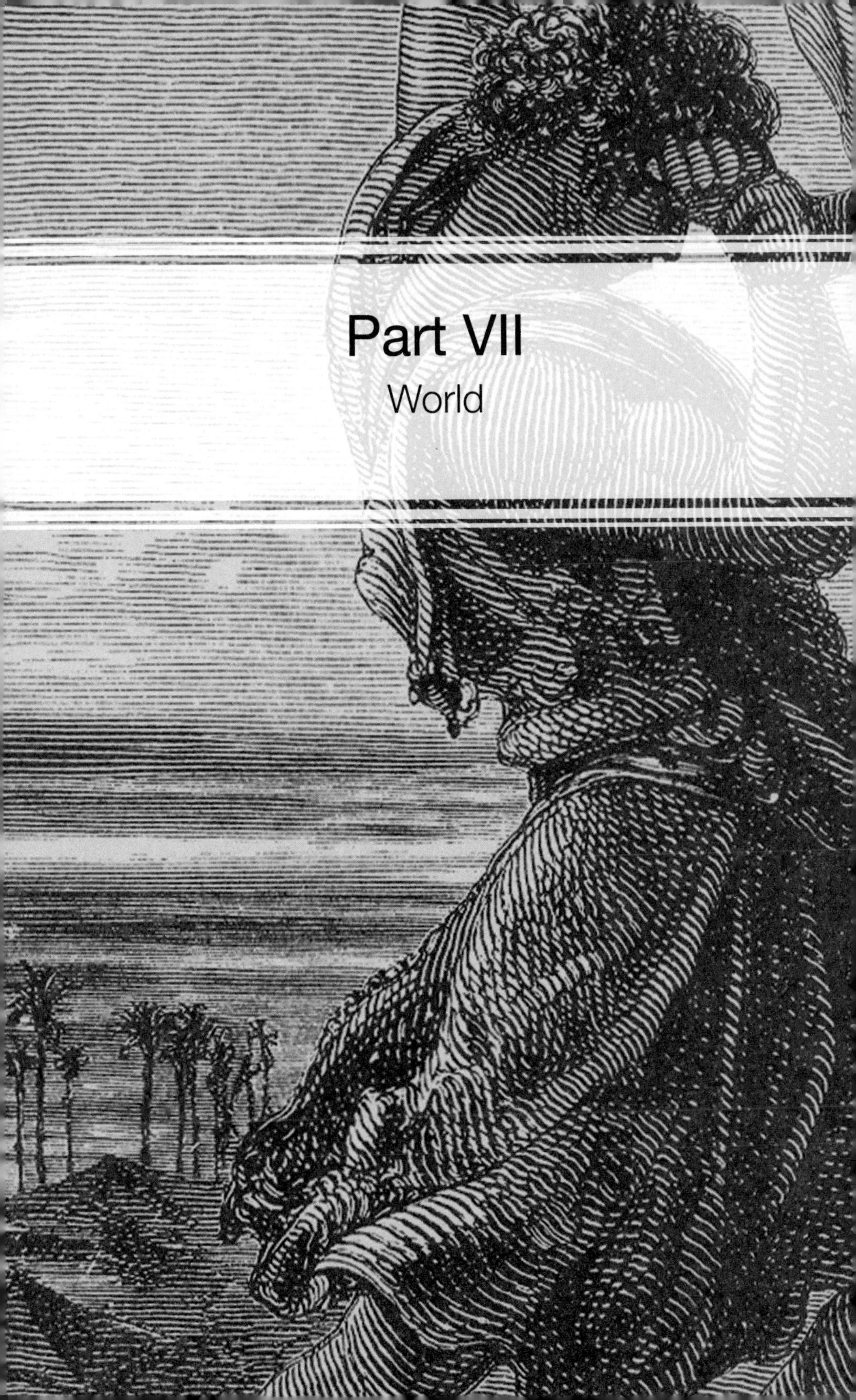

Part VII

World

33

Evangelism: Good News and Bad

All of those for whom authentic transformation has deeply unseated their souls must wrestle with the profound moral obligation to shout from the heart—perhaps quietly and gently, with tears of reluctance; perhaps with fierce fire and angry wisdom; perhaps with slow and careful analysis; perhaps by unshakable public example... You must... shake the spiritual tree, and shine your headlights into the eyes of the complacent.

Ken Wilber,
One Taste: Daily Reflections on Integral Spirituality

A huge weight was released for me the day that Bishop Thomas pronounced that he believed I was saved even though I was not comfortable saying the traditional words, "I accept Jesus Christ as my Lord and Savior." I had lived with fear of a showdown—that eventually he would tell me it was time to choose: whose side was I on? The fact that he didn't force a choice freed up a good deal of energy. And some of that energy went to tackling the remaining barriers between our worldviews.

One of those differences regards evangelism. My friends say, "I don't care what they believe, as long as they don't force it on me." Since 9/11, it seemed to me more important than ever that we all be clear on what we mean by "force."

Spreading the news

Teri: Why do Christians evangelize?

Bishop: The best hope for the world is that we fulfill the mandate Jesus left for us. His final instruction in Matthew 28:19 was, "**Go and make disciples of all nations.**" If you knew something precious that could change lives and bring peace to the earth, wouldn't you want to share it?

Teri: I can relate to that.

God's plan for my life: politeness to proselytizers

Much as I'm uncomfortable with the terminology, "God has a plan for my life," as I look back, it's hard not to think that Someone or Something spent years softening me up to keep an open mind about those who try to spread their beliefs via evangelism.

In relating my spiritual background in Chapter 3, I told about the powerful impact on me of one of the major personal growth workshop series that were popular in the late 1980s. At the end of the program I took, we were urged to enroll other people in it. And in that process of "enrollment" I began to feel what it must be like to be a religious evangelist. My life had been so enriched by the experience, how could I not want others to share it?

A trio of visions

During that period I was partly driven by a trio of visions I had during those workshops. As I've said, I am not the visions type. But long hours and intensity must have put me in a receptive state. In the first of these experiences, I suddenly imagined an image from the movie *Space Odyssey 2001* filling the room: the giant embryo floating translucently in space amidst the twinkling stars. Put into words, the feeling it gave me was something like, "I am *alive*. And I am part of the entire universe." The vision left me with a profound sense of wonder and of responsibility to make use of this awesome gift of life.

The bookend to this experience came on the last night of the workshop. Exhausted and exhilarated, I was walking out of the hotel ballroom after hundreds of hugs. I glanced to my right and spied the open doorway to a small storage room. White tablecloths were rumpled on a long table. I stopped and stared. Something about this scene fascinated me. A recessed light overhead gave the closet a soft, golden glow. And yet, I felt a terrible emptiness in that room. There was no life in it. It was completely empty of life. So empty. "*People are passing by. Why am I trembling to behold a linen closet*?" And then I heard the words, "He is not here."

It was days before I got my bearings regarding this apparent reference to the resurrection of Jesus. "Oh no," I thought. " I hope this doesn't mean I'm about to turn into a Jesus freak." Instead, I started exploring spirituality and eventually joined a church of Religious Science. And it was there, years later, that Rev. Harriet told me that my pair of visions fit a pattern described by advanced meditators: Fullness and Emptiness as the twin aspects of reality—spirit and form, being and nothingness. It seemed to fit. And yet, a little Christian seed seems also to have been planted, biding its time in the dark.

I want to mention the third "vision" also, for the profound impact it had in setting me on a spiritual path. We were doing an intense exercise in an advanced workshop in which most people had "breakthrough" moments of seeing all the love and joy that is at our core. I'm short, and I was standing in the back of a group that tightly surrounded a young garage mechanic whose turn it was. I was craning my neck to get a peek of him, but I could see only the face of a second young man who had a direct view. The look on that second man's face was the look of watching one's child be born. And the effect of that on me was like a triple reflection of a laser beam of love. It was like one of those science experiments in which light bounces from one mirror, to the next, to the next. It was as if a fire-hose worth of love and light was pouring from above into the first young man, streaming full force off him into the face of the second young man, and then gushing into me. I felt lucky that I wasn't standing directly in the line of fire; I don't know that I could have stood the full force of it. It felt like more of a privilege to be standing in the back where I could see the power of that love moving *through* each person.

That day was the beginning of finding it easy to love people who are not like me. And it was the beginning of wanting to share the good news I'd seen: It's in every one of us.

The curious case of the Krishna cookbook

Shortly after the workshop series and its visions, my softening up for evangelism was boosted by a bizarre coincidence. One Saturday afternoon I drove to the Georgetown shopping district of Washington to buy a vegetarian Indian cookbook. I parked in an open-air lot at the foot of Wisconsin Avenue, one of Georgetown's major streets. Then I walked uphill a couple blocks to the main intersection where tourists, students, and shoppers filled the streets. On the corner across from Nathan's saloon, a group of Hare Krishnas were chanting and dancing in their saffron robes to publicize their particular form of Hinduism—a form sometimes compared to Christianity. Normally I would have passed them by with perhaps an irritated thought that they were blocking the narrow sidewalk. Instead I paused, and I sensed that their proselytizing was not that different from my attempts to "enroll" my friends in my personal growth group. I may have caught the eye of one young Krishna and shared a moment's smile. Then I was on my way to visit bookstores. Unfortunately, I didn't find my cookbook, so I consoled myself with lunch at a French café.

Several hours passed before I returned to my car. There, on the hood of my car, was a vegetarian Indian cookbook. And it was published by the Hare Krishnas.

I looked around and saw no one. No other cars had books on them. I looked up. I looked under my car. I got in my car, and then I got out again and walked back uphill to where the Krishnas had been, but they were gone. Over the years, I've amused myself with a half dozen explanations. For example, maybe the person I smiled at followed me and overheard me ask a bookstore clerk for the cookbook. Or maybe one of the Krishnas actually was the bookstore clerk, quick-changing out of her orange robe and dashing to beat me to the bookstore. But in either case, how would he or she—I don't remember which it was—have known where I was parked? I know there is a logical explanation. I know that book didn't materialize out of thin air. But from that day forward, when evangelists of any kind knocked at my door, I was very, very polite to them.

Witness protection program

This openness paved the way for one of the most delightful adventures of my life: work and travel to the small Bahamian island I described previously. The family I connected with hired me to design a tourism Website based from their bakery. As I described in Chapter 5 at *Dueling Fundamentalists*, I was surprised when I learned the family was Jehovah's Witnesses because they violated all my stereotypes. Instead of avoiding discussion of religion with them, I took the opportunity to get an inside look at their beliefs and lifestyle, and to meet their brethren who passed through from all over the world. We teased each other about my interest, and we all laughed when discussion got heated and I called for the "Witness protection program."

Although many secularists think of Jehovah's Witnesses as the most hard core of the Bible-based religions (and most Christians think of them as heretics for denying the divinity of Jesus), one fact alone might make them a secularist's favorite fundamentalist: Witnesses don't vote or go to war; in many countries they have official standing as conscientious objectors. "**My kingdom is not of this world,**" and "**Those who live by the sword, die by the sword,**" were the scriptures they quoted me as explanation, citing John 18:36 and Matt. 26:52.

But of course, Witnesses do knock on doors. When I asked Anna, the petite wife of my client if it was possible to be a Witness without evangelizing, she gave me a steely look and asked, "Teri, what does the word 'witness' mean to you?"

Knowing that these lovely people were out each day knocking on doors gave me a whole new perspective when friends told me righteously of hurling insults or slamming doors on door-to-door evangelists. One friend told me proudly how a relative of hers had turned the garden hose on two immaculately dressed missionaries on her front walk.

I described in Chapter 8 at *I'm wicked, he's ignorant* the deep-seated fears that I believe lie behind such reactions and the benefits of overcoming them. In today's political climate, there is yet another reason for rethinking our reactions to evangelism: It could be worse, much worse, as we're seeing in the Middle East. And graciousness toward the peaceful kind of evangelism may be one way to head off the kind that comes with a gun.

The first step of such graciousness would be to understand that the "bad" kind is partly fueled by fear and anger at the sense that there is no place in the modern world of materialist science and achievement for the values that many fundamentalists cherish.[61] So we postmoderns have the choice to continue fueling their fear and anger or to help release the pressure. We fuel it by responding to it with suppression or fear tactics of our own. But perhaps a way to dampen it is to meet it out in the open, unarmed. To be willing to set aside everything we think we know. To quiet our own fears and anger long enough to engage its purveyors in dialogue. To seek common ground. A Christian who has respectful, open relationships with secularists will be less likely to believe the televangelist who says secularists are planning to ban Christianity.

I knew I had to cover this topic with Bishop Thomas.

Mothers who want their children to be saved

Teri: A lot of my friends hate being put on the spot by proselytizing.

Bishop: There's no reason a Christian should ever put someone on the spot. Salvation is a "whosoever will" proposition. Remember I told you 1 Peter 3:15, "**Always be prepared to give an answer to everyone who asks you to give the reason for the hope that you have. But do this with gentleness and respect.**"

And besides, there's just no point in attempting to change someone from the outside in. Romans 2:4 says it is God's "**kindness that leads you to repentance.**" The most successful evangelizers present a simple, positive message of hope. Billy Graham, for instance, touched millions of lives, and he always kept a positive focus.

Teri: My secular brother-in-law Tom feels that his mother has difficulty acknowledging anything he accomplishes or does for her; those details are lost in her overriding concern that he is not saved. Many of my friends tell similar stories. What advice would you give for Tom and his mom?

Bishop: Well on the mother's side, of course, her work as a parent training your brother-in-law was completed when he became an adult. Her job now is to love him and to leave open the way for him to someday find the truth on his own.

Teri: And for him?

Bishop: You know, I was in that situation with my grandmother who raised me after my Mom died. Grandma was one of the greatest blessings of my life, and I loved her dearly. But she was so harsh about doctrine. Her idea of evangelizing was to say to my friends, "You better get straight with Jesus, boy, or you're going to hell." And by the way, I noticed that she didn't get very far with that technique; nobody was flocking to the altar because of her.

So I told my grandmother I had a different understanding of the Word, and all I wanted was her love—as I assume your brother-in-law told his mom as well. But my grandmother was unable to change. So I had to do the changing to love her as she was—*and* I got a job as soon as I could so I could get out of Dodge and move out on my own, if you know what I mean.

Sharing the *love* of Jesus

I got a chance to see this situation from the mother's point of view at a housewarming party for one of the Highview congregation members.

I was sharing cake and ice cream with a table of women from Highview. A woman from another congregation started talking about how unhappy she was that her son isn't saved.

"We had a beautiful memorial service last week for a friend we all loved very much," she said. "The pastor didn't pull any punches about how lucky we were that this friend had been saved recently. And I was hoping that my son would get the point that he needs to get saved soon. But instead, he pulled away from us for several weeks. I kept trying to tell him time is short. But all we can do is share the Word."

Seated next to this woman was a young mother in the Highview congregation who has two teenage sons. "It's important to share the Word when the time is right," she said. "But once you've done that, isn't the most important thing to share the love of Jesus?"

"Yes, share what the Word says about the love of Jesus," the first woman said.

"Actually, I mean share the love, show the love. Especially when somebody is hurting, sometimes they first need to know we care. They need a chance to get their feelings out and know they're loved no matter what."

Mother Hafta, one of the older women at the table, said, "I certainly worry about my boy. He's a man now. I raised him to know about the Word, and that was all that I could do. Now it's not up to me, the rest is up to God. But I do worry about him getting into trouble. My prayer is, 'Please dear Lord, just keep him alive till he's through his twenties, and don't let anything happen that will ruin his mind.'"

The younger woman from Highview let out a small gasp and said, "That's my prayer. That's it exactly. Just last night I prayed that my son would be safe from anything that would permanently hurt his mind and his ability to choose."

The older woman put her hand on top of the younger woman's hand. "That's all we can do. That and just keep loving them."

34

The Interfaith Stretch... and the Muslims

If you are a Christian you do not have to believe that all the other religions are simply wrong all through. If you are an atheist you do have to believe that the main point in all the religions of the whole world is simply one huge mistake... If you are a Christian, you are free to think that all these religions, even the queerest ones, contain at least some hint of the truth... As in arithmetic—there is only one right answer to a sum, and all the other answers are wrong: but some of the wrong answers are much nearer being right than others.

C.S. Lewis, *Mere Christianity*

One of my main concerns about being associated with Highview was the implication that I believed that all other religions were wrong. And not just wrong, but bad—wicked and evil. The truth was more nearly the opposite.

9/11 and the Muslims

Like so many people in the months after 9/11, I felt a need to learn something about Islam. I looked up an institute that promotes freedom and free markets within Islam—the Minaret of Freedom based in Bethesda, Maryland. I remembered that its founder, Dr. Dean Ahmad, taught about Islam for the U.S. Foreign Service Institute, the training center for America's diplomats. Dr. Ahmad graciously invited me to sit in on one of his Honors seminars at the University of Maryland. In fact, I brought a couple friends from Celebration Center.

It was one of the best lectures I've ever attended in terms of expanding my mind to realms of history, science, and religion of which I had been totally ignorant.

What makes a civilization great?

Dr. Ahmad is a short and trim man, bald on top with tufts of white hair on each side. Trained as an astronomer, he has large brown eyes that reflect a life of gazing across the depths of space.

In the small classroom with about a dozen students, Dr. Ahmad drew two opposing arcs on the board, one representing the rise, fall, and rise of Western Christian civilization, the other representing the rise and decline of Islamic civilization. The two arcs crossed at about 1400, during the last set of Crusades, with the Islamic arc trending down and the Christian arc trending up. Among the factors that shaped these arcs, he said, the most important was the extent to which each culture was tolerating open interpretation of its sacred literature.

The low point for Christendom, he said, was in the 5th century. Not only had the Roman Empire fallen, but Constantine closed interpretation of the Bible by creating and enforcing the Nicene Creed. This created an "anti-rational streak," he said, that held back the development of science and society until Martin Luther's Reformation broke open interpretation of the Bible in 1517.

Meanwhile, while Christendom was still in its dark ages, Islamic civilization was taking off. Powered by seven development-friendly influences from the Koran, Islam spread rapidly after its founding in 622, bringing an explosive cultural renaissance throughout the Middle East. In fact, Dr. Ahmad said, these development-friendly factors in Islam spread to the West each time the two civilizations clashed, creating upswings in Western culture and becoming foundational tools for the Western Enlightenment.

Keeping the holy books open

Islam's most important promoter for development, he said, was a requirement that every individual acquire knowledge to better understand God. Islamic scholars were free to interpret Koranic law because of the value placed on *ijtihad*, the struggle to understand. This value placed on reason nurtured an integration of science and faith in which physicists were often theologians and physicians were often poets or calligraphers. While Galileo's telescope was considered a threat to religion in Christendom, the telescopes of Muslim astronomers were considered necessary to know God's works, according to Dr. Ahmad. Tragically however, a series of factors from the 13th through 15th centuries reversed most of these development-friendly factors, as Dr Ahmad explains in his book *Signs in the Heavens*.[62] Ijtihad was closed, and any further interpretation of the law based on the Koran was forbidden. Islamic society began a decline from which it has not recovered.

I had always assumed that any culture with laws based in a holy book would stagnate—and worse. The idea of holy books left open to interpretation was something new. But who should do the interpreting: king, clergy, scholar, or everyman? Dr. Ahmad seemed to trust the scholars. The problems in Islam, he told us, started when the Turkish Caliph (emperor) brought the imams (scholars) into the government. He recited the parable, "The scholar who visits the king is a bad scholar; kings have nothing to offer but power. But the king who visits the scholar is one who can be trusted."

After the lecture, we all went to dinner together at an Afghan restaurant in Bethesda. Over fragrant dishes of lamb and roast pumpkin, we learned that Dr. Ahmad is Palestinian-American, born on the boat while his parents immigrated to the United States in 1948. He showed no reaction when I shared a feeling that had welled up in me during his lecture—that the last time I remembered being so struck by the love of learning mixed with the love of God was watching the popular 80s movie Yentel, about a Jewish woman who wants so much to be a scholar of the sacred works that she disguises herself as a man to enter the seminary. It was a silly comparison, probably offensive in its triteness. But I felt like the stranger who arrives at the family dinner and quickly spots resemblances among family members that the family itself has never noticed; they are too close to each other. It was both beautiful and heart rending. (And I wondered if outsiders to both Fundamentalism and the New Age might come to a similar conclusion about those movements.)

I became a supporter of the Minaret of Freedom Institute and volunteered to redo its website. I told myself that one day I would take a full class from Dr. Ahmad.

Convert them or deport them

Shortly after the night of that lecture, I was drawn to attend another lecture series on Islam advertised by a large Christian church near my home. I thought it would be good to hear another perspective.

The main lecturer had converted from Islam to Christianity. He told many interesting facts, but the overall picture he painted was grim. He told us that Islam was a religion without a concept of forgiveness or mercy, and that the command to convert or kill infidels was present in all forms of Islam, not just the most radical. Islam was spreading rapidly in the United States, he said, with almost six million believers. Our only hope to avoid annihilation would be to convert them all or deport them.

Never in my life has the blood run so cold in my veins. "Not true!" I wanted to yell. I sensed tragedy of epic proportions. Nothing learned over the millennia; we were right back to the mentality of the Crusades.

I said nothing that night, but the following week I arrived at the second session armed with books painting a different picture of Islam. I made what statements I could in the Q&A period, and I was somewhat relieved to note that only about half the audience of 80 had returned.

Children of Abraham & Aristotle

Two years later, at a dinner given by the Minaret of Freedom Institute, I met Judith Latham, a producer for Voice of America radio who runs a salon from her home called "Abraham & Aristotle: all their children." Judith's vision is to encourage recognition of the common heritage that Christians, Muslims, and Jews have in all being descendants of Abraham. Judith brings together followers of each tradition to study the great works from all three, and to compare them with the insights of philosophy. This was shortly after Andy and I started going to Highview, and I had become acutely interested in comparisons among the "big three" monotheistic religions. I was amazed to learn that Judith lives around the corner from me, and that Dr. Ahmad frequently led the discussions. Not believing my good luck, I jumped at the chance to start attending this salon.

It was at "Abraham and Aristotle" I learned how Muslims had presided over one of history's longest periods of religious tolerance. We read together *Ornament of the World* by Maria Rosa Menocal.[63] The book tells of a period of almost 800 years when Christians, Muslims, and Jews lived together in relative peace under Muslim rule in Spain. Christians and Jews were given a status as *dhimmi*, non-believers who paid a special tax in lieu of military service, a practice that was tolerant by the standards of the time. The resultant flourishing of art, science, and commerce came to an end when Ferdinand and Isabella reconquered Spain for Christianity in 1492; they drove out the Muslims and the Jews.

These discussions made me realize what a Christian-centric view of history I was raised with. While Bishop Thomas was increasing my respect for Christianity, the salon acted as a counterweight to simultaneously build my respect for Islam.

Aristotle on the source of happiness

In addition to comparing the "big three" monotheistic religions, our salon looked at the view of ethics that came from the early philosophers. We discussed Aristotle's *Ethics*[64] while balancing on our laps paper plates of Middle Eastern food that Judith graciously prepared.

I always thought Aristotle was the first to articulate an ethical system based wholly on logic. That's an important point to my secular friends: ethics can be determined through logic alone. So I was surprised to learn that Aristotle simply asserts that we all know what's right and wrong via what he calls "intuitive reasoning"; he doesn't question where that comes from. It wasn't until much later in history that philosophers "retrofitted" this natural knowing with ethical systems based wholly on logic: John Locke's social contract, Ayn Rand's objectivism, the existentialists' self-directed ethic, among others.*

Although Bishop Thomas and I never got around to discussing Aristotle directly, he did tell me he could say "amen" to this review I found at Amazon.com by Jesse Rouse, a theology and philosophy student from Kenosha, Wisconsin.

> As a Christian, I think that it is amazing to see just how close Aristotle got to being right. Anyone reading Aristotle's work can see clearly that God has written a moral law code on all men's hearts. Should it surprise us then to see Aristotle emphasizing nearly the same morals that Judaism at the time emphasized, and Christianity does?
>
> As close as Aristotle gets, however, he is still off. His ultimate end for which all is done is happiness (by this he does not mean pleasure). As a Christian, I would have to disagree. I believe the ultimate end for our actions and lifestyle is to bring glory to God and fulfill His purpose for us. Aristotle got the means mostly right, but he ended up with the wrong end.

But what if the two ends are the same, I wondered? What if achieving the deepest happiness and inner peace will always, "bring glory to God and fulfill his purpose for us," as New Thought implies?

All of these topics provided grist for my discussions with Bishop Thomas. They also pushed me closer to the point of knowing too much. This is the cliff edge of "too many views" that I had felt collapsing under me in my experiences with C.S. Lewis and the Fig Tree sermon.

---

* Ayn Rand's Objectivist philosophy directly contradicts Plato's belief that consciousness or "ideals" existed before being. Being came first, she said. Therefore, whatever is good for individual beings is the highest and best good. And logic is all we need to discover that good.

Dr. Ahmad takes the middle-way view of a classical Muslim philosopher: all knowledge rests on the "three-legged stool" of reason, experience, and transmission from reliable sources (*aka* authority) with God as the ultimate authority. When I protested that I had learned these sources of knowing as reason, *intuition*, and authority, he said that was because I was infected by Plato. Followers of Plato tend to elevate intuition as the best way of knowing. Echoing the exact words that Bishop Thomas had said to me, Dr. Ahmad said, "Your intuition is just an experience, as fallible as any other sensory input. You must test it against reason and what has been transmitted from reliable sources."

False doctrines

Bishop: I've met a couple Muslims and been impressed by what good people they seemed to be. You know they trace their line back to Ishmael, whose father was Abraham. And they use some portions of the Bible in their Koran.

Teri: Yes. The more I learn, the more I realize Christianity has in common with Islam.

Bishop: Just because a few Muslims blow themselves up saying it's for the glory of God, that doesn't reflect on the majority who are decent people.

Teri: I am so glad to hear you say that. Can I tell you about something that bothered me a couple months ago? I know Christians believe Jesus is the *only* way to get to God. But I was uncomfortable when your visiting speaker outlined several other belief systems and attacked them as false doctrines. She hit most of my friends: New Age, Native American, Unitarians, even Jehovah's Witnesses. And she made it sound as if they were all wicked and evil.

Bishop: Mhmm.

Teri: The worst of it was that the speaker's tone was mostly fear and anger. When my husband is mad at me for something I've said, he tells me it's mostly because of the tone of voice I've used. So it was the tone of belittling that really bothered me.

Bishop: Mhmm.

My feeling about his uncustomary silence was that he saw my point but was being diplomatic in honoring and respecting the guest speaker.

Teri: I will say though, I was very happy when you followed up after the sermon by commenting that, "At least those Jehovah's Witnesses are out there on their little bicycles in the snow evangelizing. Some of us can't get up off the sofa for Jesus on a nice day." As I've told you, I have friends in the Bahamas who are Witnesses—only they're out on golf carts in the blazing sun instead of bicycles in the snow.

Bishop: Christians can't be too careful about what they let into their minds. There are a million mixed-up beliefs out there. They can turn you around, distract you from your purpose, and even take you down some pretty dark streets. We don't have time for false doctrines.

Don't you say in Religious Science it's important to keep our thoughts pure?

Teri: Mhmm.

Bishop: So, can you see my point?

Highview joins an interfaith group

The week after this conversation with Bishop, we were discussing another topic when he surprised me.

Bishop: Teri, I've been invited to join an interfaith organization that's forming locally. It will let churches work together for common concerns like our relationships with the local government. But we don't have a Muslim member. Do you think you could find one for us?

Teri: (I gulped.) You want me to find you a Muslim? (I actually didn't believe I had heard him correctly.)

Bishop: That's right.

Teri: Uh… I can probably do that.

Bishop: And I want to follow up on what you said last time about having friends who are Jehovah's Witnesses. They may do good work, but they make serious doctrinal errors you've got to be careful of. They don't believe Jesus is God. If they're such good Bible scholars, I would sure like to ask them about their translation of John 1:1. I want to know why they inserted "a" into their translation of, "**In the beginning was the Word, and the Word was with God, and the Word was *a* God.**" (nwt)

Teri: Religious Scientists love that passage. Next time I'm in the Bahamas, I'll ask my Witness friends about that.

I won't go into the conversations I had about this several months later in a little bakery in the Bahamas. But I will say I came to appreciate the care and scholarship the Witnesses put into tracing the Greek origins of words and cross referencing every instance of a particular term in the Bible. "*Teri, look at this: 'a' cross, 'a' thief, 'a' river, 'a' God.*" It was another form of love of learning… and of God.

I had always been interested in world religions. But now I was being attracted to each one I encountered. I felt like the little boy in the charming novel *Life of Pi*.[65] The hero is born in India to a Hindu mother and secular father who names him "Pi" after the mathematical formula. Growing up, Pi is enchanted by the incense and chanting in Hindu ceremonies. But he meets teachers from other religions, and then sneaks behind his parents' backs to say a rosary in a Catholic Church or to bow on a hidden prayer mat during the Muslim call to prayer. When these activities are discovered, Pi gets into very big trouble as each of his religious teachers realizes he is not the boy's sole source of inspiration.

I loved the novel, just as I found myself loving both Christianity and Islam the more I learned about them. And I began to wonder what stood in the way of being a Christian and a Muslim too. The questions I wanted to ask about this didn't fit the format of the Abraham and Aristotle salon, so Dr. Ahmad invited me to a Koran study that he conducts in his home. In addition to being a professor, he also holds the status of imam (teacher of Islam), and he has officially dedicated a room of his home as a mosque (place of study and worship).

Being a Christian and a Muslim too

I arrived on a Sunday afternoon coming directly from service at Highview. One of the associate ministers had given a talk about Jesus as "The Only Way" in which she said, "There's nothing bad about all those other religions, it's just that they're not The Way."

Dr. Ahmad and I sat on sofas in a room in which one wall was completely covered by a massive, yellowed, world map. He handed me a copy of the *Qur'an* (more correct transliteration of "Koran.") It had Arabic and English in facing columns and extensive footnotes on each page. He said this particular translation is a good one for beginners because the footnotes present several alternative interpretations.[66]

I had asked to learn about Jesus, so Dr. Ahmad had a list ready of the references to Jesus in the Qur'an. We took turns reading aloud the dozen or so passages. Here are some of the points I was surprised to learn as I flipped the parchment-like pages of his Qur'an:

- Jesus was born of Mary in a virgin birth
- Jesus was a great prophet who received revelation from God
- Jesus escaped crucifixion. God made it appear Jesus was crucified, but actually he was taken to heaven where he awaits the final days. In those final days he will come back to earth to convert Christians and Jews to Islam
- When Jesus told his disciples to await a counselor who would come after him, he was referring not to the Holy Spirit, as Christians believe, but to Mohammed, who would be the last in a long line of prophets God sent to all nations

Dr. Ahmad explained that the Qur'an teaches that God forgave Adam and Eve for their sin, and thus there was no need for Jesus to die. People are not born in original sin, he said, but they do easily forget their elevated status as agents of God. Thus, people are not inherently sinful, but rather it is this forgetting that the devil (called "Shaytan") plays on in tempting us to remain self-centered.

I realized that millions of people had died over each of these differences with Christian doctrine. But what I was most intrigued by was the similarities.

"But what about the message of Jesus, what status does it have with Muslims?" I asked.

"There is dispute among scholars whether the gospels in the Christian Bible accurately represent the teachings of Jesus. But many Muslims consider themselves Christian in the sense that they honor and follow the teachings of Jesus in addition to those of the Qur'an. Of course, most Christians would say those Muslims aren't really Christian."

When I pushed him about the extent to which the message of Jesus is represented in the Qur'an, he said that love, mercy, compassion, charity, piety, and justice are all deeply revered, with a special emphasis on brotherhood. In fact he said, many Christians who convert to Islam do so for its stronger teachings regarding brotherhood. Islam has more of an emphasis on reaching out to the whole world, he said.

"No, wait," I said, confused. "Didn't Jesus command to 'Go teach all nations'?"

"Yes," he said, "but that was only one reference. The rest of the Bible is all directed to the twelve tribes of Israel."

I still had a confused look on my face when Dr. Ahmad admitted that there is one factor that is stronger in Christianity than in the Islam—the requirement to love your enemies. "In Islam loving your enemies is a good thing, but it's not a command like it is in Christianity," he said.

"Of course, not many Christians really practice it," I offered.

"I'm glad you said that. Actually, we sometimes give Christians a little slack because their religion is so impossibly demanding that it's not surprising no one can live up to it. But in Islam, we don't have that excuse, since the goal is presented as a sliding scale. It should be easier to do a little. Of course, for that same reason it seems more reprehensible when we do nothing."

This struck me as a very "Christian" thing to say.

"So what stands in the way of a person being simultaneously a Christian and a Muslim?" I asked.

"The word *muslim* means surrendered to the will of God. So in that sense, people of any religion might call themselves muslim with a small "m." But the primary tenant of Islam is, "There is no god but God, and Mohammed is his messenger," with 'messenger' meaning the last of the long line of prophets God sent to all nations.

"So, to be a Muslim with a capital "M," he continued, "a Christian would have to accept the teachings of Mohammed along with those of Jesus. And the major stumbling block to that—besides the doctrines of original sin and the crucifixion, which we've already mentioned—is the Trinity. If the Trinity is understood as God having three centers of consciousness—Father, Son, and Holy Spirit—then that is multiple Gods, which to Islam is idolatry." As an afterthought he added, "There is one scholar who conceived a way of reconciling the Trinity with the concept of one God. John Hicks put forth that Creator, Redeemer, and Counselor are three qualities or *names* of God. And that conception does not conflict with Islam—it has 99 names for God. But Hicks is considered a heretic by most Christians."

The afternoon passed quickly as Dr. Ahmad consulted multiple references to answer my questions. At various points he turned to an Arabic dictionary, an English dictionary, the Bible—with which he seemed very familiar—and a Bible commentary, as well as to various sources online via his laptop.

"Putting together what I've learned today, it sounds like Islam sees itself as transcending and including Christianity, just as Christianity sees itself as transcending and including the Judaism of the Old Testament."

"That's right," he said. "And the Sufi mystics see themselves as transcending and including Islam. Although, of course, most Muslims see Sufis as heretics; they have too much in common with the Gnostic Christian mystics and with Eastern religions."

Just a crazy thought

Once again I was caught up by the thrill of the love of learning mixed with the love of God. How could we all have spent so many centuries hating each other when we had so much in common? Afterwards I had a crazy thought about how to save the world. We could enshrine all the world's holy books as the basis of law worldwide but *leave open to interpretation which concepts transcend and include the others.* The transcending thought always wins. I know, I know, we'd just be killing each other over the interpretations. But could it be much worse than where we're headed now?

DISCLAIMER: Just as with any other essay portion of this book, the fact that Bishop Thomas has allowed me to intermix my thoughts with our dialogues does NOT mean he endorses a single thing I say. Especially this. I don't even endorse it. In fact, just forget I said it. It's just an example of the kind of thoughts I had once I started easing my grip on my belief system so I could open myself to something new.

The Bishop confronts the interfaith stretch

Several weeks later Bishop Thomas reported to me on his first meeting with the new Northern Virginia Interfaith group.

Bishop: We had myself and several other Christian pastors, a Christian Scientist, a pregnant Rabbi, and a Muslim. When one of the Christians said the opening prayer, he ended with, "In the name of Jesus."

Teri: Oh yeah. I bet I know what happened next.

Bishop: The Christian Scientist complained that he should have said, "In the name of Love." So I had to ask myself what I will do when it's my turn to pray. God is love, so I could say, "In the name of love." I do want to promote unity, but not at the risk of compromising what I believe. I'm going to have to wrestle with that.

Teri: That's a tough one. I know you'll be guided to make the right choice.

One month later:

Teri: How did you decide to handle the prayer at the interfaith meeting?

Bishop: I had to get clear on what the purpose of an interfaith group is. Inter-faith means across all religions, whereas inter-denominational means among the various sects of Christians. So it's a given that as an interfaith group, we believe things the others won't accept. And if we are going to pursue a common goal, we have to deal with that.

Teri: So have you had a chance yet to say the opening prayer?

Bishop: No, but if I do, I will close with "in the name of Jesus." And if our Muslim member ends with "in the name of Allah," I will respect that it's his right.

Unity is a kingdom thing

The next week at Sunday service, Bishop had just returned from an interdenominational conference in Chicago that he said filled his heart with the beauty of unity. He gave us a high voltage, singsong, rocking report something like:

This is not a Black thing!

This is not a White thing!

This is a kingdom thing! (finger pointing in air)

(He had us repeat that chant while he continued.)

We are all one!

I don't care about your race, creed, or color.

It's time to put aside our petty differences.

I don't care if you are Evangelical, Baptist, Methodist, or Catholic.

If you believe in Jesus, we are brothers.

We are one, y'all!

It was not as all encompassing as a Religious Scientist might hope for; but combined with the respectful things he'd been saying about Muslims to me in private, it was enough to put tears on my face. The circle of love was limitless, and the circle of community was open to all who shared the group's values.

I redoubled my effort to appreciate where he was coming from on those issues that still bothered me.

35

McLaren Completes the Bridge

To hold beliefs that puzzle you...
is the vital sign of a vibrant faith
of head and heart, a dynamic
faith that isn't brain dead, hasn't
committed intellectual suicide,
and is in process. Real faith... is
alive, moving, pulsing, swaying,
each belief trembling in dynamic
tension with the others.
Brian McLaren, *More Ready Than You Realize*

When Bishop Thomas and I had been meeting for about a year, I proposed that we write this book together to capture the extraordinary ground we were covering. And from that point on, we were debating not only ideas but the best way to present them. Frequently when we reviewed a draft chapter, we both were tempted to change what we'd said—me because my ideas kept evolving, and Bishop because he was now sensitized to how things sounded to non-Christians. So then we'd have a new debate about the changes. I told him we shouldn't delete his early references to "the rough side of God." He told me that my first draft didn't fully capture his points.

Bishop: Where's all the other good stuff I said? We talked about this for an hour.

Teri: I'm fairly sure I got all the important points. I just condensed them. And, uh, sometimes you repeat yourself.

Bishop: No, you've missed a lot of good stuff.

Teri: If I missed stuff I'm sorry. Is it possible, though, that I got what you said, but it seems alien when you can see how it sounds to me?

It began to look like we were stuck in a loop, when someone else stepped in to shake us by our collars and point us toward a higher view.

C.S. Lewis in blue jeans

The discussion group I lead on the philosophy of Ken Wilber was meeting in a bookstore near DC's Metro Center subway station. One night I arrived early and browsed new releases at the front of the store. *A Generous Orthodoxy* called out to me.[67] It was by Brian McLaren, the author whose work I almost bought at the C.S. Lewis seminar a year earlier.

Now I learned from the cover that McLaren is a pastor working from *inside* the Evangelical movement to open it to new possibilities. His Emergent Church movement calls Christian churches to do less squabbling with each other and refocus on their core mission of bringing love and restoration to the world. *Time* magazine called him one of the 25 most influential Evangelicals, although among Evangelicals, he is considered both a hero and a heretic. He had recently given up his pastorship at a church in nearby Maryland to pursue fulltime speaking around the world.

McLaren is also a former English teacher, and it shows in the clarity and personalness of his writing. Within just a few sentences, he had me thinking, *This guy thinks the way I do.*

> For those who have accused me of being excessively original, this book should affirm my basic unoriginality. I'm saying little or nothing new, but rather I'm listening to a wider variety of older and newer voices than most people do. I'm trying to take them all seriously, which itself is, perhaps, my chief novelty.

The book felt smart, candid, and direct, but also warm, personal and humble. C.S. Lewis in blue jeans.

> If I seem to show too little respect for your opinions or thought, be assured I have equal doubts about my own, and I don't mind if you think I'm wrong. I'm sure I am wrong about many things, although I'm not sure exactly which things I am wrong about.

This book feels like a bridge.

I bought it and spent the next 24 hours wolfing down thoughts like these:

> It is so hard for us to have a feel for the word *king* even remotely similar to what people would have felt in Bible times... What would it be like to live in times of perpetual violence, horrific brutality, ever-present danger, and constant vulnerability to whichever warlord threatened us? Perhaps under those circumstances we can imagine what good news it would be that a good king had come into power.

Christian use of the word *sovereignty* makes matters worse, McLaren said, because of the way it implies *control,* which is not good news today, "a period that told us in a hundred different ways how we're already controlled"—by our genes, class struggle, Freudian psycho-social aggressions, operant conditioning, evolutionary competition, laws of physics and chemistry, linguistic constructions, colonialism, industrialism, and advertising.

Whew!

Against this backdrop, McLaren says, talking about God as the all-controlling king is just more bad news.

> *Good* news, under these circumstances, would be a leader who liberated us from all determinisms, who deconstructed oppressive authority and the self-interest of leaders and nations, who destabilized the status quo and made way for a better day, who delivered us not only from corrupt power, but also from the whole approach to power that is so corruptible.
>
> Which is exactly (I say) what is meant by the phrase "Jesus is Lord."

Is this what Bishop Thomas had been trying to say to me? I *got* this. In fact, it gave me goose bumps. Maybe this book could help Bishop and me communicate better. Remembering the low, stone footbridge I had envisioned at the beginning of my discussions with Bishop Thomas, I now saw McLaren stepping to the center of it, arms outstretched to meet the fingertips of Bishop and me, each standing at opposite sides of the small stream.

Generous Orthodoxy was still in my bag at my next appointment with Bishop.

Speaking Baptist to the Zulus

Teri: The thing is, much of the biblical language that you use sounds archaic or oppressive to people who haven't grown up in your church culture.

Bishop: That's why I'm happy to have this chance to explain what these terms really mean. I don't think we should water them down.

Teri: It's not about watering down. It's about doing whatever communicates well. I once got a great piece of advice from a friend in the Foreign Service who had served in Africa. I was complaining that I didn't feel truly myself when I had to change my language for my audience. He said, "You know, Teri, when I'm talking to the Zulus, things just go better if I speak Zulu than if I try to teach them English."

Bishop: That's what Paul meant when he said he became all things to all people so that he might save some. "**Though I am free and belong to no man, I make myself a slave to everyone, to win as many as possible. To the Jews I became like a Jew, to win the Jews… To the weak I became weak, to win the weak.**" (1 Cor, 9:19-22)

Teri: That's beautiful, wow. So my friend's advice really struck me. And to tell you the truth, I thought about it a lot when I first started meeting with you. It hurt my mouth at first to say "sin" and "Satan" instead of "error" and "ego." It took a lot of work to see the parallels in our beliefs and to appreciate why the differences are important to you. I still wince sometimes when you say "Lord" or "sovereign."

Bishop: Those are beautiful words.

Teri: Not to me. I hear domination, control, and patriarchy in those words. I just discovered the Christian author Brian McLaren who has a lot to say on this topic. He has a great explanation of why traditional church language turns off modern secularists.

I pulled out of my bag *A Generous Orthodoxy* and laid it on Bishop's desk. He picked it up. He picked it up like a teenager picks up the car keys left on the kitchen counter to his dad's sports car. It was a moment that marked the beginning of a shift—for both of us.

Bishop: Can I borrow this? (reading the cover and leafing through). It looks like this guy thinks like me. Oh man, Teri, you didn't do any highlighting. I have so many things to read, and I've got to finish my doctoral dissertation.

I took the book back from him, and I marked up passages while we continued our conversation. Then I returned the book to him. Here is one of the sections I marked.

> Let's start simply. In the Bible, *save* means "rescue" or "heal"… get out of trouble. The trouble could be sickness, war, political intrigue, oppression, poverty, imprisonment, or any kind of danger or evil…

McLaren suggested that to judge means *to name*. This reminded me of times I was in a group discussion being dominated by one person. Everyone is grateful when someone finally *names* the situation: "Charlie, you've done most of the talking. Let's give other people a chance." Judgment could be as simple as that.

> One way God saves is by judging, *and then by forgiving*. So often the danger or evil we face is self-created, self-inflicted, self-sabotaging—and we keep doing it because we are self-deluded through denial… By penetrating our denial and self-delusion (with awareness), God begins saving us…
>
> This is a window into the meaning of the cross. Absorbing the worst that human beings can offer—crooked religiosity, petty political systems, individual betrayal, physical torture—Jesus enters into the center of the thunderstorm of human evil and takes its full shock on the cross. Our evil is brutally, unmistakably exposed, drawn into broad daylight and judged—named and shown for what it is. Then, having felt its agony and evil firsthand, in person, Jesus pronounces forgiveness and demonstrates that the grace of God is more powerful and expansive than the evil of humanity. Justice and mercy kiss; judgment and forgiveness embrace. From their marriage a new future is conceived.

This was a form of salvation I could embrace.

And there was something else. Something in the last two sentences of the quote above felt familiar. It had the smell of something Ken Wilber would write as he always seeks the most inclusive way to express something. I scoured the footnotes until I found Wilber's name. McLaren was aware of Wilber's work.

The story behind the story

This was a coincidence I could relish. Wilber was working among "postmoderns" to make the sacred acceptable again, and McLaren was working among traditional religious folk to encourage them to reach out to those same postmoderns. For me, it was the last plank in the bridge.

But how would Bishop Thomas react? It was several weeks before the answer began unfolding. In the meantime, I was reading every book of McLaren's I could get my hands on. One of them, *The Story We Find Ourselves in*, showed me how to be enchanted by the Old Testament. McLaren retells the story through a preacher-turned-science teacher as he stands halfway up a volcano on an Island in the Galapagos, watching a pair of tortoises mate. A gleaming drop of tortoise semen symbolizes creation and the story behind it.

> It is a story that gives us something so much more important than textbook-style, so-called objective facts… For me, it is a story that gives us *in-formation*… A story that *forms* us *inwardly* with truth and meaning—something that we moderns seem to value far less highly than our ancestors did.

Through McLaren's telling, finally I could understand the impelling beauty Bishop Thomas sees in God's charge to Abraham, "**You are blessed to be a blessing.**" The same book by McLaren even gave me a hint how it could seem more wonderful to be separate from God than one with him.

And then another surprise. One book of McLaren's was very similar to this book: *More Ready Than You Realize: Evangelism as Dance in the Postmodern Matrix.* It is the story of a two-year dialogue between a pastor and a doubting woman named Alice. It is told from the point of view of McLaren as pastor. At the end of it, Alice is a Christian, and McLaren draws eight lessons for evangelism. The lessons encourage relationships in which both parties share not just facts but stories as part of a mutual journey toward God. [68]

Bishop Thomas and I had just lived out every one of the eight lessons.

36

Law & Politics: Seeking a Way *Beyond*

We've taken sins out of God's domain, where they can be forgiven, and put them in the domain of law, where they can only be plea-bargained.
Peter McWilliams, *Ain't Nobody's Business If You Do*

Those of us who relish the freedoms and achievements of modernity find it hard to comprehend the distress these cause religious fundamentalists. Yet modernization is often experienced not as a liberation but as an aggressive assault... Sometimes, to prevent an escalation of the conflict, we must try to understand the pain and perceptions of the other side.
Karen Armstrong, *The Battle for God: A History of Fundamentalism*

I knew that for my secular friends, all this theology was irrelevant; the only issue they were concerned about was whether Bishop Thomas wanted to put them in jail for not following the Bible. The first couple times I tried to explain to Bishop the difference between something being wrong and it being illegal, he had trouble following me.

Should law protect us from the wicked?

Teri: I want to talk about the role of government.

Bishop: That's easy. The role of government is to protect us from the wicked. I can show you the scripture on that.

Teri: That's great. I like that. Protect us from the wicked, but not to protect the wicked from themselves.

Bishop: Why would we do that? Here it is: Romans 13:4 says government is "**God's servant, an agent of wrath to bring punishment on the wrongdoer.**"

Teri: That doesn't say protect us from the wicked. That says punish the wicked.

Bishop: Hmm? I don't see a difference. Punishing the wicked is the method for protecting us from the wicked.

Teri: The difference is that when the focus is on protecting innocents, the only laws we need are those that prevent someone from harming someone else: murder, theft, fraud, etc. But if the purpose of law is to punish the wicked, there's no limit on what can be considered wicked and thus outlawed.

Bishop: The Bible spells out what's wicked.

Teri: That's exactly what I'm afraid of. That's how we got Prohibition and all the blue laws about stores being closed on Sunday, laws against premarital sex and even blasphemy. And doesn't the Bible forbid women from uncovering their heads or wearing gold jewelry? Many of the people I know are terrified of the Religious Right. They're afraid that they'll have us all in headscarves and behind bars for sex out of wedlock. And frankly I'm afraid too.

Bishop: No, that will never happen for two reasons. First, several of those things you mention are not forbidden by the Bible when the relevant passages are read in context. All Christians recognize that now. And second, the Religious Right is a very small minority. I'm not so afraid of them as I am of the godlessness in the world. You can look at so many societies, like Rome, where the lack of God in public life led to their destruction.

I took in a sharp breath at his use of the third person "them" in referring to the Religious Right. Because Highview is mostly apolitical, I hadn't recognized that most Black churches are conservative on personal morality but liberal on social issues. I had always lumped together anyone who took the Bible "literally" as part of the Religious Right.

Teri: My friends and I have seen the resurgence of religious states in the Muslim world, and we're afraid it could happen here. There's plenty of talk among fundamentalists of returning to a Bible-based legal system.

Bishop: That's interesting. I have met thousands of Bible-based Christians at hundreds of conferences for lay people and leaders. And I have never heard any call to legislate morality.

Teri: I am very happy to hear you say that, but I'm not convinced. And the reason is that human nature is the same worldwide. Christians are vulnerable to the same pressures that cause Muslims to justify repression with religion. I hope you're right that what you call the "immature Christians" are a small minority. But that could change with tomorrow's gas price.

Bishop: Teri, if anything, the pressure is coming from the other side, from secular society. What about all the laws that enforce a secularist value system, and laws that make it difficult for Christians to practice their faith?

Teri: Like what?

Bishop: Well first of all, abortion being legal. That certainly hurts an innocent.

Teri: Abortion is a special case, I'll grant you. Almost no one would deny that each abortion is a tragedy. It's just that the relative benefit to individuals and society is so great.

Bishop: You've just proven my point. The secularist value system is based on convenience to the individual, and that's what they enforce through law.

Teri: I respect your position on that. In fact, I'll go so far as to say I respect people who protest peacefully at abortion clinics. But it's such a terribly difficult issue; could we please set that one aside?

Bishop: Well, you want to justify homosexual marriage because you say some good comes out of it for individuals. But good can come out of a rape, too, when a child is produced, but that doesn't mean you justify the rape.

Teri: Huh? What? That's not a good comparison. Clear harm comes of a rape, and my whole point about homosexual marriage was that no harm comes of it.

Bishop: Hmm. Well, I guess that makes sense. But one can argue that homosexual marriages *do* harm society… (This exchange predated some discussions in the chapter, *Homosexuality Revisited.*)

After we'd been around this bush several times, my view shifted about why politics and religion are such a toxic mix. The experts my peer group follows place all the blame on the backwardness of religious conservatives. I was beginning to see that "my side" both contributed to the problem and held keys to solving it. I found some experts who agreed with me.

Both sides consider the other wicked and evil

In terms of being part of the problem, most of my friends are quick to see that they are being "demonized" by the Religious Right, but they are slow to recognize their own tendency to reciprocate. That's why I laughed when Bishop visited the movie discussion at Celebration Center and someone half-joked, "The only evil people are Republicans."

Another time I was seated at a formal Washington dinner beside two liberal political analysts. One of them said to the other, "I've tried and tried to understand what makes the neoconservatives behave the way they do. And the only thing I can come up with is that they are evil."

About that time an *L.A. Times* headline also caught my attention: "The Dark Side of Faith: *It's Official*, Too Much Religion is a Dangerous Thing." [69] It reported findings that high levels of praying, attending church, and certainty regarding the existence of God had been correlated with *higher* levels of murder and abortion. I was pretty sure those statistics needed a second look. But what struck me was the headline's tone. "It's Official"—*We secularists knew it all along*.

Projection and exaggeration stir the pot

Brian McLaren lays out the process of demonization like this:

- I have an issue with, say, my own judgmentalness so I become hyper aware of judgment in others
- I seek out the most extreme example and envision how bad things would be if that example were even worse
- I generalize that example to all people on the other side of the issue

No wonder the other side looks wicked and evil compared to us.

Psychologists call it projection when we see in others those traits we deny in ourselves. Of course, that doesn't necessarily mean the other side isn't guilty of those traits. But it does mean we need to stay alert to our biases. Research shows that when we watch the news, for example, we see bias only against our own side, and the effect *increases* as we become more informed.[70] Thus, more information is not the solution.

"Mean green" makes it worse

This cycle of demonizing each other is nothing new. But what is new is how excesses of postmodern relativism are stoking the flames. Ken Wilber first drew my attention to this theme by calling excesses of relativism mixed with narcissism "mean green." Then I found the same theme in the work of an older hero to the postmodern age, Robert Pirsig. He is most famous for *Zen and the Art of Motorcycle Maintenance*. But it's in his second book, *Lila: An Inquiry into Morals*, that he talks about how extreme moral relativism caused intellectuals to confuse protecting ideas and protecting acts.[71] He points to New York's experiment with letting drunks shout obscenities, panhandle, and relieve themselves on the sidewalk. We confused the right to *think* anything with the right to *do* anything, he said. And that left society "caught in the crossfire" between intellectuals and criminals—without a clear right to protect itself from *actions* that erode the quality of life for all.[72] I wondered how many people who enjoyed a counter-culture sense of freedom in Pirsig's *Zen* would be shocked to know he later wrote this:

> It's this intellectual pattern of amoral "objectivity" that is to blame for the social deterioration of America, because it has undermined the static social values necessary to prevent deterioration. In its condemnation of social repression as the enemy of liberty, it has never come forth with a single moral principle that distinguishes a Galileo fighting social repression from a common criminal fighting social repression. It has, as a result, been the champion of both. That's the root of the problem. [73]

Fundamentalism: *modern* response to modern times

This pressure from relativism explains much of the resurgence of fundamentalism worldwide. Religious historian Karen Armstrong calls this resurgence, "a complex and rational response to uniquely modern circumstances." [74] Her theme is echoed by other academics looking at the new fundamentalism. They call this resurgence, "a proclamation of reclaimed authority over a sacred tradition which is to be reinstated *as an antidote for a society that has strayed from its cultural moorings*." [75]

In other words, only in the last few decades have fundamentalists felt pushed beyond the breaking point by social change. And only in the last few decades have they developed the whole apparatus of mega churches and political involvement in response. Moral Majority founder Jerry Fallwell, for example, said he was opposed to politics in the pulpit until the 60s when the Supreme Court "decided to remove God from the public square, beginning with the school-prayer issue." "What could I do?" he asked.[76]

Freeze-dried religion is modern!

The irony, according to experts, is that when fundamentalists felt pushed too far by modernism, the tools they chose to fight back with were solidly modern in their rationalness. This is one of the themes that my new hero Brian McLaren has taken the lead in articulating. At the time of Jesus, he says, religion had space for visions, parables, prophets, and miracles, but no dogma. Modern fundamentalism, on the other hand, took its cue from the rational and mechanistic "modern" era ushered in by the Enlightenment. Doctrine was cast in a set of absolutist, rational proofs to meet the demands of a rationalist culture. Beginning with Calvin, according to McLaren, doctrine was "pressed, freeze-dried, and shrink-wrapped" in order to *win back* the place in society that religion lost to science in the modern era.[77]

So, as I had come to suspect in my discussions with Bishop, the problem with some fundamentalism is not that it's irrational. Rather it might sometimes be *too* rational—not open to the new, the unexpected. That's where the real clash with progressives is.

Acknowledging the other side's contribution

In Chapter 9 at *Two kinds of good*, I related Pirsig's concept that there are two kinds of quality, and we need both: "static quality" and "Dynamic quality." In politics, the contribution of orthodox religion is to bring us the rules and roles that hold society together via "static quality." The contribution of progressives is to express "Dynamic quality" by bringing us the new and unpredictable. Without Dynamic quality a society will stagnate and die. But without static quality, the gains from Dynamic quality cannot be locked in, and all we have is chaos.

Unfortunately, Pirsig notes, advocates for the two values always regard each other as evil. But both values are necessary for our survival and growth.[78] And thus, the best a society can hope for is to have its conservative and progressive forces evenly matched. Perhaps we should be grateful for how evenly split we are in the United States.

Both sides use the law to impose their values

This tendency to demonize each other heats up when either group perceives that its freedoms are threatened, as in the recent political climate in the United

States. Indeed, religious and non-religious people have plenty to fear from each other—*when the other group attempts to use the law to enforce its worldview.*

I decided to ask some friends from the Christian right about how current laws threaten their value system. Though, of course, I didn't have any such friends in my regular social circle because of the way most of us socialize within our own value systems. But I do have a fellow teacher who makes no secret of her strong religious views, so I asked her. I got an earful.

"First you take my taxes to pay for all kinds of things I'm opposed to," she said. "Then you tell me my kids can't pray in school, something that's critical to their upbringing. You remove all Christian symbols from public life while going out of your way to honor every other religion, and you even tell me it's politically incorrect to wish someone a Merry Christmas. I am afraid of being persecuted for my faith next. They'll be sending all Christians off to sensitivity training—or to prison."

I thought she was exaggerating. Shortly thereafter I saw a news report from Sweden about a Pentecostal pastor who was sentenced to jail for quoting the Bible's condemnation of homosexuality in an article he wrote for his local newspaper. He was convicted under Sweden's hate crime law.[79] That's "mean green," the pluralism that aims to honor all views, but overshoots by censoring the views of those who disagree with it.

Another expression of growing secular distrust of religion is tightened local regulation of churches. County boards that used to see churches as a benefit to a community now see them as a tax drain or even a nuisance. Fights over parking, zoning, and service fees can make churches feel besieged. McLean Bible, the mega church at which I attended the C.S. Lewis seminar, was told by Fairfax County to stop offering Bible classes that are part of a degree program until it applied for a permit as a college.[80] Actions such as these may represent legitimate concerns by neighbors. But they appear to play out some Christian predictions that the "Last Days" will be preceded by a crackdown on religion.

Brian McLaren says, "To the degree that (both sides) have sold their spiritual birthright for a political ideology, they must repent; neither left nor right leads to the higher kingdom." [81]

Ways through the deadlock: Greasing the conveyor belt

If the conflict is fed by extremism on both sides, failure to see the others' contributions, and over-reliance on government for answers, where might solutions lie? A few thinkers are beginning to point to a way *beyond* the deadlock.

In answer to postmodernism, both Pirsig and Wilber offer principles that can make the kind of moral distinctions that relativism obscures. The principles both these thinkers offer are tied to honoring the universal *stages of growth* of individuals and society. And the more I study, the more those principles sound like ones Bishop Thomas tells me he finds in the Bible. "It's in there!" he'd say.

I think this is why Wilber calls secularists to encourage religion's best side rather than fight its worst. The religions have the holy books everybody looks to. Wilber says religion is the only institution that can reach most the world's people where they are and serve as a "conveyor belt" for their growth.[82]

Moving beyond politics

Exploring ideas similar to Wilber and Pirsig, but working from the religious side of the street, Brian McLaren acknowledges that pluralism has been both good and bad, and he calls Christians to move *beyond* it. McLaren looks for "emergent Christians" who are "post-liberal," and "post-conservative." Using the language of cancer diagnosis he says,

> Emergent Christians see pluralistic relativism as a dangerous treatment for stage 4 absolutist/colonial/totalitarian modernity… something that saves a life by nearly killing it. It's dangerous medicine—but stagnancy, getting stuck too long in the cocoon, is dangerous too.

And then he gives me goose bumps again.

> Is it possible that modern, exclusivist, absolutist Christians are right—pluralistic relativism is dangerous? But is it possible that the way ahead is not to *stop short* of a pluralistic phase, but rather to *go through it* and *pass beyond it*, emerging into something beyond and better? Do you see why words like *postmodern*, *post-liberal*, and *post-conservative* keep coming up—why the word *beyond* is so prevalent these days?[83]

What if McLaren's "beyond" points to the same trend I thought I glimpsed in gender relations (Chapter 30, *A shifting midpoint*). It was secularists and liberals who pioneered expanded roles for women. They brought us the "Dynamic" good of something new. Religious conservatives were first to point out the problems and extremes; they held the pattern of "static good." But eventually most conservatives did adopt those aspects of feminism that are of clear benefit to all—equal wages, freedom for women to work, encouragement of "speaking up" in constructive ways to overbearing husbands or bosses, and so on. Religious conservatives absorbed those advances into a fuller interpretation of scripture; assertive communication skills became a "literal interpretation" of Col 4:6, "**May your speech be gracious, seasoned with salt, so that you may know how you should answer each person**."

What might happen if we took the perspective that the same scenario of re-balancing is unfolding now with pluralism and relativism? McLaren takes the view that Postmodernism is in its early stages and may not reach its final shape for generations. There's still time for us to influence that shape, he says. So perhaps we can consider that Phase One was the secularists and religious liberals bringing the benefits of increased respect for all people. In Phase Two, fundamentalists with a close eye on the Bible note that such respect has always been inherent in scripture—*it's in there!*—the Good Samaritan is a good neighbor to *all*. The fundamentalists then courageously reject the extremes of pluralism and help us all move to embrace the positive aspects of the new idea in a balanced way, in this case fulfilling the scripture, "**There is neither Jew nor Greek, slave nor free, male nor female, for you are all one in Christ Jesus**." (Gal 3:28)

From this perspective, both sides are playing important parts. Fundamentalism isn't that bad.

Where angels fear to tread

While a few philosophers, preachers, and political activists such as those mentioned above are attempting to ease tension between religion and politics, the academic experts have concluded it's all but hopeless. In a paper on "The Quixotic Quest for Civility," academics who saw all this coming warned in 1988 that fundamentalists and secularists are caught in a loop. Attempts to communicate break down into "reciprocated diatribe" (mud slinging) in which rationalists become irrational and Christians become unchristian, they say. The only glimmer of hope the academics hold out is for an intervention in which "those not so embroiled in the controversy" seek to share "undistorted communication" about the issues.[84] Or, as my Grandpa would put it, "Find somebody who can keep a cool head and cut through the bull hockey."

Bishop Thomas and I plunged ahead.

An answer in honoring the public environment

Teri: You may have noticed the two bumper stickers on my car: one says I'm "Pro choice on everything." And the other says, "Personal Responsibility is the answer." That's because I believe the only way we grow is through our free choices and facing the consequences of our actions.

Bishop: I agree with that.

Teri: And therefore, I strongly believe in everybody's right to do anything that doesn't hurt someone else…

Bishop: You don't mean *anything*. What if I wanted to have sex with a sheep?

Teri: Well, uh… I'm pretty sure there would be health implications, and we would have to be sure it was okay with the sheep. But if it was uplifting for both of you…

Bishop: I can't believe you're saying that.

Teri: Wait. You got me off track. What I started to say is that I've always been an advocate for the *legal* right of people to do whatever they want. But as a result of my discussions with you and getting to know some of the people here, I have come to see how much the public environment can impinge on the person who is trying to live a simple and chaste life. I think most reasonable people would agree that the virtues you and I have talked about are admirable for those who choose to follow them. And historically people got social support for efforts to live by those values via all kinds of voluntary arrangements—like hiding the girlie magazines behind the counter. But today, much in the public sphere either attacks traditional values or scoffs at them. It started with sexual behavior, but it has spread way beyond that. For example, there's the "everyone does it" response to cheating on tests, lying on your resume—or on your corporation's audit.

Bishop: They're making wrong right.

Teri: Yes. And the funny thing is, many secularists will admit in private that new freedoms have made possible *behavior* that serves no one. But they refrain from saying that publicly for fear of supporting a legal backlash. For example, a feminist friend of mine said, "I would say that teens are getting sexually involved too young now, but I'm afraid of giving anyone ammunition for going back to the days of total repression."

Bishop: What you call "repression" the Bible calls *gently* rebuking your brother. And I've told you how that must be done in humility and love, *not* with repression.

Teri: Well I've been thinking about something like that as an alternative. Maybe each of us has a responsibility to speak for our values, not in a judgmental way, but just honestly. The whole thing with boundary setting in the 70s was very healthy in this regard—teaching unassertive people to say "no" when they were uncomfortable with something. We called it "raising consciousness."

So perhaps we should be extending this now. Perhaps when a friend or colleague expresses an "everybody does it" attitude we should be willing to say, "I'm uncomfortable with that." Not "you're wrong" or "that's bad" which would be judgmental and turn people off. But a simple statement of our own values. I have a Jewish friend who does this, and the result is that everyone else wants her advice because they know she'll always tell it straight.

Bishop: She sounds very Christian. That's a good form of evangelism.

Teri: And maybe we should call broadcasters and tell them we won't buy products advertised on shows that degrade what it means to be human, like *Desperate Housewives*.*

Bishop: I like *Desperate Housewives*.

Teri: What?

Bishop: Cindy gets on me about my TV habits. I like those shows where a lot of things blow up. I get enough reality all day, I like to relax. We have to know our own tolerances. Remember the scripture I told you, "**All things are lawful but not all things are expedient.**" (1 Cor 10:23 asv)

Teri: *Help me Jesus.* But, but what if your kids were in the room?

Bishop: Well, I might turn the TV off; or I might sit them down and use it as a teaching opportunity. And I think people should complain about shows they find offensive if they are moved to do so. But we don't need to promote a sterile environment to be good Christians; our work is done from the inside out. Something in the world only becomes a problem when it's so pervasive that it threatens my right to control my own environment.

Teri: You never cease to surprise me.

An answer in personal responsibility

Teri: So as I started to say before, I believe the only way we grow is through our free choices and facing the consequences of our actions. So to me, passing laws that prevent us from making stupid, selfish, or immoral decisions is like asking the government to do your job as pastor. It's like you're saying," I wasn't able to persuade them to be good, so I want the government to force them."

* At the time of this discussion, I had never watched Desperate Housewives. When I finally did, I was surprised by its sensitive handling of many family issues. And it was pretty darn entertaining, too.

Bishop: Jesus didn't want to persuade anybody by force. He said in Luke 9:5, if one house doesn't listen to you **"shake the dust off your feet"** and move on to the next. In fact, he got much madder at the religious folk than at the sinners.

Teri: Yes, yes.

Bishop: So I suppose you could say I'm pro-choice on everything too.

Teri: What!

Bishop: But before you go grabbing for that notepad again, I'm only "pro-choice" as long as all involved parties get a say in the choice. So when you're talking about abortion, we can presume the unborn child would want to live. So somebody's got to speak for the child. Other than abortion, you could say I'm pro-choice on everything.

Teri: Wow. You've stunned me again. Listen, I can work with that. I would have to fight you on abortion. But I would fight you honorably, with respect and with love.

Bishop: That's a start. That's a good start. But wouldn't it be better if we didn't have to fight?

Shortly after this conversation I saw a press report about an extraordinary attempt at conciliation between two clergymen who lead rival political action groups. Liberal Rabbi and activist David Saperstein normally fights for abortion rights, and Evangelical Christian activist Rev. Rob Schenck normally fights against homosexual marriage. But in an attempt to turn down the heat on these issues, the two clergymen reached an agreement: Rabbi Saperstein promised he would promote among liberals a campaign to cut abortion in half, while Rev. Schenck began encouraging the teaching among conservatives that homosexuality is not a choice but a "predisposition," something that is "deeply rooted" in many people.[85]

Neither of these gestures is totally satisfactory, of course, to the opposite side. But they mark a potential for a new way of approaching difficult issues. Both sides say, "I'll help your side deal with effects of my hardliners."

The greatest answer: compassion

Over the year of our dialogues (which stretched into two with editing the book) Bishop Thomas and I had several conversations on law and politics. But the most inspiring solution for conflict that we arrived at had nothing to do with either.

Teri: If you don't mind my bringing it up one more time, I want to make sure I've been clear about my fears of religious-based laws. For example, among my own friends I've seen the situation where parents reject a gay child. And 30 years later when that child is dying in the hospital, suddenly the parents show up and ban the gay spouse from making decisions or even visiting.

Bishop: Well look at the Terri Schiavo case. (A dying woman whose husband and parents fought over a decision to end her care.) Was that fair to the parents who weren't allowed to see their own child?

Teri: No, probably not. It's true that in tough cases like that whichever side the law takes someone will be excluded, and sometimes that exclusion will be a terrible injustice. But in our society, we've decided that in the tough cases, preference goes to the spouse. Then we forbid gay people from being spouses.

Bishop: The problem is not the law, it's that the parties involved are behaving in a non-Christian manner. If my child were gay and had chosen that lifestyle, of course I would have compassion and do everything I could to bring us all together for a just solution.

Teri: I'm glad to hear you say that. And I know you mean it. But most fundamentalists don't see it that way, as far as I can tell.

Bishop: Well that would only be if they miss the point and get caught up in rules and dogma. As I've told you, I grew up in a very strict Pentecostal church—some of the stories I could tell! But a relationship with God is not about rules; it's about principles. It's not like somebody's standing over you with a stick waiting for you to break a rule. It's more like the principle of gravity: What goes up, must come down. And the principle here is to always seek what you call the higher good in any situation. Mature Christians know that.

One last surprise

I was continually surprised at how little real difference there was between my values and those of Bishop Thomas when we really got to the bottom of things. I was satisfied that we had gone as far as we could go, so I never tackled head-on the question of laws about homosexual marriage. But several months after our last discussion about politics, the Universe dropped the question in our laps. Acting as the church Webmaster, I was first to receive an email from the office of Virginia State Senator Ken Cuccinelli. His staff said he wanted to address our congregation regarding his support for an upcoming bill to ban gay marriage. His amendment defined marriage as the union between one man and one woman only. I took a deep breath and forwarded the email to Bishop Thomas.

It was the first topic he brought up the next time I walked into his office. He said, "Let's write back and tell them we agree that the Bible limits marriage to one man and one woman, but we don't see any justification in the Bible for legislating morality."

I took another deep breath. This is the reply we wrote together and sent.

> July 28, 2006
>
> Dear Senator Cuccinelli,
>
> Thank you for the offer to speak to our congregation regarding your support of the November ballot amendment to define marriage as the union between one man and one woman only. As a fundamentalist church that holds the Bible as the literal Word of God, we agree this is God's definition of marriage, and that the homosexual sex act is displeasing to God. However, we find no support in the Bible for legislating morality, and prefer to do as Jesus did and leave this choice to individuals and their churches who will have to answer to God.
>
> We would, however, be eager to have you speak to us regarding local legislation that limits the ability of churches to reach people with the Word of God. We are especially concerned about the requirement from Fairfax County that McLean Bible Church cannot offer Bible classes without being licensed as a college. We are also concerned with the general reluctance by many local governments to permit churches to occupy commercial space because it removes properties from the tax rolls.
>
> We believe that the growth in pressures such as these stems in part from the perception among secularists that churches seek to limit their freedoms. Of course, nothing could be further from the truth as we seek to bring them true freedom in salvation through the redemptive blood of Jesus. You will have our full support in any efforts to erase this confusion in the public mind so churches can get on with the work of bringing reconciliation, compassion, and upright living to a world in desperate need of God.
>
> God bless you with wisdom and judiciousness,
>
> Bishop Phil Thomas
>
> Pastor, Highview Christian Fellowship, Fairfax

Their letter back said the senator could make time for a discussion with us on other topics after the election.

37

Beyond Politics Part 2: Healing Our World

For I was hungry and you gave me something to eat, I was thirsty and you gave me something to drink, I was a stranger and you invited me in, I needed clothes and you clothed me, I was sick and you looked after me, I was in prison and you came to visit me.
Matt. 25:35-36

A few weeks after I handed Bishop Thomas the book by Brian McLaren, he returned from a marathon trip, and something seemed different about him. He'd spent a week at a pastor's conference in Phoenix, followed by a week on a mission in Africa, followed by a bishop's conference in Cleveland.

On his first Sunday back, he gave a passionate sermon about how Americans skip church when they're worried about paying the cable bill, while starving people in Kenya will walk miles in bare feet to worship together on Sunday. He said he wanted to organize some American churches to support a group of churches in Kenya. "We can be more powerful if we all work together," he said.

The week after that, he gave a sermon about how Christians should be known by their fruits in the world. "I know you haven't heard preaching like this before," he said, "but you're going to be hearing more."

Something was different in our dialogues as well.

Our mission: heaven on earth?

Bishop: So far Teri whenever you've talked about politics, you've only expressed fears of Christians imposing their values on others. But we haven't talked about our proactive Christian mission—to bring healing and compassion to the world. To feed the hungry and care for the sick. To be peacemakers as Jesus called us to be. To bring liberation to all people and light where there's darkness.

Teri: Yes, yes. Frankly I've been surprised that I haven't heard more talk about that from conservative Christians.

Bishop: Well then you'll like this. Before the bishop's conference last week the organizers asked all attendees to read a book, *Adventures in Missing the Point.* It's about how pastors can get sidetracked by secondary issues and miss the point of Jesus' message.[86] It's a dialogue between two Evangelical leaders who are working to change the church from the inside: Tony Campolo and that other fellow you told me about, Brian McLaren.

Teri: You're kidding me.

Bishop: No, it was quite a coincidence.

Teri: How did people respond?

Bishop: Everybody was enthusiastic. And at the conference we had speakers who shared a fantastic vision with us about bringing harmony between the left and right factors in Christianity. Tony Campolo,* and the fellow who wrote *God's Politics,*[87] Jim Wallis. You know that book?

Teri: I think I saw some reviews on it a while back.

---

* Popular Evangelical speaker Tony Campolo gives over 300 talks a year calling Christians from Left and Right to social action. He has said of the Middle East conflict, "The Jesus of the scripture transcends all nations and calls all nations into judgment…And if we think that they're the bad guys and we're the good guys, we aren't being Christian. There's goodness and there's badness on both sides of this struggle."

He was censored for two statements in his 1983 book A Reasonable Faith. He wrote, "Jesus is the only Savior, but not everybody who is saved by him is aware that He is the one who is doing the saving." He also wrote "I mean that Jesus actually is present in each other person." A Panel of Reconciliation found those statements to be "methodologically naïve and verbally incautious," but the panel stopped short of finding him guilty of heresy. (Christianity Today, 1/24/03, as reported at www.christianitytoday.com/ct/2003/001/1.32.html)

Bishop: Wallis says the Right ignores social justice in favor of personal morality. And the Left is so afraid of being associated with religion that it won't speak up for moral and spiritual values. Wallis is one of several people trying to get both sides to focus more on how they can cooperate to be a force for good in the world. Here, why don't you borrow my copies?

Teri: (He handed me both *God's Politics* and *Missing the Point,* and I flipped through them.) This time I get the benefit of your highlighting.

Spiritual progressives extend a hand

I took the books home and read them over the following weeks. Coincidentally, this was during the period that a spiritual activism conference in Washington turned press attention to the Religious Left. The conference was co-sponsored by Wallis's Sojourner group and the Network of Spiritual Progressives headed by Rabbi Michael Lerner, who is also editor of the progressive Jewish magazine *Tikkun* and author of *The Left Hand of God.* I followed the press reports and picked up the discussion with Bishop a few weeks later.

Teri: I see what you mean that folks like Wallis, Lerner, and Campolo have a great vision. They encourage the forms of common ground that you and I have talked about: calling on people of all spiritual orientations to put their love into action without demonizing the other side. I love the goals, but I can't support many of their specific programs.

Bishop: Like what?

Teri: Well first, I have to make a major disclaimer here, which is that my opinions on this are not typical for people in New Thought or New Age. We have just a very few people who think the way I do on this. And if my buddy Ed Preston were here, he'd argue with me every step of the way.

Bishop: Okay, I got ya.

Preferring voluntary action

Teri: Several of the programs these reformers support require the use of government power. The way I see it, as soon as we turn our efforts to wielding political power, we risk getting sucked into righteousness and power hunger. The lure of power distracts and distorts the good intention.

Bishop: What kind of programs?

Teri: More poverty programs, government health care, foreign aid, trade protection; and Wallis supports payments to Black Americans as reparations for slavery.

Bishop: That would be a mess.

Teri: I think so, too. So there's a huge, hidden obstacle in efforts to find common ground: the fact that both sides are unconscious of how much they depend on government to do their good works for them. And to my mind government programs are usually less effective in the long run than voluntary efforts.

Bishop: I'm inclined to think you're right. In fact, it's hard for me to focus on this discussion when I could be spending the time trying to get some help for those churches in Kenya or developing our total man ministry right here.

Teri: Yes, exactly. That was one thing that impressed me most when I came here—your vision that even a small church like this could offer counseling, career development, even shelter—not just to its own members but to the community.

Bishop: And now the interfaith group we've joined is looking for ways for churches to work together.

Teri: That's beautiful. The *leaders* of that spiritual activism conference last week impressed me as being highly mature spiritually; they encouraged speakers to keep their focus spiritual and positive. But as soon as the topic turned to political action, some speakers fell into name calling and arguing over specific programs. That's what happens when the focus is gaining political power, even for the best of aims.

To me, the real answers demand more of us. We all need to promote our values via the voluntary strategies of education, inspiration, conciliation, and dialogue. Just speaking for myself, I am much more excited about contributing my time and money to a church or other group that directly feeds the poor than to one that promotes laws forcing *other* people to feed the poor.

Bishop: Nobody's seen better than me how government handouts can backfire—destroy the will and esteem of those who receive them.

Teri: You know the Muslims may have a head start on us here. They're expected to pay a percentage of their wealth directly to charity every year.

Bishop: How's that work?

Teri: Dr. Ahmad tells me there's always been debate about it in Islam, with the Sunnis wanting it to be collected by the religious leaders and the Shiites wanting it completely on the honor system. In fact, he says that's one of the original issues that split them up.

Bishop: Interesting.

Peace begins with me

Teri: Of course we must take a stand where we see injustice, corruption or just bad decisions in politics. But so often that tempts us to self-righteousness. Take anti-war activism. If I am at a peace protest yelling obscenities at the other side or even silently believing they are evil, I am part of the problem. That's something I'm proud of as a Religious Scientist; we work to remember, "Peace begins with me." Just after the U.S. sent troops to Afghanistan post 9/11, Celebration Center held a peace circle on the Capitol grounds, led by Rev. Beckwith from Los Angeles. But we didn't protest *against* anything. In fact, we wore signs that said, "FOR peace, AGAINST nothing." The tourists loved taking our pictures, but the signs helped us remember to stay humble about thinking we knew the best answer to world problems.

Bishop: Matthew 10:16 (nkjv) tells us to be "**wise as serpents and gentle as doves.**"

Teri: I like that. Another way we can take power peacefully is by being conscious of our investments. There's a great example of that in *Adventures in Missing the Point*—I am really loving that book, by the way. Campolo and McLaren make a great team.

Bishop: I need it back for my ministerial class.

Teri: Here in the chapter on social action, Tony Campolo tells how some of his students each bought one share of stock in a company that operates in the Dominican Republic. Then they all went to a shareholders meeting and insisted that the company raise wages and offer health, education, and environmental services.

Bishop: That sounds great.

Teri: Yes, maybe. If they then invested their *own* savings into that company, then I say bravo, I'm inspired. But if they put their personal retirement funds in some other stocks that pay more, then they're just righteous hypocrites. And I'm a righteous hypocrite too, because my retirement account is still invested where I think I can get the most profit. It's so easy to blame corporations. But as long as any of us have our savings invested in stock that we pay no attention to, *we are the problem.*

Bishop: Now I'm learning something from you.

The good neighbor policy

Bishop: It all sounds interesting. But even if we wanted to encourage a more voluntary system, how do you put the government genie back in the bottle once it's out?

Teri: The easy answer is for groups to just bypass government and run their own programs where their spiritual values can be fully integrated. You have to help people see the areas in which voluntary action is more flexible and has deeper, more enduring impact. Remember Hurricane Katrina? The Red Cross got there before Homeland Security. And churches from around the country were able to help where the government couldn't.

Bishop: I can see how that could be, but how do you control people who won't contribute their share or recipients who take advantage of a voluntary program?

Teri: I don't think we should try to control them unless they're aggressing on someone else. A friend of mine, Mary Ruwart, wrote a book *Healing Our World in an Age of Aggression.* It lays out an action plan to use voluntary, "good neighbor" means to address national and international problems. She says that in order to control selfish others, we give away our power, and that always backfires—it creates resistance by those we're trying to control, and eventually they turn that same kind of power on us.[88]

Bishop: Well, that sounds like the scripture "**Love your neighbor as yourself.**" (Mk 12:31) But wouldn't there be a lot of gaps and hardships and bad decisions in a more voluntary system?

Teri: Don't we have plenty of those right now? So if you mean how do we bring heaven on earth, it seems to me the only route is to motivate people spiritually to do their individual parts. It's more demanding than just paying taxes and trying to influence how they're spent. But Jesus never said it would be easy, did he?

Bishop: Ah, you have been learning something, too. In fact Jesus said those who followed him would be scorned by the world. But he made our mission clear in Luke 4:18: he walked into the temple, picked up a scroll, and read from Isaiah, "**The Spirit of the Lord is on me, because he has anointed me to preach good news to the poor. He has sent me to proclaim freedom for the prisoners and recovery of sight for the blind, to release the oppressed, to proclaim the year of the Lord's favor.**"

Teri: That's a mission I could get excited about.

Bishop: But he also made it clear that it's a mission we can't hope to finish by ourselves. That's what the second coming of Jesus is about...

38

End Times: Fear Not

Some day the world will
be reborn, resurrected into
a consciousness of unity,
cooperation, love and collective
security. We are a part of...
the unfoldment of the Divine
Intelligence in human affairs.
(This unfoldment) has reached
the point of conscious and
deliberate cooperation with
that principle of evolution and
out-push of the creative urge
of the Spirit, to bring about
innumerable centers which It
may enjoy.
Ernest Holmes, *This Thing Called You*

Bishop's mention of End Times raised a red flag for me. The Bible's predictions for the end of the world were rarely discussed at Highview, and that was fine by me. My impression was that no good could come of discussing the last book of the Bible, *Revelations*, with its apocalyptic vision of mass destruction that would be survived by only a few true believers.

In fact, I occasionally became depressed when I got a taste of the apparent glee with which some Christians look forward to the day they "win" and everyone else is annihilated. An article in *Vanity Fair* called it a "revenge fantasy" and quoted a follower of Tim LaHaye, author of the wildly popular *Left Behind* series. The follower had calculated exactly how much blood would be spilled in the final confrontation between good and evil. Standing with a tour group in

Israel looking over the expected ground zero of Armageddon, the fellow says, "Can you imagine this entire valley filled with blood? That would be a 200-mile long river of blood, four and a half feet deep. We've done the math. That's the blood of as many as two and a half billion people."[89]

So a shiver went through me when Bishop Thomas ended our conversation about politics by saying we couldn't reach a perfect world before Christ returns. In fact, he said he was preparing a series of sermons on the topic.

Teri: Should I be afraid of what you're going to say?

Bishop: Teri, don't you know me better than that by now?

Teri: I should. But you're so full of surprises. And *Revelations* is so full of fear; I don't see what good can come of discussing it.

Bishop: But that's the point: to allay the fear. We study eschatology (end times) so people know what to expect, so they can prepare and face it when it comes. Revelations promises **a new heaven and a new earth** (Rev 21:1). It tells us that "eyes haven't seen" what God has prepared for us. That's *good* news.

Teri: But the End Time predictions just cause believers to give up on getting along with non-believers because it's already been foretold that we'll never find peace with each other. And that just makes social tension worse.

Bishop: No, no, no. The believer can never give up on the non-believer.

Teri: Maybe there is some scientific wisdom in the predictions. Science tells us that our Sun will go supernova in five billion years—if an asteroid doesn't get us first, or a series of nuclear explosions. And those events would all look like the lake of fire in *Revelations*. So in that sense, a new earth *is* going to be needed some day—even if we have to get there by space ship.

Bishop: This isn't about science, Teri. If we took our sinful selves to a new planet, we'd just mess that one up.

Did you read this? (He picks up the book by McLaren and Campolo that I had placed on his desk to return to him, *Adventures in Missing the Point*.)

Teri: Oh my gosh, I loved it. Campolo says the End Times interpretation in the *Left Behind* series has only been around for 150 years. Most mainstream theologians still interpret that Christ returns and joins the efforts of those who are trying to bring in a just social order.

And he says that Jesus warned against trying to predict when that will be.

Bishop: That's Matthew 24:36 "**No one knows about that day or hour.**"

Teri: You know, there's a metaphysical interpretation of Revelations. It says that each part of the prediction relates to us personally. So each one of us must cast our negativity and pettiness into the "lake of fire" and turn our consciousness to the infinite until we take on the mind of Christ. That would be the "New Heaven," it's the kingdom *within*. We either blow up the whole planet, or we find a way to live in peace. And *that* would be the "New Earth." [90]

Bishop: There might be something to that. But it's also a prediction of world events.

Teri: I just hope the end doesn't come prematurely because some Christian or Muslim who can't wait blows up the Temple Mount to get it started.

Bishop: No Christian would do that. Maybe some nut.

Teri: And that nut would be egged on by wild talk about the glory of Armageddon.

Bishop: Look, Teri, I thought your people always focused on the positive. There are many interpretations of the end times, but all of them predict that those who struggle to bring good to the world do not do so in vain. It's a promise to the good guys, not a threat, because anyone can be part of the good guys who chooses to.

He picked up *Missing the Point*. The book now had Bishop's highlights in green and mine in yellow. He stood up and began reading from his green in a chapter by Campolo.

> Jesus tells us that he has come first and foremost to declare that the kingdom of God is at hand… And God wants this kingdom to become established *on earth, now*! –not after the Second Coming or a future apocalypse or anything else. But right now.

I took the book from him and read one of my yellow paragraphs.

> I have come to believe that both the liberal social Gospelers and the fundamentalists were each partly right... God is at work

> in the world through faithful servants, both inside the church and outside the church. Bringing hope to the poor, liberation to the oppressed, and the creation of a new society in which love and justice reign…

He took the book back from me and read from the green.

> (But) we should not delude ourselves into thinking that whatever we can build of God's kingdom now can come to fullness without Christ's return. We are all flawed people, and only a face-to-face encounter with the eschatological Christ can make us into kingdom people. And without kingdom people, there is no kingdom—as John Milton wrote in Paradise Lost, "The mind is its own place, and in itself can make a hell of heaven and a heaven of hell."

Teri: Amen to that!

Bishop: That's it; that's our mission. We Christians should be an example to the world of how to live as we to continue the work of healing the world that Jesus started. That's why churches should be working together. That's why I keep talking about "Total Man Ministry." We can *show* the love of God by finding someone a meal or teaching them a skill before we testify about what God has done in our lives.

Teri: We can be an example of forgiveness and non-judgment so we can widen the circle to invite them in.

Bishop: We can fulfill Abraham's promise to *be* a blessing to all nations.

Teri: I'd be happy to be on your team for that vision... as long as everything about it is voluntary for all parties.

Bishop: I've told you there is no point in changing people from the outside in. But we each have to do our part to fulfill our purpose. Jesus said anyone who has faith in him "**will do even greater things**" than he did (John 14:12). He didn't mean we'd do *better* things, he meant our results could be greater because there are more of us. But a lot of people think they can run off to save the world when their own hearts are still dark and petty. And that won't work.

Teri: Yes, that's why my people say, "Peace begins with me."

Bishop: I can say "amen" to that.

39

God's Plan Revisited

And the end of our explorations
shall be to return where we began
and know it again for the first time.
T.S. Elliott

If it's true that we only grow when we encounter a problem we can't solve at our current level, then Bishop Thomas and I were lucky to be each other's problem. It was obvious to both of us early on how much we had in common. So it simply was not possible to believe the other was wicked, evil, insane, stupid, ignorant, or even blind. We had to find some other explanation for our different beliefs. For him it was that some people are genuinely seeking God outside of Christianity. For me it was that "old time religion" has more truth than I suspected, and the incarnation of Jesus demonstrates the most important truth we can all live out.

Teri: When we first started meeting and you explained Genesis to me, you asked me what better explanation I had for the relationship between Man and God. And I want you to know it made a huge impression on me that you did that. It forced me to think very carefully this past year, and I think I'm ready to answer you.

Bishop: All right.

Teri: I suspect you have had the same sense I have that despite all the things you and I have been debating, there is something remarkably similar about our relationships to God. Am I right about that?

Bishop: I have felt that. Sometimes I think you're my alter ego.

Teri: Or you're my altar ego—with an "a." (We both laughed.) So here's my theory about the similarity we feel.

Bishop: Okay.

Teri: I feel as if I've come full circle—only it's more like a spiral because I'm seeing my starting point from a higher level. As a child I started with a view of God as a judging father. Then in my twenties I lost the sense of there being anything out there at all. When I got back the sense of something out there in my thirties, it was as a force I could interact with because I am part of it, and that was thrilling.

But as I've worked with you, I'm seeing that force is also something separate from me that I can relate to, that I can love and be loved by, that I can sing, and dance, and jump for joy over in praise of.

And furthermore, that force appears to have a direction to it—a direction pointed pretty much the same way as what the philosophers call more Truth, Beauty, and Goodness—toward the highest good of all. You call it the will of God, and I am now comfortable calling it that also.

Bishop: No more "Universe"?

Teri: Well, maybe it will depend on whom I'm talking to—"Greeks" or "Jews." (We both smile at my allusion to scripture.) So I've come to see the awesome beauty in the Bible's story—not in all the details, but I don't really care about the details anymore. It's a story that offers me a part in making the world a better place, but it also calls me to account to offer my best, and to acknowledge when I have offered less.

Bishop: I notice you're not here every Sunday. Are you still going to Celebration Center?

Teri: Their approach to prayer still works best for me. And sometimes I go there to balance some of your more, uh, challenging sermons. I fantasize putting the two churches together.

Bishop: You still seem to be seeking something. So I can only counsel you to continue reading the Bible and to pray for what we call illumination.

Teri: I want to continue learning how to integrate the character strengths you've helped me to re-value with the acceptance of all people—and of myself—that I learned more easily elsewhere. I am extremely grateful to you for sticking with me—not just for the conversations, but for the role model you've provided of how to integrate those things. You have helped me see how I can have it all. I can have being and doing, faith and works, heaven and earth, conservation and progress, union with God and communion.

Bishop: This has been extremely valuable for me, too, working with you. It's forced me to question everything I believe, to make sure I really understand *why* I believe it. Everybody ought to go through that.

It has also permitted me to see non-Christians in a new light. I think I'll be able to minister to them more effectively. Since being exposed to you and to the work of McLaren and people like him, I might do some things differently. Be more careful how I say some things—as I evolve and mature in my knowing of better ways to accomplish God's will.

But overall, our work together has deepened my faith.

Teri: Mine too.

Bishop: So, are we done? I hope not, I've enjoyed this.

Teri: Me too. Let's see, we've covered religion, politics, and sex. I'm sure I'll think of something else. Maybe we'll bring some more folks in on the conversation.

Bishop: All right then, I'm ready. Any time.

Teri: I'll see what I can do.

Wrestling with an angel

Bishop Thomas and I originally titled this book, *Wicked and Evil Isn't that Bad*: *A Fundamentalist and a New Ager Wrestle for the Soul of the 21st Century*. But our Christian friends didn't like the first part for implying compromise with evil, and our New Thought friends didn't like the second part for implying conflict. We considered the compromise of *The Bishop and the Seeker: Making Peace with Religion,* but it just didn't have the bite we both value. So back came *Wrestling for the Soul of the 21st Century*. Wrestling is an honorable sport, never intended to wound. And it is, in fact, a pretty good description of what Bishop Thomas and I were doing.

While we were considering the name change, I recalled that someone in the Bible wrestled with an angel. I looked it up and found that it was Jacob—I was getting pretty good by now with those online Bible concordances. And this time, I actually read the entire chapter (Genesis 32)—Bishop would be so proud of me. What I learned brought tears to my eyes. The result of the nightlong wrestle was that Jacob decided to return to lands controlled by his estranged brother, Esau. For fear that Esau would attack him, Jacob split up his party and had each group approach by different routes. Jacob went first bringing his best sheep as a peace offering. But when Esau saw him coming from the distance, instead of attacking, he ran to his long-lost brother and kissed his neck. He welcomed Jacob to settle on his land, and he told him to keep his prize stock.

Bishop Thomas and I might each give a slightly different interpretation to how this story applied to our encounter with each other and with the social currents we each represent. But we both thought the metaphor was perfect.

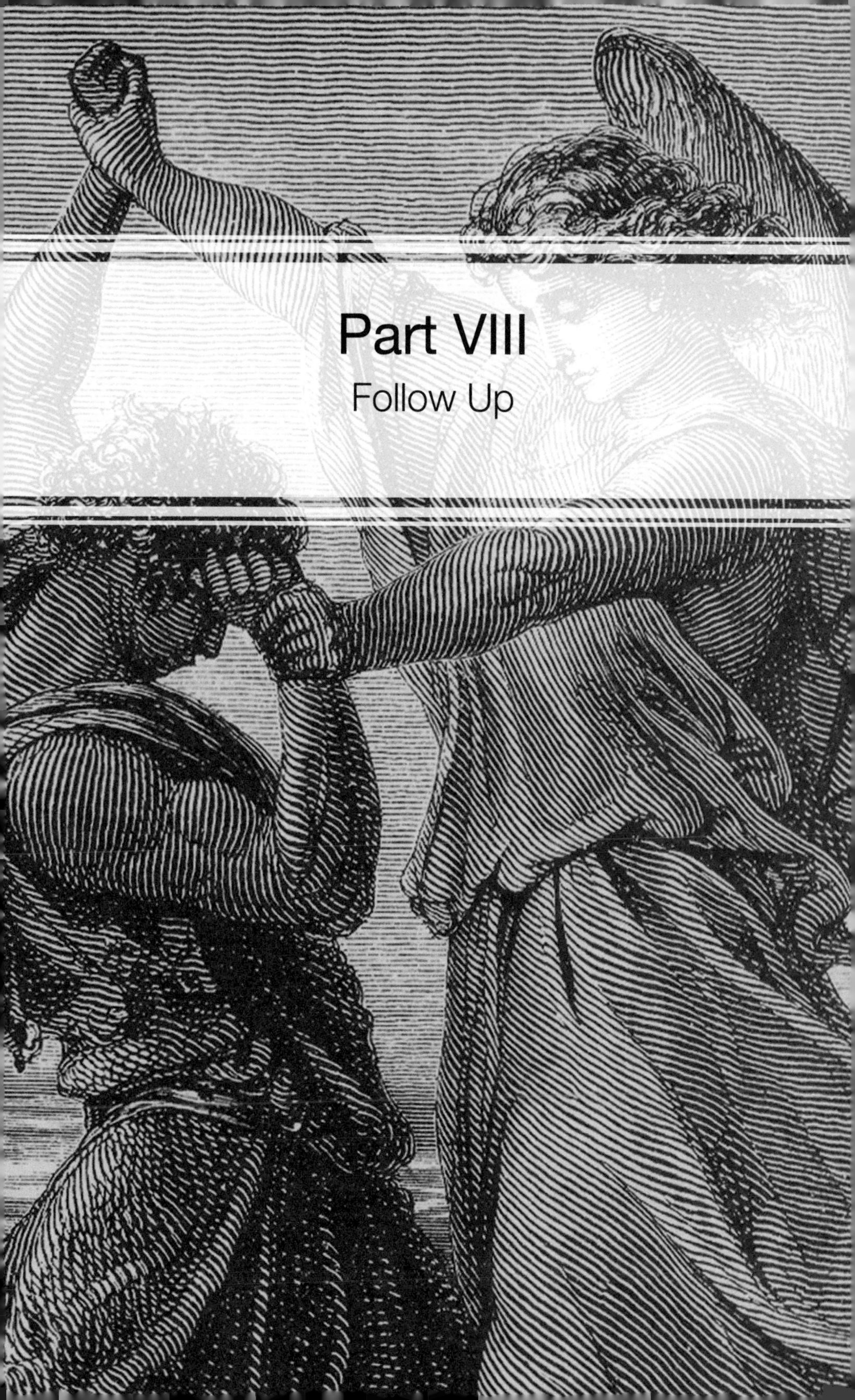

Part VIII

Follow Up

What it would take for us all to get along

One of our goals in writing this book is to mitigate the toll that religious tension can take on our families and our society. The days of believing that universal education could peacefully contain religion to the private sphere are over. It was a noble experiment, but it failed. And not only is God not dead, his followers are back kicking. We need a new strategy for integrating the positive or harmless aspects of religion into the public sphere while protecting us all from excesses. And Christians need a way of sharing their vision of a moral society that doesn't imply they might lock up anyone who disagrees.

Is there anything each of us can do to help restore balance?

As we reported in chapter 36, *Law and Politics: Seeking a Way Beyond,* the experts have concluded it's all but hopeless. The only glimmer of hope academics hold out is for an intervention in which "those not so embroiled in the controversy" seek to share "undistorted communication" about the issues.[91] The people most well positioned for this job are mature Christians and those who believe that some truth can be found in all paths. Even if the non-Christians don't "speak Baptist," any dialect in the language of faith may be enough for building a bridge. And it will help if all participants are striving for the humility that Buddhists call "beginners mind," Christians call "a teachable spirit," and Religious Scientists call "open at the top."

If you think you may be such a person, here are some lessons Bishop Thomas and I have gleaned from our work together that may help along your way.

1. Note commonalities

We hope we have convinced you that what appears as a vast cultural chasm among belief systems conceals the many values held in common by anyone who seeks the highest good for self and others. Focusing on the commonalities will help us work together in finding ways to cope with the very difficult critical differences.

2. Notice your projections

We have shown that both sides consider the other "wicked and evil": it's just a little harder to catch non-fundamentalists using those terms. Each side fails to recognize in itself many of the flaws they see in the other side; that's what psychologists call projection and Christians call criticizing the speck in someone else's eye before removing the log from your own. If you doubt that your side has been unduly harsh on the other side, try asking someone from the other side if they've ever felt judged or even demonized by your side. Ask them if you've made it hard for them to live their values. Ask them if they're afraid you would eagerly cause them hardship or shame, or even put them in jail for their beliefs. Then ask yourself if you recognize and respect the other side's attempts to live their lives the best they know how.

3. Acknowledge the other side's contributions

It's so easy to compare our group's best practice and motives to the worst excesses of the other side. Just as an experiment, try flipping that perception. What is their best and your group's worst? If you believe your group doesn't have a bad side, see item 2 above.

4. Transcend and include

We have suggested that one way to tell which aspect of a system is "higher" than another is to ask which one "transcends and includes" the other. Under this scheme, if you believe that your group is spiritually or ethically "higher," then it's up to you to do the transcending. "**To whom much is given, much is expected**." Can you transcend the shortcomings in another belief system and still tap any strengths that system may give its followers? For example, guided by moral relativism, New Agers and secularists can be extremely good at non-judgment, though not always so good at drawing "tough love" lines to keep themselves, their families or communities safe and productive. Is there room for secularists and religious liberals to be more discerning in the values they promote publicly? Likewise, orthodox Christians can be very good at holding themselves and others accountable for their actions. Is there room to do so while showing the compassion, inclusiveness, and non-judgment many moderates have perfected?

5. Beware attachment to your symbols[92]

Raising consciousness about the implications of our symbols is good. But direct attacks on symbols or symbolic acts always backfire. When we put our effort into stopping flag burning or stopping public display of the Ten Commandments, we turn up the heat on the pressure cooker of belief systems. What would happen if we ignored symbolic challenges and focused on just the things that impede us from living our values? Let's save our resources for educating both sides about laws or customs that truly prevent our side from pursuing its goals.

Similarly, secularists and religious liberals can turn down the heat by renouncing extremes of behavior in public. "**All things are lawful but not all things are expedient.**" From trash television to public rudeness to provocative fashion, taking personal responsibility to tone things down may dampen the urge to strike back by those who are offended.

6. Beyond Caesar: education, inspiration, conciliation

Our most serious tensions stem not from our different beliefs, but from the use of law by each side to enforce its beliefs. And if you doubt that both sides play this game equally, simply ask people on the other side of the fence which laws make it hard for them to live by their values. Instead of voting for laws to enforce your values, wherever possible turn instead to voluntary education, inspiration, and conciliation. Our chapter on Law and Politics includes several suggestions along these lines.

7. Reach out a hand

Here are some good ways to start practicing all of the suggestions above:

- Take a fundamentalist to lunch—or a New Ager—or a secularist. Ask the other person about his or her values and *listen*.
- Then share your hopes and fears, not your positions on the issues.
- Hold a group discussion as outlined in our Guide for Group Discussion in the next section.
- Give a copy of this book to your friends from a different belief system.

And then consider saying a little prayer—or affirmation:

There is a power for good in the Universe.
I align myself with that power. And I acknowledge the yearnings of my brothers and sisters worldwide to align themselves with that power.
I will do gladly whatever I am called to do to support the efforts of others to align themselves with that power.
I release any hatefulness or judgments I have carried, and I forgive those who have judged me or made it difficult for me to do my work.
I hold the vision of a world with more love, respect, and dignity for all.
And I let this vision go with a grateful heart, knowing it is done.

Optional close 1: *In Jesus' Name.*

Optional close 2: *And so it is.*

Afterward Teri: My Jesus

Andy's view

One of the extraordinary aspects of this story is the way my husband's reactions paralleled my own. When you fall through a rabbit hole, having someone else along helps confirm that you're not crazy—unless of course, you're sharing a *folie á deux*—an illusion for two.

I had several conversations with Andy trying to pin down what we were experiencing.

"I've asked myself many times what draws me to Highview," he said. "There's something more definite, less mushy, that I can't put my finger on. It's not just that the beliefs are more definite, because I don't necessarily buy into all the beliefs—although I have felt a growing sense of personalness and closeness about Jesus that feels deeply right."

"I feel that sense of definiteness too," I said. "And some of it is the idea that there is a standard against which feelings can be measured, which of course is the main point Pastor has been making in our dialogues. But as you said, it feels like it's not mainly the beliefs but the atmosphere. You can get a grip on things here, get a purchase. At Celebration Center we were so good at diffusing friction that there wasn't enough traction for me. I felt as though I couldn't get a foothold from which to move."

"Another thing," said Andy, "is that I feel very well loved at Highview. A dozen people come up to me after every service, and my connection with them feels absolutely genuine. I feel loved and appreciated at the Center, too. But somehow it seems more palpable, more acute at Highview. Maybe some of that is the passage of time, the way you feel a new love more acutely than an old one. And some of it is from the fact that we are still outsiders at Highview, in a way, and therefore people go out of their way to make us feel honored and welcomed. It's like an unfair advantage we have there."

Freedom, responsibility, and something else

For both Andy and me, some of the factors that attracted us to Highview were the same as those that originally attracted us to Religious Science, especially the emphasis on freedom and responsibility. Responsibility for how we *respond* to any situation and freedom from the victimhood of blaming others for our problems; freedom to be an individual within community; freedom from past habits, from destructive thought patterns and from popular attitudes. Religious Science makes a much bigger point of freedom to express yourself, but it's also there at Highview, ready to be exploited, as Andy and I found.

And then again, maybe the reason Andy and I have so much trouble articulating what drew us to Highview is that we weren't wholly in charge of the process. The

Universe had someplace else it wanted to show us, and so it gradually turned off the heat in our comfy old nest so we'd have to seek warmth elsewhere.

And then, of course, there's Jesus

And then, of course, there's Jesus. Andy came more quickly than I did to feel a connection to Jesus. He didn't talk about it much; it was low key. But one day he brought home a small cross from a yard sale and put it up in his office. Our home has multiple religious icons, and previously the only Christian ones were a contrarian painting of "Laughing Jesus" and a Virgin Mary night-light I received as a gag gift and never got around to moving off our dining room side table. It sits under a winged Balinese goddess that hangs from the ceiling.

I also sensed that Andy had a growth spurt in his sense of himself. He seemed less vulnerable to triggers that used to set off his insecurities (that would be me, mostly).

Saved by accident

Then one day at Highview, Andy got saved by accident. The altar call during Sunday service usually comes in two phases: first a call for anyone who is ready to accept Jesus as Lord and Savior, and then a general call for those who are already saved and want prayer or a renewed commitment. Frequently Andy and I participate in the second call based on our general sense that our life experience is equivalent to being "saved." But this day, Andy wasn't paying close attention and walked up to the front during the first part of the altar call. And then once he got there, it seemed like the right thing to do to answer, "Yes" when Bishop Thomas asked him if he wanted to accept Jesus. I think Pastor intuited the situation and didn't make as big a deal out of it as he sometimes does. Luckily, someone else had also come up for the call, and Pastor focused more attention on that person.

Afterwards, Andy was glad it had happened as it did.

My Jesus

And what about my connection to Jesus?

Pastor Thomas made it possible for me to heal my sense of separation from Christians when he offered me the crack in the door (I won't say "loophole") of saying he believed I was saved. When he said that some people can be saved without calling themselves *Christian*, it permitted me to explore the meaning of "salvation" without betraying my enduring sense that people of all beliefs can attain that state, whatever it is. I have no idea if the number of other Christian churches willing to make that crack available is closer to six or to six million. But it is a crack expressed by at least a few other Evangelical leaders such as Brian McLaren who says, "Stop speculating about hell and start living for heaven!"

I began to see Jesus in new ways. I saw that the soft-focus "Jesus loves me" picture from my childhood was not wholly accurate. Nor was the sharper sense I developed in New Thought of Jesus as a supreme ethical teacher and example of spiritual attainment. There is something yet more radical, more hard-edged about him.

The Jesus with me since childhood was the Jesus of love your neighbor, visit the sick, forgive seven times seventy, and turn the other cheek. It was a powerful legacy that made me a better person and that I found echoed in the best of the alternative spiritualities I studied.

But the Jesus I first met through Peter McWilliams was the Jesus who told a disciple to follow him without first returning home to tell his family he was leaving. Not compassion or "family values," but something far more radical was commanded here. And even after I decided that Jesus was exaggerating to make a point, and after I decided this command was "for those who can accept it," the radicalness still took my breath away. "**He who would gain his life must lose it.**"

Bishop's *Speak Life* sermon about Jesus cursing the fig tree permitted me to see Jesus as a role model for passionate participation in *this* life. And thus began growing my appreciation for a Jesus who integrates opposites: strong and yielding, noble and humble, compassionate and demanding… spirit and flesh. As a Religious Scientist, I believe we are all spirit and flesh. "Jesus as supreme example, not exception." And yet…I couldn't be certain that was the whole story.

Teachable spirit

I suspect I'm not seeing the whole picture yet. But one thing I am sure of, "the Universe" isn't through with me. And I am deeply, wildly indebted to Bishop Thomas for providing a role model of integration, and to my beloved new family at Highview for providing the space in which I can explore its possibilities.

The more I learn, the less I know. Bishop Thomas defined "humility" for me as having a teachable spirit. I want always to have a teachable spirit.

And then...and also...and you know what happened next?*

Another year passed. I finished the book while on our annual summer trip to my sister's in Chico, California. The town's "One Mile" must be one of the nicest municipal parks in the country. A boulder-strewn creek that flows right through the center of town has been dammed up to create a natural swimming pool surrounded by verdant grass and shaded by towering oaks. So when I saw a sign saying the Methodist church was having its annual service in the park the Sunday we were visiting, we immediately decided to go. Afterward we planned to visit my aunt who lives just a block from the park.

---

* McLaren uses this childlike language to indicate our spiritual formation is never finished.

When we arrived, the pastor and musicians were set up on a grassy knoll at the edge of a circular opening in the trees. Andy and I took folding chairs at the perimeter just as the choir began singing, "How Great Thou Art." One glance upward was all it took to put tears on both our faces—the ancient oaks spiraled heavenward like crazy corkscrews, trimmed to prevent falling limbs. We tried to sing, but when the choir got to the second verse, all we could do was squeeze each other's hand.

When through the wood and forest glades I wander,
And hear the birds sing sweetly in the trees
When I look down from lofty mountain grandeur
And hear the brook, and feel the gentle breeze
Then sings my soul, my Savior God to thee;
How great thou art, how great thou art!

I looked just behind me and saw wild grapes spilling from the brush that edged the area. I stood to pick a bunch, imagining how sweet it would be to take it to the "altar" if there were an offering. At the sermon, my eyebrows went up when the pastor talked about Ann Lamont's book in which she is drawn into a Black church by the music. When the pastor announced that he would baptize anyone who desired it after the service, I felt a glimmer of interest pass through both Andy and me. Suddenly I understood the syndrome in which congregants sneak off to someone else's church to be saved—to a place where the only interpretation of the event is your own.

At the end of the service, no one showed interest in being baptized, so the pastor pointed everyone toward the picnic tables. Andy and I stood a few moments, but no one greeted us, so we began to stroll in the opposite direction toward the creek.

I was already feeling a brimming peace when a voice began closing in on us from behind. With angelic clarity it sang a tune from the baptism scene in the movie "Oh Brother, Where Art Thou?"

As I went down in the river to pray
Studying about that good old way
And who shall wear the starry crown?
Good Lord show me the way.

As the voice got closer, we shared the thrill it gave us by squeezing hands. Then the singer, a beautiful young Asian woman, popped in front of us and gave us a broad smile before turning off in another direction. I mouthed "thank you" with all the emphasis I could muster. The tune stayed with me as we continued toward the water's edge at the upstream end of the grass-edged pool.

I did not carry out the image in my head of walking right straight down into the water. Instead I stood on the bank gazing at the reflection of fall's first golden leaves and watching a toddler play with a toy boat. Andy went back to get the car, and I said I'd meet him at my aunt's.

I strolled trance-like downstream to the footbridge over the small dam. I stood in the middle of the bridge, gazing down to the shadowed pool where a dozen trout milled in the clear waters. I plucked the grapes that were still in my hand and tossed them one-by-one to the fish, who darted for them eagerly. I tasted one—sour, vivid. Then I turned my attention to the dam's overflow spout. It served as a fish ladder, though I had never seen a fish attempt its six-foot rise.

The water gushed and tumbled, emerging in a froth of bubbles bursting and merging, bursting and merging—a fountain of life. I stared into it a long time.

Then I crossed over, and I walked slowly toward my aunt's, reluctant to break the spell, reluctant to let go of the simple symphony in my head.

And who shall wear the starry crown?
Good Lord, show me the way.

Afterwords Bishop Thomas: Lessons for Evangelism in the 21st Century

It has been said that there are two reasons people reject the message of Christianity: some people feel they are not good enough for salvation, and other people feel that the message of salvation is not good enough for them. In most of my ministry, I deal with people in the first group. In my dialogues with Teri, I learned much about the perceptions of some in the second group.

One of the main things I learned is that dealing with non-Christians in this so-called "postmodern era" is very different from dealing with the heathens in St. Paul's day. The people in those days had never heard the message of Jesus. For many, all they had to do was *hear* the Good News and they were ready to give up their idols. But today, many of the people we Christians meet adopted their "alternative religions" or even secularism because they *have heard* about Jesus—and they may have even been attracted to and absorbed *pieces* of his message. But they've heard about Jesus in a distorted way, or they've seen the centuries of bloodshed and hypocrisy that can result when scripture is interpreted immaturely or as a cover for man's jealousies and greed.

With such people, we need a new form of evangelism, one that recognizes that these "alternative religions" are often sincere attempts to approach the truth. And thus, rather than leading by attacking their mistaken beliefs, we can be more successful in engaging them in dialogue about the values that lie *behind* their beliefs. Where we find common ground in values, we may find fertile ground for the Word.

To borrow the terminology that Teri is so fond of, perhaps we can encourage those in alternative religions and even secularism to *transcend* the limits of those beliefs while they still *include* whatever golden nuggets of the Christian message may have been at their core. And of course, it is not enough for us to talk to them about the love of Jesus, we must show that love in our actions and in how we approach all people.

The main thing I hope this book conveys is that although the message of Christianity has spanned the globe, many people have not had a chance to hear it with a clarity that can reach those who feel locked out of its life-changing promises and all inclusive blessings. It is a "whosoever will" proposal, and those who *will* accept it—on its terms, are never the same again. I hope that these dialogues erase the stereotypes and present the message again as it was intended to be heard.

Guide for Group Discussion

If you have been moved or intrigued by the discussions in this book, we invite you to suggest that your church, temple, mosque, sangha, ethical society, or bowling league hold a discussion and invite an organization with different beliefs. The goal will *not* be to change anyone's mind, but simply that persons from each viewpoint will leave saying, "At least I felt they heard us for a change."

Suggested format

Find someone in your organization known for his or her even-temperedness and open-mindedness, and ask that person to be a facilitator. We offer a full discussion guide and suggestions for proceeding at the book's website: **BishopandSeeker.com**.

A few questions to get you started

1. Thinking about the factors that drew Teri and Andy to New Thought:
    - Which, if any, of those values do you share?
    - What support sources do you have for developing or expressing those values?
2. Thinking of the values that drew Teri to Highview:
    - Which, if any, of those values do you share?
    - What support sources do you have for developing or expressing those values?
3. Do you believe that it's possible or desirable to integrate the values from the two communities? How or where have you seen that done?
4. A major topic was the role in making decisions of reason, scripture, and gut feelings. Which of these do you rely on?
    - If you rely primarily on gut feelings, how important do you think it is to distinguish fleeting emotions from genuine inspiration or divine guidance?
    - If you rely primarily on scripture, how do you know when you have the right interpretation?
    - If you rely primarily on reason, how do you guard against self-serving rationalizations or ego needs?
5. What techniques or qualities did Bishop Thomas and Teri call on to get through the rough spots in their dialog? Discuss any situation in your life where these approaches might help you work through conflict.
6. What is similar in the way Teri and Bishop Thomas experience God in their daily lives? Do you think the similarities are enough for people like them to be able to work together for good, or do you think their differences will always get in the way?
7. What issue or quality in the book would you like to learn more about or have more of in your life? How might you get started toward that?

You can also join the online discussion for this book at **BishopandSeeker.com**.

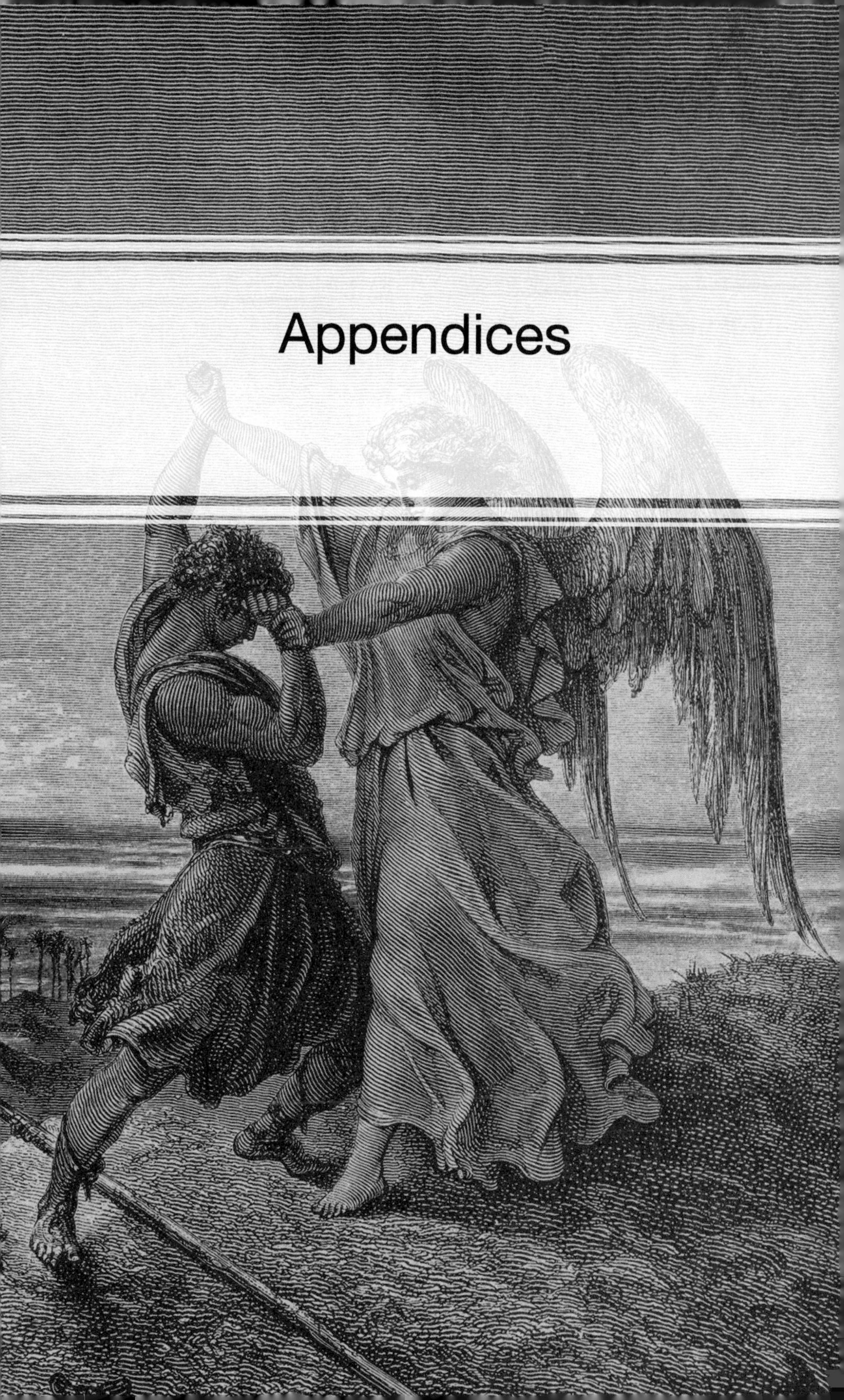

Appendices

A Glossary for Non-fundamentalists

Some definitions below will not be wholly acceptable to either "side," so we beg your indulgence. This glossary was absolutely necessary for your authors to make it through the rough parts of their dialogue. So we ask you to just hold on until you've read far enough to see how we got here.

Devil/The Enemy: That which prevents us from reaching our potential and fulfilling our purpose

God: Source, Spirit, Love, Divine Energy, Universal Mind, The One

Sin: Missing the mark, less than perfect

Perfect: All encompassing

Judgment: Consequences

Wrath of God: Extreme Consequences

Hell: Permanent, total, utter, absolute separation from Source

Confession: Consciousness that we have missed the mark

Repentance: Turning away from a dysfunctional condition

Sacrifice: To make sacred

Atonement: *At one-ment*, to make whole or perfect

Salvation: Transformation

Fundamentalists: In Christianity, we are defining fundamentalists as those who believe that the Bible is inerrant, and that its central message is that the only path to salvation is to accept the sacrifice of Jesus on the cross as *at one-ment* for our sins. This one-time choice leads to an inflow of **guidance from the Holy Spirit**—not to be confused with intuition, feelings, emotions, or instinct—that sets us on a lifetime path of **holiness** or wholeness achieved by confession and repentance and demonstrated by love of neighbor as ourselves.

And Definitions for Some Alternatives

Secularism: The belief that the universe can be best understood by reason, and that life can be best lived by applying ethics—both without reference to God. (Secularists may or may not believe God exists.)

New Age: An individual approach to spiritual exploration that emerged in the United States in the 1960s largely as an alternative to perceived shortcomings of traditional Judeo-Christianity. Followers take a mix of beliefs and practices from all world religions, and most believe the universe can be best understood through intuition.

New Thought: The high-end, intellectual core of many New Age beliefs. With roots in philosophy, the mystical traditions of world religions, and transcendentalism, it came together as a 19th century movement teaching, "There is a power for good in the universe that you can use; it works through your thinking." God is the "Universal Mind" that unfolds into form. Our human minds intersect with this "One Mind," and in this sense, we are one with God. Life can thus best be understood by a combination of reason and intuition.

New Thought churches vary in the degree to which they associate themselves with Christianity. They include Unity, Religious Science, Divine Science, and the "celebrity" led churches in Los Angeles of Rev. Della Reese-Lett's *Foundation for Better Living* and Rev. Michael Beckwith's *Agape*.

Where the authors fit

Bishop Thomas identifies himself as a non-denominational, Christian Fundamentalist using the definition on the prior page or as an Evangelical in the common understanding.

Teri Murphy identifies herself at the beginning of the book as a follower of New Thought as taught by Religious Science.

Fundamentalist Christian Belief Statement

As posted at Website of Highview Christian Fellowship
Fairfax, Virginia, HighviewCF.org

1. **We believe** in the scriptures of the Old and New testaments in the original writings as being the inspired, infallible, and inerrant Word of God; and that the Bible is our supreme and final authority in all matters regarding faith and life.
2. **We believe** in one Perfect, Infinite, Holy and Eternal God, Creator of all things, eternally existing in three Persons: the Father, the Son and Holy Spirit, each having the same nature, attributes and perfections and each worthy of the same worship and obedience.
3. **We believe** that the Holy Spirit is the third person of the Godhead; and that he baptizes, seals, indwells, regenerates all believing sinners at the moment of salvation.
4. **We believe** in Jesus Christ as the only begotten Son of God; his virgin birth; his substitutionary sacrifice for our sins; his literal resurrection from the dead; his present ministry as our High Priest in heaven; and his in-person, literal, and imminent return.
5. **We believe** that salvation by grace through faith in the shed blood of the Lord Jesus Christ is available freely to every man; all who receive him as Savior and Lord are born immediately into the family of God.
6. **We believe** that Jesus Christ gave two ordinances for his church to follow, The Lord's Supper (communion) and Baptism.
7. **We believe** in the personal, premillenial, and pretribulation rapture of the church; and that there will be a bodily resurrection of the unjust into the Great White Throne Judgment and the eventual condemnation to eternal separation from God.
8. **We believe** that each believer is an equal member of the holy and royal priesthood. Because all believers are priests, we need no mediator other than Jesus Christ to approach God directly.

Religious Science Belief Statement

As posted at Website of Celebration Center of Spiritual Living
(formerly Celebration Center of Religious Science)
Falls Church, Virginia, CelebrationCenter.org

1. **We believe** in God, the Living Spirit Almighty; One indestructible, absolute, and self-existent Cause.
2. **This One** manifests Itself in and through all creation but is not absorbed by Its creation.
3. **The manifest universe** is the body of God; it is the logical and necessary outcome of the infinite self-knowingness of God.
4. **We believe** in the incarnation of the Spirit in everyone and that all people are incarnations of the One Spirit.
5. **We believe** in the eternality, the immortality and the continuity of the individual soul, forever and ever expanding.
6. **We believe** that heaven is within us and that we experience this Kingdom to the degree that we become conscious of it.
7. **We believe** the ultimate goal of life to be a complete emancipation from all discord of every nature, and that this goal is sure to be attained by all.
8. **We believe** in the unity of all life, and that the highest God and the innermost God is one God.
9. **We believe** that God is personal to all who feel this indwelling Presence.
10. **We believe** in the direct revelation of truth through the intuitive and spiritual nature of the individual, and that any person may become a revealer of truth who lives in close contact with the indwelling God.
11. **We believe** that the Universal Spirit, which is God, operates through a Universal Mind, which is the Law of God, and that we are surrounded by the Creative Mind which receives the direct impress of our thoughts and acts upon it.
12. **We believe** in the healing of the sick through the Power of this Mind. We believe in the control of conditions through the Power of this Mind.
13. **We believe** in the eternal Goodness, the eternal Loving-kindness, and the eternal Givingness of Life to all.
14. **We believe** in our own soul, our own spirit, and our own destiny, for we understand that the life of all is God.

Author Bios

Teri Murphy is a freelance communications consultant and trainer in Arlington, Virginia, who previously worked as a writer, editor, speechwriter, and policy analyst for three federal agencies. In her first job at the U.S. Information Agency, she wrote articles explaining American culture and politics for placement in the overseas press. With her husband, Andy Murphy, she co-authored *The Husbands Manual: A Guide for Husbands and Men Trying out for the Part.*

Teri has a lifelong interest in theology, communication skills, and the delicate balance between community and individuality. She coordinates the Washington D.C. Meetup study group of philosopher Ken Wilber, and she is an occasional volunteer reviewer for the *Journal of Transpersonal Psychology*. She was previously a board member of the Celebration Center of Religious Science in Falls Church, Virginia.

Teri has an undergraduate degree in Communications and Public Policy from University of California at Berkeley and a Masters of Urban and Regional Planning from George Washington University.

Bishop Phillip O. Thomas presides over the Virginia member churches of Praise Covenant Interdenominational Fellowship (PCIF), an affiliation of independent, Bible-based churches on the East Coast of the United States.

Bishop Thomas was born in inner city Baltimore to a mother who suffered from MS, an absent father, and a grandmother who made sure he spent most of his childhood in church. He gave his life completely to God late in high school, and spent several years touring the Mid-Atlantic region preaching and performing with a gospel band. In 1999 he gave up a successful career as telecom account executive at Bell Atlantic to become full time pastor of Highview Christian Fellowship, which is currently located in Fairfax, Virginia.

Bishop Thomas earned Bachelors degrees in Biblical Studies and in Biblical Counseling from Washington Bible College in Lanham, Maryland, and The Christian College Seminary in Independence, Missouri, where he also completed the Masters of Divinity degree. He completed a Doctoral degree from Florida's Jacksonville Theological Seminary in 2008. He has traveled and done ministry work in Africa and India, and is author of *Bring it On: A Total Man's Guide to Christian Living*. He and his wife, Cindy Thomas, have three grown children.

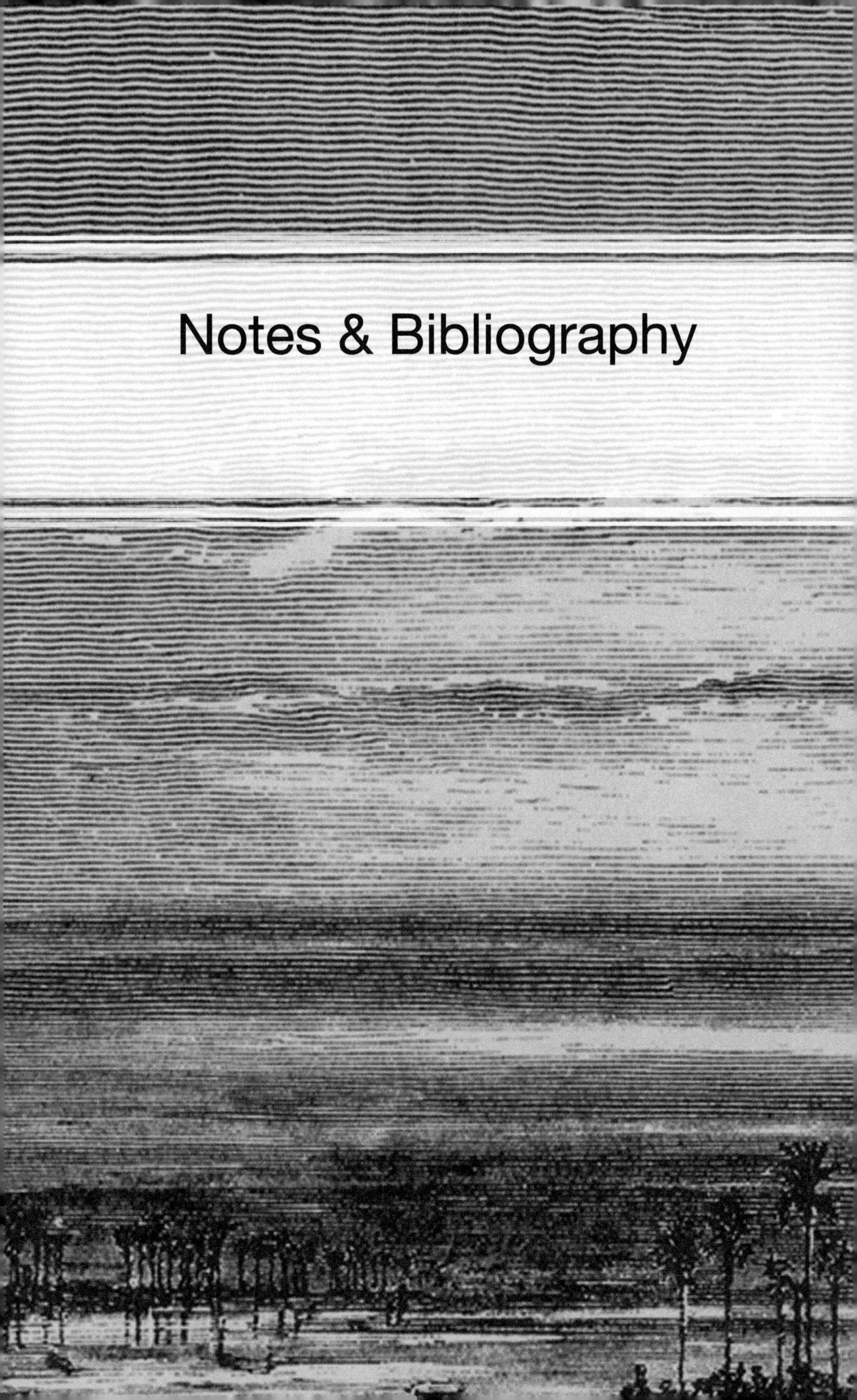

Notes & Bibliography

Chapter 3. Background, No Coincidences

[1] A Brief history of New Thought: New Thought has origins in the Neo-Platonist philosophy that "Mind" or consciousness or "Spirit" existed before anything else. Everything created partakes in the nature of that mind. Thus God is more like the soul or mind of the world than its master.

From religion, New Thought traces to an observation common to all the world's mystics. If you sit quietly, they report, you will eventually have a direct experience—clear as putting your hand on a hot stove—that this consciousness is not separate from you, it is who you are. You are one with everything.

In the late 1800s, British judge Thomas Troward was assigned as Viceroy to India where he noticed parallels between the latest science of the atom and the ancient Hindu concept of self. He came back to wow the Theosophists of Great Britain with his "Mental Science" which claimed that the essence of the Bible could be reached through the rational process of observing how life works. Influenced by these ideas, hypnotist Phineas Quimby taught Mary Baker Eddy in Boston "scientific prayer," which she developed in a Christian context as the basis of Christian Science—not New Thought but one of its precursors. This was about the same time that transcendentalists like Ralph Waldo Emerson emboldened conformists to replace "mouldered old religions" with "self reliance" by learning "to detect and watch that gleam of light which flashes across one's mind from within." Then Ernest Holmes put pieces from each of these together to write *Science of Mind*, a foundational text in New Thought.

Chapter 4. Rescuing Truth, Beauty, and Goodness from Postmodernists

[2] *A Brief History of Everything*, Ken Wilber citing the work of Lawrence Kohlberg, Shambala, Boston, 1996, Chapter 9

Chapter 5. We have Each other's Attention. Now What?

[3] *Integral Spirituality: A Startling New Role for Religion in the Modern and Postmodern World*, Ken Wilber, Shambala, Boston, 2006, Chapter 9

[4] *Ain't Nobody's Business if You Do*: *The Absurdity of Consensual Crimes in a Free Society*, Peter Mc Williams, Prelude Press, Los Angeles, 1993, p.401

Chapter 7. Metaphorical, Metaphysical, or Literal?

[5] *Learn to Live: A New Thought Interpretation of the Parables*, Ervin Seale, DeVorss Publications, Marina Del Ray, CA, 1955, pp.29-30

[6] ETB ministries at *www.etbible.org* promotes evolution of spiritual consciousness via study of the Bible as reordered into the chronological order in which some scholars believe the passages were written. This restructuring maps well with the growth of human consciousness through various levels as described by Spiral Dynamics theory, discussed here in chapter 13: Loophole #5: God Doesn't Change, but His Methods Do. For example, the account of creation found in Genesis 1 dates from the hunter-gatherer epoch and sees God as provider of game. The second version in Genesis 2 dates from the agrarian epoch and sees God as bringer of rains for crops.

[7] *Grace and Grit*, Ken Wilber, Shambala, Boston, 1991, p.81

[8] "Power of Myth," PBS documentary in which Bill Moyers interviews Joseph Campbell, 1988

Chapter 8. Loophole #1: Judgment, Hell, and Pagan Babies

[9] *Road Less Traveled, A New Psychology of Love, Traditional Values, and Spiritual Growt*h, Scott Peck, Simon and Schuster, New York, 1978, pp.154-155

[10] *A Brief History of Everything*, op cit, Ken Wilber citing the work of Lawrence Kohlberg, Chapter 9

[11] "God, Religion, Whatever," Ed Vitagliano, an article citing sociologists at the University of North Carolina at Chapel Hill, Christian Smith and Melinda Lundquist Denton, reviewing data from the National Study of Youth and Religion, *The Manna*, Marantha Inc., Princess Anne, MD, May 2006, p.11

[12] *The Five Gospels, What Did Jesus Really Say?* The Jesus Seminar, Polebridge Press, Scribner, 1993. This project brought together scholars to determine the likelihood that each quote attributed to Jesus in the New Testament was actually spoken by him. Results are presented in a color-coded version of the New Testament. Results are controversial among Bible scholars.

[13] *Rescuing the Bible from Fundamentalists,* Bishop John Shelby Spong, Harper Collins, New York, 1991

[14] *Christianity: the Great Lie, Progressive Religion and Integral Politics*, Ray Harris at www.integralworld.net/harris24.html, May 2006. (This is a website for critiques of the work of Ken Wilber.) Ray Harris is not to be

confused with Sam Harris, a Buddhist author who reaches similar conclusions about Christianity.

Chapter 9. Loophole #2: My Intuition is Your Holy Spirit

[15] *Lila: An Inquiry into Morals*, Robert Pirsig, Bantam Books, New York, 1992, p.169

Chapter 10. Loophole #3: Literal Doesn't Mean What You Think

[16] *Brief History of Everything*, op cit, p.98-99

[17] *Holy Bible from the Ancient Eastern Text*, translation by George M. Lamsa from the Aramaic of the Peshitta, Harper Collins, San Francisco, 1933

[18] *Aramaic Light on the Gospel of John: A Commentary on the Teachings of Jesus from the Aramaic and Unchanged Near Eastern Customs,* Aramaic New Testament Series Volume 3, Rocco A. Errico/George M. Lamsa, Noohra Foundation, Smyrna , GA, 2002

Chapter 11. Praise for whom?

[19] *The Common Heart: An Experience of Interreligious Dialogue*, Netanel Miles-Yepez, Ed, Lantern Books, New York, 2006, p.28

[20] *The Edinburgh & Doré Lectures on Mental Science*, Thomas Troward, DeVorss Publications, Marina Del Ray, 1989 p.40

[21] ibid p.89

Chapter 13. Loophole #5: God Doesn't Change but His Methods Do

[22] "Moral Stages and Moralization: The Cognitive-Developmental Approach," Lawrence T. Kohlberg, in *Moral Development and Behavior: Theory, Research and Social Issues*, Lickona, ed., Holt, NY: Rinehart and Winston, 1976

[23] *Spiral Dynamics: Mastering Values, Leadership and Change*, Don Edward Beck and Christopher Cowan, 2005

[24] *The New Faithful: Why Christian Adults are Embracing Christian Orthodoxy*, Colleen Carroll, Loyola Press, Chicago, 2002, p.83

Chapter 14. Learning to Love the Wrath of God

[25] "Robertson Says Town Rejects God," Reuters, *Washington Post*, November 11, 2005, p. A3

[26] *Edinburgh Lectures*, op cit, p.89

[27] JonathanEdwards.com, a site devoted to the 18th century preacher who set the standard for hellfire preaching with his sermon *Sinners in the Hands of an Angry God* based on Deuteronomy 32:35, **"Their foot shall slide in due time."** I studied and recited this text in high school rhetoric class.

> The God that holds you over the pit of hell, much as one holds a spider, or some loathsome insect over the fire, abhors you, and is dreadfully provoked: his wrath towards you burns like fire; he looks upon you as worthy of nothing else, but to be cast into the fire; he is of purer eyes than to bear to have you in his sight; you are ten thousand times more abominable in his eyes, than the most hateful venomous serpent is in ours…
>
> But this is the dismal case of every soul in this congregation that has not been born again, however moral and strict, sober and religious, they may otherwise be…

[28] *Living Enlightenment: A Call for Evolution Beyond Ego*, Andrew Cohen, Moksha Press, Lenox, MA, 2002, preface

Chapter 15. Science vs. Religion 1: Evolution

[29] *Just Six Numbers: The Deep Forces that Shape the Universe*, Martin Rees, Basic Books, New York, 1999

[30] *The Blind Watchmaker: Why the Evidence of Evolution Reveals a Universe Without Design*, Richard Dawkins, Longman, London, 1986

[31] *Darwin on Trial*, Phillip E. Johnson, Regnery Publishing, Washington, DC, 1991

[32] *The Case for Creationism*, Lee Strobel, Zondervan, Grand Rapids, MI, 2004

[33] "Blueprints: Solving the Mystery of Evolution," *Sunday New York Times*, book review by Richard Dawkins, April 9, 1989, p.34

[34] "Researcher Claims Bias by Smithsonian," *Washington Times*, Joyce Howard Price, February 13, 2005, http://washingtontimes.com/national/20050213-121441-8610r.htm

[35] *The Metaphysics of Evolution*, Fred Reed, March 9, 2005, http://www.lewrockwell.com/reed/reed59.html

[36] "The Origin of Life? All in a Day's Work," Joel Achenbach, *Washington Post*, January 8, 2006, Style section, p. D1

[37] *Ideas of Power*, Ernest Holmes, Devorss & Company, Marina Del Rey, CA, approx 1930, p.114

[38] *The Science of Mind,* Ernest Holmes, G.P. Putnam's Sons, New York, 1938, p. 337 and *Lessons in Spiritual Mind Healing*, Ernest Holmes, Science of Mind Publications, Los Angeles, 1983, p.38. These quotes may have been influenced by Swami Vivekananda 1863-1902, who wrote in *The Complete Works of Vivekananda,*

> Involution and evolution is going on throughout the whole of nature. The whole series of evolution, beginning with the lowest manifestation of life and reaching up to the highest, the most perfect man, must have been the involution of something else. The question is: The involution of what? What was involved? God.... At the beginning that intelligence becomes *in*volved, and in the end that intelligence gets *e*volved. The sum total of the intelligence displayed in the universe must, therefore, be the involved universal intelligence unfolding itself. This universal intelligence is what we call God. Call it by any other name, it is absolutely certain that in the beginning there is that Infinite cosmic intelligence. This cosmic intelligence gets involved, and it manifests, evolves itself, until it becomes the perfect man, the 'Christ-man,' the 'Buddha-man.' Then it goes back to its own source.

Chapter 20. Living for Heaven or Earth?

[39] *Brief History of Everything*, op cit, pp.253-259

[40] *Authentic Happiness: Using the New Positive Psychology to Realize your Potential for Lasting Fulfillment*, Martin E.P.Seligman, Ph.D., the Free Press, New York, 2002. Dr. Seligman is past President of the American Psychological Association and founder of Positive Psychology, a new branch of psychology that focuses on the empirical study of such things as positive emotions, strengths-based character, and healthy institutions. His research demonstrates what Aristotle laid out in *Ethics* over 2000 years ago—that lasting happiness comes not from pleasure but from using our strengths in pursuit of meaningful ends.

Chapter 21. Fundamentalists as Positive Thinkers

[41] *Making Miracles*, Paul Pearsall, Ph.D., Prentice Hall Press, New York, 1991

[42] *Living Enlightenment*, op cit

Chapter 23. A Dialogue with C.S. Lewis

[43] *Surprised by Joy: The Shape of My Early Life*, C.S. Lewis, a Harvest Book, Harcourt, Inc. Orlando, Florida, 1955

Chapter 25. Who Needs Psychology?

[44] *The Six Pillars of Self Esteem*, Nathaniel Branden, Bantam, New York, 1994, 1995, pp.40, 203-204

[45] ibid pp.53-54

Chapter 26. Spiritual Practice, Spiritual Bypass

[46] *Paths to God: Living the Bhagavad Gita*, Ram Dass, Harmony Books 2004, New York.

[47] *Integral Spirituality*, op cit, Chapter 5

[48] *The Battle for God: A History of Fundamentalism*, Karen Armstrong, The Random House Publishing Group, New York, 2000, pp. xv-xvi

[49] ibid pp.xv-xvi

Chapter 28. Prayer vs. Raising Consciousness

[50] *The Science of Mind*, op cit, p.258

Chapter 29. Hawaiian Repentance and the Three Faces of God

[51] *Zero Limits: The Secret Hawaiian System for Wealth, Health, Peace, and More*, Joe Vitale and Ihaleakala Hew Len, Ph.D., John Wiley and Sons, Inc., Hoboken, New Jersey, 2009 pp.173-174, 193

[52] "The Evolving Faces of God," dialogue between Andrew Cohen and Ken Wilber, *EnlightenNext,* September-November 2009, Issue 45, p.41

Chapter 30. Gender Roles: What are We Really Talking about Here?

[53] *Men are from Mars, Women are from Venus,* John Gray, Harper Collins, New York, 1992

[54] *Getting the Love You Want: The Guide for Couples*, Harville Hendrix, Ph.D., Harper Perennial, New York, 1990

[55] *Marriage Rates by State: 1990, 1995, and 1999-2004*, Division of Vital Statistics, National Center for Health Statistics, CDC, and also divorcereform.org/rates.html

[56] *Are Men Necessary? When Sexes Collide*, Maureen Dowd, G.P. Putnam's Sons, New York, 2005, pp.62, 66-67

Chapter 32. Homosexuality Revisited

[57] *Between the Sexes: Foundations for a Christian Ethics of Sexuality*, Lisa Sowle Cahill, Fortress Press, Philadelphia, 1985

[58] "Methodist Bishops Affirm Their Churches are Open to Gays," AP, *Washington Post* November 12, 2005, p.B9

[59] National opinion survey, April, 1996, *Personality and Social Psychology Bulletin*, Dr. Gregory Herek and Prof. John Capitanio, http://psychology.ucdavis.edu/rainbow/html/comeout1.html

[60] *Klan-Destine Relationships: A Black Man's Odyssey in the Ku Klux Klan*, Daryl Davis, New Horizons Press, 1997

Chapter 33. Evangelism: Good News and Bad

[61] *Integral Spirituality*, op cit, pp.181-183

Chapter 34. The Interfaith Stretch... and the Muslims

[62] *Signs in the Heavens: a Muslim Astronomer's Perspective on Religion and Science*, Dr. Imad-ad-Dean Ahmad, Amana Publications, Beltsville, Maryland, 1992, revised in 2006 under a grant from the Templeton Foundation. Dr. Ahmad cites seven influences from the Qur'an that promote the advancement of science and civilization: reason, observation, learning, academic freedom, absence of aversion to material prosperity, proper citation of sources, and universality—the idea that truth can be found anywhere because God is everywhere its source.

The result of universality, for example, was that Islamic scholars translated and distributed the works of most cultures they conquered. Proper citation of sources was developed in order to assess the various oral traditions about the life of the prophet Mohammed. The Qur'an provides principles, not laws; to develop, *Hadith*, a body of law that supplements the Qur'an, Islamic scholars studied the practices of Mohammed. And to do that, they needed a means of weighing the honesty, memory, and piety of individuals who handed down stories about Mohammed's life.

[63] *The Ornament of the World: How Muslims, Jews, and Christians Created a Culture of Tolerance in Medieval Spain*, Mara Rosa Menocal, Back Bay Books, Little, Brown and Company, Boston and New York, 2002

[64] *The Ethics of Aristotle: Nicomachean Ethics*, Aristotle, Penguin Classics, revised edition 1955

[65] *Life of Pi*, Yann Martel, Harcourt Books, Orlando, FL, 2001

[66] *The Holy Qur'an*, translated by Abdullah Yusufali, Tahrike Tarsile Qur'an, Inc., New York

Chapter 35. McLaren Completes the Bridge

[67] *A Generous Orthodoxy: Why I Am a post-Protestant, liberal/conservative, mystical/poetic, biblical, charismatic/contemplative, fundamentalist Calvinist, Anabaptist/Anglican, Methodist, Catholic, green, incarnational, depressed-yet-hopeful and emergent, unfinished Christian,* Brian D. McLaren, Zondervan, Grand Rapids, MI, 2004

[68] *More Ready Than You Realize: Evangelism as Dance in the Postmodern Matrix*, Brian McLaren, Zondervan, Grand Rapids, MI, 2002, chapter 18

Chapter 36. Law & Politics: Seeking a Way Beyond

[69] "The Dark Side of Faith: It's official: Too Much Religion may be a Dangerous Thing," Rosa Brooks, *Los Angeles Times*, October 1, 2005. A report on a study in the Journal of Religion and Society, a publication of Creighton University's Center for the Study of Religion by evolutionary scientist Gregory S. Paul.

[70] "Two Views of the Same News Find Opposite Biases," Shankar Vedantam, *Washington Post*, July 24, 2006, p.2

[71] *Lila,* op cit

[72] ibid p.345

[73] ibid p.351

[74] *The Battle for God*, op cit, p.xviii

[75] *Secularization and Fundamentalism Reconsidered, Vol III,* a series of papers edited by Jeffrey K. Hadden and Anson Shupe, Paragon House, 1989

[76] "Religion and Politics: American Rapture," Craig Unger, *Vanity Fair*, December 2005, p.212

[77] *A Generous Orthodoxy*, op cit, p.325

[78] *Lila*, op cit, p.140

[79] "Swedish Pastor Sentenced for 'Hate Speech,'" Dale Hurd, *CW News* (Christian World News) CWNews.org, September 10, 2004

[80] "Church Sues Fairfax County To Keep Religion Classes," Maria Glod, *Washington Post*, July 18, 2006, p.B05

[81] *A Generous Orthodoxy,* op cit, pp.151, 154

[82] *Integral Spirituality*, op cit, Chapter 9, p.193

[83] *A Generous Orthodoxy,* op cit, pp.325-326

[84] "The Quixotic Quest for Civility: Patterns of Interaction Between the New Christian Right and Secular Humanists," W. Barnett Pearce, Steven W. Littlejohn, and Alison Alexander, a paper printed in *Secularization and Fundamentalism Reconsidered, Vol III,* ed. Jeffrey K. Hadden and Anson Shupe, Paragon House, 1989, p.174

[85] "Religious Right, Left Meet in Middle; Clergy Aim to Show That Faith Unifies"; [FINAL Edition] Alan Cooperman, *The Washington Post*, Washington, D.C.: Jun 15, 2005, p.A.01

Chapter 37. Beyond Politics Part 2: Healing Our World

[86] *Adventures in Missing the Point: How the Culture-Controlled Church Neutered the Gospel*, Brian D. McLaren and Tony Campolo, Zondervan, Grand Rapids, 2003

[87] *God's Politics: Why the Right Gets It Wrong and the Left Doesn't Get It*, Jim Wallis, Harper, San Francisco, 2005

[88] *Healing Our World: The Other Piece of the Puzzle*, Dr. Mary Ruwart, Sunstar Press, Kalamazoo, 2003, p.2

Chapter 38. End Times: Fear Not

[89] "Religion and Politics: American Rapture," op cit, p 204

[90] *The Revelation: Our Crisis is a Birth*, Barbara Marx Hubbard, Foundation for Conscious Evolution, Sonoma, 1993

What Would It Take for Us All to Get Along?

[91] "The Quixotic Quest for Civility," op cit, p.174

[92] *It's a Meaningful Life: It Just takes Practice*, Bo Lozoff, Penguin, Putnam, New York, 2000. Before Teri discovered Ken Wilber, this lovely book by a longtime colleague of Ram Dass was the first place she found a grounded critique of some New Age/Postmodern attitudes that were bothering her. Lozoff gives a simple and practical prescription for a spiritual life based in kindness.

Index

Index is available online at **BishopandSeeker.com/index**

Intermedia
Publishing Group
Publishing That Works For You

Do you need a speaker?

Do you want Teri Murphy or Bishop Phillip O. Thomas to speak to your group or event? Then contact Larry Davis at: (623) 337-8710 or email: ldavis@intermediapr.com or use the contact form at: www.intermediapr.com.

Whether you want to purchase bulk copies of *The Bishop and the Seeker* or buy another book for a friend, get it now at: www.imprbooks.com.

If you have a book that you would like to publish, contact Terry Whalin, Publisher, at Intermedia Publishing Group, (623) 337-8710 or email: twhalin@intermediapub.com or use the contact form at: www.intermediapub.com.